There's No Such Thing as Crypto Crime

An Investigative Handbook

Nick Furneaux

WILEY

Published by John Wiley & Sons, Inc., Hoboken, New Jersey.
Published simultaneously in Canada and the United Kingdom.

ISBNs: 9781394164820 (Paperback), 9781394164844 (ePDF), 9781394164837 (ePub)

For general information on our other products and services, please contact our Customer Care Department within the United States at (800) 762-2974, outside the United States at (317) 572-3993. For product technical support, you can find answers to frequently asked questions or reach us via live chat at https://support.wiley.com.

If you believe you've found a mistake in this book, please bring it to our attention by emailing our reader support team at wileysupport@wiley.com with the subject line "Possible Book Errata Submission."

Wiley also publishes its books in a variety of electronic formats. Some content that appears in print may not be available in electronic formats. For more information about Wiley products, visit our web site at www.wiley.com.

Library of Congress Control Number: 2023941068

Cover images: © kyoshino/Getty Images, © Andrey Mitrofanov/Getty Images, © filo/Getty Images

Cover design: Wiley

SKY10086280_092724

Contents

Foreword

Have you heard of pig butchering?

I sure hadn't.

I also had no idea that those six words would change the course of my life.

We were about to level up our game.

I'm a prosecutor in Santa Clara County, California, and I have the pleasure of working with one of the smartest groups of local investigators in the world, known as the Regional Enforcement and Allied Computer (REACT) Task Force. During the eight years that we have worked together, we've investigated, prosecuted, and sent to prison some of the most devious and destructive bad actors who terrorize the world from behind their screens.

REACT Agent John Alldredge asked me about pig butchering because he had just received a report from a 30-year-old software engineer who had lost $300,000 in a romance scam/investment scheme. As Detective Alldredge dug into the facts, he came to understand that what happened to this engineer was happening to hundreds of other victims worldwide in a phenomenon known as pig butchering. The term is a literal translation of the Chinese *sha zhu pan*, denoting a specific fraud technique where victims are courted online and "fattened up" by scammers—and then their net worth is stolen from them during the slaughter. After the scammer establishes a trust, they introduce the opportunity to become wealthy by making cryptocurrency investments. Victims are shown a false online investment dashboard showing massive returns, which encourages further investment. What they don't realize is that their money is long gone, lining the pockets of the scammers.

Never before had we seen a fraud typology specifically designed to steal every last penny from victims. Never before had we seen victims losing their entire nest egg, their retirement accounts, and their children's college funds. And never before had we seen such an absolutely devastated group of people once they realized that they had lost their entire financial stability as well as someone they considered a beloved companion.

Embracing our "what if we could" philosophy, and at the direction of our District Attorney Jeff Rosen, who applauds innovation, REACT began a test case with that first victim. The team used blockchain investigative skills to follow the engineer's investments, watching the money hop from wallet to wallet until it landed at an exchange that accepted a Santa Clara County search warrant. Creativity and a strong work ethic drove the successful retrieval of a good percentage of the engineer's funds and the return of those funds to him. We replicated this procedure over and over and were able to help 25 victims recover stolen money.

The reports of victimization kept pouring in. A tidal wave of people from all over the world arrived (electronically) on REACT's doorstep asking for the same type of assistance. As the team solved cases in other jurisdictions and tried to hand them over to local law enforcement, we were told on repeat, "We don't do crypto." It quickly became clear that we were facing a worldwide gap in the ability to solve cryptocurrency cases. Scaling efforts and teaching others our blueprint became the REACT workload for the foreseeable future. Our victims were entitled to exactly that.

We moved forward, building an international network (now numbering 1,800!) of active law enforcement worldwide just learning how to use the blockchain as an investigative tool. We quickly found that there was a thirst for learning this new technology and a camaraderie in helping pull our fellow officers toward crypto literacy. As we taught, shared, and collaborated, we saw crypto in more and more cases. Crypto isn't just an element in fraud cases; it became how bad actors move money. Soon we were seeing it in narcotics, child exploitation, murder for hire, and even home-invasion robberies. It was imperative that local officers develop a baseline competence.

Finding resources for this educational gap wasn't easy. Authors and experts were few and far between. Our victims needed law enforcement to understand how to locate, seize, and return their lost funds. Officers were often paralyzed by the idea of mastering crypto investigations. It seemed too complicated, too time consuming, and just really difficult. We all needed someone who could explain this technology to us in a way that even a layperson could understand.

Enter Nick Furneaux.

In his initial book, aptly named *Investigating Cryptocurrencies: Understanding, Extracting and Analyzing Blockchain Evidence*, Nick uses a tool-agnostic approach to demystify cryptocurrency. In an easily digestible format, he stays out of the deep weeds and educates how the blockchain works, why it's a fantastic source of information, and how to use this tool to our advantage. Nick is able to do the unimaginable: convey complex concepts in such a manner that readers walk away with a deep understanding of both the technology and its utility.

By holding this book (or its electronic substitute) in your hands, you've acknowledged the value in learning this technology. This volume expands on Nick's first, and truly provides a go-to resource for investigators. As new blockchains and coins have developed, so too has the education he conveys. Here you'll continue to learn about Bitcoin and the methodology to investigate it, but you'll also learn about Ethereum and how to apply different principles in its tracing, all in a tool-agnostic way.

Nick's manner of education is revered by law enforcement and industry alike. He is universally respected for his clarity, and I hear over and over from peers how much they appreciate the training Nick provides. When I got a call from Nick asking me to write this foreword, I was incredibly humbled that the man I consider the gold standard for crypto education would ask for my contribution. It's an immense pleasure to be able to illustrate the demand for an updated handbook as I relate stories from the ground floor of law enforcement, deluged by victims in need of this competence.

Law enforcement can no longer afford to turn its collective head from this means of moving dirty money by using cryptocurrency. Looking away allows an avenue for wealth transfer unimpeded by government. When we don't have the opportunity to get handcuffs on overseas bad actors, we need to look to means of disrupting them. Seizing their funds is the win that our victims deserve. This book provides the jump start we all need.

Erin West

Santa Clara County, California

Introduction

I own hardly any crypto at all, just a bit of Bitcoin and some Ethereum. People always assume that since I've been around crypto for so long, I probably bought Bitcoin in 2010 for next to nothing and am now "crypto-wealthy." Sadly, that's not the case. I have never had any interest in the investment opportunities of cryptocurrencies. Just ask my friend Chris, who I advised not to bother buying Bitcoin when it was just $2,500! However, for almost a decade I have been fascinated by the technology that underpins crypto and how it can be exploited to track and trace those who would use blockchain-based funds to acquire or move criminal assets. Whatever I think about investing in crypto—and all the best to you if you have done well from it—I believe that the technology is sound and crypto is here to stay. If your work is as a criminal investigator, lawyer, legislator, compliance officer, or tax or financial investigator—really any career that touches on crime—you will come across crypto. You need to keep reading!

This book will help you to understand the ways that criminals utilize crypto in areas such as investment frauds, pig-butchering scams, money laundering, illicit financing, and more. You will learn the fundamental elements that make up different blockchains that underpin crypto such as Bitcoin, Ethereum, and the myriad of spin-off currencies, and how you can use the underlying ledgers to trace funds, attribute addresses, and seize proceeds of crime.

I suspect that you will find the first half of the book a fairly easy read, but the second half really digs into investigative methodologies, so you might want to pull your chair closer to a coffee machine! You do not need to be a computer scientist, a cryptographer, or a mathematician; you just need a good eye for patterns and a mind that can process information. I'm sure you will get on just fine.

I hope that you will also enjoy the included contributions and interviews with some of the world's outstanding investigators in the crypto space. I thank them for entrusting me and this book with their knowledge, wisdom, and experience.

I'd like to ask you to consider something as you turn to Chapter 1. If you are working in the crypto investigations space, I urge you to focus on the victims. Investigation of areas such as fraud, pig-butchering, and other such scams ruins people's lives. I've had people in tears on the phone and even reports of those who take their own lives as a result of losing all they had. Being an investigator is not all about the "tech," the prosecution targets set by our bosses, or even "getting the bad guys." First and foremost, you should focus on the victim, bringing them justice and hopefully the return of lost funds. Having a victim focus also helps to stop you from becoming jaded when wading through bureaucracy or intransigent criminal systems. Investigate for the *person*, rather than just the *crime*, and you will feel better about your life and the good you can do for others.

Use your powers for good.

1 A History of Cryptocurrencies and Crime

Driving the Harbor Freeway north out of Los Angeles toward Pasadena, you pass by the densely populated residential areas of South Park and Vermont Harbor before likely noticing the huge sporting complex that includes the LA Memorial Coliseum and the Bank of California Stadium on your left. As you pass under the Santa Monica Freeway and swing to the northeast, the vast LA Convention Center comes into view and behind it the famous home of the LA Lakers basketball team. This arena had for decades been known as the Staples Center, named after its sponsor, the vast multinational office supplies organization. However, a person driving past around Christmas 2021 would have noticed the familiar Staples signs were gone and had been replaced by a name written in blue and white. Crypto.com Arena.

For many, this would have been the first time they had seen or heard of the name of one of the largest cryptocurrency exchanges in the world. Although just five years old when they took over sponsorship of the Lakers home, the Singapore-based company had tens of millions of customers around the world and represented just one of the many cryptocurrency exchanges dealing billions of dollars of virtual currencies every day.

A few months later, during the 2022 Super Bowl, arguably one of the most expensive sporting events in the world for a company to advertise their services, five cryptocurrency exchanges ran TV advertisements or social media campaigns to coincide with it. Crypto.com has gone on to become a sponsor of the FIFA World Cup, and Formula 1 cars in 2022 displayed the logos of Binance, Bybit, Tezos, FTX, and other cryptocurrency brands. Cryptocurrencies were now squarely in the public consciousness.

At a governmental level, having long ignored or simply criticized digital currencies, countries started to wake up to the fact that these new currencies were here to stay. Although much of their early use was arguably by a mix of hobbyists, conspiracists waiting for the new world order, and criminals, now middle-class people living in the suburbs were beginning to take an interest and buy into this new investment opportunity. Newspapers and social media were running stories of the vast profits to be made, and many with some spare cash wanted in, arguably driven by a new acronym, FOMO, or fear of missing out. Anecdotal accounts of people remortgaging property to buy Bitcoin appeared in the more sensationalist press, and futures contracts and shorting options began to be made available, often by brand-new, unregulated companies.

Legislation was badly needed, and suddenly governments became more aware of the issue and started to respond. First, bodies such as the Financial Crimes Enforcement Network (FinCEN), a bureau of the U.S. Department of the Treasury, and the Financial Conduct Authority in the UK began to react to the complex issues of companies trading cryptocurrencies. Second, the tax authorities started to consider the difficulties of tracking and charging tax on the highly volatile and anonymous nature of crypto assets. Lastly, central government caught up, and by 2022, President Biden had signed an executive order (Executive Order on Ensuring Responsible Development of Digital Assets—March 9, 2022), and legislation for the "regulation of stablecoins and cryptoassets" appeared in the British Queen's Speech (`https://lordslibrary.parliament.uk/queens-speech-2022-economic-affairs-and-business`).

Other countries responded in a rather more binary way by either banning cryptocurrencies, as did China and Indonesia, or conversely welcoming them, including El Salvador, who made Bitcoin legal tender in 2021, followed by the Central African Republic.

It is notable that it is generally countries that are experiencing difficulties with their primary fiat currency that are reacting in these more contrasting ways to cryptocurrencies.

NOTE Fiat money is a government-issued currency that is not backed by a physical commodity, such as gold or silver, but rather by the government that issued it.

As mentioned earlier, El Salvador reacted to financial pressures by welcoming Bitcoin. Turkey, in the midst of crippling inflation (mid-2022) of the Turkish lira, banned the use of Bitcoin for paying for goods and services. People were turning to cryptocurrencies as a "stable" alternative to the lira, which is extraordinary when you consider how volatile the Bitcoin price can be. Governments will continue to struggle with this new challenge to their traditional centralized, government-controlled currencies for some time to come.

As I stated previously, arguably, cryptocurrencies are part of the public's consciousness in many countries around the globe, but why is this of interest to criminal investigators? To answer this question, we need to briefly look at the history of cryptocurrencies, which will help us understand their appeal to criminality.

Where Did It All Start?

English words have an odd way of changing their meaning. In the 13th century the word "silly" was someone pious or religious; however, by the late 1800s the word carried the meaning we have today of someone or something being foolish. "Crypto" has become one of those words that used to mean one thing but is now generally recognized as referring to something else. If just two or three years ago, you had asked any technologist what the word "crypto" referred to, they likely would have all responded that it was a shortened form of the word "cryptography." Cryptography has to do with the securing of data either in transit or at rest through, historically, the use of codes and ciphers, and in recent times something we will explain in more detail later known as *public/private key cryptography*. But as I'm penning this chapter, if you ask either a technologist or just a person on the street what "crypto" is, they will probably say Bitcoin, Ethereum, or cryptocurrencies, or something similar. Why has this change to the generally accepted meaning of the word happened? Certainly, in the English language we do love to shorten words (my actual name is Nicholas but the only person who ever called me that was my mum when I was misbehaving!) and *crypto* is much easier to say, and definitely easier to type, than *cryptocurrency*.

The reality is that the two meanings are closely linked. The crypto part of the word "cryptocurrency" comes from the fact that all cryptocurrencies have their transactions and transaction ledgers confirmed and protected by cryptography. In the case of Bitcoin and its derivatives, it uses a quite simple form of cryptography and it's very secure but fundamentally straightforward. It's a mistake to read online about all the hack attacks and losses of digital currencies like Bitcoin and think that there is something wrong with the code or the cryptography underpinning it. Bitcoin has never suffered from a successful attack against its source code or crypto. We will discuss in more detail how attacks against users and custodians of cryptocurrencies can fall prey to criminals in Chapter 2, "Understanding the Criminal Opportunities: Money Laundering," and Chapter 3, "Understanding the Criminal Opportunities: Theft."

Although you do not need to become a cryptographic scientist to understand how these systems work, it is still useful for an investigator to have a good idea of how cryptocurrencies are protected in order to better grasp some of the attacks against them. We will discuss this in more detail in several of the early chapters.

From a criminal perspective, cryptocurrencies offer opportunities that are difficult to achieve through the traditional banking network. We shouldn't believe that crypto is anonymous—every transaction is recorded on the blockchain ledger for anyone to study. The issue for the investigator comes from the fact that it is difficult to connect a cryptocurrency address to a user. This pseudo-anonymity provides opportunities to hide movements of assets, pay for or receive payments for illicit goods, or target others' crypto assets, in an environment that is challenging for the investigator to analyze. As this book will outline, *difficult* does not mean *impossible*.

Although this chapter is called "A History of Cryptocurrencies and Crime," I wrote a deeper background of crypto assets in my book *Investigating Cryptocurrencies* (Wiley, 2018) and I won't go into as much detail here. However, I think it's worth the investigator being aware of the accepted stepping-stones of crypto up to the present day and how they relate to the changing shape of crimes that utilize cryptocurrencies.

Most articles and books written on the history of cryptocurrencies point back to a cryptographer named David Chaum, who created an early form of electronic money called DigiCash in 1989. Others believe that the 1998 Bit Gold concept by Nick Szabo was closer to our concept of a cryptocurrency, where a predecessor of the concept of "mining" by solving algorithmic problems was implemented. Interestingly, Nick also wrote a white paper in 1994 in which he described in significant detail the concept of a digital, or smart, contract, which was an agreement between parties based purely on a coded contract with no third parties involved.

But it's the white paper published in October 2008 by the enigmatic Satoshi Nakamoto about an (arguably) new currency type that really starts the journey of crypto as we would recognize it today. Just over two months later, Nakamoto "mined" the first block, which was the genesis of a cryptographically connected series, or chain of blocks containing transaction data, which would eventually be known as a *blockchain*.

Although Bitcoin clearly is and was a brilliant piece of code, as most inventions do, it sat on the shoulders of others. We've mentioned Chaum and Szabo related to mining and cryptographically protected currencies, but the "cryptographically secured chain of blocks" was first described by Stuart Haber, W. Scott Stornetta, and Dave Bayer in papers published in 1991 and 1992 (`www.researchgate.net/publication/2312902_Improving_the_Efficiency_and_Reliability_of_Digital_Time-Stamping` and `www.researchgate.net/publication/2312902_Improving_the_Efficiency_and_Reliability_of_Digital_Time-Stamping`). Interestingly, the original Bitcoin white paper does not use the term "blockchain" anywhere. It uses the phrase in a sentence, "As later blocks are chained after it. . . ," but not the actual word "blockchain." It is unclear who first used the phrase, but some evidence points to the forum BitcoinTalk.org, where posters discussed the issues of downloading the increasingly large "blockchain" of transactions for use in their wallets. The earliest Bitcoin wallet required the user to download a full version of the Bitcoin blockchain and act as a transaction distribution node on the network.

Bitcoin grew over the next few years, with predominantly technologists and hobbyists drawn to the interesting application of technology and the promise of an online-only currency. They were soon joined by conspiracists and "preppers" (those preparing for the world's end and/or the collapse of society) who saw a kindred spirit in the decentralized, uncontrolled nature of the currency and its possibility to trade disconnected from the control and traceability of traditional banking. In those early days, the concept of a fiat currency value for Bitcoin was a bit of an anathema—it wasn't really supposed to interact or exchange with other currencies but rather stand alone, a currency for its users by its users. However, perceived dollar values rose and fell but in fairly small amounts. (In mid-2022 there was the so-called crypto winter, where Bitcoin lost two thirds of its value from its 2021 high. In percentage terms this was nothing compared to 2011, where its value reduced from the giddy heights of $15 and crashed to just $3 in four months). However, in mid-2013 Bitcoin passed the $100 value and never fell back below it again, as of yet.

It is simply logical that criminals go where the money is, and as the Bitcoin/dollar value grew and its pseudo-anonymous nature began to be more broadly understood, there was an obvious attraction for criminality to start to use the currency to store, move, and launder assets. There were very few opportunities to steal Bitcoin, as there were very few Bitcoin *whales* (large holders of Bitcoin) that were actually worth anything in the real world, but it would not be long before targets began to appear.

In January 2010, just a year after Bitcoin had appeared, a user on the BitcoinTalk forum named "dwdollar" announced that they would set up a dollar-to-Bitcoin exchange to enable users to buy and sell Bitcoin using PayPal. The unregulated and uncontrolled nature of Bitcoin would change forever; Bitcoin now had a true, demonstrable dollar value and a very early example of a cryptocurrency "bank." For various reasons dwdollar's BitcoinMarket exchange didn't last long, but in its place came a new exchange, easy to use, well constructed, and professional: Mt. Gox.

As previously stated, criminals go where the money is and arguably for the first time they had a valuable target on the Bitcoin network to focus on. The case has been reported on and written about ad nauseam, but in simple terms Mt. Gox suffered a series of successful attacks against its systems and eventually a hacker found a way to drain Bitcoin from wallets on the exchange. They managed to steal 650,000 Bitcoin over three years (850,000 Bitcoin is often reported, but around 200,000 were found in an old wallet). Attacks on exchanges had begun.

In the next few years, many exchanges would be set up; some of them were literally in the entrepreneur's spare bedroom, often turning over eye-watering sums of money, much of it criminal. Sometimes the exchange owners were the criminals, operating the exchange as a Ponzi scheme, taking payments for Bitcoin, for example, but not actually fulfilling the order and just adding the appropriate number to a spreadsheet of what the user "owned." If the user tried to cash in the crypto asset for cash, the exchange owner would use cash from another user to pay the first person, and so on. In one case I worked on, the exchange owner would often spend $60,000 of customers' money in a single weekend at a top London hotel on what we can kindly describe as "fast living." Perhaps the most notorious was an exchange in Canada called QuadrigaCX, where a reported 76,000 investors lost around C$169 million (the values vary with reports), but following the early death of founder Gerald Cotten it was discovered that he had been running the exchange as a Ponzi scheme and the company's wallets were all but empty (`https://news.sky.com/story/man-lost-500-000-life-savings-in-crypto-exchange-scam-after-trader-died-with-password-to-funds-12577397`).

The true value of losses from exchanges is impossible to calculate accurately. I've personally worked on hacks against exchanges totaling hundreds of millions of dollars that were never reported to law enforcement and no legislation existed that required them to do it. The cryptocurrency reporting website hedgewithcrypto.com has kept an unofficial list of exchange hacks since 2012 that totals $3.2 billion of losses. None of the exchange hacks I've been involved with are mentioned (`www.hedgewithcrypto.com/cryptocurrency-exchange-hacks`). Another list from ChainSec (`https://chainsec.io/exchange-hacks`) suggests $2.4 billion. Whatever, the numbers are huge.

Some of the largest exchange thefts were reported around 2016–2018, with the vast losses from Bitfinex, CoinCheck, and others valued in the hundreds of millions of dollars for each hack. Certainly, security of exchanges has improved, although we still saw reports of a $150 million loss from BitMart at the end of 2021.

Most of these early losses were in Bitcoin, but a new cryptocurrency contender would soon appear with new opportunities for the criminal to exploit.

The Rise of the Smart Contract

At about the same time that the CEO of Mt. Gox was being put in handcuffs by the Japanese police (he ended up with a suspended sentence of four years), five entrepreneurs—Vitalik Buterin, Gavin Wood, Charles Hoskinson, Anthony Di Iorio, and Joseph Lubin—were switching on a brand-new cryptocurrency that would pave the way for a whole new paradigm in cryptocurrency use. Ethereum had arrived.

Ethereum did things differently. Bitcoin made use of a very simple programming language, known as a *stack-based language*, to enable the construction of transactions. It fundamentally allowed a programmer to design the method for unlocking existing transactions and approve the locking of new ones to change the ownership of the coin. Bitcoins are never really sent or received; rather, transaction scripts merely change the owner. Bitcoin uses a UTXO model, which stands for Unspent Transaction (TX) Output. There are some great online resources to understand UTXO, but in very simple terms if you want to calculate the balance of Bitcoins held by a Bitcoin address, simply look at the blockchain and add up all the UTXOs, the unspent transactions, where the target address was the recipient. If I want to spend some Bitcoin, I can only spend unspent transactions. This might sound obvious, but it means that I have to spend the entirety of a transaction I have received.

I'll try to explain a little more simply. I assume you own a wallet or a purse? If someone gives you two $5 bills, you have a UTXO balance of $10 in your wallet. They do not magically turn into a $10 bill, but you can look in your wallet and add them up to get a wallet balance. If you want to carry out a transaction—let's say you want to buy a burger for $7—you can't tear a bill in half to try to get close to $7; you have to transact the entire value of both bills, the UTXOs, and then receive change of $3. Bitcoin works in the same way; if you have received 0.5 of a Bitcoin you have to transact that entire 0.5 and receive change.

How was Ethereum different? First, it used an account-based model. This was less like a wallet with bills and more like a bank account. Funds are paid into an address and create a balance, and then funds can be paid out in any amount up to the value of the balance. No change. No UTXOs. This is really important for an investigator to understand, and we will deal with this in more detail later.

Second, and most important, Ethereum provided a programming language called Solidity. This is known as a *Turing-complete language*, which afforded the ability for users to extend the functionality of the base Ethereum system, including building smart contracts. We will discuss smart contracts in much more detail in a later chapter, but for now know that they enable the building of other cryptocurrencies on Ethereum known as *tokens* and provide services and interactive systems. When we read about gambling using Ethereum and gaming such as Cryptokitties or Axie Infinity or even someone buying an NFT of an ape in a wedding dress for a huge sum of money, we are just talking about tokens and systems based on smart contracts built onto the Ethereum platform.

This platform was, and is, an amazing opportunity for entrepreneurs to enter the cryptocurrency market at a reasonably limited skill level and very low cost. Experienced coders could spin up a new token on Ethereum in several hours, and so often this was followed by massive social media campaigns about this new wonderful token and how great wealth and riches could be obtained by investing in it. Celebrities were paid and sometimes duped to promote these tokens before demand would usually dwindle, and the token would die a slow crypto-death (crypto-death is not a real term but I like the sound of it and so will start to use it!).

Some of these tokens were backed by genuine businesspeople and often venture capital money and have become significant businesses, but I will say it again, where the money is, the criminals will be right behind.

Smart contracts provided a rich environment for criminals, who up to this point had been enjoying the unofficial competition of seeing who could steal the most from exchanges. The small "spare bedroom" exchanges had all but disappeared, making way for the up-and-coming behemoths of Coinbase, Binance, and Kraken, to name a few. Although there continued to be some significant criminal successes against exchanges, such as the $275 million against KuCoin in 2020 and the $150 million loss from BitMart in 2021, the criminal fraternity now had many other targets to focus on.

Although we will be discussing smart contracts and how to investigate crimes that make use of them in several chapters of this book, it is worth noting at this juncture that this is something you will really need to get your head around if you intend to be involved in cryptocurrency investigations. It doesn't matter if you are a financial investigator, a fraud specialist, a lawyer, or a digital forensics expert, having an understanding of smart contracts will be increasingly important as the market develops. I started investigating crimes involving crypto back in 2015 and it was 100 percent Bitcoin. By 2017 we were seeing hacks and losses involving Bitcoin Cash (after the hard fork that created it), Litecoin, and others, but always UTXO currencies. By 2019, some 20 percent of investigations were Ethereum/token based. In 2020 it was 30 percent, and by 2021, this had grown to around 50 percent. In the past few years I haven't done one purely Bitcoin-based examination this year. Although I am by no means an investor in crypto—I literally have less than $10,000 in a total of three or four crypto assets—I do believe that Bitcoin is here to stay, but also that contract-based tokens are the future.

NOTE It is probably worth mentioning that you shouldn't reach out to ask me anything about cryptocurrency investing. When I was writing *Investigating Cryptocurrencies* in 2017, a good friend asked me how much of this "Bitcoin thing" they should buy. The price was about $1,300 per Bitcoin at the time. I suggested that it was all criminal money and not to bother. As you can imagine, that friend had some choice words for me in 2024 when the price topped $69,000 per Bitcoin. The lesson here is not to take investment advice from an investigator!

Since Ethereum, almost all new cryptocurrency blockchains either are direct emulations of the code of Ethereum such as Binance Smart Chain or are based on a smart contract architecture such as Cardano, Tron, VeChain, Internet Computer, and a host of others. Just like Ethereum, these smart contracts have been exploited in a host of ways.

Initially, the smart contract feature in Ethereum was used to generate new tokens or coins based on a standard known as the ERC-20 protocol (ERC stands for Ethereum Request for Comment and is similar to the Bitcoin BIPs, or Bitcoin Improvement Protocols. You can find more information on ERCs at `https://eips.ethereum.org/erc` and on BIPs at `https://github.com/bitcoin/bips`). These new tokens were often called initial coin offerings (ICOs), which as previously mentioned ranged from the legitimate attempt at a business idea through deluded attempts at wealth generation to outright fraudulent coin offerings. We will discuss *rug pull* scams and what investigators should be looking for in more detail later.

It would be wrong to discuss the history of Ethereum related to criminality without mentioning the DAO hack in July 2016. This is another event for which hundreds of articles have been written, and it set the pattern for significant criminal hacking activity afterward. In simple terms, a hacker managed to extract 1.5 million ETH (Ethereum coins) from tens of thousands of users into a separate DAO (decentralized autonomous organization). Eventually Ethereum users voted overwhelmingly to "hard-fork" (more on forks later) Ethereum into a new blockchain. The resulting new chain was to retain the name Ethereum and the original, which many wrongly thought would die out, would be called Ethereum Classic. What I find the most interesting about this case is the absolute denial by the hacker that they had done anything wrong. In an online post they explained that they had used a feature built into the smart contract and that they had done nothing criminal, even explicitly threatening that they would take action against anyone who tried to get the ETH back! In part they wrote:

> *I am disappointed by those who are characterizing the use of this intentional feature as "theft." I am making use of this explicitly coded feature as per the smart contract terms and my law firm has advised me that my action is fully compliant with United States criminal and tort law.*

You can read the entire post here: `https://pastebin.com/CcGUBgDG`.

So, theft or not theft, that is the question. They even sign the post "The Attacker," with the quote marks seemingly designed to engender a sarcastic tone.

Perhaps a better question is "When is a hack not a hack?" As we discussed earlier, English words have a way of changing their meaning over time, and "hacker" is one of the those words. (Actually, a "hack" was originally a horse in Old English, and a hacker was someone who would do unspeakable things with an axe!) Back in the 1960s and 1970s, a hacker was a person who would deconstruct some piece of technology and work to improve it or adjust it in some way. Hacker workshops still exist where people who are as comfortable with a soldering iron in their hands as a mouse gather to hack different products. There is no suggestion of theft or criminality. However, by the time the film *Hacker* was released in 2016 it definitely carried a nefarious meaning.

The website Deepgram.com carries an excellent list of "hack" words and indicates whether they are good or bad: (`https://blog.deepgram.com/the-history-of-the-word-hacker-2`):

- Hack (coder), n./adj.—bad
- Hacker, n.—good or bad
- To hack (code), v.—ambiguously good or bad
- Hacked (code), adj.—ambiguously good or bad
- Hacky (code), adj.—usually bad

In the case of the DAO hack, the "feature" was there in the smart contract code but at the same time there wasn't a big red button saying "Get free ETH here!"

I asked my friend and reverse-engineering expert (read—good guy hacker) Jesse D'Aguanno where the line is between a person simply using built-in code to do something the developer didn't mean it to do and manipulating code to force an application to do something it wasn't designed to do—is it ever okay? In Jesse's view, which is likely the view of your local police department, taking something that isn't yours is wrong, and in some ways it's a shame that the assertions of "The Attacker" were not tested in court.

The reason for sharing some of these early losses of crypto is that it sets a basis for criminals exploiting code for profit. Sometimes, organizations that lose funds just shrug and move on, and I worked on a few of those; other times they engage with law enforcement, but the third way, which I always find fascinating, is where they reach out to the attacker and offer to pay them for the information on how the attack was done as a bug bounty. I guess it's no different from the FBI employing the infamous "Catch Me If You Can" fraudster Frank Abagnale as he was simply very good at what he did.

How do you reach out to a hacker that has just stolen your coins? Well, you can follow the flow of funds to the receiving address and encode a message to that address. A good example was after the Wormhole Bridge hack in February 2022, when an attacker was able to mint, or create, new coins and then move/steal them.

Just after the attack the Wormhole administrator sent a message to the attacker offering $10 million to tell them how they carried out the attack! The message read:

> *This is the Wormhole Deployer:*
>
> *We noticed you were able to exploit the Solana VAA verification and mint tokens. We'd like to offer you a whitehat agreement, and present you a bug bounty of $10 million for exploit details, and returning the wETH you've minted. You can reach out to us at <email>.*

Notice that Wormhole framed this offer as a bug bounty. Bug bounties are normally paid to researchers who expose a vulnerability and notify the company and generally do not walk away and hide with $325 million of Ethereum (the value at the time of the theft). I don't say this to criticize Wormhole in any way, but simply to highlight that paying criminals rather sends the wrong signal. If the Wormhole attacker accepted the payment, does this indemnify them from prosecution—does law enforcement now have to walk away because a deal has been done? Of course, this wouldn't stop the police from investigating and taking action if they chose to, but if Wormhole now categorized this event as being a service to them, this means there is no complainant and hence they won't engage with the police and provide evidence. If there is no expectation that the company will take this indemnified approach, then there is no reason for the attacker to comply and accept the bug bounty. This creates a tricky situation and sends a message to attackers that there is big money to be made.

NOTE Having "acquired" \$114 million from Mango Markets in 2022, the stakeholders of Mango agreed with the "attacker" that they had played by the rules of the smart contract and allowed him to keep \$67 million. The attackers was later found guilty of commodities fraud, commodities market manipulation, and wire fraud.

This chapter is supposed to be a history of crypto and its associated crimes, and I appreciate that the Wormhole hack was only in early 2022, thus hardly ancient history, but these events shape the future. They teach other would-be criminals what is possible, and the losses from exchanges, tokens, blockchains, and DAOs continue.

Of course, I have been remiss in discussing examples of money laundering, illicit payments for child sexual abuse material (CSAM), and the exchanges who were not victims of crime, as mentioned before, but rather active facilitators of crime. BTC-e, run by Alexander Vinnik, a Russian national, reportedly received \$4 billion in payments between 2011 and 2017, with a significant percentage related to money laundering (`www.justice.gov/usao-ndca/pr/russian-national-and-bitcoin-exchange-charged-21-count-indictment-operating-alleged`). Indeed, it is only in the last few years that exchanges that are now household names were receivers of significant criminal funds and were very hesitant and sometimes downright obstructive in dealing with law enforcement. I'm not going to name anyone here; you know who you are!

Although we looked in shock at the \$3.2 billion approximate losses in exchange hacks alone, this rather pales in insignificance when we look at DeFi exploits. DeFi, or decentralized finance, is a catchall term related to the ability to stake or deposit funds into contracts that promise a return on the investment. This will be discussed in detail later, but a simple example can be the ability to deposit funds into a liquidity pool that facilitates exchange from one token to another. When users use the exchange contract, a small exchange fee is paid and those with funds in the "pool" make some profits. Less popular token exchange contracts will tend to pay a higher rate and the primary tokens pay less.

People are often surprised to learn that the $3.2 billion losses from exchanges cover a 10-year period but that losses from DeFi contracts in just the past two and a half years as of this writing total $3.4 billion of disclosed losses. The values lost are eye-watering. In March 2022 the gaming-focused Ronin network related to the crypto-based game Axie Infinity announced a loss of $625 million from a single hack against its DeFi environment. Remember that these are just the disclosed losses, although thefts from these contracts are harder to hide.

The Next Targets?

Many reports are written every year on the state of cryptocurrency crime. Good examples are by Europol, the U.S. Department of Justice, and investigation companies such as Chainalysis and TRM Labs. All these reports detail vast sums of cryptocurrencies laundered, drug financing, CSAM, hacks, and thefts—the list is almost endless. In many ways, the numbers are meaningless; the concerning reality is that there are an increasing number of ordinary people who are victims. In the early days of crypto, criminals stole from criminals and illicit payments were just another form of the traditional envelope full of cash between lawbreakers. Many of the crypto assets stolen from exchanges were funds that were already related to criminality. In the past five years I've been involved in the investigation of over $21 billion of cryptocurrencies related to criminality, and one of the most concerning developments is not the "calculator numbers" from each hack and theft, but how the victims are increasingly normal people.

We stated earlier how criminals go where the money is, and as cryptocurrencies began to impress themselves on society's consciousness and newspaper articles detailed the vast profits being made as Bitcoins' value grew beyond imagination, ordinary people began to invest. The problem?

I believe that 99 percent of them didn't understand how the technology worked that they were investing in. This made them easy targets.

In 2021 I received a call from a man in Florida who had lost over $250,000 worth of Bitcoin. He was wealthy, had significant investments in the U.S. stock market, and sat on the board of several successful companies. He was a clever, interesting person and he was seemingly no easy target for a criminal. The notable thing was that the $250,000 was not much to him. Don't misunderstand me; he didn't want to write it off and was keen to understand how to get the stolen funds back. What was interesting was the manner in which he had been defrauded. He had crypto on deposit at a major exchange that only ran online support. He Googled for the support details and found a Telegram channel where you could speak directly to a support team. He connected to a woman purportedly in Singapore (actually, thinking about it, purportedly a woman!) who said that he needed to "authenticate his account" before she could help. Of course he had to—that's normal for financial transactions, and it made sense to him. . . .

Now, some of you will be new to this and are waiting with bated breath to find out what happened next and what incredibly clever and under-handed method they used to steal crypto from this sophisticated investor. Others of you who have been involved in crypto-oriented crime for a while will be well ahead of me and you know what's coming!

"We need to authenticate you, Mr. X, so please provide us with your wallet seed words," said the fraudulent support person. And he did.

If you don't know what *seed words* are and want to invest in or investigate crypto, *please* keep reading this book. For those of you who know, the seed words provided the criminals running the fake support group with access to his entire wallet, and his funds were gone before he finished the support call. What was the issue? My intelligent investor victim simply didn't understand how crypto worked and hence how to protect his assets; he didn't understand that the list of 12 seed words was a representation of his private key. The clue is in the name—*private*—and handing the seed words over was akin to giving them his bank card and PIN.

Examples like this are reported to us weekly. Speaking off the record, an investigator working with the developer of a browser-based wallet said that they receive hundreds of reports of crypto losses per week, not as a result of flaws within the program but usually because of social engineering attacks where users do not understand the simple security mechanisms that protect their funds.

The Future? More Crime!

Where does this leave us as investigators? We are going to get even busier than we are already. The concepts around cryptocurrencies—whether it be blockchains, distributed ledgers, or cryptographically protected transactions—are here to stay and as you have learned in this chapter, where the money is, criminality will follow. In fact, you could argue that with Bitcoin it was criminality that led the way, rather than followed. They recognized the possibilities of the pseudo-anonymous environment early on and then found and exploited weaknesses to carry out some of the largest thefts in history, not just in cryptocurrency history.

This means that investigators of all types—frontline officers searching premises, digital forensics practitioners, financial investigators, open source investigators, lawyers, prosecutors, compliance specialists, and the list goes on—will need to understand how cryptocurrencies work, how they relate to criminal activity, and how to investigate them. It is always interesting to me that when I'm teaching a crypto-investigation class you have the keen students, sitting forward, taking it all in, and then the people with their arms crossed who don't want to be in the room. We are always appreciative to receive so many five-star reviews for our training, but two weeks ago we got two stars from a student with the review "Not for me." Unless they are six months from retiring, they are going to struggle. It is akin to a heating engineer refusing to learn how to install air-source heat pumps. Sure, combination boilers, otherwise known as combi boilers, are not going anywhere for a while, but the direction of change is clear, and they need to keep up.

A financial investigator was speaking to me a few months ago about the rise of crypto. He shrugged and said, "Traditional bank accounts are not going anywhere soon." I'm sure he was right, but I know 15-year-olds with crypto-wallets, a 22-year-old being paid half their salary in crypto, and small businesses taking payment in stablecoins. The writing is on the wall: drug dealers who have used cash for decades are now taking payment on the street in crypto. Your role as an investigator will involve crypto whether you like it or not, so you might want to keep reading!

One of my guilty pleasures is a movie called *Ferris Bueller's Day Off*. The main character, played by Matthew Broderick, breaks the fourth wall when he speaks directly to the camera and says, "Life moves pretty fast. If you don't stop and look around once in a while, you could miss it." The same principle exists with our work and career. Just because financial investigations have been the same for the past decade does not mean they will be the same a decade from now. Stop, look around, and ask what criminals are doing and what they are focusing on.

I've been told by numerous police officers from various countries over the past few years that they don't really have any crimes involving crypto assets. The only reason for that statement is that they are simply not looking for it. To adjust the Ferris Bueller quote slightly, "Crime moves pretty fast. If you don't stop and look around once in a while, you could miss it."

2 Understanding the Criminal Opportunities: Money Laundering

AN OUTLINE OF SCAMS AND CRIME IN CRYPTO

By Erica Stanford

Risks and Crime Are Constantly Changing and Evolving

Exposure to crypto assets involves risks. Volatility, market manipulation, false and misleading advertising, loss of assets, phishing links, Ponzi schemes and other scams, and theft by hacking are, unfortunately, as much a part of the industry as the many benefits brought by financial freedom, privacy, transparency, and freedom from state actors that crypto brings.

The scale and types of crime and scams involving crypto assets have dramatically changed. Today, the percentage of crypto used in crime stands at less than 1 percent. In the early years of Bitcoin since 2009, around 30 percent of crypto transactions are estimated to have been for crime, the majority of which was for buying drugs on the dark web. Estimates in 2016 suggested that Bitcoin constituted approximately 97 percent of the crypto involved in criminal activities. By 2022, the percentage of crypto crime involving Bitcoin had dropped to around 16 percent. Criminals do not like the volatility of Bitcoin. Furthermore, Bitcoin is one of the most traceable and transparent currencies. Again, this is bad news for criminals. Now, stable coins, with the greater privacy they tend to bring, are the primary go-to for criminal transactions, mainly due to the ease of purchase. Unlike other cryptocurrencies, which one can acquire by mining but primarily by trading another cryptocurrency or paying digitally by bank transfer or card, all of which leave a digital trace, stable coins can be exchanged for cash. All over the world, although mainly in jurisdictions with higher-than-average rates of money laundering, are OTC (over-the-counter) desks where one can exchange bags of physical cash for stable coins with no questions asked and no ID checks.

Risks in crypto are continuously evolving. As one exchange, dark web marketplace, or currency collapses or is closed by authorities, another takes its place. To give just one example, Bitcoin was once the exclusive cryptocurrency used for terrorist financing. Currently, assets on the TRON blockchain, notably stable coin Tether, are reported by crypto analytics platform TRM Labs to be behind 92 percent of terrorist financing (see `www.trmlabs.com/report`). As such, specific platforms or projects are here left unnamed.

The pace of crypto innovation has outpaced the law and regulators' ability to minimize some of the industry's risks. The substantial financial rewards of crime and the speed of knowledge sharing between the bad actors in crypto have far outpaced attempts to address the problem of crypto scams and crime. That being said, crypto analytics and tracing software tools are becoming increasingly powerful and able to track down the identities behind an ever-growing percentage of transactions.

Here follow the main risks, crimes, and scams in crypto. This list is far from finite. As the nature of these crimes and scams is multifaceted and fast-evolving, there will almost certainly be new types of crimes, scams, and trends by the time you read this.

Many crypto crimes are not so much crypto crimes as traditional crimes or fraud using the medium of cryptocurrency instead of fiat currency.

Risks of Centralized Power and Store of Value

One of the fundamental choices in crypto is whether to store assets on a centralized or a decentralized platform, or on a hard wallet. All options carry risks, but the risks are very different.

Concentrating power or monetary value on centralized platforms carries inherent risk. We have seen this all too often in crypto. The collapse and subsequent findings of fraud in the centralized exchange FTX is, as of this writing, the most recent case. However, there have been many centralized crypto platforms found to be operating fraudulently. There may be several more such collapses by the time you read this.

There are many risks to centralized crypto platforms. These include the founders or core team making poor investments or choices, neglect, carelessness, or other mistakes leading to financial loss for their users. The main problem here is when the founder or team is, unbeknownst to them, fraudulently using users' crypto assets, potentially for other investments or purchases, resulting in a loss to users. One mistake in a transaction can cause the permanent and irretrievable loss of users' crypto assets, which unfortunately happens often.

Another risk posed by centralized crypto platforms is the founder's or founding team's direct theft of customers' assets. This happens either by siphoning off funds for personal gain or by what is known as an exit scam or "rug pull," with the founder suddenly closing up shop and disappearing with customers' assets.

The last main risk facing users of centralized crypto platforms is that of hacks or other thefts. Centralized crypto platforms are like a red flag to a bull for hackers, or more pertinently here, can be compared to the old bank robber days, where all a robber needed to do was hold a gun to a bank employee and make off with sacks of cash. Centralized crypto platforms hold lots of value in one digital pot. It is important to add that while bad actors can be highly sophisticated, the fault in the case of a hack often lies with the platform. They must mitigate such risks by implementing thorough security audits, penetration testing, cybersecurity, and insurance.

One of the first ways centralized platforms can reduce incidences of crypto crime is by taking a firmer stance on security and better protecting their customers' assets. Too often, lapses in due diligence, overconfidence, negligence, or reluctance to invest in security inadvertently contribute to breaches that result in users losing their crypto assets.

The crime lies as much in the negligence of the platform as in the hack.

Risks of Decentralized Platforms

Decentralized crypto platforms pose different risks. One trend has seen several so-called decentralized offerings not being as decentralized as they claimed. This leads to users losing their funds through misrepresentation and misplaced trust when their funds are either lost or stolen by the founder or team through negligence, theft, or hacks. If a platform is truly decentralized, this would not be possible.

Users of decentralized platforms are also more likely to lose their crypto assets to malware or phishing by being tricked or persuaded into clicking on a phishing link or inadvertently downloading malware onto their devices.

The most significant risks facing DeFi (decentralized finance) platform users are the frequent thefts, hacks, and exploits targeting them.

Bridges

A critical risk in crypto, specifically DeFi, is crypto bridges, also known as decentralized or cross-chain bridges, used to transfer crypto assets between blockchain networks. For various technical reasons, crypto bridges are often the most vulnerable point and have suffered many hacks and exploits. In several cases, hackers have stolen hundreds of millions of dollars of crypto assets per exploit. Other risks of crypto bridges include insufficient investment in cybersecurity.

Risks of Self-Storage in Cold Storage, Such as Hard Wallets

Hard wallet safety can be a contentious issue. Some hard wallets are safer and more impenetrable than others. Safety aside, the most frequent issue affecting users of hard wallets is not a safety threat but user error. Many users have lost or forgotten the private keys needed to access their crypto holdings, rendering their crypto inaccessible. Here, the adage "not your keys, not your coins" becomes "no keys, no coins." Users of hard wallets can also more easily be tricked into sending their assets to fraudulent addresses without the stops or checks offered by the leading centralized platforms.

Risks of Online Self-Storage

Individuals and entities should generally refrain from storing cryptocurrencies in online environments. Storing crypto online in "hot" wallets necessitates stringent security measures. Notably, while convenient, online wallets expose assets to a higher likelihood of experiencing risks, including cyberattacks, hacks, exploits, and unauthorized access. The other risk facing online storage users is the frequency of phishing attempts, whereby users click on links, resulting in hackers emptying their online wallets by various means.

Hacks and Cyberattacks

Unfortunately, threats, including hacks, security breaches, cyberattacks, and exploits, are frequent occurrences in crypto. These are made more frequent by platforms with insufficient cybersecurity checks, controls, and safety measures, resulting in vulnerabilities easily found by hackers waiting to exploit them. There are two crimes committed against users here: the theft of crypto assets, signifying monetary loss, and the resulting data breach.

Theft of crypto by hack is the most significant overall crime affecting crypto by frequency and volume. The best hackers are incredibly sophisticated and are evolving their craft faster than crime prevention efforts can keep up. Some of the most sophisticated hacking groups are state-sponsored. They are under immense pressure to do a good job, have access to any technology and resources they might need, and can act with impunity in their home countries.

State-sponsored hacking groups and hacking collectives have the best hackers, tools, technologies, and resources money can buy. These groups are behind most of the world's largest hacks and work in sophisticated, coordinated ways to steal billions from crypto exchanges, bridges, protocols, and platforms.

Nevertheless, hacking is not an insurmountable risk. Hacks can be prevented or mitigated by crypto platforms such as wallets and exchanges employing the best cybersecurity, having ongoing and extensive penetration testing to check for weaknesses, buying digital asset insurance, and having experienced digital asset and smart contract lawyers and auditors check smart contracts for all loopholes, weaknesses, and flaws. Users can be educated against opening messages or emails, clicking on unknown links or potentially compromised sites or sending crypto to unknown or unverified entities. Research shows that much of the crypto lost to theft would not be lost if its owners were more selective about where they sent and stored their crypto.

Data Breaches

The second threat to users from hacks is theft or breaches of data. The theft of users' data and data breaches is an increasing problem, with some estimates indicating that up to 80 percent of all our data is now available for sale for very little money on the dark web. This data is then, in turn, used to scam individuals en masse for their crypto and other assets. The more data scammers have on an individual, the more convincingly they can scam them, and the more likely they will fall for it. The more people fall for their scams, the more data scammers get, and so on. It is a self-perpetuating cycle until crypto (and other) companies prioritize cybersecurity above all else.

Criminal Knowledge Sharing

Knowledge sharing among crypto criminals is also a big thing. Individual hackers frequently share or sell their new learnings and tools in dark web forums or privacy-focused messaging channels such as Discord or Telegram in groups dedicated to sharing known exploits, vulnerabilities, and security flaws of software platforms or computer systems. Hacking forums also share information on hacking, vulnerabilities, leaks, and the latest tools and also run marketplaces selling the tools needed to carry out exploits. These forums and marketplaces sell criminal toolkits of everything needed to commit crime. These networks also bring together the different roles needed to run scams effectively, comprised of malware coders, hackers, phishing experts, money mules, identity thieves, social engineering experts, and more.

These trends make it increasingly difficult for cybersecurity and law enforcement to keep up.

KYC and AML Get-Arounds

KYC (know-your-customer) and AML (anti-money laundering) scams are increasing. As fast as new advances in KYC checks develop, fraudsters develop more ways to get around them. On the one hand, there are benefits to KYC and AML checks. They might stop or slow down bad actors from cashing out stolen crypto funds or funding terrorism, for example. On the other hand, they prevent financial inclusion, privacy, and freedom. There are many ethical and moral arguments both for and against such checks. There is no clear correct answer.

Crimes around KYC and AML controls involve using some form of false ID or employing or forcing someone else to be the face of a scam. False and stolen identity documents can easily be fraudulently acquired on the dark web and used on registration. Where more sophisticated onboarding checks are in place, criminals use fake IDs convincing enough to be indistinguishable from the real thing. State-sponsored hackers, among others, fly around the world on such identity documents with airport security checks unable to register that the person traveling is not the same as, or the real identity of, the name shown on the document. Anything can be bought for a price.

Marketplaces now exist, typically on the dark web, where real people sell their services to scammers and criminals wanting to get around the most detailed onboarding controls or for those running more sophisticated frauds. This might be people letting their name or address be used for a fake ID, passing video checks, or receiving an ongoing weekly salary for their name and face to be used to maintain an identity or as a made-up role in an attempt to make a fraud look legitimate. Others are tricked or coerced into letting their identity be used. The more vulnerable people are, the more likely they fall victim to these circumstances. The individuals who exchange their identity for money are not the ones to blame. These are typically individuals in developing countries who lost their incomes during the pandemic or have no other viable choice they are aware of to earn money legally. It is the criminal gangs and an untransparent system that allows and facilitates this. Many do not even know their identity is used for fraudulent purposes.

The lack of adequate KYC and AML checks on some platforms has drawn regulators' concern, with the UK's FCA writing a "Dear CEO" letter hoping to address this.

Impersonation Scams

Here, criminals mask as known individuals or organizations to trick victims into sending crypto funds or revealing sensitive information, such as personal data or their private keys. In crypto, criminals often convincingly pretend to represent crypto platforms or influencers. One example of a convincing scam was a criminal entity hacking the third-party email provider of a known crypto provider to send an email from the correct email address to trick users into downloading an update to the legitimate app. The "updated" app was fraudulent and cost users their crypto assets, but it was indistinguishable from the real one.

Impersonation scams on social media are also frequent. One example is the 2020 Twitter (X) security breach that gave scammers access to tweet from real high-profile accounts offering a fake Bitcoin giveaway if only users first sent in some of their Bitcoin to be doubled. This was not so much an impersonation scam as using real profiles against their owners' knowledge or will to promote crypto fraud.

One frequent trick is to use the names and faces of real, legitimate people to promote scams. Here, victims fall for scams or send their crypto to fraudulent addresses, believing the platform is good because of the people or entities listed on the team. Of course, the individuals or entities do not give their permission for this and know nothing of this until it is too late. The rise of artificial intelligence (AI) and the increasing sophistication of deepfakes has added to this issue.

Phishing

Phishing scams are as pervasive in crypto as in every other digital sphere. Crypto phishing links lead to drained wallets and downloaded malware. Phishing scams take many forms. Some involve links, emails, social media accounts, or sites that might look legitimate but trick users into logging on and inadvertently giving away their passwords and credentials. Some involve tricking a user into clicking on a malicious link, leading to theft of credentials, draining their crypto assets, or installing malware. In crypto, phishing scams involve tricking users into revealing their seed phrases, allowing the scammer to drain their victims' crypto wallets. Phishing links might be sent from what appears to be a genuine email address or social media platform from a known provider or might be on an app or website that looks real to an unsuspecting user. An individual cannot be too careful. If there is any doubt, or you are not 100 precent sure of the sender or receives a message from an unknown sender, it is always best to auto-delete and not take any risks.

Phishing scams also take the form of giveaways, fake technical support, employment offers, or claims to help with retrieving funds after a collapse or hack of a crypto platform. Any unsolicited message or email might be a scam or contain a phishing link. Airdrops, where free crypto tokens are sent out en masse, can contain malware or phishing links that infect a user's device or drain their crypto wallets when downloaded or clicked on.

Address Poisoning

Address poisoning is one of the newer types of phishing scams. Here, a scammer creates a crypto address similar to one to which their victim has either previously sent funds or is known to intend to send funds. In sending a crypto transaction, typically users will only check the first few and last few digits of a crypto address to ensure it is the same address to which they intend to send their funds. This is a mistake. Scammers will create addresses where the first few and last few digits are the same, but only a few digits of the address in the middle are changed, meaning the victims' funds get sent to fraudulent addresses controlled by the scammer. Alternatively, scammers will send a small payment to their victim in the hopes that the victim will see the similarities, assume it is the same as their intended address, and send their more valuable transaction to the fraudulent address. Here, all you can do is check every digit of a crypto address when sending a transaction to be sure. AI checks can now help with this.

Personally Targeted Phishing Attacks: Spear Phishing

Spear phishing is where phishing attacks are targeted directly to the user. Here, scammers will have access to users' data and records from the dark web and will target an individual directly with enough knowledge and detail to appear legitimate. The best you can do is delete any unsolicited emails or messages with the expectation that they are fraudulent.

Malware

Malware downloaded onto a device, frequently because of clicking on phishing links, can record keystrokes, take screenshots, or access clipboard data to steal a wallet and other records without the affected user knowing. Malware might also replace wallet addresses when copying, pasting, or entering to divert funds to a hacker's wallet or track when users paste their wallet data and private keys.

Ransomware

Ransomware—malicious software that encrypts its victims' files or data, rendering them inaccessible—is a known and growing problem and a threat to individuals, companies, governments, and global corporations. Hackers typically demand ransom payments in cryptocurrency. Some ransom demands charge up to a 20 percent premium if the victim pays in Bitcoin over the relatively more private Monero. Major organized crime gangs, state-sponsored hacking groups, and hacking collectives are behind the most significant ransomware attacks.

Malware, Ransomware, and Scam-as-a-Service Packages

For anyone lacking the sophistication or connections to be in a state-sponsored hacking group or organized crime gang, criminals wanting to take part in malware and ransomware attacks can buy malware-as-a-service or ransomware-as-a-service (or phishing-as or scam-as-a-service) packages on the dark web. Packages for sale offer custom malware and ransomware strains, technical chat support on how to run them, scripts for conning and extorting their victims, call center infrastructure and scam training manuals, videos, and mentoring. These strains will not have the sophistication of those orchestrated by the most successful hacking groups but still exert colossal damage on a volume basis and to their victims.

One challenge of these as-a-service scams is the ease at which they are now accessible to any petty criminal, whereas before such scams needed a degree of technical expertise to run. One trend has seen real-world criminals, such as burglars of physical goods, turn to buying and running these scam and malware packages with no need for technical understanding of how they work. This has happened more since COVID-19 and the lockdown, resulting in people spending more time at home and thus being more challenging to rob, increasing online scams and crime. Real-world criminals, such as petty burglars, are attracted to these online crypto scam offerings as they present fewer risks and potentially greater rewards.

Ponzi Schemes

Crypto-related crimes take many forms, and yet all share a common trend of aiming to part their victims from their money. Most crypto scams are not directly crypto scams, as traditional scams that just happen to part their victims from crypto instead of from a different type of asset. Perhaps the largest crypto scam by volume stolen so far was OneCoin, which lost its victims at least $4 billion, up to an estimated $15 billion. However, OneCoin did not even have a cryptocurrency. It said it did, but its so-called cryptocurrency was nothing more than the founder manipulating numbers on a traditional SQL spreadsheet, where the numbers its victims saw were nothing but a shared account on a screen. OneCoin was a traditional Ponzi scheme playing on people's hopes to make their crypto wealth.

On the surface, all crypto Ponzi schemes look different. Some claim to offer crypto mining or cloud mining. Some position themselves as investment funds or advisers. Some claim to be exchanges, purporting to be the most regulated or safest or offer the best returns or cheaper access to buy new tokens. Some claim to have a new trading algorithm that guarantees returns. Some claim to have invented a new cryptocurrency. Some might be stable coins. Typically, crypto Ponzi schemes offer unsustainably high returns, with some offering returns in the double figures daily and/or compound interest. Often, they will claim to promise or guarantee high returns, but not always.

What all crypto Ponzi schemes have in common is that they will initially pay out, giving the vestige of legitimacy so that enough people believe them to be good. Some have gone on for years. The more obvious Ponzi schemes use multilevel marketing (MLM) and offer high commissions for bringing in new investors. Those who get in early or who are the best at promoting frequently make extreme amounts of money from these commissions and employ aggressive and pressurized sales techniques to convince more vulnerable people to invest. Because of how far the tentacles of this type of MLM Ponzi scheme spread, this type of scam can be the hardest to trace and work out for sure who is guilty of knowingly promoting a Ponzi scheme and who is just an unknowing victim looking to maximize their gains by sharing what they think is a legitimate investment.

Numerous crypto exchanges and lending platforms, especially those that have already failed, can be accused of having acted in a Ponzi-like manner, using the money from new investors to pay returns to the old or to invest in other dubious schemes.

Investment Scams

Investment scams solicit funds for fraudulent purposes. They perhaps fall under Ponzi schemes but deserve their own section because of how frequently and pervasively they occur. The range of sophistication varies widely; however, the most advanced among these have been notably convincing. In crypto, these have evolved from centring around fake or fraudulent initial coin offerings (ICOs) to now being more commonly seen in unregistered securities or fraudulent investment platforms. Investment fraud involving cryptocurrency has increased enormously in recent years.

Pump-and-Dump Schemes

Entities running pump-and-dump schemes have taken advantage of the lack of regulation in crypto to run what would be, in any other context, a fraudulent offering. There are thousands of chat rooms on social channels and messaging platforms and on the Internet and dark web dedicated to running pump-and-dump groups, some with millions of subscribers per single room. These groups operate deceptively on several levels.

On the first level, crypto pump-and-dump schemes urge a group to buy a cryptocurrency at a set time to cause an artificial price surge, manipulating the market. This triggers other more naïve investors and bots to buy into that cryptocurrency, believing they will miss out if they do not buy in while its price increases. Of course, that cryptocurrency then collapses, typically back to its initial starting value, often due to a lack of new investors buying in, or on the instruction of the pump-and-dump organizers. Pump-and-dump groups frequently also disseminate false or deceptive information about the token they are pumping on chat rooms and social media to lure other investors and bots to pump up the price of the cryptocurrency in question. The vast majority of participants in pump-and-dumps lose out. Typically, only the organizers, and perhaps their chosen few, make money.

On the second level, organizers are the first to buy in, often days before they announce the pump, ensuring they have bought as much of the intended token at its lowest value as they want. They are also the first to sell out, ensuring they have made a good profit before advising their followers to do so. They also frequently charge high fees to join these groups, despite knowing that most of their members will lose money on the pumps and the group fees. On a third level, pump-and-dump schemes are nothing more than market manipulation and have been frequent in crypto.

Crypto pump-and-dump schemes remain big business. An academic team at UCL (University College London) concluded that online crypto pump-and-dumps take in $120 billion a year (see `www.chainalysis.com/blog/podcast-ep-44-everything-you-need-to-know-about-pump-and-dump-schemes`).

Romance Scams, or "Pig Butchering"

The phrase "pig butchering" comes from a Chinese expression, where pigs are fattened up before slaughter. Scammers are now more sophisticated than ever at separating individuals from their money. There are now numerous scammer schools, a trend that seems to have started in Africa and is now spreading to the United States and Europe. Here, would-be scammers, mostly disillusioned youth needing work or looking for easy income, pay tuition fees to learn how to scam. These schools teach how to write in the style of different genders and different ages, how to put on different voices and accents or use tools to disguise their real voice, how to text to string people along for months on end, what excuses to give when their victims ask to meet or video chat, and how to extract money and crypto from their victims. In these schools, thousands of scammers hone their craft. Schools train would-be scammers to lurk on social media, dating apps, online games, and forums—anywhere they can meet their potential victims. They lurk most frequently on dating apps, which are considered to be particularly effective for meeting the vulnerable. These schools train scammers to spend weeks or months grooming their victims, building trust, friendship, and often a relationship. Many victims believe they have fallen in love with their scammers' fake profiles. Some have proposed, without ever meeting in real life. Others have left real-world relationships to be with their new online love.

Pig butchering romance scams focus on getting their victims to send crypto over other currencies. It is easier to steal crypto than FIAT; crypto does not give away that it is crossing borders on transactions, and transactions are typically irreversible.

These scammers know that just asking for crypto will not generally work. People will be too suspicious. Romance scammers take time to build trust and establish a virtual relationship. They will only mention a new investment or crypto offering after building a virtual rapport, sometimes days, weeks, or even months after initiating a conversation. They word it cleverly, not asking for money but dropping hints as to how much money they have made or painting the dream of a future together if only they can both make these great returns from this investment. Once they have persuaded their target to get involved in crypto, the next step is typically getting their victims to send money to a real, legitimate crypto exchange. Only then do they mention an even better return or product and incite their victims to send their crypto from a real exchange to a different platform. The scammers inevitably control this next platform, but it might look superficially like a real crypto platform or exchange. Of course, once the scammers receive this crypto, they are off. Sometimes, they stay in communication, but only to coerce more crypto from their victims. This type of scam is the most damaging, as it frequently causes emotional pain as well as financial loss.

Pig butchering scams are founded on psychological manipulation and social engineering. They aim to drain victims of their life savings by any means of manipulation possible, using crypto merely as the means of separating their victims from their money. The full scale of pig butchering, especially romance scams, is still being determined due to a general lack of reporting of this type of scam. There is a tendency not to want to report when one has fallen victim to one.

One notable feature of pig butchering scams is their interconnectedness with other scams and frequently with organized crime gangs. Over half of pig butchering scams studied by crypto analytics platform TRM Labs, for example, showed links to international organized crime gangs (see `www.trmlabs.com/post/pig-butchering-scams-what-the-data-shows`).

The Human Trafficking Link in Crypto Scams

Despite many claims that human trafficking networks use crypto as a method of payment in human trafficking, research indicates that if this is the case, it is minimal. In contrast, research shows that the primary link between crypto and human trafficking is the use of human trafficking victims to fuel pig butchering scams. These victims are held prisoner, forced to serve as the unpaid call centers behind crypto scams.

A huge problem, particularly in Southeast Asia, is that false job ads lure victims to unfamiliar destinations. On arrival to their destination country, human traffickers bundle their victims into vans and confiscate their passports and other personal items. Once at their destination, guards lock the human trafficking victims up in buildings with bars covering all windows and no escape route. Police raids have helped to release some of these victims, but the problem is ongoing and fueled by corruption. Chinese criminal syndicates are accused of running many of these scam sweatshops, in which police raids have found torture devices, electric shock devices, and handcuffs. Reports of torture and even killings in these compounds are, sadly, frequent. Unfortunately, there is no sign of this crime abating. With criminal syndicates sharing intelligence, human traffickers can quickly empty compounds and send their victims in busloads to the next prison compound in advance of police raids. Consequently, the abuse of these victims and the scams they are forced to sustain persist.

Scams of Scams

The dark web has a myriad of interesting sites and offerings. Hitmen offering murder, torture, and disfigurement or "accident"-for-hire services are perhaps the most extreme. There are also numerous ransomware- and scam-as-a-service providers, hacking and hacker-for-hire services, money laundering services, crypto mixing services (used to obfuscate crypto transactions), carding shops (dealing with stolen credit cards or credit card details), drug and weapons dealers, market manipulation offerings, and more. Some of these are real, though typically not the murder-for-hire services. However, these offerings are frequently just scams, scam offerings of their real (but criminal) equivalents. Typically, these services ask for payment in Monero, a cryptocurrency known for its enhanced privacy, though not wholly untraceable, or Bitcoin that has undergone a series of obfuscations through various mixers and other obscuration tools. These offerings indicate how deeply crime inhibits parts of the dark web.

Follow-on Scams

There is a scam version of almost every crypto activity—both legal and illegal. One of the most pervasive type of crypto scams affecting victims is the follow-on of crypto scams and collapses. Almost every crypto scam or collapse is followed by "victim support" offerings, purporting to get the victims their money back, offering free legal aid, or other such claims. Of course, there are legitimate offerings intended to help victims in class action suits or otherwise. Unfortunately, victims who have fallen victim to fraud or collapse cannot be too careful. Details of all victims or investors who have lost money are frequently illegally obtained and sold on the dark web. These details are then bought by criminal networks and used to target the already vulnerable victims. These scams will eventually ask victims to pay more to regain their lost investment. Should an individual be solicited with any proposition that necessitates divulging personal information or making a payment, irrespective of the offer's persuasiveness or the accuracy of details possessed by the solicitor, it is advisable to refrain from sharing any information, engaging with any links, or conducting further financial transactions. Instead, promptly reporting the incident to law enforcement authorities is the best action.

Some Words to Finish

With all this being said, crypto gets a perhaps unjustly poor reputation for its share in global financial crime. While there have been and will continue to be many crypto scams, fiat currencies, particularly the U.S. dollar, dominate illicit transactions. The inherently transparent and traceable nature of crypto assets brings multiple benefits in the fight against financial crime. Crypto transactions are more traceable than FIAT currency, with the uniqueness of every crypto token meaning transactions can be tracked back throughout that coin or token's life cycle and all other addresses and wallets with which a transaction may be associated. In investigations, following the money is faster, easier, and more effective in crypto than FIAT money digitally, and certainly much more straightforward than following cash or other tangible assets. Crypto analytics tools enhance the ability to follow and understand criminal networks and trends and "watch" their stolen crypto. Many who have used crypto for criminal purposes and got away with it are now discovering, when the FBI or other law enforcement come knocking at their door, that their entire transaction history has been traced and linked back to them, often years after they committed the crime. It was true at the onset of Bitcoin and now: Using cryptocurrencies for illicit activities is ill-advised due to the high likelihood of detection.

Former CIA director Michael Morell, in a 2021 report titled "An Analysis of Bitcoin's Use in Illicit Finance" by (see `https://cryptoforinnovation.org/wp-content/uploads/2022/07/An-Analysis-of-Bitcoins-Use-in-Illicit-Finance-By-Michael-Morell.pdf`), which includes research from industry experts, summarizes his findings in two main points:

> *[B]ased on our research and discussions with industry experts, I have confidence in two conclusions:*
>
> - *The broad generalizations about the use of Bitcoin in illicit finance are significantly overstated.*
> - *The blockchain ledger on which Bitcoin transactions are recorded is an underutilized forensic tool that can be used more widely by law enforcement and the*

> *intelligence community to identify and disrupt illicit activities. Put simply, blockchain analysis is a highly effective crime fighting and intelligence gathering tool.*
>
> Other quotes included in this report further highlight this point. Blockchain technology is a "boon for surveillance," and "catching illicit actors is 'magnitudes greater' using blockchain than in the traditional banking sector," and "if all criminals used blockchain, we could wipe out illicit financial activity."

There Is No Such Thing as Crypto Crime

Back in 2021 I started giving a series of conference talks titled "There is no such thing as cryptocurrency crime." We were in the middle of the pandemic and so all conferences were on Zoom or similar and so it was easy to say yes and simply log into a conference being held in Vancouver or Washington, rather than having to get on a plane. I have paid my proverbial dues flying around the world and I'm more than happy to be presenting from my warm office with just a 10-second commute time from my kitchen! The talks seemed to be very successful, and the principal point from the 60-minute presentation was well received and formed the basis and title of this book.

The talk title was originally designed to be deliberately contrary and argumentative, a clickbait title. "Of course there is cryptocurrency crime," people would tell me, "it's all over the newspapers and our police force now has a crypto-crime unit."

The point I was making was simple, but the lesson you should take away from it is profound and important. There is a 2,500-year-old Bible proverb that sums it up pretty well. It is presumed by some scholars to have been originally penned by the well-known Israelite King Solomon (of the movie *King Solomon's Mines* fame—although I don't believe he was actually cast in the film) and was later quoted by Shakespeare, but the last line is still a well-known English saying today:

> *What has been is what will be,*
> *And what has been done will be done again;*
> *There is nothing new under the sun.*
>
> **(Eccles. 1:9)**

In Chapter 1, "A History of Cryptocurrencies and Crime," we discussed how criminals go where the money is and cryptocurrencies have been no exception. But even though the concept of a cryptocurrency is new (although maybe not so new if you read about the stone money used on the Pacific island of Yap covered in my first book), and although there have been new opportunities created by smart contracts, for example, I still challenge you to come up with a "new" category of crime.

Money laundering, Ponzi schemes, social engineering attacks, computer hacks, terrorism funding, illicit payments, even sanction avoidance—all these things have existed for decades and, in some cases, millennia. What is even more interesting is that when you boil down a crime that involves crypto, you will see similar techniques that have been used by criminals and that law enforcement has learned to investigate successfully.

What is the takeaway?

> *Do not forget tried and tested investigative methodology just because the crime involves cryptocurrencies.*

This statement was, in part, driven by the growing tendency of law enforcement and investigation companies all over the world to begin to form specialist crypto investigation teams. This isn't a bad idea in itself, but their role needs to be carefully considered. When I wrote *Investigating Cryptocurrencies* back in 2017/2018, I made a fundamental error. Because my background was digital forensics—which is mostly just extraction and then analysis of data from phones and computers—I thought it was logical that crypto investigations would be done by those teams. Cryptocurrencies needed artifacts such as private keys to be extracted from forensic images (copies) and then analysis carried out. I felt it was obvious that the people who would do computer investigations related to crypto would be my friends in digital labs around the world. The book was oriented in that direction, with tools and methods for data extraction and open source searches. I was wrong.

In the past five years, we have realized that "there is nothing new under the sun," that yes, we have the people who can extract data in the form of digital forensics experts, but we also have skilled analysts who understand following money movements and complex laundering methods in the shape of financial investigators (FIs), specialist fraud investigators, and others. I mentioned in Chapter 1 the appearance of decentralized finance (DeFi) cryptocurrency products related to futures and shorting. Financial investigators already understand these often complex concepts and how to follow the money. These products are not really that different from their namesakes in traditional finance, and FIs simply need to learn how it relates to cryptocurrencies and then apply their existing wealth of investigative knowledge.

We also already have the skills to carry out open source online investigations in the form of cyber investigators. Many investigation teams have specially trained dark web investigators. In addition, specialists in money laundering and fraud already understand the generic methodologies used in these areas; they just need to learn the cryptocurrency specifics and then apply their existing knowledge. Basically, everyone needs to learn about how crypto impacts their area of criminal interest.

As we already have available the foundational skills needed to investigate all types of crimes involving cryptocurrencies, we have to wonder at the reason for creating specific, siloed teams. There is a real danger that a crypto-specific team becomes isolated and only gets to see crimes specifically related to digital currencies. This is problematic in two ways. First, crimes that involve crypto but are actually much wider in scope may not be investigated correctly in the narrow perspective of a crypto investigation department. Second, cryptocurrency evidence may be missed at the discovery stage purely because the team didn't know what to look for to identify crypto artifacts or signs of use.

Let me give you two examples of this; these are both real crimes:

- A man selling Bitcoin online sold several small sums to a buyer. The buyer was friendly and offered to meet the seller. The seller invited the buyer to his home. The buyer arrived with a friend, cable ties, and a pistol. They beat up the seller and forced him to transfer them all his Bitcoin. What type of job is this? Is this a crypto investigation?

  This crime had a number of potential charges associated with it: bodily harm, perhaps attempted murder, false imprisonment, theft. . .the list goes on. And of course, there is the crypto element!

  There is the risk that this job could be considered a crypto investigation and pushed on-to the crypto investigation department. After all, the seller was dealing crypto and it was Bitcoin that was stolen. But is this really the case? Think of the many other evidence points that may have been possible. Phone records, CCTV, doorbell camera footage, fingerprints, eyewitnesses of the suspects on the street, tracing the route taken to the scene of the crime and away from it—the list is extensive and we haven't touched on the cryptocurrency part yet.

- Surveillance officers are watching a midlevel drug dealer and witness a number of deals taking place on the street with the street dealers. They move in for the arrest but find no cash on the suspect. A digital forensics person finds a crypto-wallet on the suspect's device that contains $250,000 of crypto assets and logs indicating that the street dealers were paying the suspect in crypto rather than cash.

  Is this a cryptocurrency job? Please don't misunderstand me; there could be much to learn by tracing the path the funds took, where they came from, and where they went, but this is a drug job, and we know how to investigate drug dealers. Again, there is the risk that this lands on the desk of the crypto people, but there is once again a list of other evidence points that should be considered and investigated.

So, what's the lesson? In my experience, crimes that involve cryptocurrencies are never "stand-alone" in that the only evidence is the blockchain evidence. This means that crypto investigators need to work closely with frontline officers, cyber officers, open source investigators, and financial investigators, among many others. We should not fall into the trap of thinking that any crime with a crypto element is a "cryptocurrency" crime and so we give it to the person who has been trained on the new and shiny crypto investigation software and think that will be sufficient.

I was speaking to the head of cyber investigations in a South American country just a few months ago and he was telling me about their new national crypto investigation team. I asked what skills they had in the team, and he sounded a little confused and told me that it was a team of cyber people who had done their training on their chosen commercial tool. It's one of those moments where you know that you have to say something but for the life of you can't find the words. I mumbled something like "Don't forget to work closely with other departments," but in reality, that team has to have a collection of digital forensics, cryptocurrency-trained track-and-trace people, financial investigators, open source investigators, and so on—or they need to embed their people within the departments that specialize in those skills. Being a crypto investigator is not just about putting a crypto address or transaction ID into a commercial intelligence tool—it is so much more than that. I equate it to being a traditional forensics person who only knows how to lift fingerprints. It's a very useful skill, but there is so much more to find.

So how do cryptocurrencies get used, applied, or exploited in different crime types? Let's look at some common examples and begin to understand what an investigator is looking for.

Money Laundering

DEFINITION Money laundering involves the process of making illegally obtained funds (dirty) appear legitimate (clean) by disguising their true source and mixing, or blending, them.

In case you have ever wondered, money laundering gets its name from the technique of blending funds. As traditionally criminal funds were in cash, you would feed, or blend, illicit money into cash businesses such as casinos, strip clubs, or laundromats. Because it was very hard for the authorities to clearly know the numbers of clients that these types of cash businesses had, and also the value of payments made by those clients, it was very easy to inflate the legitimate income with illegitimate funds. As long as the business did not "overblend" (e.g., a laundromat doing $50 million is obviously a large clue) and did its accounting properly, paying taxes and so forth, the profits could be removed cleanly from it. Laundered.

From very early on in the history of cryptocurrencies, criminals saw the potential for the hiding, converting, and moving of illicit funds. The pseudo-anonymous nature of Bitcoin provided an easy and low-risk way of turning criminal money into crypto via the many unregulated exchanges that existed for about the first 10 years of Bitcoin's history. Whereas traditional money laundering had numerous steps, or layering, to make it successful, moving the funds through a variety of sources, asset switching, and blending, a criminal could simply convert the funds into crypto through an exchange that took no customer information and was unregulated with regard to anti-money-laundering capabilities and that was it. The crypto sat in an anonymous address and could be moved to any recipient with ease or simply cashed back into fiat currency from another exchange. Laundering could now be achieved in a single step with just a laptop and an Internet connection.

I hate to be so glib, but stealing is relatively easy; it's what you end up doing with the proceeds of theft that is most likely to get you caught. Breaking into a millionaire's mansion and making off with a Monet painting just takes some good planning and a variety of skills, but once you have the Monet in your hands, what do you do with it? Every art buyer will recognize the painting and a good number of them will call the police. Unless you have stolen it to order, actually turning it into dollars or sterling so that you can enjoy the proceeds of your life of crime will be very difficult indeed. Its analogous to the climber who will tell you that climbing the mountain is the easy part; it's the getting down that kills most people.

Money laundering used to be complex; now, with a cryptocurrency like Bitcoin it feels easy to the criminal. Criminal gang members can be paid in crypto, ransoms paid in crypto, payoffs made in crypto, then turned back into fiat currency with a single mouse click through an exchange or even on the street. I worked on a case where the perpetrators never even sent the Bitcoin anywhere. To prove the ability to pay for criminal services, they deposited Bitcoin in an address, provided the master public key to prove they owned the funds (more on that later), and then when an agreement was reached a physical courier handed over the private key in person. The exchange of funds was invisible because on the blockchain the change of ownership never happened. Quite clever.

A change was needed—legislation aimed at the exchanges. By 2022 legislation similar to banking legislation was levied against any organization trading cryptocurrencies, with the requirement to implement anti-money-laundering checks, maintain know-your-customer (KYC) on clients, and provide suspicious activity reports (SARs) when unusual activity was detected.

Has this solved the problem and stymied the criminals' use of crypto? Far from it. Fit-for-purpose legislation has only been implemented in a handful of countries, and even those places have nowhere near the number of trained investigators needed to keep up with the reporting from compliant exchanges. When one country's financial intelligence unit received its first SAR from the Coinbase exchange, I got a phone call asking what they were supposed to do with it! Although by 2022 most of the large exchanges were compliant, there are still many territories in the world where they can still act with impunity. Other countries have hidden their heads in the sand by simply banning cryptocurrencies. They probably banned the ownership of hard drugs, too, and that's worked well, hasn't it? Any country that bans its citizens from owning cryptocurrency simply hasn't read the manual. Crypto doesn't care where a person is and the blockchain is ambivalent to geographic location—you might as well ban air.

Chainalysis reported that in 2021 criminals laundered $8.6 billion. The problem has not gone away, but robust legislation accompanied with an increase in trained investigators will help to level the playing field.

The next piece in the money laundering puzzle for the investigator is detection and tracking. Thankfully we now live in a world with software tools such as TRM Labs, Chainalysis, and Elliptic that use techniques to uncover the ownership of crypto addresses and simplify the ability of tracking and tracing funds across the blockchain, or increasingly, many blockchains. Money launderers now realize that just moving funds into Bitcoin is not enough, and we see an increasing use of bridges to jump blockchains and mixers to obfuscate funds. The right tools can help to solve that puzzle. Although I will teach some of these techniques in this book, you will definitely need to invest in a commercial track-and-trace tool, preferably two, to benefit from their address attribution databases.

What Is an Investigator Looking For?

Following on from the biblical quote earlier in the chapter, please excuse the religious symbology, but there are no virgin births of crypto coins on the blockchain. All coins were mined or minted at some point in the past and, in many cases, can be tracked from birth to their current resting address. This is especially the case with UTXO coins such as Bitcoin or Bitcoin Cash. Whereas physical cash is very difficult to trace once it leaves the printer, the public record of the blockchain is unchangeable, enabling the investigator to know where funds have come from and where they are going. As I stated previously, there is "nothing new under the sun" and so the typologies related to money laundering in crypto are the same as or similar to the typologies that you will be used to seeing as an investigator.

In this section, we will consider examples of what investigators can look for to identify possible money laundering typologies. Keep in mind this is by no means an exhaustive list.

Centralized Exchanges

As mentioned in Chapter 1, exchanges have become a key element of the broader cryptocurrency infrastructure, enabling bank-style accounts to be maintained and conversion between fiat and crypto currencies and even exchange between cryptocurrencies themselves. We differentiate a centralized from a decentralized exchange as a centralized exchange works in a similar way to a bank. It is generally owned by a company or individuals, has internal liquidity, will provide services such as technical support, and is often subject to regulation.

Whereas exchanges have been targets of criminal activity, many have been directly and knowingly involved in receiving and laundering funds. Others have knowingly ignored and still others have facilitated the movement of illicit funds unknowingly because of a lack of anti-money-laundering capabilities.

Many exchanges are now working actively with government and law enforcement to provide SARs and are responding quickly to requests for KYC information and freezing and seizure orders. However, there are still a large number of exchanges, large and small, that outright ignore requests for assistance or make a show of compliance while putting up roadblocks at each step. If we are following a trace of crypto payments and are able to identify assets transferred to addresses owned by noncompliant or unlicensed exchanges, then we can make a pretty good assumption that the funds are being hidden. To a lesser degree, suspicions can also be raised when funds move to exchanges in high-risk jurisdictions.

We will not cover here the triggers that exchanges should be looking for to identify money laundering. There are some outstanding books, white papers, PhD dissertations, and other sources that cover this complex subject in the detail it deserves. It is worth noting, still remembering the "nothing new under the sun" quotation, that the triggers will be very similar to the prompts used by the banks. In addition, commercial software tools designed to automatically identify suspect addresses in a customer's history or actions that carry the signature of criminal money laundering are available from many suppliers such as TRM Labs, Chainalysis, and Elliptic.

Needless to say, the identification of an exchange in the downstream of a criminal's address is very useful. Whether we are law enforcement, government, or a lawyer, we should then be able to produce legal paperwork to request or force an exchange to freeze or seize assets. Of course, exchanges are unlikely to simply roll over and send you $1 million of crypto simply because you suggest that it belongs to a victim or because you believe that it is criminal. A significant weight of evidence or judgment by a recognized court of law is likely to be needed. We will discuss this in more detail in Chapter 17, "Crypto Seizure."

However, for many investigations the identification of an exchange either sending or receiving funds to a suspect address can help to move your analysis forward, if the exchange is willing to cooperate.

Of course, the use of an exchange by a suspect address is not necessarily evidence of money laundering. However, if you have strong or definitive evidence that funds held in an address are the result of fraud or theft and then you observe movement of those funds into an exchange, you are certainly looking at criminal movement of illicit funds and possibly money laundering if you discover that funds are changed into other currencies or split into different addresses, or their transmission is otherwise obfuscated.

It is important to note that you cannot track through centralized exchanges. It is analogous to paying a $20 bill into a bank and then going back the next day and asking for the same $20 bill back. That will likely be impossible as the cash has been collated with other cash from the day and you will never see it again. Without help from the bank, it would be impossible to trace the bill through the bank. It is the same with exchanges. When crypto is paid into an account at Coinbase, for example, that crypto is not physically moved into your account; rather, your account is credited with the correct amount and the actual crypto moves into the hot/live wallet or the cold/offline wallet of the exchange. When the customer wants to gain access to their crypto, the correct amount is sent to them from the hot wallet. This means that we as investigators trace the funds into the exchanges wallet and. . .well that's it; we can go no further without the explicit assistance of the exchange.

However, most primary exchanges, willing to work with an investigation, can provide records of crypto paid in, crypto withdrawn, internal currency exchanges, fiat bank account information, name, address, email, phone, photo, proof of address, and usually IP addresses. This data can be vital in tracing the funds beyond the exchange and potentially identifying money laundering.

NFTs and NFT Gaming

An NFT, which stands for "non-fungible token," is a unique digital fingerprint that can refer to another digital asset such an artwork, text, music, or pretty much anything. There is no suggestion that someone playing a blockchain-based game or buying an NFT is automatically guilty of money laundering. However, games often have their own currencies/tokens on the blockchain and you can buy characters, skill cards, land, and objects in that token or standard crypto. Many games generate in-game elements as NFTs and may store them on *side chains*, alternative chains connected to a primary chain such as Ethereum. This can make them trickier to trace. You may be asking how someone buying a skill card, for example, on the game Axie Infinity for a few dollars can be seriously money laundering. However, browse to `http://sandbox.game` (live as of this writing). Select the Marketplace icon and then Land & Estates. Things may have changed since this book was published, but take a look at the price of the land on this virtual world. As shown in Figure 2.1, there are parcels of land for thousands of dollars.

I'm currently buying a house in the real world and have to provide detailed proof of the source of the funds I will using to pay for it. No one is asking me that question if I buy a parcel of land on sandbox.game for $150,000. I can then transfer the land to another user anonymously on

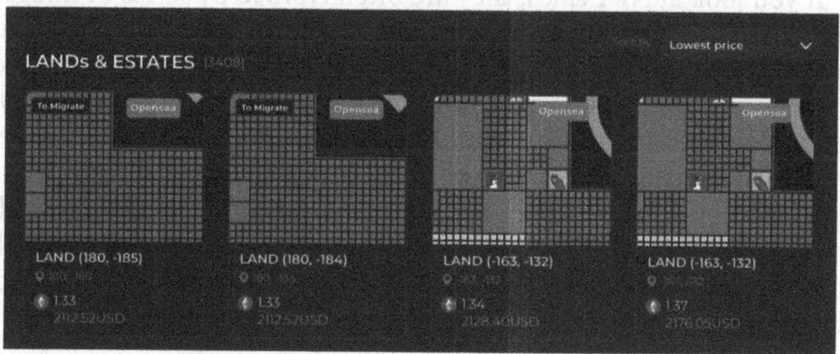

Figure 2.1 Examples of Virtual land for sale

the blockchain or sell it for significantly less without anyone noticing or any reports being made to government agencies.

I am in no way suggesting that there is anything wrong with sandbox. game or that they would knowingly be involved in criminality. Indeed, they may even generate SARs to law enforcement. But wherever significant funds or assets can change hands in a pseudo-anonymous, unregulated environment, there is a potential for money laundering that should be considered if tracing of suspicious funds follows assets to gaming sites.

The same is true of other gaming and gambling sites. Unregulated casinos have been used for decades for both company-sanctioned and -unsanctioned money laundering. Their blockchain-based versions are no different and the methods used are virtually identical. Blockchain-based gambling also has the benefit to the criminal of often being automated using smart contracts, and so funds can be deposited and withdrawn with impunity and anonymously.

I've included NFTs in this section as the typology of money laundering via anonymously buying and selling an asset is similar to the gaming sites just discussed. We will be discussing investigating NFT transactions and their history in more detail in Chapter 12, "Ethereum: Investigation Methodology." If you've been living under a rock and haven't heard about NFTs, then it might be time to put this book down and visit a site such as `http://opensea.io`. OpenSea is a broker for NFT sales and as of this writing was trading an average of around 1.5 million NFTs per month for a value of about $2.5 billion. Did I mention that was *per month*? (You can check out the current sales numbers for OpenSea here: `https://dune.com/rchen8/opensea`.)

If you look at NFT sales, they are often typified by series of images, which are generally procedurally created with specific features—rarer special features demand higher prices. One of the more famous collections is the Bored Ape Yacht Club, a procedurally generated collection of cartoon apes in different clothes and head gear. Feel free to search for it. As I'm writing, a Bored Ape Yacht Club ape image with pink hair and weird eyes just sold for 78 ETH. That's just under $100,000 in old money. Apparently, it's the pink hair that makes this one particularly rare. See the properties in Figure 2.2. I'd love to include the image of the ape, but it's worth $100,000 and I don't want to be sued!

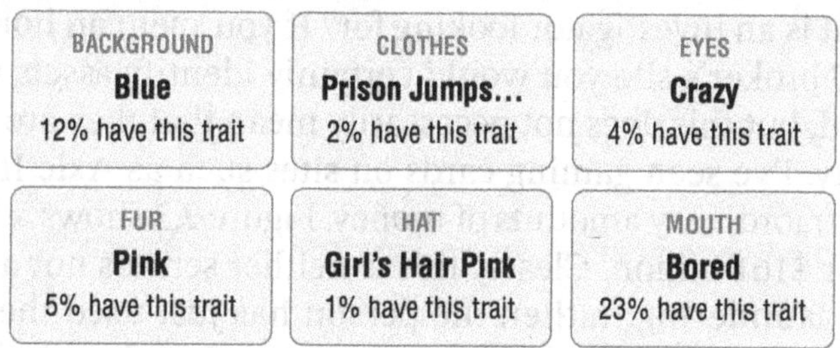

Figure 2.2 Example of traits that make up a generated NFT

Of course, it's important to mention that OpenSea and other NFT brokers are doing nothing wrong—they're just handling sales of an artistic token. However, art has been used for the laundering of money for a long time due to its esoteric nature when it comes to valuation. Why is the Bored Ape worth $100,000? Of course, someone may answer because that is what someone is prepared to pay for it; others may try to convince me that it's "art." But this provides an opportunity for those looking to launder assets.

In the simplest example, the person looking to receive criminal funds takes an "artistic" picture of their dog, posts it on an NFT broker site for $250,000, and then the holder of the criminal funds buys the NFT, neatly moving $250,000 through the broker proxy to the receiver of the funds. The same has been done with auction houses and art dealers for decades, but of course auction houses are now seriously regulated.

As my solicitor friend Syedur Rahman put it recently:

> *Unlike traditional art, NFTs are not subject to specific regulations [as of this writing] that have been designed to prevent money laundering, including providing ID documents to assist in validating ownership of property. The prices of digital art are less influenced by factors that affect the price of a traditional piece of art, such as age or condition. This means that pricing of NFTs can be more subjective, giving criminals the opportunity to launder their money through NFT trading without arousing as much suspicion as they would if they bought more traditional assets.*
> `www.rahmanravelli.co.uk/expertise/nfts-non-fungible-tokens-risks-regulation-and-the-law`

So, what is an investigator looking for? If you spent an hour looking at an NFT broker's site you would certainly identify assets that seem overvalued, but this does not necessarily mean that they are related to criminality. I've seen gaming cards on sites such as Axie Infinity for sale for extraordinary amounts of money. Figure 2.3 shows a *Snack Box* for sale for $161 billion. Clearly this is neither serious nor an attempt at money laundering; rather, the person has just used the figure of 123,456,789 ETH as a placeholder. However, an item bought for a small amount and quickly sold for a large amount could be interesting.

The reality is that no investigator in the world has the time to sit and scour OpenSea or sandbox.game for random evidence of criminality. But if you have an address that you suspect, or know, is related to criminal activity and you see evidence of transactions with gaming sites or NFT sites, it is definitely worth looking at those transactions and following the assets, looking for evidence of wrongdoing.

Mixers

Back in 2018 I was contacted by an officer at a UK Regional Organized Crime Unit who had carried out one of the earliest Bitcoin seizures. However, an easy oversight was made and they hadn't checked for the existence of Bitcoin Cash. In August 2017 a fork in the Bitcoin blockchain meant that any Bitcoin you held prior to the fork meant that you now held the same number of coins in Bitcoin Cash. If you didn't check when assets were held, it was easy to forget to check for the existence of the forked currency. The investigation team realized the

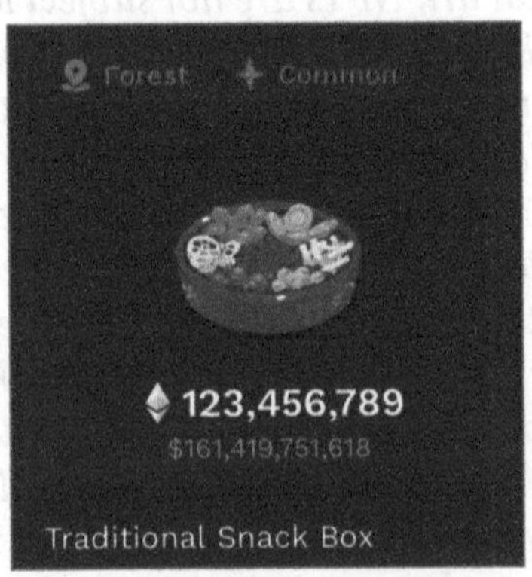

Figure 2.3 NFT from a game for sale for a massive sum

oversight but when they checked, the Bitcoin Cash had been moved out of the suspect's wallet, interestingly following the suspect's arrest. The funds were transferred straight into a mixer. At the time there were no commercial tools for tracking and tracing Bitcoin Cash and certainly no cool artificial intelligence (AI) systems for analyzing mixers such as exist now in some commercial software. The only option left was to do it manually, following each transaction, watching the funds split and split and recombine. Within 20 hops or so we realized we could predict the next transaction and how it would split and where the funds would go. Within a few days we had traced all the funds, on lots of pieces of paper, to a single destination address. The more time passes, the more I remember it as a positive, fun experience. At the time, the work made me feel like my brain was in a vise! It was tough but doable.

Investigators often assume that once funds hit a mixer, then it's game over. Of course, it's hard to do, but there is still useful work to be done that can generate positive results. Over the past few years we have worked with other researchers to analyze a number of mixers on both the Bitcoin and Ethereum blockchains, including the old Bitcoin Fog, Wasabi, and Tornado Cash.

There is a fundamental difference between the ways that mixers work on a UTXO blockchain like Bitcoin and an account-based blockchain like Ethereum. However, the rules of the blockchain are not broken and all transactions are still on the public ledger, so no matter how convoluted or obfuscated the transactions become, they can still be seen and hence the path of funds deciphered.

On a UTXO blockchain, generally the mixing comes from carrying out a very large number of transactions, splitting the original funds into many smaller parts and then combining them with coins held by other users. There are many techniques to follow the money and end up with an output address candidate, but we will not be covering these techniques in this book as there are commercial and government sensitivities. Commercial tools such as TRM Labs (who I work for) and other tools are available that enable AI-based deconstruction of mixing chains and are worth having if you have critical cases where mixers are in use by the suspects.

Before the acquisition of my company CSITech by TRM, we used their software to solve the theft of Bitcoin from an Eastern European exchange. The funds were stolen, split a few times, and then recombined into a single input address belonging to the Bitcoin Fog mixer. A quick manual attempt at following the funds quickly highlighted that we were dealing with a attempt at mixing that involved hundreds, possibly thousands of transactions. Using the TRM function of following mixing/peel chains, we deconstructed the entire mix and were able to identify where the primary output addresses were and, in two of the three cases, who they belonged to. It was a real win for the investigation. The rather vast graph was the largest the tool had produced at the time. If you look at Figure 2.4, you can see the huge number of transactions but also where the outputs clustered. It was not a job I would wanted to have done manually, even though it was technically possible with a big enough piece of paper—a really big piece of paper!

Other Bitcoin mixing systems are based on wallet providers. Good examples are Wasabi (recently deprecated) and Samurai wallets, which produce transactions often with large numbers of inputs and outputs,

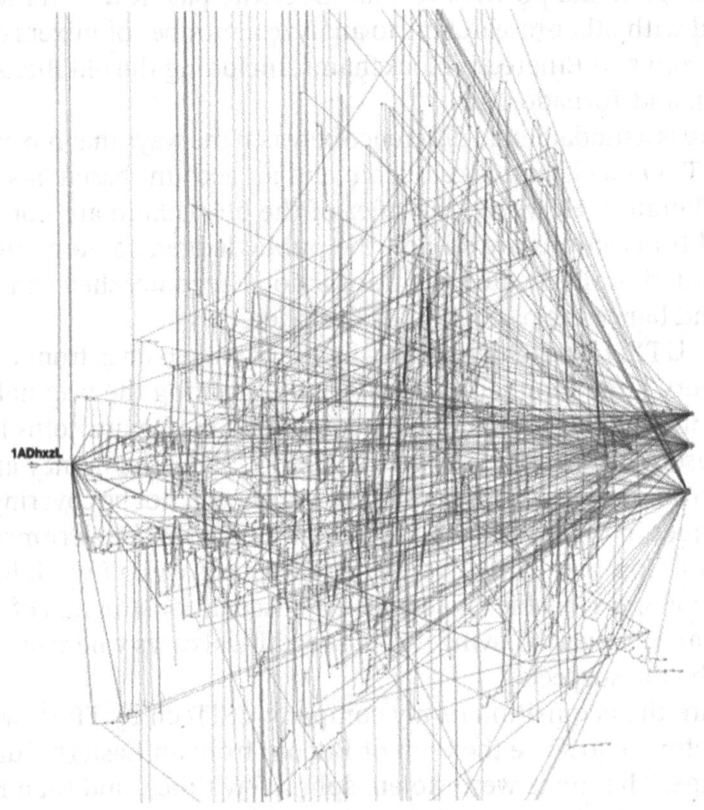

Figure 2.4 Large link graph of mixed funds

making it complex to connect the input address with the output address. Again, mathematical techniques enable us to do a pretty good job of unraveling these transactions.

Mixers for account-based blockchain currencies such as Ethereum work in a different way. Because each address has a balance—unlike Bitcoin, which only has a list of unspent transactions (wallet software looks at the blockchain and works out your balance from the unspent transactions; the blockchain does not have a balance for an address)—the Bitcoin method of splitting and combining would not work. Hence, mixers such as Tornado Cash obfuscate the path through the mixer by dumping the input funds into a "bin" full of transactions of the same value. We can easily see the path into the mixer but not which output corresponds to the input. If you are struggling to picture that, imagine a bucket of tennis balls, all identical. A criminal wanting to break the chain of the illicit funds can add a tennis ball, say 10 ETH, to the 10 ETH bucket. They can wait a little while and then extract 10 ETH. If many people are adding tennis balls and removing tennis balls, how can you connect the input to the output? It is sometimes possible, but it's very hard. You will appreciate that this is a rather simplistic explanation, but I don't want to get into "zero-knowledge proofs" and the like in this book.

Tornado Cash was used as a privacy tool by some wanting to move illicit funds, but it was the vast amounts of illicit funds that were channeled through the service that resulted in the U.S. Treasury's Office of Foreign Assets Control (OFAC) sanctioning it. There had been notable uses of Tornado Cash by the perpetrators of the $196 million BitMart exploit and the almost $34 million hack of Crypto.com, but these paled into insignificance with the 2022 exploit of the Ronin Bridge by the North Korean state group Lazarus when they managed to extract $625 million, with around $7 million being moved through the mixer.

So, what is an investigator looking for to identify mixer use? I would hope that your commercial intelligence tool of choice would identify possible mixer use in the address or cluster inputs and outputs or even further up or downstream from the address. Otherwise, you can use simple pattern recognition to identify the split and combine patterns of UTXO mixers and research the well-known addresses that are the inputs for mixers such as Tornado Cash. Even recognizing Wasabi transactions is straightforward as they follow a specific pattern known as *coin-join transactions*. These transactions simply take the crypto from a large set of people and put them in a single transaction with seemingly indecipherable outputs that do not appear to relate directly to the inputs. As mentioned previously, a Wasabi transaction will have a large number of inputs and outputs, and the outputs will have a large number of the same output value, which often appears to double several times. See Figure 2.5 for an example. This shows a snapshot of the 136 output addresses in the transaction, and you will note that many of the values are the same. Connecting the inputs to the outputs relates to a mathematical mixture of this "base" value and change values. But we will leave that there.

Being able to recognize patterns like this can be helpful if you are working without a commercial tool or if the tool fails to tag the transaction as being related to mixing or coin-join.

I recommend some caution with tagging an address as criminal or suspect if it received funds from a known mixer or coin-join wallet. Some users may simply have wished to remain anonymous moving funds because of the threat of persecution in their country, and they perhaps desired to send funds to a human rights organization, for example. Also, criminals are known to send small amounts of funds to legitimate addresses after the illicit funds emerge from Tornado Cash, effectively putting innocent people in the crosshairs of the authorities for "receiving" illicit currency. Of course, those people have no control over this any more than I have control over a malevolent person paying drug money into my bank account if they know my account number and then seemingly connecting me to criminality.

bc1quhhc7qvmzhudazvl6cwxwhp7z03u6xe87gg7r8	0.10018862 BTC
bc1qhkvvwksnv8zq4dtvz2xx8fulnc88rmhqfxaz0r	0.10024776 BTC
bc1q5eexwdwcwr4pm4y0grz4qg63wwvejpqhs8...	0.10026868 BTC
bc1q6fhqmayhy6htayrztq02yfd0gm8e8tf9gr9xwd	0.10039958 BTC
bc1qx8h7k4vp0nw3kzatu2j43h34k9ykxu7rl0686h	0.10039958 BTC
bc1q47mgu636wj4wr5lxc2lj0c88gnav34ruges3kg	0.10039958 BTC
bc1qe3e0dquhhy47gdtzjcqufm7aqlx73unhxykwed	0.10039958 BTC
bc1q3gyn9sxez8t0t8ux74q69mccnawrvvgtq42u8h	0.10039958 BTC
bc1qkak69kqryccru98a8zjzukle62cp9ahy2h60j3	0.10039958 BTC
bc1qnkv0f3mt30wwlqeu3wjkuldmlv34utyr6y66we	0.10039958 BTC
bc1qyj857u82d7em490ktv50rz89l8xpxsdp6rk9yv	0.10039958 BTC
bc1qv257cv6ec8vuqtn2e5ahgqa6ljtgwk9yldwux8	0.10039958 BTC
bc1qu2kldcyqxhenh5nqmwh29y0fm078rm5vd72p...	0.10039958 BTC
bc1qqyzdcqtacuwt20k7pvxnuyag88ukhqm2m6th5s	0.10039958 BTC
bc1qer4cfxzj9vjxhjj85p5whdl9vgrdf43ygc2xkx	0.10039958 BTC
bc1qv4ahjkntmzw2p4w9rqyx0u4862zzuhluqa953y	0.10039958 BTC
bc1q99l78ewlfmxx3wftnp2p2w03jdvgn88684th4j	0.10039958 BTC
bc1q4c9tvf0cm3ch9uxzpcfnc96f4qpjjy99j3t82w	0.10039958 BTC

Figure 2.5 Outputs of the same value identifying a coin-join transaction

This issue became crypto-headline news in August 2022 when funds from the newly U.S.-sanctioned Tornado Cash were sent to a list of celebrities, including Jimmy Fallon, Shaquille O'Neal, and Logan Paul. As the crypto news website cointelegraph.com noted:

> *It is illegal for any U.S. persons and entities to interact with Tornado Cash's smart contract addresses, blockchain or business-wise. Penalties for willful noncompliance can range from fines of $50,000 to $10,000,000 and 10 to 30 years imprisonment.*
>
> *Source: https://cointelegraph.com/news/anonymous-user-sends-eth-from-tornado-cash-to-prominent-figures-following-sanctions*

I would argue that the receivers of the funds had not interacted with the smart contract address as they had not triggered a transaction. If a bus knocks me off my bike, I haven't knowingly "interacted" with the bus. However, this didn't stop some agencies and organizations such as exchanges temporarily deny-listing the celebrity addresses and effectively blocking them from trading crypto. A minor outcry ensued, and the addresses were unlocked again.

However, it can be useful to track back from an address—for example, on the Ethereum blockchain. Where does the crypto come from to fund a fraudulent scam, for example? If the funding crypto comes from a mixer, that would be useful intelligence.

Recognizing the patterns related to mixers such as Blender, ChipMixer, and CryptoMixer as well as the services already discussed can help you to identify when crypto is being laundered.

Decentralized Exchanges

There is a scene in the 1987 movie *The Princess Bride* where a character keeps using the word "inconceivable" in a variety of situations. Eventually the sword-wielding Spaniard Inigo Montoya says the line, "You keep using that word, I do not think it means what you think it means." I rather feel the same about the word "decentralized."

The word used to be used in the sense of moving power and responsibility from a central body to other offices or regions and so was used by government or large companies looking to move decision making away from the center. The *Merriam-Webster Dictionary* uses the definition "the dispersion or distribution of functions and powers," which makes good sense.

Bitcoin was called the first decentralized currency and it's actually true for a number of reasons. Bitcoin is run not by the owners of Bitcoin but by the miners that verify the transactions through proof-of-work (more on that later). There is not just one miner run "by" Bitcoin, which would make it centralized; within reason, anyone can mine, meaning that the mining is, by the definition above, decentralized.

However, there are other elements of Bitcoin that can make it decentralized. Anyone running a full node wallet such as Bitcoin Core becomes a distribution node on the Bitcoin network and also a holder and appender to the full ledger of every transaction going back to 2009. Again, this is not a single centralized ledger such as we would find in a bank but a "distribution of functions," hence once again, decentralized.

But we find ourselves in a cryptocurrency world where everything seems to be called decentralized and I'm often led to make the same statement as Inigo: "You keep using that word, I do not think it means what you think it means." Many new currencies use proof-of-stake rather than proof-of-work, which is very good for the planet due to the massively reduced power usage compared to Proof of Work, and have a small number of miners otherwise known as validators. Binance Smart Chain has 21, Tron has 27, Avalanche 28, and Polygon just 3. I'm in no way suggesting that this makes them less secure or less effective somehow—that's a whole different discussion—but can they really be described as truly decentralized?

Anyway, that brings us to decentralized exchanges. We know what centralized crypto exchanges do, as discussed in the last section, and you may have personal experience if you have an account with someone like Coinbase, Binance, or a myriad of others. However, a decentralized exchange (DEX) is based around a smart contract that handles the exchange of digital assets. They are generally non-custodial in that they do not store funds on your behalf. There are no user accounts and no KYC information is taken; the contract simply allows a user to swap from one currency to another, for example, from Wrapped Ethereum to Wrapped Bitcoin. If we see this activity in a suspect's flow of transactions, why might it be of interest to us?

Obviously, swapping from one currency to another can confuse an investigator, and this can help to obfuscate what is happening with illicit assets. Later in the book we will look at transactions involving DEXs and you will see how easy it is to lose track of funds when they are repeatedly swapped for other crypto asset types. So although the use of a DEX is standard behavior for a sophisticated crypto user, when associated with an address that is already suspect, we would want to watch the swaps carefully as they could be a basic attempt to clean the funds.

Although DEXs are by nature noncustodial, increasingly DEXs are offering more than just the ability to swap from one asset to another but are providing DeFi products like the ability to stake or deposit funds into finance products that provide a return, such as providing liquidity to a coin swap.

This is fairly straightforward to understand. Imagine a currency exchange at an airport. If you want to change from dollars to euros, the exchange teller will need to have euros in the till or safe to carry out the swap. If they have none, or not enough euros, they can take your dollars but can't complete the swap. To enable these swaps to happen, the company that runs the exchange ensures that they have enough notes, known as enough liquidity, to cover any exchanges that travelers want to make.

Now imagine if the same exchange wasn't run by a company but was simply a stand-alone, automated ATM with no liquidity, no notes inside. How could swaps take place? The ATM could ask users to deposit funds in the form of euros, dollars, sterling, and so on and in return the customer would make a small amount of interest. So, you as a customer and others deposit a variety of bills into the ATM. The ATM now has liquidity. Other customers can swap between currencies and will be charged a fee, and some of that fee goes to the depositors.

Simply translate that ATM logic to some code on the blockchain known as a *smart contract*. Users can deposit funds to provide liquidity in the contract and earn interest from the deposit. Usually, the user can withdraw the funds as needed. I'm sure you are way ahead of me, but if we see this behavior in a suspect's address, then it may be an attempt to generate clean funds from dirty funds and careful calculations need to be made as to payments made by the DEX to the suspect alongside their deposits and withdrawals. We will look at examples of this on the blockchain later in Chapter 12.

DEXs in themselves should not be considered suspicious. They are used by crypto users and traders for completely legitimate reasons, but where you have a suspicious address, perhaps related to a suspect, and you see movement of funds through DEXs like Uniswap, PancakeSwap,

Bisq, and many others, these trails should be carefully to followed to keep track of the funds.

Casinos

People gamble, lots of people, it just seems to be no one you know! It is something that few will readily admit to but will happily line up in a convenience store and buy a lottery ticket or lay a few bets on a trip to Las Vegas. In my home country of the UK, 44 percent of adults have likely gambled in some form in the last four weeks, and from April 2021 to March 2022 have gambled £14.1 billion (`www.gamblingcommission.gov.uk/about-us/statistics-and-research`).

The large gaming companies were quick to see the benefits of gaming systems that used the blockchain and smart contracts. Using public blockchains and smart contracts, they could give the impression, rightly or wrongly, of being transparent. There are benefits for the player, too; they do not need to provide any personally identifiable information and games can be played with crypto funds in anonymous wallets.

The initial systems were decentralized applications (dApps) based on the Ethereum platform, which had a large user base and robust development capabilities. However, network congestion led to higher transaction fees, and dApps eventually began to migrate to blockchains with small fee structures such as TRON—which has become so popular with gambling dApps that Dapp.Review called it "Las Vegas on the Blockchain" in their 2019 Dapp Market Report (`https://dapp.review/article/238/2019-Dapp-Market-Report`).

Gambling online or offline is not illegal in most countries, and as we have stated, many people gamble, so why have we included it in our section on money laundering typologies? As I previously stated, where the money is, criminality will also be there, and the vast sums that move through gambling systems make them perfect for the blending of criminal and legitimate funds. Many gaming companies have realized the need to protect themselves against sanction by bringing in identity checks and other vectors to dissuade the money launderers. However, there are still many gaming sites out there that require no KYC information and that allow depositing of significant funds. Just do an Internet search for "crypto gambling no kyc" and you will find plenty of sites listing gaming options that enable completely anonymous play.

For the investigator this is the key. Gaming sites that require no KYC should always be a red flag in an investigation. Although use of these sites is not necessarily illegal, large sums of crypto being transferred into known gambling addresses should be enough to arouse suspicion. This is especially the case if a gambling site offers the ability to withdraw funds, including any winnings, to a second address. This then almost acts as a pseudo-exchange, where funds can be deposited, a few games played and perhaps a little money lost, and then the funds withdrawn to another address.

Although I'm not a fan of gambling due to the social problems that can result, it is not my desire or intention to vilify gambling sites that support crypto. However, casinos and related gaming companies have long been associated with criminality, and although I'm aware that gaming associations and governing bodies in some countries have been working hard to enact regulations and legislation, large deposits into gaming sites should be viewed as suspicious by an investigator. Sites that require no KYC should always be viewed critically, but even legitimate gambling services that require proof of age and identify are no guarantee that funds are legal. Identities can be stolen or spoofed, and the proof-of-identity requirements by different companies operating in countries with lower levels of legislation can be little more than a "box-ticking" exercise to show to regulators with little actual protection.

If you see gambling site transfers from your suspect, look harder!

Chain Hopping

When I was about 10 years old I would run home from school every day. I used to run to school, too, and even run around my paper delivery round before my dad built me a racer-style push bike. My run home from school took me down a short lane between some terraced houses that opened up into a driveway of sorts that had a chain across with a "No Parking" sign slung from it. Every single day I hurdled that low chain, hundreds of times, except the one time when I didn't. For some reason I stepped slightly left to where the chain was higher as it rose up to the wall it was connected to, but muscle memory meant I only jumped enough for the low middle part of the chain. I caught my foot and slammed down on my face on the pavement. It hurt.

This brief section is about money laundering through chain hopping and has absolutely nothing to do with hopping over actual chains, but the name always reminds me of pain. In fact, investigating crypto-based chain hopping is also painful, but in a different way. By "chain" I'm using a shortened form of blockchain, and "hopping" simply means moving funds between one blockchain and another. You may think that we covered this issue in the "Decentralized Exchanges" section; however, we discussed swapping between coins and tokens but always on the same chain, such as swapping between Wrapped ETH and Curve tokens but staying on the Ethereum blockchain. However, if we want to swap from ETH to Solana, then we have a problem. Ethereum and Solana are two different blockchains and actually work quite differently, so if I want to swap tokens I need to use something called a *bridge*. A bridge will accept input coins on one blockchain and generate a commensurate value in the other token on the destination blockchain. The bridge for ETH to Solana used to be called the Wormhole bridge but changed its name to Portal Bridge not too long after a hacker made off with $325 million. Technically, the bridge software team say that the name hasn't actually changed and Wormhole is now a "protocol" and Portal Bridge is a dApp based on the protocol.

It is a mistake to picture a bridge such as the original Wormhole bridge as somehow physically connecting the two blockchains over the Internet. No tokens are actually sent or received. If I want to convert 1 ETH to Solana, I would send my 1 ETH to the Wormhole bridge and it accepts the token. It then sends approval to the Solana blockchain to release new coins to a Solana address. Some bridges, such as the original Wormhole bridge, use a "mint and burn" model where coins sent to the bridge are burned and new coins minted on the destination chain.

NOTE In February 2022 an attacker discovered a way to exploit the bridge contract to convince something called the Validator Action Approval (VAA) to mint new coins without receiving coins on the other side of the chain. The attacker was able to acquire $325 million in the hack. To learn more, visit `www.theverge.com/2022/2/3/22916111/wormhole-hack-github-error-325-million-theft-ethereum-solana`.

As investigators, why are we interested in this money laundering typology? Specifically, because it's harder to follow the money. In a DEX that swaps tokens on one blockchain we are able to follow the contract to see what funds are swapped and where they go. When a chain hop occurs, we need to trace the funds into the bridge and then use the destination chain to locate the output of the transaction. Some chains make this relatively easy, but some are very hard, hence my comment about the pain. As of this writing some commercial investigation tools such as TRM Labs, Elliptic, and Chainalysis support tracing across the primary chains, which makes life significantly easier.

Hackers are regularly using chain-hopping techniques to obfuscate movements of stolen coins. In August 2022 the crypto analytics company Elliptic reported that over $540 billion of stolen crypto had passed over a bridge called RenBridge (`www.cnbc.com/2022/08/10/crypto-criminals-laundered-540-million-using-renbridge-elliptic-says.html`). This included $156 million paradoxically stolen from another bridge, called Nomad Bridge.

The reason for chain hopping becoming popular in recent times is likely the increase in regulation around exchanges. With primary exchanges now requiring significant customer identity proof, the decentralized and pseudo-anonymous nature of cross-chain bridges means that they are becoming a fast, inexpensive, and safer way for criminals to launder funds out to other chains and then to off-ramps such as gambling sites and exchanges.

Investigators need to watch suspect addresses carefully to ascertain if there are transactions that relate to bridges. Find out what bridge is being transacted with and then try to locate the output transaction on the destination chain. We will cover this more fully later in Chapter 12.

Privacy Coins

This is a tricky section to write; you know by now that I'm an investigator and you may assume that privacy coins like Zcash and Monero are difficult to investigate and hence, by definition, must be a bad thing. However, it's more complex than that. Most of us would agree that we have a right to privacy in our lives, including our financial decisions and transactions. But if I pop to the local shop and buy a drink and chocolate bar by waving my card or phone over a payment terminal, a record of that transaction will be stored, under my name, by my bank. If the government took an interest in my chocolate-buying habits, then they could make a request to the bank and in most circumstances my purchasing history would be duly handed over. We accept this breach of privacy for the price of security and convenience.

In 2009 the advent of Bitcoin provided users with an enhanced level of financial privacy. With disconnection to any bank or government-controlled entity, funds could be moved and trades carried out using private software wallets controlling anonymous transactions on a distributed ledger. The appearance of exchanges watered down this anonymity somewhat as it provided investigators with identifiable on- and off-ramps that otherwise anonymous transactions could be traced to. Investigation tools began to use a number of techniques to identify primary addresses and clusters of addresses, providing further deanonymization of the currency. Soon Bitcoin became known as pseudo-anonymous rather than boasting the truly anonymous nature it had started with.

As is almost always the case when gaps appear in technology, the void was filled and so-called privacy coins started to appear, notably Zcash and Monero. Although they are still cryptocurrencies in that they are based around cryptography and have elements of blockchain/decentralization, they use some ingenious techniques to enhance the public/private key concept to make transactions fundamentally closed to a third-party viewer and metadata almost nonexistent. I won't pretend that these coins do not provide a challenge to investigators, and the U.S. Treasury's Financial Crimes Enforcement Network (FinCEN) often mentions coins such as Monero in its advisories. The Internal Revenue Service (IRS) awarded several blockchain investigation companies contracts to look for methods to find exploits to enable tracing, with bonuses for those who were successful.

Cryptocurrency analytics company CipherTrace filed for two patents in 2020 for Monero tracing capabilities and released tools, but only for qualified government agencies and certain financial institutions.

Privacy coins have been sometimes termed as "criminal coins," which is inaccurate and unfair. There is no suggestion that the teams involved in their development created them specifically or even indirectly to facilitate criminality; they would argue that it comes back to an individual's right to privacy. Privacy does not equate to illegality. However, their enhanced privacy functions are certainly attractive to technically savvy criminals.

Justin Ehrenhofer, a developer with the Monero Space Workgroup, told the website Newsweek (`www.newsweek.com/monero-developer-criminal-groups-use-crypto-ransoms-justin-ehrenhofer-1600884`): "Monero is increasingly used for ransomware payments. In 2020 and 2021 the adoption of Monero increased significantly. . . .While we are disappointed that ransomware groups increasingly demand payment in Monero, we understand why they do, and we expect them to use Monero significantly more in the future."

How we view privacy coins depends on our perspective. As an investigator following conversion of criminal funds, perhaps when you make a request for information about a suspect from an exchange like Kraken and then have reported to you in their response documentation movement of coins into Monero, your heart sinks as you know that your day just got harder. However, if you switch proverbial hats and take a privacy perspective, then the technology is superb and provides strong anonymity of transactions. Often, law enforcement officers that I'm teaching will make a sweeping statement that if you have anything to hide, then you are clearly involved in criminality. Even not taking into account the generic privacy arguments, this completely ignores the fact that there are governments around the world that will use financial data to persecute, imprison, and do much worse to people who, from a human rights point of view, are doing nothing wrong.

However, if you are investigating movement of funds from a suspect that moves coins into a privacy coin, I suggest looking harder! You may also want to reach out to your favorite crypto analytics company to help you trace the potentially laundered funds. Later in the book in Chapter 11, "The Workings of Ethereum and Derivatives," I'll show you how to read the contracts that help you to identify coin swaps. In the meantime, a quick Internet search will identify services that support conversion to and from Monero and Zcash, for example.

It is worth keeping an eye open for localmonero.co. It is a service based on the original model for localbitcoins.com where buyers and sellers are directly connected. Localbitcoins.com works hard to be in line with regulations, but this does not appear to be the case for localmonero.co. As of this writing there were a number of offers to buy or sell Monero with no ID or other KYC (see Figure 2.6).

KINGOFCRYPTO (86; 100%)	Seen just now	Cryptocurrency NO KYC - NO ID REQUIRED - SWAP YOUR COINS FOR XMR	444.11 XCD	Up to 711.79 XCD	BUY
COMPRATUDO (430; 100%)	Seen just now	Cryptocurrency BUY CRYPTOCURRENCIES WITH AN ANONYMOUS GUARANTEE	444.11 XCD	60 - 5654.44 XCD	BUY

Figure 2.6 Monero coin swap requiring no KYC information to be provided

NOTE Although not fully live as of this writing, `http://haveno.exchange` is due to be released soon, which is a noncustodial, decentralized exchange for converting between crypto and fiat currencies all built on Tor and Monero. As their website states, "It doesn't get any more private than that!" It appears to use much of the Bisq code, so we are hoping that the knowledge we have of tracking through Bisq will help with Haveno.

Crypto ATMs

In October 2013 a slightly odd-looking terminal appeared in a coffee shop in Vancouver. It looked a little like a standard cash ATM, but on closer inspection it displayed icons on the screen related to cryptocurrencies. This was the first crypto ATM installed, and it enabled the conversion of fiat currency to Bitcoin. As of this writing, coinatmradar.com (`https://coinatmradar.com`) reports that there are now nearly 40,000 crypto ATMs in 79 countries around the world, with the majority in the United States. Of course, these are the only ones registered with the site.

Coinatmradar is a great site for finding ATMs in a particular area and discerning the fees charged and so on. For example, I have a good friend in Baltimore named Andrew. If Andrew wants to buy some Ethereum, he has about 300 crypto ATMs to choose from in the Baltimore area. As you can see in Figure 2.7, Andrew could buy Bitcoin for between a 9.8 percent and a 14.7 percent fee.

This means that if he wants to take $1,000 cash down to the ATM at the Discount Tobacco Shop, then almost $150 of that will go to the ATM provider as a fee. This should be raising the question in your head as to why anyone would use an ATM when they can go to the Coinbase exchange, for example, and pay a flat 1 percent fee. You read that right: 1 percent. The answer is anonymity. If Andrew wants to convert his cash into crypto anonymously, then an ATM that takes no or very limited ID information is the only way to go. There is a lack of uniform KYC requirements among the many companies that manufacture crypto ATMs, with many requiring only a phone number. Others require additional personal information as the amount of the transaction increases. In addition, there is little communication among the various companies. As a result, if I wanted to launder $20,000 of dirty money, I could simply use four different ATM machines with daily limits of $5,000 each to transfer the illicit funds to my desired wallet.

Eastern Carroll Fuel (Eastern Blvd) Buy fee: 9.8%
Lowest Fee BitcoinATMs

7-Star Mini Market Buy fee: 14.7%
COINFLIP

Discount Tobacco Shop Buy fee: 14.7%
COINFLIP

Orbit Beer & Wine Buy fee: 14.7%
COINFLIP

4 Trees Smoke Shop Buy fee: 14.7%
COINFLIP

Figure 2.7 Example of crypto ATM fees

In 2019, UK-based drug enforcement officers were staking out a midlevel drug dealer. They had observed a number of meetings with both suppliers and street dealers before they moved in for the arrest. To their surprise, they found no cash on the dealer at all; intelligence had suggested that he would be carrying more than £50,000. It was only when a cell phone analyst looked at the dealer's phone that they found over £250,000 available in a crypto-wallet. Whereas drug deals had traditionally always been done in cash, street dealers were selling to users for cash, converting to Bitcoin at the local corner shop ATM, and then moving that crypto anonymously to the supplier. In the years that followed, other gangs were found that were asking for payment for drugs on the street in crypto. This is now a fairly normal occurrence.

Although we tend to think of money laundering as criminal bosses moving and hiding large amounts of money, this drug supply model is quite clever as it brings the laundering down to the level of the street dealer. The illicit cash acquired from the drug deals on the street is effectively laundered straight into the ATM and then moved up the supply chain. This massively reduces the obfuscation of those funds further upstream. As financial investigators, this means we need to start looking at laundering starting earlier in the illicit flow of funds and also for smaller amounts. It would be easy to ignore these small movements of funds into crypto without realizing that if the whole network is doing the same, then we could be missing significant sums of illegal monies.

NOTE In March 2022 the UK Financial Conduct Authority stated that as no companies running ATMs in the UK were registered with them to provide financial services, the ATMs they were running were illegal and must be shut down and registration sought. You can read the judgment here: `www.fca.org.uk/news/news-stories/warning-illegal-crypto-atms-operating-uk`.

Peer-to-Peer Platforms

We have already discussed decentralized exchanges and also mentioned peer-to-peer (P2P) services such as Bisq and the upcoming Haveno exchange for Monero. Instead of a coin swap or trade being handled by a smart contract where the funds increase or decrease liquidity in the contract, the P2P system connects two physical users, one who wants to buy and one who wants to sell.

The first site that I was aware of that offered P2P transactions in the crypto space was localbitcoins.com, which is still a very popular exchange. A few years ago, localbitcoins.com was a challenge for investigators as users were not required to provide any ID information, but they now work to comply with KYC regulations. When you attempt to sign up, the current site states:

> *Financial service providers have a statutory obligation to identify and know their customers. During your registration process we will ask for information about your primary address, reasons of use, financial status and activity type. We will also need you to verify your ID with* ***a valid government-issued identification document*** *(*`https://localbitcoins.com`*.)*

This means that a legal approach to localbitcoins.com should result in a reasonable amount of information if you are able to comply with the legislative requirements.

PEER TO PEER TRADING RISKS

Trading peer to peer is not always safe. Many traders will post a WhatsApp or Telegram number on their account, enabling a user to break out of the site and communicate and trade directly. This is all fine, except the example I gave earlier of a seller being assaulted when selling Bitcoin started when he used a peer-to-peer site and then contacted buyers directly.

The example in the redacted image Figure 2.8 shows where a user has put their WhatsApp number in the payment method metadata field.

Figure 2.8 A coin swap on the 1Inch service

However, other P2P sites such as Bisq.network does not require any information to be provided at all. The site is very clear that no registration is required. This is problematic for investigators, and although it is possible to track transactions through Bisq, doing so is complex and you will not be able to get any useful data from the Bisq organization to assist.

Some swapping contract providers such as 1inch also provide a pseudo-P2P capability. Using 1Inch, which is based on the Ethereum network, you are able to sell tokens in exchange for other coins, such as Wrapped ETH to DAI, and specify a third-party taker address. This all happens on a chain and so is not difficult to trace. However, the transactions can be difficult to read, and we will cover this later in the book in Chapter 12.

It is important to note that like many of the services we have covered in this chapter so far, P2P exchanges are not in themselves illegal for users to access. This is the same for DEXs, for privacy coins, or for chain hopping. However, like these other services, when we have a suspect address or addresses and they are actively moving coins that we suspect are illicit funds, then we have to take an interest and follow the money. Money laundering with crypto is not necessarily more complex, but there are certainly many typologies available to the criminal and we have to be aware and able to track and trace these movements. As you will see as the book progresses, although this process can be complex, it is rarely impossible.

3 Understanding the Criminal Opportunities: Theft

Crypto Thefts

I've called this section the rather unhelpfully broad title of "Crypto Thefts." There are so many methods by which criminals steal crypto such as phishing, investment fraud, smart contract hacking, pig butchering/romance scams. . .and the list goes on. Although all these crimes have victims and generally result in financial losses, some tend to have a longer and more complex process associated with them whereas others are a "short con." In this chapter, we will look at each primary category, with some examples of their modus operandi to help us to understand how criminals think. Of course, by the time this book is published, someone will have come up with some other clever ideas. I often speak to investigators who agree with me in that they often feel a degree of wonder at the creativity of criminals in the crypto space. An investigator is tasked with deconstructing a crime that someone came up with from scratch. Although many crimes are straightforward, some of the hacks, the smart contract manipulations, and others can be incredibly clever. If you are a criminal reading this, I appreciate your intelligence and creativeness, but, please stop—if you could use your powers for good you would be amazing investigators!

Social Engineering

Although this is not a category I want to focus on, I want to clarify what I mean when I use the term "social engineering," as it is used in many of the criminal techniques we will discuss in this chapter. Christopher Hadnagy, author of *Social Engineering: The Science of Human Hacking*, 2nd ed. (Wiley, 2018), defines social engineering as "any act that influences a person to take an action that may or may not be in their best interest." If you want to learn more about social engineering in all its various forms, I strongly recommend reading any of the books by Hadnagy.

Note that the quote says "may or may not be in their best interest" since social engineering techniques are not always about coercion and can be used positively in everything from child discipline to PTSD rehabilitation. In the context of this chapter, I will use the term in its negative sense, where an attacker uses manipulative or misdirection techniques in order to achieve the acquisition of seed words, private keys, passwords, and so forth.

In its simplest form, a text message telling you that "your Coinbase account has been hacked," with a link to some dubious authentication page, is an example of social engineering. At the more complex end, a romance scam, now often rather ungraciously included in the category of "pig-butchering" scams (I'm not a fan of the term), may take many months for a person to be drawn into a fake romance before the scam is perpetrated. Almost all the thefts against individuals that we investigate involve some form of social engineering.

Phishing

Phishing is a catchall term for attackers sending malicious electronic communication designed to trick people into falling for a scam. This started with email, but today we see more attacks via direct messaging such as text messages and WhatsApp, among others. Although these are often defined as "smishing" (named after SMS messaging), I more often see "phishing" used as a generic term.

Historically these attacks have been designed to try to get you to share authentication information such as your bank details, your PayPal account, and even your Amazon login, but as we have stated several times in this book, where the money is, criminality will follow. The first example of crypto-oriented phishing that I had any involvement with was a phishing website set up in 2017 to help users generate a wallet (private key/seed words) for a cryptocurrency named IOTA. Although the website correctly generated wallet seeds, it also gave them to the owner of the website. The value of the amount stolen is open to some debate due to the fluctuation of fiat values, but it's fair to say that millions of dollars' worth of MIOTA coins disappeared from victims, wallets in late 2017. What I particularly "like" about this case is that progress was made in the investigation through cooperation between the IOTA Foundation, Europol, and the UK's Southeast Regional Organised Crime Unit (SEROCU), among others. SEROCU especially did an outstanding job in the investigation of a cryptocurrency where no tools existed to help and all had to be done manually (you know who you are, Rob and Emma!) and at the time of writing a 36-year-old male from the Oxford area of the UK is awaiting trial.

The significant increase in the general public wanting to be involved with crypto investments has provided a vector for scammers to diversify from PayPal or Amazon phishing attacks and begin to orient them toward exchanges. The communication via a text message or similar will usually take the form of something like this: "Your cryptocurrency wallet has been breached. visit: [INSERT FAKE URL] immediately to secure your account and move your funds to a safe account."

The URL will direct the victim to some fake website. Some make little attempt to look like the true website, whereas other sites are cleverly and carefully crafted. I saw a very impressive URL that was similar to `www.binänce.com` using an alternative character set (note the ä with the dots, for example) for one of the letters. The site scraped the main Binance site so that it always attempted to look identical. That takes a lot of work by an attacker but can be very successful.

SIMPLICITY IS OFTEN THE BEST POLICY

A more slickly produced scam doesn't necessarily generate more money. In 2017 I was asked to be on a team tasked with "stealing" $1 million from a Middle Eastern bank. (Obviously we were being paid by the bank!) A huge amount of work was done by an extremely knowledgeable and professional team. We had people on the ground, photographing the headquarters and carrying out Wi-Fi scans for open routers; open source investigators locating and profiling key people; financial experts looking for loopholes; and hackers scanning for vulnerabilities. Eventually, in a carefully crafted and executed sting operation against a senior person, we were able to acquire virtual private network (VPN) credentials, enhance our stolen login to have some administrator rights, and carry out an extraction of $1 million to an external account. Success.

However, a week after our successful operation (of which I was a very small cog in the machine, focusing on open source information) and while the methods were being discussed and mitigation against future attacks implemented, an account manager at the bank received an email. It simply said, "Please pay $1.2 million to the following account – *<ACCOUNT NUMBER>*" and was signed by the name of the CEO. What made it more extraordinary is that the email was not cleverly spoofed to look like it was from the actual CEO of the bank but was from something similar to `CEOMiddleEastBank@gmail.com`. What did the account manager do? Paid it! All that planning and work and we could have just sent an email from an appropriately named Gmail address asking for the money!

One of the more interesting phishing scams in recent times has been the *airdrop* scam. One of the techniques many new tokens have used to raise awareness of their offering has been to provide free tokens to website registrants or just send tokens to random crypto addresses prelaunch. Although most of these come to nothing, it's a good way of marketing, as a new token appears in your wallet, sometimes unrequested, and many people will research what it's all about and maybe buy more tokens. The many transactions and holders of the token on the blockchain also make the coin look "busy," or popular.

A particularly successful airdrop scam happened in mid-2022 against the decentralized exchange Uniswap on the Ethereum platform. What is interesting about it is that it targeted advanced crypto users, not new, inexperienced crypto investors as had been the case previously. There was no text message or email sent; using a rather clever technique, the attackers did the ultimate in social engineering and sent existing investors free money!

To show you how this worked, first here's a bit about *liquidity pools*. As we have explained previously, swapping tokens on Uniswap requires a smart contract to have its own liquidity, so there are, for example, sufficient wrapped ETH on one side of the swap and curve on the other side to enable swaps to take place. Investors can add funds to the liquidity pool and will receive in return liquidity pool/provider (LP) tokens, which essentially represent one share of the fees earned by the pool. When fees are earned in the pool, shares held by a user get a commensurate amount as a reward.

The attackers sent a transaction to existing Uniswap investors (anyone who had Uniswap LP tokens in their wallet), which essentially promised 400 UNI (Uniswap tokens) to each user for free. This was a phished group of about 74,000 investors. All the victims had to do was visit the Uniswap website, connect their wallet to the site, and approve the transaction. As I have said before, there is nothing new under the sun and the scam website used the domain `uniswaplp.com`, which impersonated the official Uniswap website `uniswap.org`.

Investors just had to connect their wallet to the site, which is normally a safe thing to do, but signing the transaction triggered a `setApprovalForAll` function that provided full approval rights of the user's wallet to the scammer. Essentially, the function enabled the rather creative attacker to withdraw all Uniswap v3 LP tokens the user held. Did it work? Several users were taken in and their wallets drained, to a dollar value at the time of $8 million.

To an investigator new to crypto, this might sound complicated, but when you think it through it is just a combination of scam techniques used for years—like the Nigerian prince scams where they want to send you money but ask for an advance payment, the PayPal scams to obtain your authentication and empty your account, and so on. The Uniswap attack just used a smart contract to bring it all together. It's important to reiterate that as investigators we know how to investigate scams and phishing attacks; it only takes a small amount of new knowledge to apply this to the crypto space.

Hacks

In Chapter 1, "A History of Cryptocurrencies and Crime," we talked about hacks that have been primarily against exchanges. Although the original Bitcoin code was solid (apart from some minor issues in the first year), exchanges ended up becoming the unofficial banks on the Bitcoin network and to operate had to implement systems that had nothing to do with the blockchain or the cryptocurrency itself. They had to set up customer management systems, private key management systems, systems to enable transactions to take place while not exposing keys to users, and so forth. Accomplishing these things was not in itself particularly technically difficult, but every line of code written or third-party software implemented by the exchange added a layer of insecurity, a layer that could be attacked. You might think that this will be a lengthy section of this book, but it isn't. Whole books have been written just on crypto-based hacks, and understanding them, and especially investigating them, takes some very specific skills. Generally, the attacks have not been against the blockchains themselves, although there have been some notable exceptions, but against the integrated systems used by the exchanges. This means that if you are a cyber investigator with experience investigating financial attacks and have the appropriate ethical hacker–type training, then you are good to go with crypto-oriented hacks; few new skills are needed.

When we think about a hacker, we tend to imagine a nefarious person or team sitting at their keyboards writing malware code, port scanning, injecting vulnerabilities, and using all the standard cracking methods to gain access to otherwise private digital material. All these techniques can be used in attacks against exchanges, but in my experience hackers against crypto exchanges tend to use primarily social engineering techniques and, more often than not, involve people working for the company. We investigated a hack against an exchange in Eastern Europe a while ago, in which some millions of dollars were stolen. The culprit ended up being a disgruntled employee with access to the exchange wallet's private keys; they sent coins to a mixer in an attempt to cover their tracks. Interestingly, in this case the evidence did not come from the blockchain and tracing the funds. Tracking through mixers can be tricky and time-consuming, but working with a team, we used good old-fashioned log files on the company systems to identify the actions of the attacker and eventually find their user ID to identify them. The investigative processes we used were hardly any different compared to a noncrypto investigation of one of the world's primary mobile phone providers where several million user records were hacked and leaked to the Internet. Again, our analysis of log files on the network eventually identified a consultant working with the company who was stealing the records and selling them on the dark web.

This brings me back to something I mentioned earlier: that being a crypto investigator doesn't just mean tracking some funds to an identifiable off-ramp. There is much more to it than that, and often a variety of skilled people are needed to locate all the evidence to find a suspect.

This section could easily be a book in its own right, and so I'm not going to attempt to cover everything an investigator needs to know to investigate hacking attacks because the skills are too varied. However, in Chapter 11, "The Workings of Ethereum and Derivatives," we will discuss in more detail a variety of hacks against smart contracts.

Fraud

Recorded fraud would appear to stretch back to 300 BCE when two Greek traders, Hegestratos and Zenosthemis, carried out a straightforward insurance scam, insuring their boat and cargo and then deliberately sinking it. Hegestratos drowned in the attempt (perhaps learning to swim should have formed part of the plan!) and Zenosthemis was arrested. Due to the propensity of greed in human nature, I can't believe that fraud has not formed part of civilization since the very dawn of time, but it's Hegestratos who takes the dubious privilege of being the first.

Whether it's Charles Ponzi (the father of the Ponzi scheme) making money from investors in his postal voucher investment fraud in 1920 or Eduardo de Valfierno paying to have the *Mona Lisa* stolen in 1911 so he could sell his fakes to underground art collectors, fraud has been around in varying forms for a very long time. I never fail to be surprised and sometimes impressed by the techniques of subterfuge used by criminals who are often very successful in their endeavors.

Although the Internet and traditional news outlets love the "big" stories of fraud with huge dollar losses, the reality is that many frauds are carried out for fairly small amounts of money. If you steal $1 million from someone they are definitely going to the police, or if you steal the money from another criminal, which is surprisingly common, you may find yourself meeting the same fate as Hegestratos! However, a fraud that takes just a small sum but from large numbers of people tends to be more successful. If I lose $50 in a fraud, I'm very unlikely to go to the police, meaning there are likely no complainants, making it a bit of a victimless crime. Even if I go to the police station and bang my fist on the desk demanding an investigation into my $50 loss, it is very unlikely that anyone is going to do anything about it. The reality, though, is that the same fraudster may have hundreds or even thousands of victims, and if the victims are all losing $50—well, you can do the math. It becomes a *big* fraud, but no one is reporting it. Incredibly, we are seeing this problem applied to fraud losses in the many thousands of dollars.

If I lose $25,000 in a crypto fraud, I will struggle to get any police force to investigate; it's a lot of money to you and me, but just not "enough" to trigger a full investigation. If you go to a private investigation company, there will be costs for the investigators to try to trace the stolen funds to an off-ramp, and a law firm will need to be appointed who will create legal letters to freeze or seize the located funds. In an interview with the CEO of Asset Reality, Aidan Larkin estimated that an investigation and legal process would have a likely cost of around $75,000, with most of that figure being the legal costs.

Although we have all read about the multi-hundred-million-dollar crypto frauds, we are already seeing this attempt at mass, low-value, victim fraud in the crypto space, with phishing attacks requiring a "fee" to authenticate your fake crypto wallet to hacked smart contracts that move a small amount of crypto to the scammer in each, otherwise legitimate, transaction.

There are many different categories of fraud, but I'll cover the key ones that you as an investigator are likely to come across involving crypto. Please remember that these are just the key categories and that there will be many varieties and subvarieties that use similar techniques.

Rug Pull

The expression "to have the rug pulled out from under you" can be applied to frauds where you believe that you are safe in an investment only to "have the rug pulled out from under you," usually when funds are withdrawn from an investment pool by the criminal, leaving the investment fund empty. In similar scams called *pump-and-dump*, the value of a token is artificially raised or pumped, and then the funds are withdrawn by the scammer, driving the remaining tokens' value to zero. In an exit scam, the scammer literally exits the investment with all the money! Although the details of the methods can be slightly different, they are all essentially rug pull scams.

Rug pull scams in the crypto space have been far too easy to build and implement. The ability to create a new token on chains such as Ethereum, Binance Smart Chain, or Tron offers a simple process for defrauding investors. (Although rug pull scams generally affect crypto investors, I have differentiated this from investment company scams, which work in a very different way.) There are several tried and tested methods, but different processes are appearing all the time, such as the following:

- A token is designed and launched; then social media and other marketing sources are used to promote it, perhaps paying a celebrity or influencer to post about it, growing its perceived value. Once the value is high enough, the scammer (who will own a significant percentage of the coins) will sell them and exit the token. The exit of funds back into another coin such as ETH will likely drop the value of the currency to zero.
- A new token is created and a swap contract set up using a service such as Uniswap. Uniswap enables the simple creation of swaps between tokens. If I set up a new token called NickCoin on Ethereum, I can define a *swap pair* on Uniswap to enable investors to swap from ETH to NickCoin. The swap contract on Uniswap requires liquidity in both tokens. The scammer supplies the NickCoin liquidity and some ETH liquidity. Next, I "pump" the reputation of the token as the "next big thing," and the only way to access the amazing new NickCoin token is by using the Uniswap contract. As investors who are sold on the investment idea of NickCoin swap from ETH to NickCoin, that positively affects the value of NickCoin and creates a growing pool of ETH in the contract. Once there is significant ETH, I, as the scammer, swap all my NickCoins for all the ETH in the swap contract and take my money. With nothing left in the ETH liquidity pool and following the result of the massive sell-off, the value of NickCoin will go to zero or close to it. The scammer walks away with all the ETH in the contract!
- A scammer sets up a new token; in the smart contract code anyone is allowed to buy the token but there's a limit as to who can sell the token. Once again, the scammer markets the token, convincing investors that it's worth buying into it. Once the value of the token is high, the scammer sells all the tokens. As no one else can sell, the value is driven to zero.

An interesting real-world case of the third example is a token called Squid Game, which was built on the Binance Smart Chain blockchain.

The token rode on the back of the popularity of the violent Netflix series of the same name. Although Netflix was quick to say that they had nothing to do with the token, investors bought into the new coin, with the value rising from little over a cent to over $2,800 in just a few days. Soon afterward reports began to appear on social media that users were unable to sell the coins, which were related to a secondary coin called Marbles about which little was known. The scammers then drained the liquidity, pocketing around $3.3 million.

The token has continued to run on the Binance Smart Chain. The developers were blacklisted, but it continues to ostensibly be run by the remaining holders of the coin, albeit with a value as of this writing of just $0.0006 per coin (`https://coinmarketcap.com/currencies/squid-game`).

Identifying that a new token is a scam can be difficult technically, but most new coin releases that are legitimate are careful to have a strong and public development team, third-party contract validation, and other strategies to highlight legitimacy. However, it is useful for an investigator to be aware of the signs that may relate to a token being a scam. In the case of Squid Game a number of indicators should have raised suspicions:

- The white paper released by the developers was full of spelling and grammatical errors.
- The named developers did not exist on sites such as LinkedIn.
- Telegram and Discord groups were closed.
- Twitter (X) comments were blocked.
- Tokens could not be sold (examination of the contract code may have revealed this).
- A large number of tokens were owned by the developers. Blockchain explorer sites such as Etherscan enable you to see the holders of tokens, and if you see a large percentage of the tokens owned by a single user address, that is often a red flag.

Pig-Butchering/Romance Scams

I feel bad connecting something as crass sounding as a pig-butchering with romance, but when it comes to scams they are often connected. The phrase comes from the practice of fattening up a pig, not because you really love the pig and want to give it lots of treats, but because you are planning to kill and eat it and want it as fat as possible! In a scam, this means "fattening" up the victim before stealing all their money and can be related to many types of scams.

Investment scams will often demonstrate growth of the victim's money and even allow them to withdraw small amounts of profits. This makes the victim feel safe and happy, but the scammer's proverbial knife is waiting. This process of allowing removal of profits is then usually followed up by the scammer convincing the victim to deposit even more money: "Look how much money you have made—imagine if we had 10 times as much!" You get the idea.

The term "pig-butchering" is regularly related to romance scams. Romance scams work by convincing a victim that the scammer—who is normally represented in pictures stolen off the Internet of good-looking people—is in a relationship with the victim and then socially engineering them out of money. They will talk online, sometimes on the phone, and will always have a reason why they can't do a video call. With female victims, it is usually a "heart" relationship, and with men, the scammer is usually a younger woman who will send more and more revealing pictures to demonstrate their "love" for the victim. These images are usually stolen from social media or more recently OnlyFans feeds of adult models, as these will tend to be more revealing and not immediately available if a suspicious victim does a Google search. This social engineering phase is the "pig-butchering" part where a relationship is built and emotions become involved. Next comes the request for money, often in the form of crypto. For female victims, the scammer may purport to be in the army and serving in some far-off country with limited Internet and need money to come home. Other versions of the scam are the "female" scammer needing money for a flight to come and see the victim; then their grandmother becomes sick and needs an operation that they need money for, and the lies carry on.

SCAM PACKS FOR SALE

Several years ago, I worked with a TV production company that was investigating romance scams for a documentary. We were attempting to follow the flow of crypto paid by the victims to scammers. They interviewed an adult model who had her images stolen to be used in romance scams, and they ended up being included in a "scam pack" that you could buy on the dark web that gave you all the tools you needed to become a romance scammer. This pack included sets of images of people, directions for setting up social media, scripts to use with the victim, and even where to send the victim's crypto so it could be laundered. Her images ended up being used hundreds of times in romance scams. Although there will be some readers who will have little sorrow for a person putting nude images of herself online, this misuse of her images negatively affected her life in the real world. Men who were being scammed using her images found her actual home address, her phone number, and her real social media. Some thought that she was scamming them herself and made threats; others believed that they were in a real relationship with her and began to stalk her on- and offline. Although the scammers have moved on to other image sets, the problem has not completely gone away several years later.

It is notable that when we followed the crypto funds from victim to scammer, we often saw the funds move into wallets upstream that were known to be associated with scams, money laundering, drugs, and other badness, showing that this was likely part of organized crime rather than a lone scammer.

I have to say at this juncture that romance scams make me angry. It's bad enough for a victim losing money, but some of these scammers are brilliant at the social engineering aspect and leave people feeling that they are in a relationship and even in love with this person. I dealt with a case of a middle-aged woman who had been scammed out of about $150,000 by a man she honestly believed was in the military and needed money to "buy body armour to keep him safe as the armour they were given was no good." She really believed it. Even when we presented the facts that he wasn't who he said he was and that the money was going to a scammer in Eastern Europe, she still sent him more money! She really wanted the relationship to be real. It was heartbreaking for her and upsetting for her family and even those of us involved in the investigation as we desperately tried to convince her of the scam.

Unless you're a psychologist, you may find it difficult to understand why these scams are successful and why people fall for them. The reason is that they reach out to basic human emotions and often those who are the most vulnerable. The Federal Trade Commission reported that romance scams just related to crypto resulted in $139 million in losses in 2021 in the United States alone, so they definitely work (www.ftc.gov/news-events/data-visualizations/data-spotlight/2022/02/reports-romance-scams-hit-record-highs-2021).

As investigators, we will likely not have to figure out a scam of this type; a complainant will usually come to us, and the signs are often clear right away. There is often a significant amount of other evidence to be considered, such as social media, chat history, phone records, and bank details. However, the crypto evidence can be very useful. Although romance scams have been around for years, the crypto part is fairly recent. The reason for asking for crypto tends to fall into several camps; the person asking for money, for example, "can't receive a standard bank transfer" normally because they are pretending to be in the army, or a woman in a fake abusive relationship who needs secret funds to escape. The examples go on. Over the last few years the romance scam has combined with investment scams where the relationship is used to coerce the victim into investing into a new token, DeFi scheme, or crypto business. The scammers are very adept at talking people through the steps of buying crypto and having it transferred to them or to the scam investment. In recent months, I investigated a romance scam where the scammer convinced the victim to sign a transaction with a malformed smart contract that enabled the scammer to empty the victim's wallets completely. More on that later in Chapter 11.

Romance scams are on the rise and payments being requested in crypto are becoming the primary mechanism. If you are investigating crypto or working toward doing so, you will come across them. Remember, there are always a lot of other categories of evidence. Don't get too focused on crypto tracing; it is useful but forms only part of an investigation.

Investment Scams

Throughout the last few years, I have found myself almost always having one or two investment scam investigations on the go, and the values were rather eye-watering considering that they were individual, rather than corporate, losses. Although quite a number were under $100,000, the majority were significantly more, with losses north of $250,000. These were rarely single payments to the scammers, but drip-fed amounts over time, usually ending with the victim trying to withdraw "profits" and being told that they had to deposit more to be able to withdraw. The most creative excuse I heard from a scammer was that the "customer's withdrawal account lacked liquidity and so had to be primed with funds to allow the customer to withdraw profits as all their funds were invested." If I were allowed to use a confused emoji in the book I would use one now! Sadly, even though we warned the victim that this was a scam, he thought that this was quite a reasonable request from the "investment company" and sent them more money. I think another confused emoji is needed.

What was notable about the victims, for the majority of the investment scams that I worked on, is that they were not the vulnerable 90-year-old grandma being scammed out of her life savings but wealthy, otherwise sophisticated investors who were seasoned risk takers and had usually done well from it. One victim said to me that "the language the scammers used was right, the concept of futures investing was well understood to me, the investment website with its graphs and data was exactly what I was used to in the fiat investment world—it felt right." This was often the story. The scammers used the right language, had real advisers who would befriend the investor (pig-butchering again), usually had legitimate addresses in London or New York, and even had phone numbers answered by corporate-sounding voicemail systems. The websites were often modeled on legitimate investment sites, and the live crypto data simply embedded from authentic sources, all lending to the credibility of the offering.

In 2019 I received a phone call from a woman who was a household name in the UK as a news broadcaster. She was calling under some pressure from friends who believed she was being scammed out of her significant crypto holdings, although she disagreed. She was hugely likable and very intelligent, and in the first five minutes of the conversation I was confident that she was in the midst of a live investment scam. Even though I talked her through their methods, she still didn't believe the company was criminal. We carried out some open source searches on the investment company. We found that the website was one month old, and the company was registered two months before with an address in the city of London. The website had been built using a template from a "scam pack" that you could buy on the dark web. I showed her other fake investment companies that had nearly the exact same site design. She still didn't believe it. She even told her "investment company" contact, who would phone her every few days with "new opportunities," that she had an investigation team looking into them! We recommended that she remove a good percentage of her funds, knowing that the scammers wouldn't allow it. She came back to us to explain that, according to the investment adviser from the firm, she would lose a lot of profits if she cashed out now. On a video call, I opened a sealed envelope containing a note I had written the day before predicting what the scammers would say. She still wouldn't accept it. In the end we convinced her to visit the registered address in Central London with a colleague. Rather cleverly for the scammers, there was a company with almost the right name trading on the second floor of the address, but they were not an investment company and they had never heard of the woman contact.

You would think that surely that was that and she was now convinced. She now accepted that the company was a scam but still didn't believe that the investment consultant—she was almost at the point of inviting him to dinner—was aware of the scam or otherwise involved. "I think he's a victim too," she said. "I need to warn him that he's working for a scam company." You can't make this stuff up.

The reason I tell this story is that the social engineering aspect of scams that involve personal relationships can be strong, as you learned in the section "Pig-Butchering/Romance Scams." Otherwise sophisticated investors, presented with overwhelming evidence of a scam, can become defensive of their decisions and even start defending the company. I've seen that many times and even worked on a case brought to us by the wife of an investor who again refused to believe that his investment decisions had been wrong.

We have worked on investment scams that originate in Eastern Europe, West Africa, and China. One scam investment company was registered to a rather rundown Chinese restaurant in a UK seaside town. This should have been a red flag for investors, but none of the victims I dealt with had even bothered to do cursory background checks of the company! As with other person-to-person scams, there is always a lot of evidence to consider. Obviously where crypto has moved we are able to follow the money, look for patterns and clusters of addresses, perhaps extend the investigation with the identification of other victims, contact off-ramps for KYC information, and so on. However, the contact numbers provided to victims, the KYC surrounding domain names, and website hosting services can often provide a lead to a real-world suspect. Although I will not go into detail since the case is ongoing as of this writing, we worked on a case involving a website that provided wallet seed words for a particular cryptocurrency, which were then stolen by the website owner. The thief had been careful to use burner email addresses and fake KYC when setting up the web infrastructure, but just once, a service provider refused to accept a ProtonMail address and requested a verified address. The scammer provided a Gmail address. Once we had recovered this from the service provider, this led to a mobile phone number, which in turn led us to the suspect. This takes us back to the point I keep repeating that crypto evidence is never siloed—there are always other threads of investigation.

As I've already alluded to, open source evidence can be useful and quite straightforward to acquire. We were contacted by a group of victims who had lost crypto in an investment scam; they had set up a Reddit group, had found each other, and had made good progress in the investigation. Just using Google searches and some clever reverse social engineering when the scammer called, they had identified the person's real name, where they lived, and a real-world business address as well as possible co-conspirators. It was quite impressive. What they didn't have was the track-and-trace ability to follow their funds, which we were able to help them with. We were able to put a case together and get it reported to law enforcement, who then effected an arrest. I have over the years received some quite extraordinary bottles of whiskey for thanks for services rendered, and that was one of those times.

Investment scams are easy to spot:

- They are often promoted on social media.
- They often use celebrity endorsements, which can be real but are often fake.
- Websites are usually very new.

TIP If you have the technical know-how, searching for unique code blocks on sites such as `http://publicwww.com` and Google Code Search may identify similar sites using similar code.

- Registered companies are usually very new.
- Investment returns are unreasonable. If it's too good to be true, it probably is.
- The salesperson refuses to meet in person.
- Profits are not returned.
- There is no way of cashing out.

Support Scams

Cryptocurrency support scams are a type of fraud that target users of crypto and other digital assets. The scam typically involves a person or group claiming to be a customer support representative from a legitimate cryptocurrency platform such as an exchange. This is usually advertised via social media and uses chat systems such as Discord, Telegram, and WhatsApp. They will then attempt to gain access to a user's funds by asking for their private keys or other sensitive information. Strong social engineering techniques are used to maximize the chance of fooling the victim. The scammer may also offer "support" services such as helping users reset passwords or withdraw funds, but of course, they are just trying to steal the user's crypto.

Cryptocurrency exchanges have historically been very difficult to contact. Finding a contact number for even the tier 1 exchanges such as Binance or Kraken was, until recently, virtually impossible, and obtaining support meant finding a useful Reddit group or similar source. This provided an opportunity for scammers.

I first came across this method following a call from a man in Florida. He was a wealthy, sophisticated investor and had some significant crypto holdings, which he subsequently had stolen in their entirety, with a dollar value of over $250,000. He had been looking for some support on his Binance BNB (Build and Build) holdings as he was struggling to swap between two tokens. He found a Discord chat group that purported to be from Binance. He was answered by a helpful support person who said the victim had to be authenticated and asked for his seed words. He handed them over and of course this gave the scammer access to all his crypto and it was all stolen minutes later. This was just due to a lack of technical understanding on the part of the investor; had he understood the importance of the seed words, then he would still have his crypto in his possession.

Another support scam we investigated was even cleverer in that they asked the victim to provide just words 3, 7, and 10 of their seed words. Of course, we are all used to the questions from banks and others to provide the first and third letter of our password to the support person, so this question did not feel wrong to the victim. The victim supplied the words but the support person said that they hadn't been accepted, so perhaps try words 1, 8, and 11. Within a few minutes they had all 12 words. Pretty clever approach.

During 2022 we saw the primary exchanges becoming easier to contact as they became keener to be viewed as "banks" on the blockchain and provide personal support. But then toward the end of the year, the industry was rocked by the failing of the exchanges FTX and Genesis. This spurred on the appearance of more "support" scammers pretending to be liquidators, or staff there to help you if you had lost funds in the aforementioned company's demise.

Where the money is, the scammers will soon follow.

Simple Theft

We have been looking briefly at some of the more complex categories of crimes that can involve crypto, but we have ignored the fact that just like any asset, crypto can simply be stolen. Of course, the public/private key infrastructure that protects crypto on the blockchain is solid, but if someone can get hold of your private key, your seed words, or your login to your preferred exchange, then the assets can simply be taken.

There was a man who kept his seed words in his wallet in his jacket at work and told his boss about them, resulting in his crypto "disappearing." Recall the person we referred to in Chapter 2, "Understanding the Criminal Opportunities: Money Laundering," who was selling Bitcoin online and invited the buyers to his home, where he was tied up and forced to send the thieves his crypto. There are other ways of stealing digital assets without the complexities of investment scams and phishing attempts.

These types of crimes usually require the criminal to get close to the victim, and this provides many more evidential details to consider in your case. In the case of the victim who was tied up in his home, there would likely be phone records, neighborhood CCTV, doorbell camera footage, fingerprints, eyewitness reports, vehicles used, and so on, before we look at the crypto element.

Perhaps the most brazen case I worked on came at the start of 2022. I will adjust some details to protect the person. It was a weekend and I answered the phone to a woman who asked if I could help her with a crypto loss. Although I don't normally take calls on the weekend, I was not busy so I nonchalantly asked her what the details were. When she said that over $18 million of her personal crypto had just disappeared that morning, I almost fell off my chair!

TIME TO BE CAUTIOUS

I'd like to share a word of warning. Certain nation-states, journalists, and even criminals may use fake investigations to get into communication with you, to get you talking and sharing information, to understand how you work on crypto cases, the tools you have at your disposal, and more importantly what you can and cannot do. This information can be very useful to them. (Even this book will omit significant details about operational capabilities of certain tools and agencies.). Be very cautious with LinkedIn requests, overly interesting or valuable investigations, and offers of payment that are too good to be true.

In the case of the $18 million loss case, the value, the emotional young lady on the phone, and a check of social media showing me a very attractive "influencer"-styled woman on private jets and tropical islands felt too good to be true and set my "scam senses" tingling! However, in this case, amazingly, it was legitimate.

The woman shared the transaction ID, which did indeed show a vast amount of crypto moving that morning from an address she claimed was hers to a third party she didn't know. I called friends at the metropolitan police and they stood ready to take a look at it, but I said I would get the evidence together and see where it progressed.

The following day, the crypto still sat in what was a new Ethereum address. The suspect had used a small amount of the funds to try to get the mixer Tornado Cash to work, but it seemed that they were unsure whether to trust it. On day 3, the crypto was still in the third-party address. I wonder if some of you are already beginning to think the same way that I was on day 3. Why hadn't the crypto moved? Why couldn't they get Tornado Cash to work? A strong candidate for an answer is that the suspect didn't know what they were doing. The crypto should have been laundered away within hours, but nothing by day 3. So, who would have the extraordinary knowledge to hack the woman's computer and steal a vast sum but have no plan how to launder the money? She believed that she had been hacked, but it just didn't add up. Perhaps the person had stumbled on her crypto-wallet following a hack of her computer, but it didn't feel right to me.

I called her and said we were going to try something before embarking on an expensive investigation. She should contact everyone close to her—family, close friends, assistants, employees, anyone who had physical access to her and her technology—and tell them about the theft, that she had contacted a renowned investigation firm and that they were working with the police and were confident that the thief would be identified quickly.

She immediately realized that I was suggesting that someone close to her was responsible and she wouldn't accept that as a possibility, but I pressed that we would not take on the investigation unless she did as we asked. Twelve hours later she called me back. A very trusted person close to her had confessed and "didn't want to go to prison." She was devastated at the break of trust, but 24 hours later the crypto was returned. I was delighted for her—she was a genuinely lovely person—but it reminded me that with all the knowledge and the technology and tools at our disposal, you sometimes just need to sit back and ask the good investigative questions.

With all the clever criminal schemes, sometimes proximity to a victim, the right circumstances, and good old-fashioned greed will prompt a person to steal what is not theirs, and crypto is no exception.

Contract Manipulation

We will discuss smart contracts in much more detail in Chapter 11, and we have already explored attacks on contracts such as the DAO hack in 2016 discussed in Chapter 1 and the fake Squid Game coin contract mentioned a few pages ago. There is nothing inherently wrong with the smart contract ecosystem, but where there's code there are vulnerabilities. Criminals can exploit smart contracts in a number of ways, and there is probably enough to write a whole book on the subject, but we'll just look at a few examples.

Fake Contracts

Fake contracts are not fake in that they are not real, but fake in that they do not do what they promise to do. Perhaps the simplest example of this is a scammer setting up a new crypto token on Ethereum, Tron, or Binance Smart Chain, for example, and then convincing people to buy into it and finally profiting criminally from the purchaser funds. This can be achieved in a number of ways:

- A token could contain a very high buy fee, which will steal the majority of your money at the buying phase. Think of buying a token for $100 but $99 is the token buy fee.
- The tokens are not able to be sold (Squid Game Token is a good example) and only the owner may sell, as we discussed previously.
- The token code may contain a very high sell fee, which will steal the majority of your money at the selling phase. Similar to the first bullet point, think of selling a token for $100 but $99 is the token sell fee.
- The contract code may allow the owner to create more coins in their own wallet. Once the token has grown and acquired value, the criminal mints more coins and sells them. This will also have the effect of putting too much liquidity in the token's ecosystem and result in a fall of the token's value.

Fake contracts are difficult to identify before the scam is under way and users start to complain that they can't sell their tokens. Once there are complainants, then simply the fact that a token is blocking sales, as an example, is enough to usually signify that you are dealing with a fraud. Of course, it is very useful to be able to read the raw source code; an experienced Solidity programmer (Solidity is the programming language used to build smart contracts on the Ethereum platform) would likely be able to ascertain the fraudulent aspect of the code by identifying the code blocks that blocked sales, set high fees, or enabled the owner to mint coins. Most crypto or financial investigators are not programmers and will likely have to rely on an expert to assist.

Exploiting the Contract

I guess that you could call this section *hacking* the contract rather than *exploiting* it. This relates to attacks where criminals find and manipulate the code in a third party's smart contract to cause it to act in a way that it wasn't designed to. This topic again could be another book in its own right. Hackers have been finding and abusing vulnerabilities in code for as long as there has been code to hack. Smart contracts are a hugely attractive target because they are related to the transaction of assets, hence those assets can potentially be stolen. As of this writing, a quick look at the darker corners of the dark web revealed people willing to hack smart contracts to order or who were selling existing vulnerabilities in contracts for other hackers to exploit.

Some of the largest-value thefts have come from exploiting contract code. In 2021 the DeFi protocol Compound suffered a loss of around $150 million following a system update. A change in the code allowed the attackers to claim many more of Compound's governance tokens (COMP tokens) than they were permitted to. By manipulating the code, they were able to trigger a distribution of the COMP tokens to addresses of their choosing.

We can't talk about exploitation of contracts without mentioning the hack on the Ronin Bridge in 2022 carried out by the Lazarus Group, a hacking team run by the North Korean government. The hack netted $615 million in just two transactions. The Ronin Bridge was used by the game Axie Infinity to move funds and assets from and to the game's blockchain. The vulnerability was due to issues with the validation code that managed the movement of funds on and off the bridge, which resulted in the eye-watering losses.

A clever form of contract hacking is called a *reentrancy attack*. It's helpful to think about a normal transaction of a token. Consider, for example, a pretend token called NickCoin on the Ethereum blockchain. To send 100 NickCoin, I send a request to the NickCoin contract to move 100 NickCoin from my address to a third-party address. The contract checks that I have the funds and then sends the funds to the destination address while the balance on the NickCoin contract address and the sending and receiving addresses is updated.

However, I (as the hacker) can potentially ask the NickCoin contract to send the funds to a malicious contract that I've built. Once this nefarious contract receives the funds, it will carry out a callback function to the vulnerable NickCoin contract *before* the contract has updated the balance. The cycle repeats until all funds are effectively drained from the NickCoin contract.

This type of attack has been used many times, including the DAO hack of 2016, the attack on Cream Finance in 2021 (with losses of $130 million), and the Meerkat Finance hack in 2021 (with losses of $31 million). The Meerkat Finance hack is a bit of an odd one. They set up their service on the Binance Smart Chain and then experienced the hack attack just one day after its official launch, losing 73,000 BNB coins and $14 million BUSD. A day later a person on Telegram posted that it had been "a test of the system," a claim that was widely disputed by the community, who feared a rug pull scam. The Binance security team did a super job of recovering the funds, and the majority of victims got their money back.

Sometimes the vulnerabilities are not actually in the smart contracts but rather in the systems that allow users to interact with the contract. This was the case in the Badger DAO hack in 2021 where the DAO protocol suffered an attack worth $120 million, losing both Bitcoin and Ethereum. Although the hack was due to malicious permissions passed to the contract, the issue that enabled the attackers to create and pass the malevolent permissions was due to vulnerabilities in the software's user interface, not the contract itself.

Phishing

I've already mentioned phishing as a concept earlier in the chapter in the "Social Engineering" section, where I explained that the word has become a colloquial term for emails, text messages, and other messaging that contains links that are malevolent in some way. How is this related to smart contract vulnerabilities?

It is notable that the hack against the NFT broker OpenSea was due to a combination of a smart contract flaw associated with a phishing attack against users. OpenSea is estimated to have lost 254 NFTs with a combined value of around $1.7 million. The hackers undermined OpenSeas's Discord channel and posted in the announcements that OpenSea had "partnered with YouTube to bring their community into the NFT Space." The announcement included a link that when clicked would compromise the victim's OpenSea account and the attackers were able to use an old OpenSea contract to steal the NFTs.

Back at the start of 2022 when the attack happened, users interacted with what was known as the "Wyvern contract." Users gave a proxy contract the authority to withdraw their NFTs using a `setApprovalForAll` permission. (This was fixed in May 2022 with the new Seaport contract).

The phishing link connected to an exploit that encouraged users to sign a transaction that gave the attacker ownership of the proxy contract. This allowed attackers to steal users' NFTs from their wallets.

Phishing attacks remain a firm favorite with criminal groups. When questioning a victim, always look for emails or text messages that the victim has clicked on.

Flash Loans

A *flash loan* is generally a zero-collateral loan. A user interacts with a smart contract to take a loan and repay the loan all in a single transaction. That might sound pointless, but a sophisticated trader can use those funds to take advantage of arbitrage opportunities and margin trading, and they can also be used to fund liquidity mining operations.

NOTE Arbitrage is a trading strategy that exploits pricing discrepancies between different markets. By simultaneously buying and selling an asset on different exchanges, traders can take advantage of the price difference and make a profit. This can be done in the same way with cryptocurrencies, and flash loans can provide the necessary capital to make these high-speed arbitrage trades.

Because there are so many exchanges around the world, determining a single true price for digital crypto assets is nearly impossible. This pricing disparity is what makes arbitrage trading appealing.

A flash loan attack is when a malicious actor takes out a crypto flash loan, uses it to manipulate markets or perform other dubious or criminal activities, and then repays the loan without penalty. Or the effect of taking the loan can result in driving the lending market to zero, enabling the criminal to walk away with the "loan." I use the word "dubious" as well as "criminal" as some of the flash loan attackers have argued that they are doing nothing wrong and only playing by the rules of the contract. In a moment, we will look in more detail at the Mango Market attack, which is a good example of this.

The flash loan attacks have grown in popularity in the past couple of years and now account for many of the significant losses experienced by crypto markets. The financial concepts behind some of these attacks are highly complex, and I strongly recommend involving financial investigators in these investigations because they should already have an understanding of market manipulation strategies. Some flash loan attacks benefit from creating large price swings by carrying out large-scale trades, some result in stealing the loan itself, and others create a financial effect elsewhere. In the bZx attack in 2021, the attackers used flash loans, yet their aim was not to steal the loan funds but to create massive price slippages in decentralized exchanges (DEXs) that had low liquidity. The initial attack caused price slippage on the DEX Uniswap, which bZx used as an "oracle" to set its prices. (Blockchain oracles are programs that connect blockchains to external systems. This enables code running on the blockchain such as smart contracts to execute based upon data from the real world.) By reducing the value of the sUSD token with this manipulation, the hacker took two flash loans, forcing bZx to issue money to them to balance the loan and collateral. As a result of manipulating the pricing, the hackers stole a total of $55 million.

Another example is the flash loan attack against the token BUNNY on the Binance Smart Chain. The BUNNY team described on Twitter (X) [`https://twitter.com/PancakeBunnyFin/status/1395173093333680136`] how the attack unfolded:

1. The hacker used PancakeSwap to borrow a huge amount of BNB.
2. The hacker then went on to manipulate the price of USDT/BNB as well as BUNNY/BNB.
3. The hacker ended up getting a huge amount of BUNNY through this flash loan.
4. The hacker then dumped all the BUNNY in the market, causing the BUNNY price to plummet.
5. The hacker paid back the BNB through PancakeSwap.

If you are interested, the primary transaction can be found here: `https://bscscan.com/tx/0x897c2de73dd55d7701e1b69ffb3a17b0f4801ced88b0c75fe1551c5fcce6a979`.

An interesting detail of the transaction is that the attacker embedded a short message in the transaction code with a subtle rabbit-themed joke: `ArentFlashloansEaritating`.

As mentioned previously, it can be very important to involve financial investigators in these generally complex investigations because they understand the complexities of flash loans and their associated price fluctuations. Criminals in this space can be incredibly creative in their ability both to uncover vulnerabilities in contract code and to understand how to exploit price movements and profit from it.

Playing by the Rules

Some significant losses from contracts and markets have come from an attacker arguably playing by the rules. What I mean by this is that they use the contract or market against itself, perhaps making it work in a way that is functionally what the programmer intended, but the results of the actions are certainly not within the expected parameters of the contract.

The first example I can think of is the 2016 DAO hack, which I have referred to a couple of times. As I highlighted in Chapter 1 when discussing bug bounties, the attacker posted on note-taking site Pastebin that

> *I am making use of this explicitly coded feature as per the smart contract terms and my law firm has advised me that my action is fully compliant with United States criminal and tort law.*

Note that the attacker described the methods used to extract funds as an "explicitly coded feature." He believed that he was playing by the rules. (I use the male gender as most sources point to an Austrian man as being the perpetrator.)

In more recent times, a very clever attack was carried out against Mango Markets during 2022, resulting in losses of around $114 million. Mango Markets is a trading site that enabled lending, borrowing, swapping, futures, and spot margin trading, enabling the creating of long and short positions against crypto tokens.

SPOT MARGIN TRADING

Spot margin trading is a type of crypto trading that allows traders to use margin combined with their existing crypto balance to increase their buying power and open positions larger than the amount of crypto they already have available.

Futures trading is a type of derivative trading that allows traders to speculate on the future price of a certain cryptocurrency asset. This type of trading involves a contract between a buyer and seller, in which both parties agree to buy or sell an asset at a predetermined price and date in the future.

A short position is a trading strategy in which a trader sells an asset, expecting its price to fall so that they can buy back the asset at a lower price and make a profit. It is the opposite of a long position, which involves buying an asset with the expectation that its price will rise.

In the case of Mango Markets, two separate accounts were used to carry out the attack. On account A the trader initially used 5 million USD coin to buy 483 million MNGO and go short, or effectively bet against the asset. Then on account B the trader used another 5 million USDC to buy the same amount of the internal Mango coin MNGO, using 10 million USDC in total to effectively hedge their position.

The attacker then used more funds to buy up spot MNGO tokens, taking its price from just 2 cents to as much as 91 cents within a 10-minute span. This was possible as MNGO was a rarely traded token with quite low liquidity, which allowed the rogue trader to manipulate prices quickly.

As the MNGO prices increased, the trader's account B quickly racked up some $420 million in profits. The attacker then took out a loan of $114 million in liquidity from all tokens available on Mango, which effectively wiped out the liquidity in the protocol.

Figure 3.1 shows the increase in MNGO token value from 2 cents to 91 cents in a very short time.

Within days a trader named Avraham Eisenberg went public about the attack and described it as a "highly profitable trading strategy" that was allowed by Mango's code, effectively playing by the rules. To my amazement Mango's token holders grudgingly accepted Eisenberg's assertion that he was just playing by the rules and voted to let him keep $47 million on the condition that he would return the other $67 million.

A few months after the attack, I was in a meeting with a cross-section of UK law enforcement investigators at the U.S. embassy in London, where we discussed the details around the Mango case. My colleague Chris Janczewski, previously an IRS investigator, asked the assembled group if they felt Eisenberg had broken the law. He raised his hand but only a few hands in the room rose with him. It is incredibly difficult to get your head around whether a law has been broken when the rules of the market were followed. However, there are existing laws that cover market price manipulation. The U.S. Department of Justice, along with the Securities and Exchange Commission (SEC), obviously agreed with Chris because in January 2023 they charged Avraham Eisenberg with the theft of funds from Mango Markets. In a statement, David Hirsch, chief of the Crypto Assets and Cyber Unit, said:

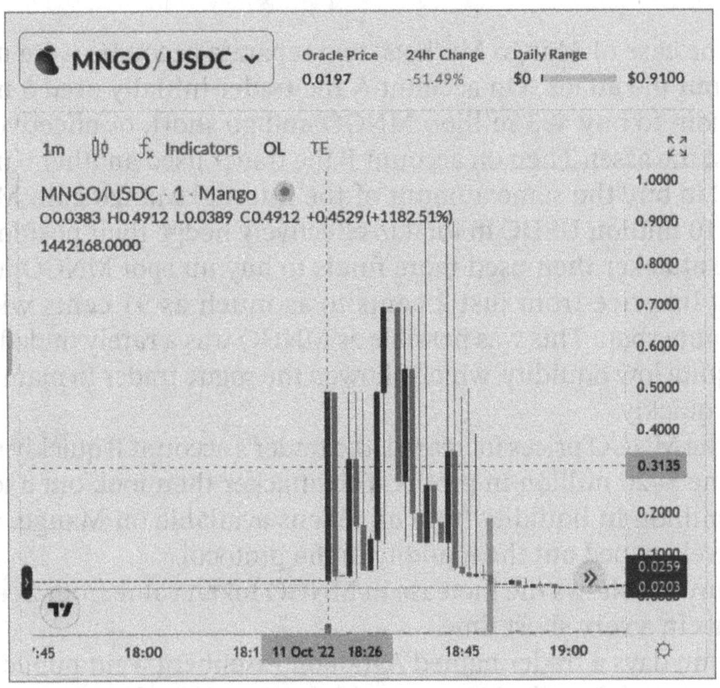

Figure 3.1: Graph showing the change in value of the MNGO token

> *As we allege, Eisenberg engaged in a manipulative and deceptive scheme to artificially inflate the price of the MNGO token, which was purchased and sold as a crypto asset security, in order to borrow and then withdraw nearly all available assets from Mango Markets, which left the platform at a deficit when the security price returned to its pre-manipulation level. . . .As our action shows, the SEC remains committed to rooting out market manipulation, regardless of the type of security involved.*

The SEC's complaint, filed in federal district court in Manhattan, charges Eisenberg with violating antifraud and market manipulation provisions of the securities laws and seeks permanent injunctive relief, "a conduct-based injunction, disgorgement with prejudgment interest, and civil penalties" (see `www.sec.gov/news/press-release/2023-13`).

This clearly demonstrates that the authorities are not going to take "playing by the rules" as an excuse for illegality.

VALUE FRAUD

Value fraud, otherwise known as wash-trading, can easily be accomplished with NFTs. A criminal takes an artistic picture of their dog and mints it as an NFT, then using another account buys it from themself for $100,000. They wait a week and buy it again for $150,000, then again for $175,000. Next, they promote it on social media as the next big thing and then put it back up for sale for $225,000. Investors will see the fast growth and may be tempted to buy this wonderful dog NFT. All it will have cost the criminal is the very small fees from the broker, and they see $50,000 in profit.

Another form of playing by the rules is exploiting a contract to force the contract to create, or *mint*, new coins. This type of attack is normally carried out against bridges, which connect different blockchains together. In Chapter 2 we briefly referred to the hack against the Solana blockchain bridge called the Wormhole bridge. The attacker discovered a way to exploit the bridge contract to convince something called the Validator Action Approval (VAA) to mint new coins without receiving coins on the other side of the chain. The attacker was able to acquire $325 million in the hack. This wasn't a direct hack against the code in the strictest sense, but rather using the contract to do something the programmer had not really intended it to do.

A similar technique was used in the Ronin Bridge hack used by the Axie Infinity game, carried out by the North Korean Lazarus Group. Bridges similar to either Wormhole or Ronin generally work by locking up crypto in smart contracts on one chain and then minting those tokens in a "wrapped" form of the token on a destination chain.

The Ronin Bridge had a vast amount of ETH in a single address, which made it a highly valuable target. The Ronin attacker obtained five of the nine validator private keys that were used to secure the bridge. By holding a majority of the keys, the attacker was able to withdraw the crypto straight from the Ronin Bridge to their own wallet. The crypto-analysis firm Chainalysis reported that Lazarus used over 12,000 addresses in the subsequent laundering of the funds and that $30 million had been recovered (`https://blog.chainalysis.com/reports/axie-infinity-ronin-bridge-dprk-hack-seizure`). If you examine the attack in detail, you'll see it used a number of techniques we have discussed in this chapter, including social engineering, hacking, and even playing by the rules when they used the validator keys to transfer funds.

Other Criminal Opportunities

Although not directly related to theft as in the title of this chapter, there are a few other criminal opportunities that you should be aware of when looking at crypto addresses that are involved in criminality.

Yield Farming

Cryptocurrency yield farming is a form of passive income that involves providing liquidity to specialized cryptocurrency markets such a token swap contact. The process of yield farming requires users to deposit their crypto assets into a liquidity pool in order to collect interest payments or to receive rewards from the exchange. This is a straightforward way for a criminal to earn clean funds from dirty money. If you deposit large amounts of capital into an interest-bearing bank account, the bank will ask all sorts of inconvenient questions about where the money came from, but in a smart contract, no one asks and to be frank, generally no one cares. The interest payments or rewards are essentially new, clean funds generated from the proceeds of crime.

Investigators need to look carefully at crypto addresses that are related to criminality and watch for function names such as `deposit`, `reward`, or `withdrawal`, which may indicate the earning of new crypto. We will look at this in a practical way in Chapter 11. Figure 3.2 shows transactions with function calls that could indicate that the user is yield farming.

0x5310ee308a451fc326...	Remove Liquidity...	11621876
0x90d43afb5e68580505...	0x415565b0	11617471
0x42d50b342cfcf7fa64cc...	Remove Liquidity...	11615258
0x8a2a5cede52a9c03bd...	Withdraw Token	11615179

Figure 3.2: Transactions with function calls that could indicate that the user is yield farming

Funding of Groups

When building the elements of this chapter I actually wondered whether the use of crypto for the funding of criminal groups along with areas such as sanction avoidance should be a chapter in its own right. However, this is a highly complex area that affects only very specialist investigators, and techniques and investigative capabilities are rightly closely guarded by the law enforcement and government groups concerned. This is an area I have had some contact with but I certainly would not call myself a specialist.

The pseudo-anonymous nature of crypto has meant that criminal and terrorist groups see the technology as a significant opportunity to enable funds to be donated globally and in an anonymous way. In recent years a number of Islamic terror groups attempted to advertise Bitcoin addresses for donations, but there was little in the way of operational security and funds were sent straight to exchanges with no attempts at obfuscation. However, recently both Islamic terror groups and far-right groups have made strong use of social media to spread their message, and with it the use of crypto as a means of acquiring donations has also grown.

In July 2021 the U.S. Congress heard evidence from law enforcement about terror funding in a session titled "Terrorism and Digital Financing: How Technology Is Changing the Threat." You can read about it here: `www.congress.gov/event/117th-congress/house-event/LC67196/text?s=1&r=18`.

In his statement to Congress, John Eisert, Assistant Director, Investigative Programs at Homeland Security Investigations (HSI), stated that less than 1 percent of terror funding was related to cryptocurrencies, but he went on to say in his statement:

> *HSI led a global cyber operation with IRS and the FBI related to 24 cryptocurrency accounts, all of which were identified as sources of influence for al-Qaeda. The HSI undercover operation was initiated to investigate the unlawful use of cryptocurrency to support terrorism. The result of the investigation—ending result of the investigation, HSI seized 60 virtual currency wallets, worth $80 million, and illuminated the illicit financial network.*
>
> **Source:** `www.congress.gov/event/117th-congress/house-event/LC67196/text?s=1&r=18`

One percent may sound like a small amount but when it's one percent of a global criminal funding effort, it is a considerable amount, as can be seen by the seizure of the $80 million worth of crypto. Hence, antiterrorism teams need to be aware of and trained in identifying crypto use and tracing both the donors and the off-ramps that will turn these donations into fiat currency that can more easily be used by the groups to fund the bombs and bullets of their trade. The 2022 Europol Terrorism Situation and Trend Report (`www.europol.europa.eu/cms/sites/default/files/documents/Tesat_Report_2022_0.pdf`) stated in part:

> *The use of digital currency, cryptocurrency and virtual assets service providers (VASPs) enables terrorist and extremist groups to increasingly misuse crowdfunding activities, while maintaining a higher level of anonymity for donors and recipients. With regard to jihadist terrorism, there have been cases of financial support or requests for support from IS and al-Qaeda involving cryptocurrencies. Spain, for instance, has reported a shift from money business services to crypto assets and virtual platforms since 2020, which further increased in 2021. Right-wing extremists also use funding platforms operating with cryptocurrencies. Moreover, prepaid cryptocurrency coupons or premium tickets that can be bought*

> *legally in Member States for values comprising between EUR 50 to 250 have been used for transferring money abroad.*

Rather concerningly, the report also highlighted that

> *the pro-al-Qaeda media outlet Jaysh al-Malahim al-Elektroni published the second issue of the* Wolves of Manhattan *magazine. The publication provided guidance on how to infiltrate protests in western countries for the purpose of targeting police officers and promised a cryptocurrency reward to the first individual who would send photos documenting the killing of a police officer.*

So, although cryptocurrencies may not be the primary methodology of these groups for financing, they are certainly aware of their potential, and I suggest that these attacks will only increase as crypto becomes more widely used globally and more secure privacy coins become easier to use.

Sanctions Avoidance

Although there have always been government sanctions in place against organized criminal gangs, terrorism groups, and rogue states, sanctions avoidance has become a hot topic since the invasion of Ukraine by Russia. Before the donation of weapons had begun in early 2022, governments moved to sanction both groups and individuals that were seen as being supportive of the Putin regime.

In July 2022 the UK National Crime Agency (NCA) published a Red Alert document for law enforcement, private industry, and financial crime regulators to consider and implement:

`https://nationalcrimeagency.gov.uk/who-we-are/publications/605-necc-financial-sanctions-evasion-russian-elites-and-enablers/file`

The document outlined four primary areas that investigators need to consider:

- Detection of frozen asset transfers
- Detection of enablers of asset transfers
- Detection of suspicious payments
- The role of private industry

If you are involved in any crypto investigation, I suggest giving this document a read as it's a useful and open source overview of the role of different groups in the detection of sanctions avoidance. Although it is related to the UK in some of its phrasing and governmental department names, it is still helpful to understand how a government requires investigators to be engaged and aware of sanctions avoidance.

So can cryptocurrencies be effectively used by bad actors in the avoidance of sanctions? Helpfully, or should I say, unhelpfully, the answer is both yes and no.

First, why would we say no? Let's take the theoretical idea that we are a sanctioned country, and we want to buy some planes. The problem is that we still do not have a cryptocurrency that is globally and ubiquitously accepted for buying and selling goods—that's the case whether you want to buy a pizza, an Airbus airplane, or even an anti-aircraft missile system! Even if an aircraft manufacturer from another rogue state agreed to accept Bitcoin or similar for payment of a $50 million aircraft order, where would that company cash out? That company needs to pay its staff, pay the electricity bill, and so on, none of whom will accept the Bitcoin and will require fiat currency. So, theoretically, on paper, I could use Bitcoin to pay for my planes, but the reality is that when the manufacturer needs to turn the crypto into fiat they are going to have a real problem because all of the exchanges big enough to even look at $50 million are going to ask rather a lot of questions about the provenance of the Bitcoin. This makes using crypto for high-value sanctions avoidance very difficult indeed.

However, why would we say yes to the same question? When we look at lower-value transactions, perhaps between individuals, then crypto becomes more useful as a sanctions avoidance tool. If I reside in a sanctioned country or am a sanctioned person, then moving funds via the banking system becomes very complicated indeed. Of course, even in the case of Russian oligarchs at the moment, there are plenty of banks around the world that will be willing to ignore international sanctions and route the money for them; however, significant expenses and risks are involved. Simply moving Bitcoin from one wallet to another doesn't actually cross any borders. We always think about "sending" Bitcoin, but in reality all we are doing is updating the blockchain ledger—nothing actually moves anywhere. This makes it straightforward to "move" crypto from one wallet to another. The major exchanges are still going to ask for KYC and provenance but significantly less questions will be asked when depositing $250,000 than $50 million, and KYC can be fairly easily faked or routed via a proxy person. That aside, there are plenty of brokers in the world willing to exchange your crypto with no questions asked for a slightly enhanced fee.

As I'm not an expert in this space I reached out to my friend and colleague Ari Redbord. Ari was previously Senior Adviser to the Deputy Secretary and the Undersecretary for Terrorism and Financial Intelligence at the U.S. Treasury before taking up the role of Head of Legal and Government Affairs at TRM Labs, so he is well placed to have an educated opinion. I'm sure you will find the interview interesting.

INTERVIEW WITH ARI REDBORD

Nick: Hey Ari, we need to better understand the use of sanctions in the crypto space, so I was hoping you could answer a few questions.

Ari: Sure thing, Nick, happy to help.

Nick: So first, what are economic sanctions and what's their purpose?

Ari: Governments and multinational bodies impose economic sanctions against an adversary in an attempt to alter or deter behavior. Sanctions can take a variety of forms, including travel bans, asset freezes, arms embargoes, capital restraints, foreign aid reductions, and trade restrictions. Sanctions can be comprehensive—taking the form of an embargo against an entire country such as Cuba, Iran, or North Korea—or may be more targeted, going after a specific person or entity engaged in malign activity. In recent years, the United States has expanded the use of economic tools, with sanctions becoming the go-to nonkinetic response to national security threats around the globe. Sanctions are generally viewed as a lower-cost, lower-risk way to isolate bad actors and resolve conflicts than boots-on-the ground alternatives.

Sanctions are imposed by both national governments like the United Kingdom and the United States and multinational bodies such as the European Union and the United Nations. Oftentimes countries will work in concert, taking action together such as in response to Russia's invasion of Ukraine. Sanctions have been used to advance a range of foreign policy and national security goals, including counterterrorism, counternarcotics, nonproliferation, human rights promotion, conflict resolution, and cybersecurity.

Government agencies, such as the United States Treasury Department's Office of Foreign Assets Control (OFAC), implement sanctions against countries, regimes, entities, and individuals that are seen as a threat to national security. In the United States, OFAC administers and enforces economic sanctions against targeted foreign countries, geographic regions, entities, and individuals to further U.S. foreign policy and national security goals. As part of these efforts, OFAC maintains a specially designated nationals (SDN) list that includes designated entities and individuals. Generally, if OFAC places an individual or entity on the SDN list, it means that the person's assets and/or property in the U.S. can be blocked and that all U.S. persons and/or U.S. entities are prohibited from transacting with the designated party.

Nick: That was interesting, Ari, but what if someone, for example in the U.S., was to knowingly or even unknowingly trade with a sanctioned person or company?

Ari: The consequences for sanctions violations are severe. OFAC may impose civil penalties for sanctions violations generally based on a strict liability legal standard. This means that a U.S. person or business may be held civilly liable for sanctions violations even without having knowledge or reason to know it was engaging in such a violation. There is, however, a substantially higher standard when it comes to the criminal prosecution of a sanctions violation, in which the government must prove a violation beyond a reasonable doubt.

Nick: So, how has OFAC used economic sanctions in specifically the cryptocurrency space?

Ari: In the last few years OFAC has taken a number of actions in the cryptocurrency space in an attempt to cut off illicit actors, stop the flow of laundered funds, and curb malicious activity from cybercriminals, terrorists, and nation-state actors like North Korea. As part of this effort OFAC often adds cryptocurrency addresses to its SDN list as a way to taint those addresses and alert cryptocurrency exchanges and other cryptocurrency businesses not to transact with them. Since 2018, OFAC has added 388 blockchain addresses to the SDN list.

When it comes to the cryptocurrency space, OFAC has taken action to thwart malicious activity such as terrorist financing, ransomware, darknet market activity, and cyber threats. For example, in July 2021, OFAC designated a Tajik national named Farrukh Furkatovitch Fayzimatov for his involvement as a terrorist financier for Hay'et Tahrir Al-Sham (HTS). In September 2022, OFAC issued a round of cyber- and Iran-related updates that included cryptocurrency addresses linked to individuals affiliated with Iran's Islamic Revolutionary Guard Corps (IRGC).

Nick: At this current time the Ukraine-Russia conflict is still ongoing, with many sanctions in place against Russia and individuals. How has OFAC used sanctions in the Russian illicit finance context?

Ari: Some of OFAC's most impactful actions over the past few years have targeted Russian illicit finance. For example, OFAC has used sanctions against four Russia-linked cryptocurrency exchanges for their lack of anti-money-laundering (AML) controls that allowed the free flowing of illicit proceeds from ransomware, darknet markets, and other illicit activities.

Even before the war, in September 2021, the Treasury designated its first cryptocurrency exchange, SUEX.io, a concierge cryptocurrency exchanger incorporated operating in Russia. SUEX was operated as a so-called nested or parasite exchange, meaning SUEX did not directly custody its clients' crypto. Instead, it fed off the infrastructure of a large global cryptocurrency exchange to conduct its transactions. Using this relationship with a large exchange, SUEX was able to convert the illicit monies of its clients to physical cash at an alarming scale. Under two months later, OFAC took action against a second Russia-based exchange, Chatex, again for a lack of AML controls and in April 2022 Treasury added Garantex, another Russian exchange to the SDN list for its involvement with darknet market Hydra, which was also sanctioned by OFAC. Russian-language Hydra, the world's largest darknet marketplace at the time of the takedown, sold illegal narcotics, forged documents, stolen credit cards, and other illicit materials. Prior to the takedown, Hydra was doing about $1 billion annually.

OFAC has also used sanctions against other Russian illicit finance risks. In October 2022, OFAC designated individuals and entities for their "involvement in Russia's invasion of Ukraine" and Russia's attempt to find new ways to "process payments and conduct transactions." Specifically, OFAC took action against Task Force Rusich, which was described by OFAC as a "neo-Nazi paramilitary group that has participated in combat alongside Russia's military in Ukraine." OFAC also added individuals affiliated with the group—"two of its senior leaders"—and five cryptocurrency addresses linked to the group to its SDN list.

Nick: We have mentioned several times in this book the role of the North Korean Lazarus Group and their attacks against crypto services. How has OFAC used sanctions against North Korean cybercriminals?

Ari: According to TRM analysis, 2022 was a record-setting year for crypto hacks, with about $3.7 billion in stolen funds. Attacks against DeFi projects were particularly common, with approximately 80 percent of all stolen funds, or $3 billion, involving DeFi victims. TRM Labs has identified 10 "mega hacks" in 2022, which we define as hacks involving $100 million or more. These 10 hacks account for almost 75 percent of the total amount stolen in 2022. Arguably most concerning is the involvement of North Korea, which has continued to attack cryptocurrency businesses at alarming speed and scale. In the age of cryptocurrencies, stolen funds can be used directly by nation-state actors like North Korea to fund weapons proliferation and other destabilizing activity.

For example, the year's largest hack was perpetrated by North Korea's Lazarus Group against the Ronin Bridge—a $625 million infrastructure attack on a bridge associated with the play-to-earn game Axie Infinity. While North Korea has long engaged in cyberattacks on cryptocurrency businesses to raise funds to fund its weapons programs, nuclear proliferation, and other destabilizing activities, the Ronin hack was unprecedented.

In the wake of the proliferation of hacks and other exploits, we also saw increased regulatory action. We saw Treasury's OFAC use sanctions to go after threat actors. For example, following the attack on the Ronin Bridge, OFAC used blockchain intelligence to trace the stolen funds sanctioning both the blockchain addresses to which the funds moved and the mixing services that North Korean cybercriminals utilized to launder over a billion dollars of cryptocurrency— including blender.io, a centralized Bitcoin mixer and decentralized Ethereum mixer Tornado Cash.

Nick: But how can sanctions work in a truly decentralized space?

Ari: The Tornado Cash designation is the first time OFAC sanctioned a set of smart contracts on the Ethereum blockchain. A smart contract is basically a software program that is uploaded to a blockchain and that usually anyone can interact with. Smart contracts can be programmed to be "immutable," which means that they cannot be taken down or updated.

Historically, when an individual person is added to the SDN list—whether in TradFi [traditional finance] or crypto—anyone who sends funds to that person or receives funds from that person is typically in violation of sanctions law. This is because, in the vast majority of those cases, it is clear that an individual has intentionally transacted with a sanctioned person or entity.

What makes the Tornado Cash designation challenging from a compliance and enforcement perspective is that any person who deposits funds into Tornado Cash can trigger the Tornado Cash smart contracts to send funds to any other Ethereum address(es). Theoretically, someone could send funds to Tornado Cash and then specify that those funds be deposited into a totally unrelated cryptocurrency address belonging to a random, unsuspecting, or even unwilling person.

In the days following the designation, we saw actors take advantage of this capability—presumably as a protest against OFAC's novel decision to sanction a smart contract—by sending funds, unsolicited, from Tornado Cash to cryptocurrency addresses associated with high-profile individuals and celebrities.

In the wake of sanctions against decentralized Ethereum mixer Tornado Cash, many in the crypto ecosystem blanched at the idea of OFAC sanctioning a smart contract or software rather than a "person or entity," as have been targeted before. In fact, OFAC went on to change and clarify the designation with a FAQ explaining that a "person" includes "an individual or an entity, defined as 'a partnership, association, trust, joint venture, corporation, group, subgroup, or other organization.'" In other words, OFAC made clear that it could, in fact, target and sanction a decentralized mixer. But questions remain about how OFAC, and other authorities, will use sanctions in a more and more decentralized space.

Nick: For an investigator reading this book, what guidance has OFAC provided to the cryptocurrency space and what have we learned from enforcement actions against cryptocurrency businesses?

Ari: As discussed already, over the last few years, we have seen OFAC focus on cryptocurrency. OFAC has used sanctions and enforcement actions to go after those facilitating money laundering and sanctions evasion, sending a clear message to crypto businesses that sanctions compliance is foundational infrastructure. Specifically, OFAC has taken a series of enforcement actions against cryptocurrency businesses for having a lack of OFAC sanctions compliance controls in place.

For example, in December 2022, OFAC announced a settlement with cryptocurrency exchange Kraken for violations of Iran sanctions. According to OFAC's release, Kraken failed to implement appropriate geolocation tools in a timely fashion, thus allowing access to users who appeared to be in Iran when they engaged in virtual currency transactions on Kraken's platform.

Specifically, the settlement letter explains that, while Kraken maintained an anti-money-laundering and sanctions compliance program, "between approximately October 14, 2015 and June 29, 2019, Kraken processed 826 transactions, totaling approximately $1,680,577.10, on behalf of individuals who appeared to have been located in Iran at the time of the transactions. . .as a result, Kraken engaged in 826 apparent violations of the Iranian sanctions program." The Kraken settlement is simply the latest in a line of actions that includes enforcement activity against Bitgo, Bitpay, and Bittrex for failing to comply with U.S. sanctions.

Nick: So, how can a cryptocurrency business ensure that it is not engaging with a sanctioned individual or entity? How does an exchange know that a customer is located in Iran, North Korea, Sudan, or another sanctioned jurisdiction? What does OFAC expect when it comes to crypto sanctions compliance? Sorry, that's a lot of questions!

Ari: No problem! In October 2021, OFAC published its "Sanctions Compliance Guidance for the Virtual Currency Industry" (October 2021 guidance) at `https://ofac.treasury.gov/media/913571/download?inline`, which outlines how long-standing OFAC sanctions guidance applies to the cryptocurrency space in the same way it does for traditional financial institutions. The October 2021 guidance also provides digestible guidance for financial institutions and cryptocurrency businesses on best practices to combat the use of virtual currency by sanctioned persons or jurisdictions.

OFAC Associate Director of Compliance and Enforcement Lawrence Scheinert explained how the agency is thinking about crypto sanctions compliance when he appeared on the TRM Talks podcast. I'll quote him directly: "The growing prevalence of virtual currency as a payment method brings greater exposure to sanctions risks—like the risk that a sanctioned person or a person in a jurisdiction subject to sanctions might be involved in a virtual currency transaction."

He continued, "Accordingly, the virtual currency industry—including technology companies, exchangers, administrators, miners, wallet providers, and users—plays an increasingly critical role in preventing sanctioned persons from exploiting virtual currencies to evade sanctions and undermine U.S. foreign policy and national security interests."

The guidance highlights a number of key areas, including the use of geolocation tools to prevent IP addresses that originate in sanctioned jurisdictions. It also highlights the need to employ monitoring and investigations software that can identify transactions involving cryptocurrency addresses associated with sanctioned individuals and entities listed on the SDN list.

Nick: So, looking forward, what can we expect from OFAC and other sanctions regulators?

Ari: Over the last few years OFAC has been active in the digital assets space using its sanctions and enforcement authorities to go after both illicit actors and cryptocurrency businesses that lack compliance controls. As the cryptocurrency ecosystem grows, and state actors like North Korea and Russia attempt to use cryptocurrencies to evade sanctions, we are likely to continue to see activity. However, the nature of blockchains allows regulators like OFAC to trace and track the flow of illicit activity and ultimately seize back hacked, stolen, and illicit proceeds.

Nick: Ari, that was superb. Thank you for sharing your insights with us.

Summary

In this chapter we have primarily discussed the opportunities for criminals to steal funds. It has been in no way a complete list, and many of the categories of criminality related to crypto could have entire books written specifically about them. However, I hope that this chapter has given you a taste of how criminals can use often old types of fraud and scams but apply them to the world of crypto. We started Chapter 2 by discussing the title of the book, that there is no such thing as crypto crime, and I hope that these two chapters have helped you to see that crypto never stands alone, that it is almost always based on categories of crime that we have been investigating for decades before crypto came along and, in some cases, they have been around for millennia. Whenever you come across a case involving crypto, remember that there will always be other evidence and that the concepts and processes used by the criminal are likely known to you. Work with other specialists such as financial investigators and cyber and fraud experts and never let the "crypto" part concern you.

But who should be a cryptocurrency investigator? In the next chapter we will examine this question.

4 Who Should Be a Cryptocurrency Investigator?

When I wrote the book *Investigating Cryptocurrencies* (Wiley) back in 2017, the vast majority of cases were Bitcoin oriented and there were very few people confident to do investigations. In the UK I could count on one hand the police cyber teams that had a person who had some knowledge or capability to take on a case with a crypto element. One or two regions were beginning to purchase track-and-trace tools, but there was a debate as to where the responsibility for a crypto case should lie.

My personal perspective was that crypto cases needed digital discovery skills, computer, and cell forensics skills and then the ability to leverage some freeware command-line tools that we and others were writing. Of course, by 2018 track-and-trace tools like Chainalysis and CipherTrace became available and were beginning to revolutionize the way we visualized crypto transactions, and they also had a pretty reliable way of identifying some addresses. When I was writing the first book in 2017, the first full version of Chainalysis had only just been released. It was a fairly complex tool to use, and results could be easily misinterpreted by someone who didn't understand the underlying crypto transaction technology and hence what the tool was trying to visualize for you. In my mind, this put the skills primarily with the digital forensics people who had the technical skills to understand this new fangled technology as well as the existing tools and software to carry out the discovery and data extraction that would be required.

It turned out that I was wrong, which is not in itself unusual, but this was a big thing to be wrong about. I actually wrote the second half of the first book as a technical manual for digital forensics and then went on to construct a training course that contained lots of coding and discovery tools and of course the concepts around track-and-tracing.

Although the first year of teaching we had primarily computer crime practitioners, suddenly I found that the room was filling with fraud specialists and then financial crime analysts. It was notable that the technical aspects left them cold and it was a massive learning curve, but as soon as we got into the mechanics of tracing transactions, they came alive and absolutely crushed the quizzes in that section. By 2020 we had to drastically adjust the class to orient toward the skills of nontechnical people, and I realized that it was these officers and investigators who understood the concepts around financial crime, scams, and frauds and that crypto was just adding a different payment vehicle to criminal techniques that they already understood.

So, in the later part of 2022 when I started writing the early chapters, I knew the book couldn't be intended just for the technical geeks but had to be readable and understandable by those with the many skill sets that would be involved in an investigation involving crypto.

In this chapter we will discuss the variety of job roles that exist in the crypto investigations space as well as the skills that a person should develop. We will also look at how departments could structure their human resources to ensure that crypto investigations are not dominated just by track-and-trace skills.

At the time I started writing this chapter I was playing around with the capabilities of ChatGPT for research and content generation. So I asked the AI system, "Who should be a cryptocurrency investigator?" I was not expecting anything of note; however, the response got me thinking:

> *A cryptocurrency investigator should have a strong grasp of technological systems and digital currencies, and an understanding of the cryptocurrency market. Additionally, they should have extensive knowledge of computer networks, network security systems, cryptography, and financial crime. They should also have experience in financial fraud investigations, security auditing, or cybercrime and network investigations.*

The AI then concluded:

> *A good cryptocurrency investigator should also possess strong analytical skills, excellent research abilities, and the ability to use data-driven insights to draw conclusions.*

Those are a lot of skills! Let's look at the second group first. The role of analytical, research, and data analysis skills is absolutely vital in most types of investigations, but cases with crypto can be complex and require strong analytic thinking, and the ability to make assumptions based on likely human behavior and both mathematical and technical probabilities. I appreciate that sounds scary, but they are probably skills you already have that can transfer to crypto and its vagaries.

The first part of the AI response wasn't bad either, but it is extremely unlikely that you are going to have a "strong grasp of technological systems and digital currencies, and an understanding of the cryptocurrency market. . .an extensive knowledge of computer networks, network security systems, cryptography, and financial crime. . .and also have experience in financial fraud investigations, security auditing, or cybercrime and network investigations." Well, if you do have all those skills then you might want to give me a call! In reality, these skills call for a number of job roles working together to be able to analyze and piece together each element of a case such as a complex fraud or multi-victim scam. We will look at some job roles required in a crypto department when we hear from a contributor in the section "Building a Crypto Team" later in the chapter, but now let's look at some skill sets.

Individual Skills

When building your personal skills because crypto investigations is something you want to be involved with or if you have the job of building a department to carry out crypto work, the skills required are certainly varied. Let's break down the skills that our friendly AI system highlighted as well as a few others. Almost all of these skills are not essential in isolation; if you asked me if knowledge of the cryptocurrency market was essential to the investigation of crypto-oriented crime, then the answer is both yes and no. It can be useful in some cases but not always.

Knowledge of Technological Systems

Knowledge of how computers work is not needed in the vast majority of cases, but there are times where investigations do need some computer-related knowledge. A good example is ransomware, which infects and encrypts a computer and then asks for crypto as a ransom. Understanding how the ransomware works and how systems are infected, even at a basic level, can be very useful. I believe that all crypto investigators should be computer literate at the very least.

Knowledge of Digital Currencies

All investigators should have a basic working knowledge of digital currencies. From a frontline police officer, to a track-and-trace expert, lawyer, or legislator, it is almost impossible to visualize how a crime was committed using or stealing crypto unless you have some understanding of how it all works. This is not overly complex and we will be covering the basics in upcoming chapters, so keep reading! Learning can also be achieved yourself by setting up wallets and buying and moving small amounts of crypto or by taking industry-approved classes such as the ones offered by TRM Labs, Chainalysis, among others. Although these professional classes can be expensive, they are built on the back of considerable experience and many carry certificates that may be accepted by some courts as proof of a level of expertise.

I suggest that this is a key skill to develop.

Understanding of the Cryptocurrency Market

As I've said before, I'm not a crypto investor. I know people who have done very well buying and selling at the right times, but it's not my expertise and I focus on what I'm good at. I was called by a man who had bought 5,000 ETH at $1 per ETH during the launch crowd sale and still owned the majority of them. He had borrowed the money from his mother. At the time of his call, his holdings were worth over $17 million. Not bad! I do not think that a deep knowledge of the cryptocurrency market is a prerequisite for an investigator, but it doesn't hurt. I wouldn't spend a huge amount of time on it unless you want to do some investing. The only exception to this is gaining an understanding of how the more complex financial products work, such as shorting and other futures-type trading in crypto. Understanding how these systems work could be useful if a case comes up in that area.

There are a vast number of YouTube videos, Reddit channels, and websites that can help you get a handle on how the markets work.

Extensive Knowledge of Computer Networks

I worked on a case where the suspect had installed crypto mining software on every computer in his employer's office. We will discuss mining in a little more detail in Chapter 6, "Mining: The Key to Cryptocurrencies," but essentially the software would attempt to "mine" blocks on a crypto blockchain, netting him money every time it was successful. Although it was possible to mine from just one computer on the blockchain he was targeting, putting the software on hundreds of computers and having them work like a hive massively increased his earning power. There was some discussion about whether this was illegal or just a disciplinary offense. Given the fact that a huge amount of power was required to run and cool each computer as well as "stealing" processor cycles from the computer that may have needed to do other things such as backing up files or running antivirus, it was my belief that he had stolen from his employer. It was an interesting case but is the only one in six years that required a knowledge of computer networks.

However, crypto does generally run on a distributed networking model and so a basic understanding of the way distributed ledgers communicate can be helpful when rare crimes such as mining hacks and even mining-based money laundering come up. I don't cover those crimes in this book, but do an Internet search for them if you are interested.

NOTE Cryptocurrency mining fraud is a scam whereby a user is deceived into paying for an unprofitable or nonexistent cryptocurrency mining service. This fraud often involves a company that claims to offer cloud-based mining services, but in reality, they are either stealing or misappropriating resources or charging users for completely fake services.

The case I just mentioned also required some knowledge of the way hive computing worked where disparate computers are tasked to work together on a single task. So it's a useful but not a key skill.

Cryptography

There are entire university courses and books aplenty that deal exclusively with cryptography (which we used to call crypto before cryptocurrencies came along and acquired the abbreviation), and of course cryptography itself makes up half of the name of cryptocurrencies. Although a knowledge of cryptography is useful, I have not found it game-changing as an investigator.

Financial Crime

When financial investigators started attending my training back in 2019/2020, they clearly were not too interested in the discovery and underlying digital forensic aspects of the class. But when we got to the track-and-trace elements or reading suspicious activity reports (SARs) from an exchange or even considering attacks on a smart contract providing financial services, they simply "got it." This was because they understood the concepts of transaction flows, the mechanisms used to traditionally launder money, and so on; when we simply added in the crypto element, they understood it and were comfortable with how to investigate it.

Understanding financial crime is a significant skill set to have, and financial investigators are already experienced in the complexities of fraud, investment scams, and more difficult crimes such as market manipulation. Although there are some benefits of, for example, open source investigators also qualifying as financial investigators, it is certainly quicker for financial specialists to learn the extra element of crypto.

If this is an area of particular interest to you, check out university degree courses available specifically in the area of financial investigation. But if you are already employed in an investigative role such as with a police department or government department, then there are usually training and career development opportunities to be found.

Fraud Investigators

As fraud is, by definition, usually a financial crime, there is a significant crossover between financial and fraud investigators; in some investigation environments, they are virtually one and the same. However, there are specific qualifications that you can gain in the fraud arena. As previously mentioned, it is good to understand how frauds work and how they are investigated and then adding the crypto part to it. This knowledge can be gained by obtaining appropriate qualifications or on-the-job experience.

I got into fraud investigation from the digital investigation angle, identifying the digital evidence on computers and phones and building the criminal picture from those elements. When I started to look at crypto-oriented fraud, it again generally came from the digital and open source direction.

Open Source Investigations

"Open source intelligence is the collection and analysis of data gathered from open sources to produce actionable intelligence." At least, that's what Wikipedia says and for once I agree with it. I won't write too much about this as we have a whole Chapter 15, "Open Source Intelligence and the Blockchain," coming up on open source investigations, but I suggest that it is a vital skill in cryptocurrency work. By definition, blockchain distributed ledgers are open source, and often it is the work of connecting the crypto evidence to other online open source evidence and then on to real-world intelligence that is needed to build a complete picture.

Conducting online searches is not just a case of typing a name or some other text into Google. There are many advanced tools and techniques used by professional open source investigators that enable the location of often key intelligence. There is also the issue of legislation around open source evidence, how it's collected and reported as evidence. Laws related to privacy, collateral intrusion when data is gathered about a person not related to the investigation, and surveillance regulations often have to be applied to the collection of online data.

I would estimate that half of the investigations I have worked on in the crypto space have included some type of open source research, aside from the blockchain data. I remember one case where a dark web trader selling drug paraphernalia for Bitcoin was using a pseudonym, which also turned out to be their *Call of Duty* game name. That alone was not enough to connect them—I've had quite unusual aliases turn out to be different people—but the suspect's first language was not English and they always spelled "doing" as "duin." We found this error on the dark website and also in *Call of Duty* forum posts. With the same alias and such an unusual spelling error, confidence was high that it was the same person. We tracked the alias to another game forum where he was selling game cheats for crypto. One forum post contained a Bitcoin address, which turned out to be an address that he would send funds to from his dark web activities. It's interesting just how often you can make these connections.

Learning open source search techniques can be done in a number of ways. There are some excellent books on the subject, including *Hunting Cyber Criminals* by Vinny Troia (Wiley, 2020) and *Open Source Intelligence Techniques* by Michael Bazzell (Amazon Digital Services, 2012)—anything by Michael Bazzell; all his books are superb. There are also university courses that include open source elements and a number of private courses run by specialist companies. A search of Twitter (X) and YouTube will also reveal a number of podcasts and video series that deal with open source search techniques.

I mentioned it previously, but often police and government investigators must gather open source information under very specific methodologies and guidelines. Here in the UK, as a civilian I have much more freedom in the information I can search for and record than a police officer, who will need to acquire a particular warrant for some types of information gathering. Even as a civilian I also have to take great care to comply with General Data Protection Regulation (GDPR) legislation. It's vital to make yourself aware of the rules and laws that cover privacy in your country.

Cybercrime Investigations

As cryptocurrencies run on computers and communicate over networks, any crypto investigation is, by a broad definition, a cybercrime investigation. So, yes, cybercrime skills are required at least to some extent. However, for most investigators who are only involved in the financial aspects or track-and-trace of assets across the blockchain, and although it is a cybercrime investigation, a detailed knowledge of the workings of computers and networks can largely be ignored. Electronic discovery of evidence or intelligence from computers will be the job of the digital forensics experts, and any network analysis will be the work undertaken by network and cyber investigators who specialize in packet-level investigations. Crypto investigators do not need this type of skill specifically, but it would certainly be useful for existing network analysts to build an understanding of how cryptocurrencies communicate. Many network analysts are amazed to learn that primary Bitcoin data traffic is completely unencrypted and is transmitted in clear text via port 8333. If you work in the covert world and have a wiretap running against a suspect, then being able to extract Bitcoin traffic can be extremely useful as it may enable attribution of addresses to your suspect.

NOTE Some wallets that run on computers or phones support encryption from the device to a blockchain node. An example is the Wasabi wallet, which enforces transmission of transactions via the encrypted Tor network. Also, users may make personal use of Tor or VPNs to encrypt and obfuscate the origination of a transaction.

So, although network investigations may form part of a crypto case and in many investigations digital forensics would be involved, these skills are pretty specialized and adding crypto knowledge is rudimentary. However, because these cases are by definition cyber related, there is much benefit in having a foundational understanding of computer systems and networks that will enable you to better understand the fundamentals of crypto, encryption, and transmission.

If you are considering a degree or similar in cybercrime, just a word of warning. While researching this topic, I reached out to several universities and asked for any degrees they teach related to cybercrime and each time was provided information on cybersecurity. Remember that courses such as cyber/network/computer security tend to focus on stopping bad things from happening whereas investigation of cybercrime comes when something bad has already happened. Knowledge of computer security is not useless, of course, but is not specifically helpful in this arena. Instead, look for criminology and cybercrime combined courses for something more useful.

Setting Up a Cryptocurrency Investigation Department

I have had the opportunity to consult with several large police forces who were looking to set up cryptocurrency investigation units. They sound very grand and exciting, and they receive a lot of applications to work within the department. Having seen it done badly, I've appreciated the opportunity to give my opinion to see it done well. One South

American team did it badly; they bought several crypto investigation commercial tools, put some cyber people on the tool training program, and then put them in a room and called it the Crypto Investigation Unit. No. It isn't. As the title of this book reminds us, there is no such thing as crypto crime and you need a variety of skills to make a holistic department.

Although I have been able to consult on this and ran a very small team myself, I'm no expert in building and running a crypto investigation department, so I reached out to Phil Ariss, a good friend and colleague who has huge expertise in this area. As of this writing, Phil is the Director of Public Sector Relations in the UK for TRM Labs, having taken a career break from the police service where he served for 15 years. As a police officer, Phil specialized in cryptocurrencies and virtual assets, providing some of the first written guidance, policies, and procedures for UK law enforcement, standardizing the approach to investigations and how assets should safely be seized and stored. Between 2019 and 2022, Phil was the national coordinator for cryptocurrencies and virtual assets for policing, working for the National Police Chiefs Council (NPCC) Cybercrime Programme, and was posted to the City of London Police, who run the national fraud reporting program.

Perhaps Phil should be writing his own book? Anyway, I asked him to consider the skills and issues when building a department. This is what he had to say.

BUILDING A CRYPTO TEAM

With the increased adoption of cryptocurrencies for almost all thematic threats across criminality, not to mention the increase in civil cases, having a team to investigate these cases, effectively, efficiently, and diligently is vital. While there are some very mature investigation teams across the globe, there is clearly going to be a need to see this capacity increase in line with the adoption of these assets by the wider public, especially if the adoption of Central Bank Digital Currency (CBDC) reaches its potential.

Building an investigation team can be an exciting and rewarding opportunity, but not without challenges! There is more to investigating cases with a cryptocurrency element than simply having a staff member who has access to blockchain forensic tools. Sure, that's a starting point, but it's certainly not an effective model, and if staff members are working in isolation, it's certainly not sustainable, nor scalable. So, what does an investigation team look like? What capabilities will it need? What roles need to be created, recruited, trained, and then integrated into the team?

Before we can talk about building a team, we need to address the elephant in the room, the topic that is often the single greatest challenge to building a successful team: the budget. Having a generous budget affords the gift of flexibility, whereas smaller budgets will often mean a more streamlined approach, with staff members carrying out multiple roles and some areas will simply be deemed a luxury, or having to utilize existing resources elsewhere within the organization, which brings the challenge of competing demands.

For most public sector organizations, the structure of a team can usually be broken down into three distinct areas of roles and responsibilities to ensure the team is working toward the same vision, purpose, and goals. These are strategic, tactical, and operational, often in a pyramid format, with the base of the pyramid being the larger volume of resources dedicated to the operational response, working upward toward a smaller tactical team, and even smaller strategic team.

Having a clearly defined command structure provides a clear overall leadership structure, setting out the vision for the team, the areas of responsibility and remit, and how the team can contribute to the wider benefit of the organization. In the UK, strategies for serious and organized crime are usually aligned with the 4 P principles: Prepare, Protect, Prevent, and Pursue.

Prepare is the organization's ability to be ready to meet a call for service, such as a ransomware strain against critical national infrastructure. Protect is the approach to target harden businesses and individuals from being victims of crime. Prevent is working with individuals on the cusp of criminality and making meaningful interventions before they go on to commit crime—after all, prevention is better than cure! Last is Pursue, the ability for the organization to effectively investigate and bring to justice those who cause harm, which is often the most resource intensive.

So what resources are required to make the ideal cryptocurrency investigation team? Let's take a look at some of the roles and responsibilities that would be required.

Suspicious Activity Reports (SARs)/Suspicious Transaction Reports (STRs) Analysts

Nearly 500,000 SARs are generated each year in the UK. The contributor here has been introduced as an expert in the UK; he does not have US knowledge primarily from the traditional financial sector, but as cryptocurrency businesses start to fall under regulation, an increasing number will be generated by crypto-native businesses. Resources working on the SARs database are vital to understand the type of reported suspicious activity but also the volume. Having analysts working on these databases is a must, as it will give public sector agencies the perfect opportunity to build intelligence-led cases, with confirmed identities and accounts held in the native region.

Financial Investigators

Financial investigators often bring a wealth of experience to any team, but the move from traditional finance to cryptocurrencies and decentralized finance can often be a steep learning curve. That said, their familiarity with financial systems, money laundering methodologies, and utilizing their expertise and experience to make the evidential links between financial accounts and criminality are vital requirements. Outside of the evidential parameters, having experience in managing cash and property in regard to the seizure, restraint, and confiscation process, on a procedural or legal basis, is also an absolute necessity, considering the often complex legislation that governs the processes.

Digital Forensics Specialists

Having a wide organizational understanding and strategy in place for digital forensics is key for all areas of investigations. In large police forces, digital exhibits are seized and examined on a routine basis, but vital intelligence and evidence could be missed should they not form part of the digital forensics strategy. Uncovering cryptocurrency usage during examination allows the case investigation parameters to be extended. An example would be for suspects under investigation for Child Sexual Abuse Material (CSAM); extending the digital forensics strategy to consider cryptocurrency usage may uncover other suspects and lead to potential safeguarding opportunities. The potential cryptocurrency investigative leads that may be sitting in evidence property stores are a wasted opportunity from both an evidential perspective and an asset denial perspective.

Open Source Intelligence (OSINT) Investigators

Having experienced and well-trained open source investigators can enhance any investigation, but with blockchain-based investigations, a good open source investigator is worth their weight in gold. Overlaying OSINT data with blockchain data can contextualize and add depth to what would otherwise be sterile data. Considering the movement to Web3 and the embracing of tokens and NFTs, it's an area that any cryptocurrency investigation team will need to be invested in. Away from the enhancement of blockchain data, the added value to building a suspect profile is also highly advantageous and can be a significant benefit at the time of enforcement.

On-Scene Knowledge and Briefings

For large-scale enforcement, often additional resources are drafted to help with searches or deal with a variety of other procedural issues that may arise. Whenever individuals or small groups temporarily join niche teams with a level of expertise it can prove challenging, as the usual performance expectations are clearly unreasonable. Extensive briefing packs and briefing videos are required to bring these valuable additional resources up to speed as quickly as possible, so they know that what they are seeing in front of them is a hardware wallet and not a USB stick or that they know not to power down digital devices, but most important of all, that they know where to go to get help and that they can ask questions in an environment that doesn't judge and that is supportive.

Tactical Advisers

Tactical advisers are a great way for a specialized team to support the wider organization and help bring value to other crime business areas. A tactical adviser provides key pertinent information and initial actions when initial support can't be provided. Let's take the scenario of a spontaneous incident at 3 a.m.; nearly all the support functions are not going to be available to provide information or advice to staff who are fast asleep! There may be consideration of having an "on-call" function, providing a 24/7 service, but the benefit of having tactical advisers is that it starts to bring a little bit more knowledge, experience, and willingness to individuals outside the main investigation team, which can only start to increase the overall organizational knowledge and understanding of cryptocurrencies.

Seizure Expertise

Without a doubt, the area of any operational team that carries the most risk, be that personal, organizational, legal, or reputational risk, is in the role of carrying out asset seizures. Having a cadre of staff who are highly trained, highly experienced, and well drilled, and who know their subject matter well, is vital to ensure that any cryptocurrency seizure is done in a manner that mitigates identified risk and follows any policies and procedures that have been set. Staff members should have a background in live digital forensics and a broad understanding of various cryptocurrency protocols and be able to adapt their processes to any challenges that arise.

Blockchain Forensics

Of course, a cryptocurrency team isn't complete without staff members who are dedicated to blockchain forensics. Depending on the size of your organization, sufficient resilience should be built in, with a clear succession plan for potential future demand and attrition. This has the benefit of not only ensuring that staff members are not overwhelmed by volume of cases but also preventing the crippling of the functionality of the team should a staff member move on to another organization or otherwise become unavailable. Resilience also allows for peer reviewing, a functionality that should be seen as mandatory, rather than a luxury, and can allow "cross-pollination" of learning, experience, and best practice, ensuring that a consistently high standard of intelligence or evidential product is maintained.

For supervisors, having a sound understanding and overview of the work that is undertaken is paramount. Providing clear and unambiguous instructions, parameters, and investigative strategies is vital, as is the ability to effectively supervise this work, including challenging the findings when appropriate. An effective supervisor must also be able to audit the investigative approach and be able to share any audit findings with another investigator who can replicate the case with the same findings.

Thanks, Phil; that was very useful indeed.

Other Roles

We have been focusing on what you might describe as a standard investigative department that might exist in a police force, but there are many other roles that would require skills in the crypto arena, and they are expanding every day. A short list might include:

- Tax avoidance identification: Tax authorities like the Internal Revenue Service (IRS) have been at the forefront of financial investigations involving crypto; however, a huge job lies ahead as tax authorities find ways to identify when crypto is being used for tax avoidance. The focus has been on the multimillion-dollar frauds, but what of the people stashing away a few thousand dollars to avoid tax? Those investigations will take a lot more work, people, and dare I say it, artificial intelligence capability.
- Anti-money-laundering scoring: Any finance houses, banks, or businesses that accept crypto are going to want to check that they are not being used as a deposit service to bounce criminal crypto onward.
- Sanctioned funds identification: There is a requirement by all businesses to check that payments made to them are not involved with or related to sanctioned people, businesses, or countries. Crypto skills will be needed in this space.
- Regulators: Legal regulators in many countries are involved in granting and then monitoring licenses for businesses to trade in the crypto space. This will require specialist crypto investigation skills.
- Due diligence: Check potential business partners or customers for illicit activity or illicit crypto funds. This applies to any VASP (Virtual Asset Service Provider).

- Proof of funds/provenance of funds: Exchanges have to do a lot of this, but so do finance houses and businesses that accept crypto.
- Auditing: Accountants are already having to determine the tax implications of crypto buying and selling by businesses. I've been involved in a number of investigations where companies in trouble have tried to hide funds from auditors and company administrators/receivers by moving assets into crypto.
- Operations security and counterintelligence analysts: Increasingly, operations security and counterintelligence are having to consider crypto assets in their understanding of the opponent's financial holdings and transactions.
- Defense analyst civil affairs: This would include mapping the economic environment of a country and its stability/vulnerability to malign influence.

Building a new type of team brings challenges, but in this increasingly crypto-centric world of financial crime it is when, not if, you will be faced with building something within, or distinct from, your investigation departments. Consider all the skills that are required and the tools that are needed.

In our next chapter we will look at the role of commercial tools and whether they are vital to an investigation.

5 The Role of Commercial Investigation Tools

Before we start talking about the history and use of commercial crypto investigation tools, I should make it clear that as of this writing I cannot be considered completely independent. In 2022 my company CSITech Ltd. was bought out by one of the leading companies in the space, TRM Labs. Although I am a massive fan of the TRM Labs tools, I am also an admirer of other tools in the space and have benefited greatly in the past few years by having access to them. It's only right that I specifically offer my thanks and gratitude to:

Jonathan Levin at Chainalysis
Steve Ryan at CipherTrace
Tom Robinson at Elliptic
Zalan Noszek at Bitfury Crystal
. . .and of course, my friend Esteban Castano at TRM Labs

I have great respect for each of these people and their tools and wish them all success.

I have not attempted to cover each and every tool, and I'm aware that there are other tools on the market that I have not had access to. This is simply a history of my own experience with commercial tools. If you are in the market for a tool, do your own research, try before you buy, and ensure that the tool is fit for purpose for the types of investigations you are involved in.

In the summer of 1998, I found myself in the campus of the University of Florida in Gainesville, Florida. With me in the physics lab was the head of department, Haniph Latchman, a fabulously interesting and intelligent man who at the time was on President Clinton's federal task force for education. We were discussing the technical possibilities of remote teaching using video, voice, and shared screens using webcams. In the current age of Zoom and everyone working remotely, it will seem strange to younger people that this would be a discussion, but one must remember that at the time Internet connections were just coming out of the age of dial-up connections and such luxuries as fiber to the door was a long way in the future. This meant that we were working with users having, at best, just 56 kilobits per second (even the physics department was only "blessed" with a 2-megabit Internet connection!); hence, moving real-time video and audio to students was a major challenge.

Following our discussion, we started talking about some hacks that the U.S. government had recently experienced and that he and his department had been tasked with assisting law enforcement with the investigation. Latchman turned to a display and showed me a new piece of software written by a U.S. programmer named Shawn H. McCreight. The software was called Expert Witness but within a year it would be renamed EnCase, and it changed my life.

Although investigators and hobbyists had been building tools to enable data analysis and reconstruction at the code level for several years, there had been no single tool that would enable computer hard disks to be copied and analyzed without making changes to the contents or operating system—in other words, in a forensically sound manner. (Some of the early command-line tools would by 1999 form part of a free kit of software called The Coroners Toolkit, which became the Sleuth Kit and then Autopsy.) EnCase was the first real attempt at a commercial, well-supported tool, to help investigators with the burgeoning world of computer crime. From the first time I saw that predecessor to EnCase I was hooked on the concept of the investigation of digital crimes—that moment literally shaped the next 25 years of my life.

What EnCase did was not in itself new. As I mentioned there were different tools around for disk copying and hexadecimal analysis and deleted file re-creation (known as *carving*). But this was the first time it was all packaged up into a single tool and automated many of the complex tasks. It soon enabled investigators to write their own plug-ins in a language called Enscript, forensically copy drives over a network, and the list goes on. Although there were many of us who would be more than happy to write a bit of code or fire up a tool in a command line, EnCase just made things easier and faster and thus efficient.

Within a few years, other disk analysis tools appeared, such as FTK Forensic Toolkit and X-Ways, and then mobile phone analysis tools such as Cellebrite. Arguably, none of these tools did anything you couldn't achieve in a command shell with the right software, but they did it so much faster, in a graphical interface and with automated reporting, they simply shaped the way we investigated cyber crime.

Why have I told you this story? Bitcoin was celebrating its sixth birthday before someone released a similar commercial tool to assist with blockchain forensics. As we reviewed in Chapter 1, "A History of Cryptocurrencies and Crime," there had during those six years already been a number of high-profile and high-value crimes, often hacks against young exchanges, but hardly any investigators knew anything about crypto crime and the few who did had learned the hard way. Those investigations had been done with a blockchain viewer and a pen and paper. Attribution of addresses relied on pattern analysis and dead reckoning, and at least a few agencies had begun to record their own list of addresses that related to the major exchanges such as Binance. However, in 2014 a British entrepreneur named Jonathan Levin co-founded a company with Michael Gronager to investigate the Mt. Gox hack and later released a tool that, like Encase before it, would shape my future and the future of an entire investigative genre. It was called Chainalysis Reactor.

If you haven't heard of, or used, Chainalysis, welcome to the world of crypto crime as you are obviously very new! For a couple of years, it was the only tool available to enable the automatic graphing of transactions and implemented and extended the concepts of clustering as had been suggested by Sarah Meiklejohn and her coauthors in the white paper titled "A Fistful of Bitcoins: Characterizing Payments among Men with No Names" (see `https://cseweb.ucsd.edu/~smeiklejohn/files/imc13.pdf`).

We will talk about clustering in more detail in a later chapter, but in simple terms a UTXO-style cryptocurrency such as Bitcoin requires the owner of the transaction to own the private key for all the addresses that are inputs into the transaction. This means that if you have five addresses that are inputting/paying into a transaction, in most cases it can be assumed that all five belong to the same person. We can then extend our analysis to see if those addresses exist in any other transactions as input with yet more input addresses. Also, Bitcoin uses a system of payments and change that we have explained previously. It's similar to paying a whole $10 bill for a $9.50 transaction and then receiving change from the cashier. Bitcoin requires that you spend whole amounts and receive change. If you can figure out which output address is the change, then that also is owned by the person triggering the transaction. All these addresses would form a cluster that, on the balance of probabilities, are owned by the same person. If you can identify the owner of just one of those addresses, you know who owns them all. If we scale this up to the tens of thousands of addresses used by an exchange and can cluster them all, we only need to identify one to know the owner of them all.

To achieve this, Chainalysis started making payments into and withdrawals from services such as exchanges, mixers, and online stores. This exposed addresses that they knew definitively were owned by that service. They would then apply their clustering algorithms, scanning for transactions that included these known addresses and creating huge address clusters that were attributable to a service. Although many of the techniques had been used by researchers and written about by academics before, Chainalysis spent vast amounts of time and money building the world's leading attribution engine at the time.

It was the only and best tool of its type, and everyone who could afford it bought it, and like EnCase of forensics history, it wasn't cheap. Everyone assumed you were paying for the slick link graphs and animated pie charts that described the connections addresses had to identified clusters, a technique known as *exposure*. However, although the user interface was slick, the money was in the constant development of the attribution database. With Bitcoin being much more popular into 2017 and 2018, the blockchain was growing fast and it was like painting the Golden Gate Bridge in that it was a job without end.

Other tools were quick to come to market, notably Elliptic and CipherTrace, which, although similar to Chainalysis, attempted to do things in slightly different ways. Tool choice came down to the way an investigator wanted to work and the depth and accuracy of the address identification database that supported the tool.

The next investigative spanner in the works was the release of Ethereum in 2015. Rather than the UTXO model with clusterable input and change addresses, Ethereum worked on an account-based model, with a wallet usually containing a single address and enabling exact payments. On top of that, Ethereum offered a tokenization engine, which enabled the building of other systems and currencies on its blockchain, as we explained in the last chapter. Although the existing tools had been built with UTXO protocols in mind, it was not too difficult to integrate the one-to-one or one-to-many account-based model of Ethereum. In fact, often the graphs were much simpler to understand. However, most tools struggled with the new smart contracts that Ethereum offered as they were built using embedded code in a contract address that could almost do anything. It was also difficult to adjust the tools built around UTXO's to segue into a new way of understanding the data. The commercial tools available were going to have to make some significant adjustments to cater to the new protocols and tokens.

From this crypto new world order, tools began to appear such as TRM Forensics from TRM Labs, which was released in 2018. This app was built with tokenization and smart contracts in mind and fundamentally sidelined the clustering model that had dominated the market for several years. TRM focused on the transaction-to-transaction model; although it often created more complex (read, busier) graphs, it enabled the investigator to see the flow of funds from address to address rather than cluster to cluster. (I know that a Chainalysis Reactor user will say that you can do address-to-address analysis in Reactor. Indeed you can, and you can do cluster-based analysis in TRM Forensics too, but it is not their primary modus operandi.)

By 2023 there were a significant number of tools designed to support an investigator in a crypto investigation. Some tools are simpler to use than others and thus useful for a nonfinancial investigator to use. Some are more complex and aimed at trained crypto investigators. Others have a focus on anti-money-laundering and enable companies to automatically scan incoming transactions to ensure that there is no exposure to illegality or sanctioned funds. As always, do your research and invest in tool(s) that work for the type of investigations you are doing. If you are just doing Bitcoin investigations, then choose tools that are strong in that area. If you are involved in account-based transactions and crimes involving smart contracts, then other tools might fit your needs better. I'm not going to specifically recommend tools you need to do your own research.

Do You Need a Commercial Tool?

Yes. Well, no. But really, yes. I should explain my rather unhelpful indecision.

A year or so back I was contacted by a university student wanting to do intern work. She was very bright, motivated, and knowledgeable. I asked her if she had done any real or test investigations in the crypto space, but her response was concerning. "We did a couple of investigations at Uni using *<name of commercial tool>* but I don't have access to that now so I can't do anything." This was a troublesome answer because yet again the mistake was being made that teaching someone how to use a tool was the same as teaching the student to be an investigator. We had the same in digital forensics in that investigators were taking Encase or FTK courses and thinking they were ready to be let loose on cases. Knowing how to use a commercial tool does not make you an investigator. I am a firm believer in being able to carry out an investigation manually without having to rely on an expensive, if capable, tool. This knowledge enables you to carry out investigations on blockchains that perhaps your commercial tool doesn't cover, but also to be able to give testimony in court using findings that you had achieved without a tool. This may be vital, as results and reports from a commercial tool may or may not be accepted in court as evidence. In later chapters we will help you understand how to track transactions manually in both UTXO and account-based blockchain viewers. However, there is a problem with the purely manual approach.

Every cryptocurrency has a blockchain viewer to enable you to track transactions. The original purpose was to enable a user of the currency to check that funds had gone to the right address and to see how many blocks had been confirmed to ensure its irreversibility. Investigators started using these blockchain viewers to manually follow funds from address to address. With Bitcoin-style UTXO transactions, it is easy enough to follow specific funds, and with an account-based currency, we can still see the flow of funds from address balance to address balance. If you wished, you could graph transactions manually on paper or by using software tools such as Maltego or GraphViz. This takes time, whereas a commercial tool is almost instant, but it is perfectly achievable, and I have done dozens of investigations this way.

The problem was, and is, understanding where the funds have gone. Obviously, we can follow from address to address, but how do we know when the funds arrive at a virtual asset service provider (VASP) or other type of off-ramp? How do we know if the funds have gone to a far-right group donation address or simply are a donation to their local animal shelter? The answer is that we don't. There are patterns that we can recognize on the Bitcoin blockchain, for example, that help us to identify an address that "looks" like it could be an exchange or could be a ransomware address, but unless we have done the hard work of building a massive address identification and clustering database we will fundamentally be in the dark as to who that address belongs to. If you are tracking stolen funds, it is vital to know if they have gone to a VASP so that proceedings can be put in place to freeze and ultimately recover that crypto. If you are investigating Bitcoin, then I suggest that it is essential to have a commercial tool available.

Ethereum and other account-based currencies are slightly different. Their blockchain viewers, such as Etherscan.io, contain significant metadata about a transaction and will often identify off-ramps such as exchanges and other VASPS. Figure 5.1 shows an address on the Ethereum blockchain identified as belonging to the Exchange Binance.

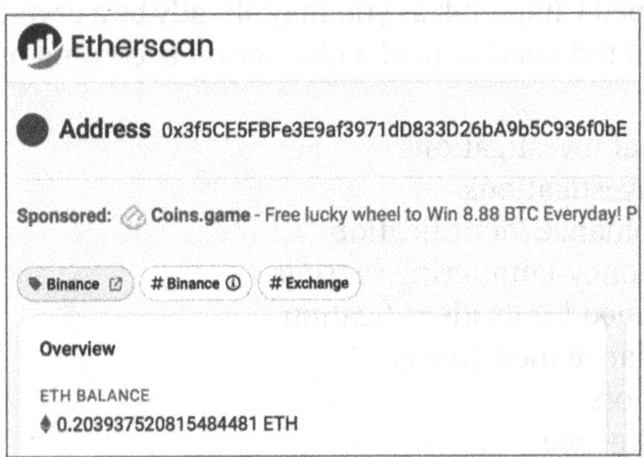

Figure 5.1: Etherscan showing an address attribution of Binance

Etherscan has a version for Binance Blockchain that is very good, and even working with the TRON cryptocurrency viewer Tronscan, the VASP identification is often enough to provide the off-ramp information you may be looking for. So, if Etherscan is so good, do you need a commercial tool? It's really not a straightforward answer. I have done many investigations involving Ethereum and Ethereum-based tokens just using Etherscan, but it's like wading through molasses. That's not a fault of Etherscan—it wasn't designed as an investigative environment. It provides all the information you need, but collating all that information and reporting it is a completely manual, and rather tedious, process. Add to that the regular need to graph out the connections between addresses and it can become very time-consuming indeed.

As of this writing, I believe that TRM Forensics is the best tool available for tracing coins over non-Bitcoin blockchains and even between blockchains across bridges, which is a fairly new capability and extremely hard to do manually. It is in no way the only tool with these capabilities, but it best fitted the way I work. This is extremely important and brings me back to the advice I've mentioned several times: identify the types of investigations you will be doing and test the commercial tools to see what fits best.

What is your primary and secondary investigation focus? The following is a simplified list from Chapter 4, "Who Should Be a Cryptocurrency Investigator?" but highlights the wide array of roles where crypto investigation or analysis needs to be done. All would certainly benefit from having commercial tools available. (I've included it again here in case you skipped Chapter 4, as you may already be a crypto investigator and didn't feel the need to read a chapter on becoming one!)

- Criminal investigations
- Civil investigations
- Tax avoidance identification
- Anti-money-laundering scoring
- Sanctioned funds identification
- Compliance monitoring
- Regulators
- Due diligence
- Proof of funds/provenance of funds
- Auditing
- Operations security and counterintelligence analysts
- DoD civil affairs
- Financial journalist

I suggest that all of these roles require access to a commercial crypto investigation tool. I thought long and hard about the word "require" in that sentence. The reality is that although *some* aspects of those categories could be done manually, and absolutely should be understood as to how they can be done manually in a blockchain viewer, especially track-and-trace work, it will be, at best, time-consuming and, at worst, impossible. As I've mentioned, you are not just buying pretty graphing tools;

you are primarily buying access to the backend identification database. In the case of TRM Forensics, they also apply considerable artificial intelligence to the data to identify patterns of transactions such as mixers or cross-chain swaps in addition to the identification of VASPs, criminal addresses, and so on. So, for example, I was asked by a law firm to check the provenance of the crypto that was being used to buy an island. Yes, you read that right, buy an island. . .with crypto. You can't make it up. It was in a tropical part of the world, too. I wasn't in the slightest bit envious! But obviously the owners of the island wanted to know where the buyers had earned their crypto and were understandably resistant if it had come from criminality. In a commercial intelligence tool, checking the historical exposure of the crypto is almost a single click whereas to do it manually would have been viciously time-intensive and likely impossible without the tool's identification and exposure data.

Perhaps you are beginning to understand my "yes, but no" answer at the start of the section as to whether you should buy a commercial tool. Many of the investigative tasks can be accomplished manually with blockchain viewers, but in reality, a commercial tool is required to make the work efficient and rapid and to provide more intelligence than it would be likely possible to acquire without it.

Two Is One and One Is None

Before crypto had been invented, some of my early skills included the covert extraction of data. We would teach some cool methods and tools for the quiet extraction of files from target computers while leaving no digital trace. I got to meet and work with some very interesting people from the specialist police and intelligence communities of several different countries. Sometimes the students would have come from agencies that, as they would put it, were a little more "kinetic" in their methods. After a few days of trust building and some beer and pizza, I would sometimes learn that "Jeff" wasn't from the police after all, but was either serving or ex–special forces from the UK or United States, who were bringing their ability to work in hostile environments to the intelligence field. I learned to recognize them eventually—hugely capable, intelligent, and very tenacious in learning and practicing what they were being taught, as well as being irritatingly fit. They would also have rather good sayings that I often repeat to sound worldly. One such saying was "Slow is smooth and smooth is fast." I have been trying to teach my mother-in-law this for years as she has a tendency to do everything at high speed, normally resulting in something getting broken! Slowing down a little makes you carry out a task smoother with fewer errors, and the smooth action results in a faster result. It's a pretty cool life lesson.

However, there was another saying that has some application to our discussion of commercial crypto tools: "Two is one and one is none." This saying can be applied to many things in life, including everything from how many weapons you should carry in a military application, to corporate strategic planning, or even the number of toothbrushes you should take into the jungle. The saying is simple; if you only have one of something and it fails, is lost, or simply proves to be a bad plan, then you essentially have nothing. However, when you have two of something you are pretty assured that one of them will come through for you. Perhaps you can see where I am going with this?

When working in the digital forensics field, it was generally accepted that just one commercial tool was not sufficient but that reports should be checked in a second tool. For this reason, many departments had both Encase and FTK software or perhaps FTK and X-Ways. The same applies to crypto investigation software. My colleagues at TRM are going to scowl at me for saying so, but you should be considering having two tools available to you. The problem, though, is one of time and cost. The tools are pretty expensive and because each tool works in a slightly different way, engaging with training is essential. If you can only afford to have access to one tool, then do your research and make sure it's the tool that best works in the way you need it to. However, if you can have access to two different tools, then you should. This is not a small thing as there can be significant differences in the ways that the tools report. The identification databases can differ, for example.

A good example of this is where two tools disagree on the identification of a VASP but both are right. Confused? Some exchanges offer custodian services to third-party companies, so, for example, I could set up a decentralized exchange or offer crypto loan services, but I need somewhere safe to store all the various tokens and cryptocurrencies I receive. Hence, I may decide to sign up with an exchange to handle the surplus assets for me and to quickly enable conversion to fiat currency so I can pay my employees. One tool may correctly identify the address as belonging to the exchange; however, another may have detected that the company's assets flow to a specific address at the exchange and so tag it as the name of the company. This results in two different identification tags for the address in the two tools, but both are technically right.

Another example is where a service is owned by a parent company or is part of a group of VASP-oriented companies. There are lots of examples where often decentralized exchanges or other types of VASPs with different names and branding are actually owned by the same entity. This can be useful to know when applying for freezing orders. One tool may correctly identify the name of the service, but another may identify the other services in the group. Both tools are different, and both are technically right. Two software tools can help to identify errors or just expand your horizon regarding a case. The assumptions made by any algorithms may differ, and the open source data may vary—in short, two is better than one.

When I first considered the topic of this chapter, my plan was to review the primary software tools with their individual pros and cons. But they are changing so fast and new software is coming to market every month, and anything I wrote about would be out of date within a few months. As an investigator or department head, you need to consider the current case load, the types of crypto being investigated, what functionality you are looking for, and of course the price point. Also remember that most tools work on an annual renewable contract—this means that if a tool isn't working for you anymore because your focus or case work is changing, then it is perfectly possible to switch to a different tool. You would just need to consider the training overhead of that decision.

The Future of Investigation Tools

I was tempted to just write a question mark under this heading and end the chapter! Seeing into the future for anything to do with cryptocurrencies is virtually impossible, and of course, much will be driven by the way crypto use develops in the coming years. If I return to the example of digital forensics tools, nothing changed significantly in the way the original software tools worked until a friend of mine, Jad Saliba, launched what is now called Magnet Axiom. This took a different approach to the traditional forensics tools and instead automated many of the difficult tasks facing investigators, such as carving deleted files, extracting chat data, timelining file use, and generating straightforward reports. Although tools such as Encase are still in wide use, you will struggle to find a digital forensics lab that doesn't run Axiom as a primary triage and investigation tool.

The same is likely to happen within the area of crypto investigation tools. Some tools are already implementing AI to recognize patterns on the blockchain that are indicative of particular services or methods, and I see this trend continuing. Any blockchain is a massive resource of data with which to seed machine learning algorithms, and as these systems get better, I believe that AI will play a major role in cutting through the morass of data to help an investigator get to the core datasets (mostly addresses and transactions) that are pertinent to a case.

In my early conversations with Esteban, CEO at TRM Labs, before the acquisition of my company, he asked me what I felt the future of crypto investigations may be. My answer, which I still hold to, is "predictive" investigations. With enough data, can we begin to identify criminal activity before there are even victim complaints? Could AI "see" an address on a blockchain demonstrate the data shape of a romance scam, or a ransomware address, or a terror funding address early on? In the Philip K. Dick short story and movie *The Minority Report*, murders are predicted before they happen by some traumatized-looking people lying in a big hot tub. Large data and AI have the possibility, I believe, of recognizing criminal addresses and transactions early in the crime life cycle. Although this may not lead to arrests, it opens the way for very interesting opportunities for disruption of criminal activity.

Due to the scope of international organized crime, resources are stretched and many agencies are seeing the need for disruption of groups to frustrate plans to carry out criminal acts. In the crypto realm, this has a very real potential to enable the cutting off of funding and realization of funds into fiat currency if we can be quicker at identifying criminal resources on the blockchain. I believe that AI will be able to help sort the proverbial wheat from the chaff and target disruption operations earlier and more effectively.

A key to this working is the role of exchanges and other VASPS. Although most have gone from being very hesitant to work with law enforcement to actively engaging and having departments designed just to assist investigations, they are still a blind spot to investigators who rely on data supplied by the exchanges to understand the onward movement or exchange of funds.

KYC DATA FROM EXCHANGES

Although some exchanges provide significant data in easy-to-use files, there are still exchanges that supply user data in PDFs, which cannot be copied and pasted from. This means that investigators have to physically retype long and complex addresses and other data into their investigation tools. Exchanges, you know who you are and you need to stop it! I know that the argument is that the files need to be hashed for evidential reasons, sure, but then you should provide the data in both an uneditable hashed form and a form that's of use to an investigator. Anyone would think you are deliberately trying to be obstructive. I'm sure that's not the case! Rant over.

Is there a world where data is more freely available from exchanges to law enforcement, and how does that relate to privacy laws and concerns? These questions are above my pay grade.

The future of commercial crypto investigation tools is interesting to say the least, but hopefully the new machine learning and AI capabilities that are taking quantum leaps at the moment will help investigators be proactive with disruptions and faster at bringing offenders to justice.

6 Mining: The Key to Cryptocurrencies

Back in my first book in 2018, we talked at some length about the currency used on the island of Yap in the South Pacific. They use huge stone coins made of calcite, which they use as currency by sharing who owns each stone through word of mouth, essentially creating the world's first decentralized ledger. The "ledger" exists in the memories of each villager, very similar to how cryptocurrency decentralized ledgers work. What is interesting about the Yap system is that the stone coins are not mined on the island, but rather on the island of Palau, which is a 310-mile round trip by boat across a dangerous stretch of Pacific Ocean. This is notable because it's the difficulty of creating new stones that gives them an inherent value.

To mine a new stone, you have to employ boat builders, sailors, miners, and other staff. Having built your oceangoing boats, you have to sail them to Palau, mine and cut new stones, and sail them back to Yap, where they are unloaded and positioned somewhere on the island. The very fact that the stones are on the island is proof of the work that went into obtaining them. In fact, that phrase, *proof of work*, is key to understanding traditional cryptocurrency mining. It is the significant cost of obtaining a new coin, the proof of work, that gives the stones their inherent value.

When Satoshi Nakamoto, the enigmatic designer of Bitcoin, was working on the original Bitcoin code, they had two significant problems to solve.

THE SATOSHI MYSTERY

The name Satoshi is a Japanese name and does not have a specific gender assigned to it. In Japan, names are not typically gender-specific, so Satoshi could be used as a name for a person of any gender. In 2012 Satoshi Nakamoto claimed to be male and living in Japan, although the claim has been widely disputed. In fact, the true identity of the individual or group behind the pseudonym remains unknown to this day. There have been various speculations and theories about who Satoshi Nakamoto might be, but no one has been able to definitively identify them or their gender.

Several people have claimed to be Satoshi, and a couple have taken their claims to the courts with a variety of successes and failures. The only way that someone can truly prove to be Satoshi or associated with Satoshi is to move Bitcoin from the early blocks on the Bitcoin blockchain, proving that they own the private key. Several of the people who have claimed that they are Satoshi also state that they have lost the original private keys. This is not the place to get into those court cases or to discuss those claimants. If any of them are indeed Satoshi, then I wish them every success as their concept, and the code that created Bitcoin, is truly magnificent.

Problem 1 was the issue of cryptographically confirming or authenticating transactions on the blockchain in a way that was not only distributed—as in not done centrally by some "Bitcoin God Server"—but also completely securely. Problem 2 was how to inject new coins into the Bitcoin ecosystem. Both problems were solved through the process of mining.

Cryptocurrency mining became a cornerstone of the blockchain ecosystem for solving these two issues but also for enabling users of the cryptocurrency to get involved in validating transactions by closing blocks on the blockchain in return for a reward, which injects new coins into the system. Not only does mining maintain the integrity of most digital currencies like Bitcoin and Ethereum, but it also helps prevent double spending of coins, which is tricking the blockchain into thinking a user still owns coins they have already spent, and other malicious activities. In this chapter, you'll learn how cryptocurrency mining is vital to the crypto ecosystem and why its important for an investigator to understand the fundamentals.

What Really Is Mining?

As we have mentioned, at its core, cryptocurrency mining serves two primary purposes: validating transactions and minting new coins. Back in the early days, miners could use their normal PCs to carry out mining because the calculations were simple enough for standard processors to be able to find the solution to the mining problem within the 10-minute limit set by Bitcoin. As more miners got involved, the difficulty set by the Bitcoin ecosystem increased. More calculations were needed to find the solution to a block, and so graphics cards, which boast a large number of processors, came to the rescue. Very soon, though, even computers with multiple parallel high-end graphics cards were not up to the task. Miners started to use specialized hardware mining rigs to solve these complex mathematical problems. No matter how many calculations were needed, the result would always need to be found in 10 minutes and Bitcoin constantly adjusted the difficulty to ensure this would happen.

Validating Transactions

As you have learned, cryptocurrencies, unlike traditional currencies, do not rely on centralized institutions like banks or governments to validate and record transactions. Instead, a decentralized network of miners work together to verify the legitimacy of transactions before they are added to the blockchain. Well, perhaps to say they work together is a bit misleading, in the same way as saying runners in a marathon are working together is a little disingenuous. They are all on the same track, but someone is going to win. The Bitcoin method of mining, proof of work, means that the first person to find the solution to a mathematical problem will win, but it was only the combined efforts of all miners that enabled a solution to be found within the 10 minutes. Also, other miners are required to verify the solution found by the winner.

The process is actually quite simple. Once a transaction is initiated by a user, it enters a pool of unconfirmed transactions known as the *mempool*. Miners then select transactions from this pool, verify their authenticity, and compile them into a new block. The new block is added to the existing blockchain, ensuring that the transaction is permanently recorded and visible to all users.

Minting New Coins

Mining also serves as the primary method of creating new coins. As a reward for their processing efforts, miners are granted newly minted coins, along with the transaction fees paid by users for transactions in that block. This incentivizes miners to continue supporting the network, while simultaneously controlling the rate at which new coins are introduced into the system. Because of the way the math works, there will only ever be 21 million Bitcoin produced by the system and hence the amount of Bitcoin minted is not constant but is cut in half every 210,000 blocks, which equates to approximately 4 years. As of this writing, the reward for each successful mining of a block is 3.125 BTC, and this will halve again in about mid-2028.

Proof of Work (PoW) Mining

Proof of work (PoW) is the original and most controversial consensus algorithm in the world of cryptocurrency mining. This method of mining, developed by Satoshi for Bitcoin, requires miners to solve complex mathematical problems to add new blocks to the blockchain. The process is actually quite simple.

How PoW Mining Works

In a PoW system, miners compete with each other to find the correct solution to a mathematical problem. The first miner to find the correct solution broadcasts it to the network, and other miners verify its correctness. If the majority agrees, the new block is added to the blockchain, and the successful miner receives a reward in the form of new coins and transaction fees. This all sounds very straightforward, but the number of calculations required means that running some mining software on your PC or Mac just isn't going to cut it.

To understand how this works, you must comprehend one technical piece of information: hashing. Hashing is quite a simple concept; you provide some data to a hashing algorithm and it yields an output of a fixed length that is unique to the data you gave it, a bit like a fingerprint. The clever part is that you cannot re-create the original data from the hash.

Browse to a hash calculator such as `https://xorbin.com/tools/sha256-hash-calculator`. Type in any string of text and click Calculate. It will generate the hash, which is unique to the text you provided.

So the text input **Nick Furneaux** provides this SHA256 hash (the hashing algorithm used by Bitcoin):

```
d0fa0db02f533682325a3ed466a031b402138a5c01d393b174118d802b
42105a
```

Now just change the text by one letter or change an uppercase letter to lowercase. If I try **nick furneaux**, with lowercase letters, you now get the hash

```
9ed3cecd6b0998ce6e72975db6ea06e1eb5f43ba62c4b1f97e2e103c4
fe0f387
```

You will note that the smallest change created a new hash that bore no seeming relationship to the original input. No matter how many times you enter my name with lowercase letters, that will always be the SHA256 hash.

Notice that the first hash started with a letter d and the second with the number 9. If I asked you to take the string **nick furneaux** and keep adding a number to it—**nick furneaux1**, then **nick furneaux2**, and so on—until you got a resulting hash starting with a 0, how long do you think it would take? I got bored at **nick furneaux35**. But if you found that **nick furneaux112** started with a 0 and you were the first to find it, how long would it take me to validate that you were right? Almost instantaneously! I could just type **nick furneaux112** into a hash calculator and I would know immediately if you were telling the truth.

This is exactly how PoW mining operates. In slightly simplified terms, the miner takes some transactions from the mempool, hashes them into a resulting SHA256 hash, and then starts adding data and rehashing them until they find a resulting hash with a 0, or actually lots of 0s at the beginning of the hash (I wonder how many readers have now skipped ahead to the next section!). The Bitcoin network dictates how many 0s there should be; the more 0s, the harder the solution is to find. As of this writing, a miner has to find a hash value with 19 zeroes at the beginning to successfully mine the block. If you browse to a site like `blockchair.com` and navigate to the most recent block, you will see the hash value that validated the block—in my case right now the hash that mined the last block is

```
000000000000000000018fac047b5c3970aedbcde4e6942a09ae737c665e
836b
```

The problem with having to find a value with so many 0s is that you have to make a vast number of attempts to find it. At the moment I'm writing this chapter, miners will have to try 312.67 exahashes per second—that's 312,667,846,052,947,000,000 hashes every second to find a hash value with 19 zeroes in around 10 minutes. That number is only slightly less than the estimated number of stars in the entire universe, having to be tried every second.

To achieve this, powerful mining rigs are needed, which are expensive to buy, expensive to power, and expensive to cool. A single Antminer S19 costs between $2,000 and $4,500 depending on the version. This means that there is no one "cost" to mining a new Bitcoin. In mid-2022 it was estimated that it cost $24,000 to mine a Bitcoin in Iceland compared to $49,000 in the UK, purely down to the difference in energy costs. The reality, though, is like the difficulty of mining a new coin on the island of Yap: creating a new Bitcoin costs real money and hence they have an inherent value.

But this method has come at a price (see Figure 6.1).

Figure 6.1: Example of an Antminer crypto-mining rig

Energy Consumption and Environmental Concerns

One of the primary criticisms of PoW mining is its massive energy consumption. The process, as you've seen, requires specialized, energy-intensive hardware that consumes a significant amount of electricity to power and to cool. As a result, PoW mining has come under fire for its environmental impact and contribution to climate change. It's extremely difficult to quantify the actual environmental cost of PoW mining for any cryptocurrency, although many have tried, because it has to relate to the eco-cost of generating the power that runs and cools the mining rigs. This means that a country generating 90 percent of its power from coal-fired power stations will have a much greater eco-cost per Bitcoin than a country like Iceland, where 100 percent of its electricity comes from hydro- and geothermal power.

How much power does Bitcoin actually use? If you search this on the web, you will get many scientific-sounding articles with wildly differing numbers. This was typified in a report on Whitehouse.gov in mid-2022 stating that

> *the total global electricity usage for crypto assets is between 120 and 240 billion kilowatt-hours per year, a range that exceeds the total annual electricity usage of many individual countries, such as Argentina or Australia. This is equivalent to 0.4% to 0.9% of annual global electricity usage, and is comparable to the annual electricity usage of all conventional data centers in the world.*
>
> *Source:* `www.whitehouse.gov/ostp/news-updates/2022/09/08/fact-sheet-climate-and-energy-implications-of-crypto-assets-in-the-united-states`

Between 120 and 240 is not exactly close, and of course the cost depends on where you are in the world and how the energy is being generated. No matter what the numbers really are, power usage is power usage, and in this day and age it seems like there should be a better way. Enter the new method, proof of stake.

Proof of Stake (PoS) Mining

As an alternative to PoW mining, proof of stake (PoS) mining aims to reduce energy consumption and improve network security. In a PoS system, miners, also known as validators, are chosen based on the number of coins they hold and who are willing to "stake" a certain amount of cryptocurrency as collateral.

How PoS Mining Works

In a PoS system, validators are chosen at random to create new blocks and validate transactions based on their stake in the cryptocurrency. The more coins a validator holds and is willing to stake, the higher the chance they have of being selected to create the next block. Once chosen, the validator verifies the transactions, creates a new block, and adds it to the blockchain. It's fundamentally a very simple system.

Advantages of PoS Mining

PoS mining offers several advantages over PoW mining, including massively reduced energy consumption, arguably enhanced network security, and a more equitable distribution of rewards. Since PoS mining does not require any specialized hardware or massive amounts of energy, it is a more environmentally friendly alternative to PoW mining. Additionally, PoS systems typically have lower barriers to entry, enabling a broader range of participants to contribute to the network's security and stability. Although a number of minor cryptocurrencies implemented PoS, it wasn't until Ethereum changed their mining system from PoS to PoW in 2022 that it really appeared in the crypto user's consciousness. Anyone able to own and stake 32 ETH (approximately $55,000 as of this writing) can become an independent Ethereum validator and earn coins when they are chosen to validate a block.

Does an Investigator Need to Understand Mining Technologies?

This is one of those yes and no answers. In this section we will provide a brief overview of some frauds and scams that include or exploit cryptocurrency mining, but in my experience, they have been very rare.

I have been investigating crimes involving crypto for about 8 or 9 years and all but one of the cases where mining was involved were in the first couple of years where people were getting interested in creating "money" out of thin air. Criminals go where the money is, and this was an obvious place to create complex frauds. In the last few years, the frauds have tended to move to tokens and De-Fi, as mining has become very costly and victims are less likely to be taken in by extraordinary, get-rich-quick promises.

However, the brief overview I have just provided is simple enough to understand and should provide you with enough information to at least understand the concepts and provide a foundation for you to build on if you wish, or if you are faced with a crime or financial investigation that involves any type of mining.

Cryptocurrency Mining Frauds and Scams

As cryptocurrency mining has grown in popularity, so too have the opportunities for bad actors to exploit unsuspecting individuals. Fraudulent schemes and scams related to mining are increasingly common, and it's crucial for investigators to be aware of the potential risks.

Cloud Mining Scams

Cloud mining services offer users the opportunity to rent mining hardware and participate in cryptocurrency mining without having to invest in, and run, expensive and fairly complex equipment. It should be noted that there are many services offering cloud mining and that they are by no means all scams. However, not all cloud mining services are legitimate. Scammers may create fake cloud mining platforms, promising unrealistic returns and taking investors' money without providing any mining services in return. As an investigator, you'll find these complex to unravel.

I worked on a very complicated mining scam, and what made it more difficult to unwrap and understand was that the scam was not a complete lie. The criminals did indeed have large mining facilities in Eastern Europe and the United States. They were selling mining services to people all over the world via a very professional website, and at the start of the business they were paying customers their share of successfully received coins. Everyone seemed happy. After a number of months, the payments became smaller and less often, until eventually they dried up completely. The business-owners-turned-scammers engaged with the investigation and said that they had become less successful in their mining and that costs had increased and that this had meant that the payments to customers had dried up. Untangling the numerous wallets that received funds from the company mining facilities was a massive headache, but in due course we were able to discern that mining rewards had actually significantly increased as had the expensive lifestyle of the two business partners running the business. Villas in Italy and shiny Italian supercars, all proudly displayed on Instagram (why do criminals often do that?) were somewhat eating into profits. As their materialism increased, the mining actually became even more successful and they also became greedier, which eventually resulted in them stopping paying customers altogether. It was one of the first cases where I worked with a very experienced financial investigator, who had little knowledge of crypto but had seen the pattern, the methods of laundering, and the results of greed all too many times before, and she was indispensable in unraveling the case.

The case fundamentally depended on us proving that mining rewards had not declined, and this meant locating all the wallets that were receiving coin rewards and calculating the fluctuating values. The scammers provided us with some wallet addresses that appeared to show declining rewards; these funds would then be moved into several VASPs. We noted that there were other incoming amounts into deposit addresses at the VASPs and some of those could be tracked back just two hops to mining rewards (known as coinbase transactions—nothing to do with the exchange of the same name). This enabled us to find other wallets receiving mining funds and to carry out more accurate calculations as to their income and prove that their profits were significantly higher than they stated. It was an interesting case because it was a business that started legitimately and became a scam over time.

Ponzi and Pyramid Schemes

Ponzi and pyramid schemes are also prevalent in the world of cryptocurrency mining. These schemes typically promise high returns on investment and rely on new participants to pay off earlier investors. Once the flow of new investors slows down or stops, the scheme collapses, and most participants lose their investments. Unraveling Ponzi mining scams tends to be a little easier than my previous example, as it is rare that the scammers are running any mining at all but are simply paying "mining rewards" at very low levels from other investors' money to keep victims on the hook. This means that the flow of funds is straightforward. Money comes in from investors and often is moved to others who carry out laundering and, as mentioned, sometimes small amounts are paid back to customers to keep them engaged.

Malware and Cryptojacking

Some bad actors use malware and other methods to take control of victims' computers and use their processing power for cryptocurrency mining without their knowledge or consent. This process, known as *cryptojacking*, can slow down computers, increase energy bills, and potentially expose your personal information to hackers. A few years ago there was a huge amount of malware around that simply stole processor cycles to carry out cloud-based mining, but as mining became more difficult and with Ethereum moving to PoS, this has become less attractive.

I worked on a case pre-pandemic where a company employed an IT person who loaded mining software onto every computer in the business he worked for and then set them to work cryptomining after everyone had gone home. I gave evidence in court on this case in 2023. The question was less about whether he had installed the programs and more about whether it was illegal. It was almost certainly a disciplinary matter for the company, but the police got involved and he was charged with computer misuse and theft. It's a rather interesting case as the computers were not actually hacked since he had rights to access them. He certainly added unapproved software, but was this criminal misuse? The company's energy bill would have risen drastically due to the increased power requirements for processing and cooling, so he certainly misappropriated power. There was also the question as to whether the crypto that was mined was actually owned by the company since their computers had been used to mine it. Sadly, I had to submit this chapter before the end of the case, so I can't tell you how the court ruled. It's an interesting one to ponder in line with the laws of your country.

Asset Discovery

Although this category is not necessarily related to criminal investigations in its own right, many investigations require discovery of financial and other assets and this would of course include crypto assets. This might be a tax inspector looking for taxable assets, due diligence being done for a company acquisition, or indeed looking for criminal assets or money laundering as we have discussed before.

Mining is a quite clever way of creating new assets that won't appear on a balance sheet. As you are, by definition, creating new coins from thin air, there will be no purchase record or obvious provenance. So what can you look for?

- Sales of crypto that were not previously purchased or received as payment for goods. If you cannot find the purchase of or payment in crypto, then where has it come from? Mining is a possibility.
- Payments to companies that offer mining. Payments to VASPs or unknown companies could be investigated to understand what they provide. If they offer cloud mining services, then this could be investigated.
- Payments for mining equipment. Mining equipment such as Antminers is very expensive, and so should there be purchases for this type of kit, it would obviously lead you to a conclusion that mining has been done and so it's likely that crypto assets have been created.

Will Cryptocurrencies Always Be Mined?

Cryptocurrency mining plays a crucial role in securing and validating transactions within the blockchain ecosystem while enabling a method for the injection of new coins. While proof of work mining was the dominant consensus mechanism for a number of years, proof of stake mining offers a more sustainable and an arguably inclusive alternative. PoW and PoS are not the only ways of achieving these aims, and other technologies are certain to emerge as crypto finds its place in the world. As with any emerging industry, cryptocurrency mining is not without its share of frauds and scams, and so the investigator needs to understand the fundamentals of the processes to be able to identify any criminal exploits that might appear in a case.

As I mentioned a few pages ago, mining frauds have been few and far between in my experience, but the ones I have worked on have ranged from the simple "jacking" of their employers' computers at night, which was worth a reasonably small amount to the criminal, to vast mining company scams where the victims were counted in the thousands and the lost funds in the millions of dollars. Make sure you understand the basics and be aware of the potential for fraud in this area.

7 Cryptocurrency Wallets

If you are, or are planning to be, involved with crypto investigations, you will at some point need to recognize, analyze, and perhaps use crypto-wallets. No matter if you are a frontline officer, a digital forensics examiner, or a financial investigator, wallets are the mechanism whereby crypto is sent and received by users and so are a vital link in an investigative chain. The common assumption is that crypto investigators are just trained users of transaction link tools such as TRM Labs or Chainalysis, but a much broader scope of skills is needed in many crypto investigations and that includes knowledge of wallets.

During a search phase of an investigation, whether that be a premises search or a digital examination, it is vital to identify crypto usage. One of the primary notifiers is the identification of the use of software or hardware wallets. Digital forensics investigators need to know how to *recognize* wallet software running on mobile phones or computers, even if the application names are not familiar. An Internet search engine will be your friend. Recall the example from Chapter 2, "Understanding the Criminal Opportunities: Money Laundering," of a phone being taken from a drug-dealing suspect and the only reason that around $300,000 in crypto was located was because the mobile phone investigator Googled an app name they didn't recognize and identified a crypto-wallet.

Although we will not be covering digital forensics in this book, the ability to forensically *analyze* wallet software and hardware is a new area of research. One of the problems is that when searching for articles and research on the digital forensics aspect of wallet analysis, you get muddled up with the fact that the term *forensics* is being used to mean blockchain transaction link analysis rather than the traditional digital forensics examination of software and hardware tools. I recommend that any digital forensics professionals do their own research. RAM (random access memory) analysis is a very good place to start.

NOTE Here are several good research papers:

- A framework for live host-based Bitcoin wallet forensics and triage: www.sciencedirect.com/science/article/pii/S2666281722001676
- Mobile Cyber Forensic Investigations of Web3 Wallets on Android and iOS: www.mdpi.com/2076-3417/12/21/11180
- Forensic Analysis on Cryptocurrency Wallet Apps: https://dr.lib.iastate.edu/entities/publication/b967140e-90ec-472d-9902-a7dad7273c02
- Memory FORESHADOW: Memory FOREnSics of HArDware CryptOcurrency Wallets—A Tool and Visualization Framework: https://dfrws.org/wp-content/uploads/2020/10/2020_USA_paper-memory_foreshadow_memory_forensics_of_hardware_cryptocurrency_wallets_a_tool_and_visualization.pdf

There could be many occasions that an investigator would need to *use* a cryptocurrency wallet. Perhaps the primary instances would be checking crypto holdings or transaction history on a live suspect device, or seizing assets from a suspect from their phone or computer. Seizure of crypto assets will be handled in its own chapter (Chapter 17, "Crypto Seizure") but if you are in a position where you may be an on-scene search officer, it is possible that you may locate a device that is already logged in or be provided with a password or PIN to log into a device. This may present a crypto-wallet that you haven't seen before, and so understanding the basics of most wallets' workings puts you in a good position to be able to work on the problem.

As you read this chapter, you will learn more about seed word lists, hardware devices, PINs, and passcodes. If you are not massively technical, don't worry—wallets are becoming easier and easier to use as they reach a larger mass market audience, so you shouldn't need to know too much to be able to use any wallet you come across.

NOTE Please note that accessing any data on a live running device risks compromising the forensic integrity of that device. Although most countries' legal frameworks now allow for live, on-device investigations, this is usually connected to specific regulations and methods. Please be aware of those laws and accepted procedures in the country in which you operate.

If you are already working with crypto investigations and have used different types of wallets—hot, cold, web-based, and so on—then this may be a chapter you will feel happy skipping. But it's not very long and there may just be a detail that is useful, whether having to recognize wallets, using a suspect's wallet for seizure, or setting up your own wallets for receiving crypto or for use in covert purchasing operations.

When a Wallet Is Not Really a Wallet

Wallet, as in the description of a cryptocurrency wallet, is not really a good name because it can be rather misleading. We all know what a traditional wallet is: a folding, typically leather pouch that usually has space for notes, perhaps some coins, and slots for bank and credit cards. If you look in a physical wallet, you can see the funds you own and can spend the funds as you wish. This rather leads people to believe that a crypto-wallet holds, or stores, the crypto funds. However, a cryptocurrency wallet never contains or stores any crypto funds at all; it only holds and secures the private cryptographic keys that enable funds on the blockchain to be identified and spent. A crypto-wallet doesn't even technically have a balance of funds—the stored keys enable the blockchain to be queried and any funds that are controlled by the keys are totaled into a balance. In the case of UTXO currencies like Bitcoin, the wallet uses the private key stored in the wallet to identify unspent funds that can be controlled by the private key. In account-based currencies, it just queries the address balance.

In some ways it's better to think of a wallet with no cash in it, just a bank card. The bank card is essentially a private key to your funds and enables you to go to an ATM and look up a balance or to carry out a transaction with a vendor. It's a much closer simile.

A software or hardware wallet has a fairly small list of key features:

- It protects the private keys. If someone can get the private key, they generally have control of the funds controlled by the wallet. This may not be the case with multi-signature wallets that require multiple private keys to move the funds.
- It provides a running balance.
- It may provide a transaction history.
- It enables the building of transactions.
- It communicates with the appropriate blockchain to send transactions or receive information about the currency or crypto holdings.

For a basic wallet, that's pretty much everything, but many wallets can now do much more, such as display NFTs, track currency prices, enable transactions with financial products (DeFi), enable swapping between currencies, and many other things. However, virtually all these features are just an extension of the last bulleted item. Swapping currencies is just a type of transaction, buying and selling NFTs is just a transaction, staking money in a DeFi contract is a transaction, and the list goes on. Most of these enhanced wallet functions are an extension of being able to read the blockchain to identify assets you own or to generate a transaction to make something happen on the blockchain.

Wallets are simply designed to provide convenience, security, and control over one's digital assets, making it crucial for investigators to understand their functionalities and types.

First, let's delve into the variety of cryptocurrency wallets and outline the different types available, their key features, and how they work. I will avoid talking at any length about specific wallets, as by the time you read this there will be 100 more on the market. You just need to understand the fundamentals.

Types of Cryptocurrency Wallets

The kinds of cryptocurrency wallets can be broadly categorized into two types: a hot wallet and a cold wallet. The distinction lies simply in their connectivity to the Internet.

Hot Wallets

Hot wallets are connected to, or able to connect to, the Internet, providing users with an always-on view of their crypto assets. However, this connectivity also makes them more vulnerable to attack. If a wallet is live on a computer that has been compromised, then by extension the wallet is also at risk. Malware designed to steal seed words or wallet passwords may also be a threat. In recent years I have heard of several examples of thefts simply by attackers shoulder-surfing the victim to see them log into their wallet and then stealing the device. An always-connected wallet will generally be a vulnerable wallet.

Let's look at the main types of hot wallets.

Desktop Wallets

Desktop wallets are software applications installed on a computer, offering a user-friendly interface for managing digital assets. Some wallets are stand-alone programs whereas others can be added as a browser extension. The latter type has become very popular as a means to authenticate with a website offering crypto services. A good example of this is the NFT broker OpenSea. You do not set up an account or define a username and password for OpenSea as you would when logging into a site such as Amazon or PayPal. Instead, you simply connect your browser-based wallet to the website and your hidden private key acts as the authentication.

For an investigator this means that any digital forensic investigation should always include the extraction of a list of installed software wallets and also ensure that they identify any browser plug-ins that may be related to crypto. Correlating this with the user's Internet history should enable an investigator to understand what sites crypto was likely being used to transact with.

It is also worth noting that not all wallets need to be installed and thus would not exist in an installed software list. An example of this is the Electrum wallet. It can either be installed or run from a stand-alone executable file. This would enable a suspect to run the wallet from a USB key or other removable storage device. External storage devices should also be scanned for wallet files along with any primary computers or handheld devices.

Full-node wallets run a complete copy of the blockchain and act as nodes on the blockchain network. A good example of this is Bitcoin Core, which acts both as a personal wallet and as a node on the Bitcoin network. This means that your computer with Bitcoin Core installed and running adds to the number of decentralized ledgers running around the world (`https://bitcoin.org/en/download`).

Ethereum does not have a user wallet with a built-in node; instead, you install a node client specifically (`https://ethereum.org/en/run-a-node`). As of this writing, you can also run validator nodes to make money from the proof of stake process—if you have 32 ETH to stake, that is!

Mobile Wallets

Mobile wallets are smartphone applications that allow users to access their cryptocurrencies from phones and tablets. Back in 2020 I would have written that mobile wallets were quite simple and limited, but now it seems that there is a new mobile wallet being released every week, all with new features and capabilities. The inherent security of operating systems such as iOS with code entry, fingerprint, or face scan authentication and so on arguably makes the platform a more secure environment than a desktop and certainly more accessible if you want access to your crypto all the time. This is offset by the reality that a mobile device is taken with the person, often wherever they go, and so it is easier for a criminal to acquire the device, even if they are unable to access it once they have it. (In Chapter 10, we will discuss a seizure that took place on a train where the officers waited for the phone and the crypto-wallet to be accessed and logged into by the suspect before they moved in for the arrest.)

Accessing wallets on mobile devices can be tricky because of the aforementioned security. Gaining access to an iPhone, for example, with a long PIN can be extremely difficult without the cooperation of the suspect. As we will go on to discuss in more detail, whenever a wallet is set up, seed words are generated to be used as a backup. Sometimes it's easier to find the seed words and re-create the wallet than it is to break into the device.

Web/Online Wallets

Web or online wallets are accessed through web browsers and shouldn't be confused with the browser extensions/plug-ins mentioned in the

"Desktop Wallets" section. An online wallet may likely be accessed through a browser or software tool, but rather than the private keys being hosted locally, they are held by a remote server. Because the company has custody of the private keys, these types of wallets are often known as *custodial wallets*. The best example of this is hosted wallets provided by exchanges such as Coinbase, Binance, Kraken, and many others. All the capabilities of the wallet tend to be the same, but you must trust the company to protect your funds rather than keeping your private keys safe personally. I'm not going to get into the pros and cons of online wallets in this book—do your own research if you are going to use crypto personally or for your department.

NOTE It is worth remembering that exchange wallets are not really wallets in the same way as a self-hosted solution. Funds are held by the exchange centrally and users can set up accounts and buy, sell, and transfer crypto as they wish, but notably the user never really "owns" the crypto directly. If I set up an account with Exchange A and buy 1 ETH, the exchange doesn't actually transfer me an ETH but metaphorically just adds a 1 to the ETH column in the exchanges database against my name. This is not necessarily bad, but if an exchange is fraudulent, this lends itself to a Ponzi scheme environment.

Finding evidence of an online wallet hosted with an exchange can be quite a good thing for an investigator. Local wallets often need to be accessed via PINs or passwords, which can be difficult with an uncooperative suspect. However, it can be more straightforward to get your paperwork together and apply to an exchange for know-your-customer (KYC) information, freezing orders, and so on. The exchange will usually have full access to the user's account information, and the data they can provide can be invaluable. This may include transactions in and out of the account, currency swaps, currency purchases, identity information, IP addresses used to log into the account, and so on. Although KYC is often falsified in criminal investigations, other data such as IP addresses can be incredibly useful. Although IPs used by a criminal will often be obfuscated by using VPNs and Tor, for example, as was mentioned in an earlier chapter, it's incredible how often technical failures or just human error will expose a "true," geolocatable IP address of the suspect.

Cold Wallets

Cold wallets are wallets that are not connected to the Internet, providing a more secure environment for storing crypto. Let's take a look at the main types of cold wallets.

Hardware Wallets

Hardware wallets are physical devices designed specifically for storing crypto private keys securely. They often look like a USB key or small USB device and almost always have a small screen and buttons for entering a PIN to mount the device (see Figure 7.1).

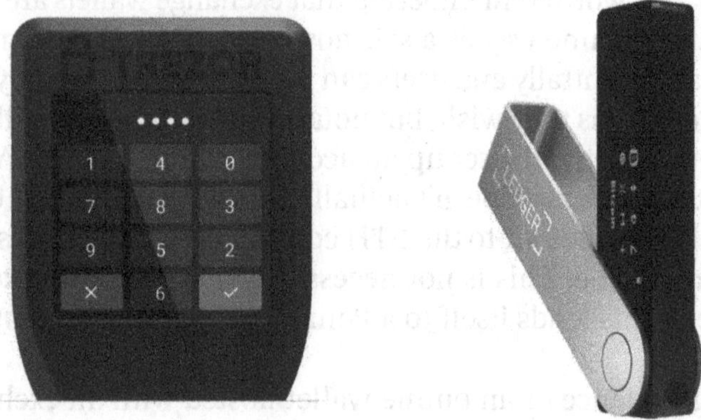

Figure 7.1: Examples of hardware wallets

Source: James Northcote/Royal Academy in Plymouth/London/Wikimedia Commons

NOTE A note for digital forensics people: imaging hardware wallets can be very tricky. Most will not mount as a drive until the PIN has been entered on the device. The Ledger Nano X, for example, won't appear in a drive list at all as either a mounted or unmounted device until the PIN is successfully entered. Most also have a lockout once the PIN is incorrectly entered a certain number of times. There have been some attempts at "chip-off" imaging and analysis of hardware wallets, but you will need to look up the latest research on that.

Popular hardware wallets include the Ledger Nano series, Trezor, SafePal, and KeepKey, and others will certainly appear.

I will almost certainly mention this again in Chapter 17, but most hardware wallets ship with cards to write the seed words as a backup to re-create the wallet should you lose the device. It is much easier to set up a new wallet with the seed words than it is to try to "crack" the hardware wallet belonging to the suspect. The first place to look for the seed word cards is in the box they shipped in. We find them there all the time!

Paper Wallets

Paper wallets are wallets (pause for dramatic effect) on paper. They are often a physical printout of a user's public and private keys, sometimes in raw alphanumeric form and often in the form of QR codes. While not as convenient as other wallets, they are a low-tech, yet very secure option for long-term storage.

Although it seems counterintuitive, you are able to set up a crypto-wallet that has never been online. Funds can be sent to the public address (Bitcoin, Ethereum address, etc.) that you have created and the wallet only ever needs to appear online when the funds are moved. If you would like to try this, browse to `https://iancoleman.io/bip39` (you can download the file from the latest GitHub release at `https://github.com/iancoleman/bip39/releases/latest`) and download the page. Disconnect from the Internet and then generate a new wallet seed phrase (see Figure 7.2).

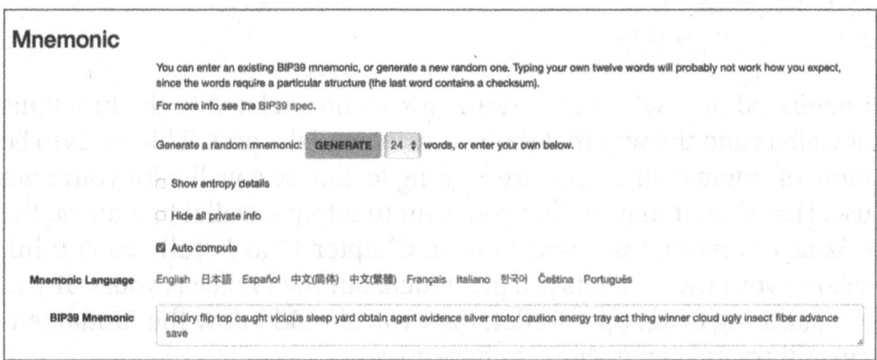

Figure 7.2: Generating a seed word list on iancoleman.io

Source: British Library Board / Public Domain / CC BY 4.0

If you scroll down the page you will find generated addresses that you can publish and have funds sent to, all without using a standard online wallet (see Figure 7.3).

Table CSV

Path Toggle	Address Toggle
m/44'/0'/0'/0/0	14oakiaK8fyCEC1xEXHXqqKvNCmCWPup4K
m/44'/0'/0'/0/1	1F1qThvZ2N313zKSAuRt1txc6ajK4FXB89
m/44'/0'/0'/0/2	1LyHbASn9KSn9QgEs9tnTJp3vxZnq8d4CW
m/44'/0'/0'/0/3	1GnKhDmbSA4vuCaAnbLTHQWcdeLEEq6qek
m/44'/0'/0'/0/4	18xtoftMKH4niRy1HXiZttviMoKsVZxiyo

Figure 7.3: List of addresses (public keys) generated by the private key

When you want to transact funds, you can use a software wallet such as Electrum or Exodus wallet. To set up a new wallet, enter the seed words and that will give you access to the received funds.

Paper wallets are, by definition, cold wallets in that they can't be online if they only exist on paper. I did see an article that defined a paper wallet as being "printed"; however, we often see handwritten seed words, private keys, and notes related to wallets. We will discuss more on this topic in Chapter 8, "The Importance of Discovery."

Software Wallets: Functionality and Security

I pondered over whether to write this section related to the functions of wallets and the way that their security model works. This tends to be more of interest when you are looking to choose a wallet for your own use. However, it may be that you want to set up a wallet to manage the seizing of crypto. I will cover this in Chapter 17 as I really don't think seizing your own wallets is a great idea, but the choice is yours. If you are planning to set up a wallet, then you should know the fundamentals. I'll try to keep it short, so here goes.

Software wallets are popular for their convenience and ease of use. As mentioned, they are available across various platforms (desktop, mobile, and web) and offer different levels of security and functionality, depending on the user's requirements.

Functionality

The primary functions of these wallets include:

Creating and Managing Multiple Addresses Software wallets enable users to create multiple addresses (public keys derived from their private key) for receiving cryptocurrencies. This practice enhances privacy on UTXO blockchains by allowing users to avoid reusing addresses for different transactions.

Sending and Receiving Transactions Users can initiate and receive cryptocurrency transactions using the wallet's interface. The wallet software signs the transaction with the user's private key, authorizing the transfer.

Backup and Recovery Software wallets offer backup and recovery options, such as seed phrases and private key exports. These features allow users to restore their wallets on new devices or recover their assets if the wallet is lost or compromised.

Security

The security of a software wallet depends on the user's device and the measures taken to protect the private keys. Some security features commonly found in software wallets include:

Encryption Wallets encrypt the private keys with a user-generated password, preventing unauthorized access.

Two-Factor Authentication (2FA) Many wallets offer 2FA, which requires users to provide a second form of authentication, such as a one-time code sent to a mobile device, before granting access to the wallet.

Multi-Signature (Multisig) Support Multisig wallets require multiple private keys to authorize a transaction, providing an added layer of security against unauthorized transactions.

Regular Updates Developers of reputable wallets release updates to address security vulnerabilities and improve functionality.

Hardware Wallets: Functionality and Security

Hardware wallets are physical devices that securely store a user's private keys offline as cold storage. They provide a high level of security, making them an ideal choice for long-term storage and large cryptocurrency holdings.

Functionality

Hardware wallets offer similar functionality to software wallets, with a few key differences:

Secure Element Hardware wallets use a secure element, such as a microcontroller, to store the private keys. This isolates the keys from the Internet and other potential attack vectors.

Offline Transaction Signing Transactions are signed within the hardware wallet itself, ensuring the private keys never leave the device.

Integration with Software Wallets Hardware wallets usually work in tandem with software wallets, providing users with a user-friendly interface for managing their cryptocurrencies.

Support for Multiple Cryptocurrencies Most hardware wallets support a wide range of cryptocurrencies, allowing users to store multiple assets on a single device.

Security

Hardware wallets are designed with security in mind. They provide various features to protect users' private keys and digital assets:

PIN Protection Hardware wallets require a user-defined PIN to access the device, preventing unauthorized access.

Physical Buttons Many hardware wallets have physical buttons that must be pressed to confirm transactions, adding an extra layer of security.

Firmware Updates Hardware wallet developers release firmware updates to address security vulnerabilities and improve the device's functionality. Users should keep their hardware wallets updated to maintain the highest level of security.

Backup and Recovery Like software wallets, hardware wallets provide backup and recovery options, such as seed phrases, allowing users to restore their wallets if the device is lost or damaged.

Choosing the Right Wallet

When selecting a cryptocurrency wallet, users should consider their needs, preferences, and risk tolerance. Factors to consider include:

Security Cold wallets, such as hardware wallets, provide the highest level of security. Users with large cryptocurrency holdings or those concerned about security may prefer this option. If you were to decide to hold seized crypto within your department, then using a hardware device with appropriate protection of seed words may be the best option.

Convenience Hot wallets, particularly mobile and web wallets, offer the most convenience for everyday use. Users who frequently transact with cryptocurrencies may find these wallets more suitable.

Supported Cryptocurrencies Some wallets only support specific cryptocurrencies or a limited number of assets. Users should ensure that their chosen wallet is compatible with the cryptocurrencies they own or plan to acquire. This is very important for investigators to consider if they are going to store their own seized crypto. You simply don't know what currencies a suspect may be holding, and thus having a wallet that will support a wide variety of currencies and tokens is essential.

User Experience The user interface and overall experience can vary between wallets. You may want to test out different wallets to find one that aligns with your preferences.

Backup and Recovery Options You should ensure that your chosen wallet provides backup and recovery options to safeguard their assets in case of device loss or failure. Backup of seed words to multiple locations is vital! Remember the "Two is one and one is none" principle we discussed earlier in the book.

Wallet Vulnerabilities

This is not a hacking book and in no way purports to be, but a section on vulnerabilities in wallets should be briefly explored. It is worth remembering that although I will describe these vulnerabilities from the perspective of a user, these can also provide opportunities for an officer, with the right legal framework in place, to exploit these issues to gain access to a device or wallet to enable the securing of proceeds of crime. Let's explore some of these vulnerabilities, in no particular order.

Weak or Reused Passwords

If a user chooses a weak or reused password, it can, in some instances, be easily guessed or otherwise cracked by attackers, allowing unauthorized access to the wallet. Vulnerable passwords could be at different locations. A user's operating system password may be weak, enabling access to the system and simplifying the process of breaking the wallet. Or the user may reuse the same password for the operating system login and the wallet software; we see this regularly. This is particularly troublesome with mobile wallets where the wallet may be protected by the same PIN as the login to the device. If an attacker can shoulder-surf the victim and see the PIN, it may provide access across the device. Countering this is easy; enforce strong passwords and always use two-factor authentication wherever you can.

Phishing Attacks

Attackers may trick users into visiting malicious websites, downloading fake wallet apps, or clicking on phishing links, which can lead to the compromise of the user's wallet and private keys. Most of the primary wallets have seen this attack against them. For a while in 2022 there were several malevolent "versions" of the MetaMask wallet available that would result in funds being stolen once the wallet was installed. The wallet Electrum suffered several fake update attacks, where users were directed to a fake site to update the software and it contained malware that drained the original wallet upon installation. My team worked on the loss of £14 million from a single victim in an Electrum fake update attack. The case was still ongoing as of this writing, but the majority of the funds had been located and a likely suspect was in the crosshairs of law enforcement.

Malware

Malicious software, such as keyloggers, Trojans, or other types, can be used to steal wallet data, including private keys and seed phrases. Although this rather connects with phishing, it should be isolated in its own paragraph too. The phishing part is usually the "hook" that drives victims to a fake wallet website or wallet download that is malign. Malware can also be sent in a scattergun approach via email or SMS messages. I regularly get text messages telling me that "There has been a transfer from your Coinbase account, if this wasn't you please login immediately." The link is fake of course. Although I can't understand anyone being taken in by it, I have worked on many, many cases where victims have clicked, logged in, and lost all their crypto. I worked on one case where a man in New York had bought crypto with the inheritance from his parents and had clicked the link in an SMS message warning him of a breach in his online wallet, downloaded the software to "recover" his funds, and lost everything. His wife was eight months pregnant, and he was about to sell the crypto (which he had done well out of) to buy their first house. The man was literally in tears on the phone. Breaks the heart.

On-Path Attacks

An *on-path attack* is when attackers intercept and modify data being transmitted between the user's device and a wallet service, potentially allowing them to gain unauthorized access to the wallet. The way that standard crypto-wallets and the primary blockchains work means that on-path attacks are not terribly effective, but this is very different when you have a web-based crypto account, perhaps with an exchange. The easiest way for an attacker to achieve this is with a Wi-Fi access point that they control. If the attacker can get you to connect to "Airport Free Wi-Fi," for example (which I see a lot), they can intercept all the traffic between your wallet and the endpoint. Although strong encryption generally makes this ineffective, tools are available that can attempt to drop the encrypted SSL connection and leave the traffic in plain text and thus readable. New protocols make this attack difficult to pull off.

Vulnerable Wallet Software

Some wallet software may contain security vulnerabilities that can be exploited by attackers, such as bugs in the code or weak encryption methods. Do your research on wallets before installing and using them. Although vulnerabilities are, by definition, not always known, if you are reasonably technical it can be worth searching the web for known issues. I often use the search system at `http://cve.mitre.org` for vulnerability searches. If you want to try it, do a search for Electrum, which is a wallet that works on multiple operating systems.

Lack of Two-Factor Authentication (2FA)

Wallets without 2FA are more susceptible to unauthorized access, as they rely solely on a password or private key. If you are setting up wallets for use within your department, you will need to have wallets with 2FA available. However, this can cause complexity with management and security of funds. Once again, we will discuss this in more detail in Chapter 17, but we have seen many problems where only one officer/crypto admin has access to the funds. People get fired, leave, or get hit by proverbial buses, and if only one person has access to a wallet, then you are putting those funds at risk. Remember the principle we discussed previously: "Two is one and one is none." This is the same issue when dealing with wallet security; you need at least two people involved, preferably with different aspects of the key. Also, if funds go missing, then it puts a single person in the firing line, which is tough on the one individual if they had nothing to do with it. We had an issue a few years back where an officer set up a Bitcoin Core wallet personally to handle a seizure (this was before there was any process in place). He carried out a successful seizure of the funds but then forgot the password to the wallet. This was also before the time where seed words were used to back up a wallet. It was the one and only time I have been asked to password-crack a wallet outside a classroom, and sadly we were not successful. At the time Bitcoin was only worth around $2,500 and it was only about 1.5 Bitcoin, if I remember correctly. It felt worse a few years later when Bitcoin was worth $60,000! I spoke to the officer on another matter a year or so back and he still has the wallet. They have recently invested in new password-cracking hardware, so he was planning to have another go at cracking it.

As you will discover in Chapter 17, I am not a fan of self-storage of crypto, but if you would like a secure way of holding seed words, try this: Browse to `http://iancoleman.io/bip39` (if you are doing this operationally, download the page and be offline when you do this). Either generate a new seed mnemonic or enter a seed string. Next, select the Show Split Mnemonic Cards check box. This will split the seed words up into three lists, each with words missing. Each list can be copied onto a different card/paper and given to a different person. Only two of the three lists are needed to create the entire list. This method means you have a two-of-three system, where three people have the list, no one person can access the wallet, but only two of the three are needed to re-create the wallet and move funds. If someone leaves the company/department or doesn't see our proverbial bus coming, you are still able to access the funds. It's pretty good security (see Figure 7.4).

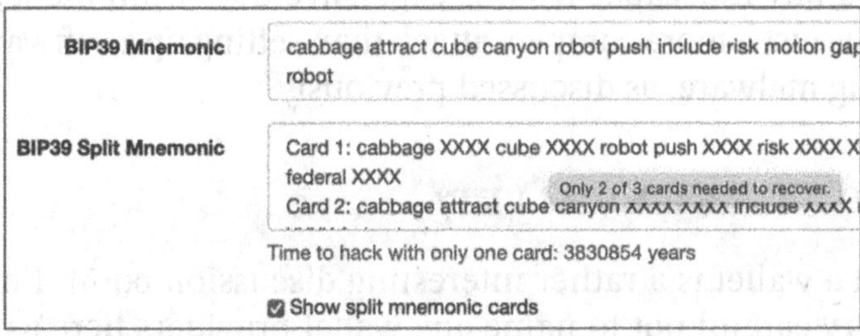

Figure 7.4: A seed phrase split into different cards

Social Engineering

Attackers can deceive users into revealing their private keys or wallet passwords or other sensitive information. We discussed some of these techniques earlier in the book so I won't go through it all again, but we see scammers impersonating exchanges or wallet support teams, or indeed many other creative tactics.

SIM-Swapping Attacks

In this type of attack, the hacker manages to convince a mobile carrier to transfer the victim's phone number to a new SIM card, allowing the attacker to bypass 2FA or to access wallet recovery options. This is a complex area that I will not explore in this book, but you should do some research to understand the mechanism and methodologies used.

Supply Chain Attacks

Malicious actors may compromise hardware wallets during the manufacturing process, making them susceptible to future attacks. This is an interesting one, which, I'll be honest, I've never seen in the wild. I think more likely than an attacker undermining a supply chain is them building their own devices that look identical to a legitimate device. Imagine a criminal team reverse-engineering a hardware device, then building a basic hardware wallet that looks identical to a real one but with a subroutine that sends seed words to the attacker when new wallets are set up. Most people would just see the picture of a device on an online retailer's site that looks like the real one, with the "name" the same, and buy it because it's less expensive than from the legitimate site. This is just a more complex attack than setting up a software wallet containing malware, as discussed previously.

CAN YOU TRUST A WALLET?

Trust in a wallet is a rather interesting discussion point. I'm going to be very careful not to name any wallet providers here as I don't want a legal letter arriving in the mail, but how do you know if you can trust a wallet? If you take a look at where most of the hardware wallets are produced or where their chipsets come from, this may be a concerning detail from a Western law enforcement perspective. It's the same issue with software wallets. Do we know who is writing them, and can we be sure that information is not being fed back to the writers? In simple terms, we either have to do our own assessments or trust the work of others. There are many pieces of research available on the Internet of research labs that have stripped down hardware wallets or carried out risk assessments on software wallets and have published the results. I suggest that you research carefully if you are planning to store your own or your department's crypto.

Cryptocurrency wallets play a crucial role in a department's ability to both manage their own assets and secure criminal digital assets. Understanding the different types of wallets, their features, and their security measures is vital for an investigator who will at some point be required to recognize, analyze, and perhaps use crypto-wallets. As we will discuss in the next chapter, it is important that even frontline officers/investigators recognize when crypto is in use. This can often be by recognizing a wallet name on a phone or device, or even realizing that the "USB device" in a drawer is actually a hardware wallet and should be treated as a financial device to be seized appropriately.

Let's learn more about the importance of crypto discovery.

8 The Importance of Discovery

The history of my surname, Furneaux, has a number of interesting explorers in its past. Notable is Captain Tobias Furneaux (August 21, 1735—September 18, 1781; Figure 8.1), who accompanied Captain James Cook on his second voyage to the South Pacific. Tobias was captain of the HMS *Adventure*, while Cook captained the *Resolution*. That voyage resulted in the discovery of a number of island groups, especially the Furneaux Group of islands near Tasmania. Cook is known as "the Circumnavigator," as it is thought that he was the first man to circumnavigate the world in both directions. (Coincidentally, I've ended

Figure 8.1 Captain Tobias Furneaux (August 21, 1735—September 18, 1781)

up living not far from the family home of Tobias in the southern UK county of Devon. However, it is not a coincidence that we named our son Tobias!)

Although the so-called Age of Discovery ran from the 1400s to the 1600s, it is rather typical that it was predominantly focused on discovering America rather than other equally nice areas of the world. America, of course, had been discovered by the indigenous peoples millennia before Christopher Columbus set foot ashore, but they hadn't put a flag in the ground and so it didn't count. Columbus did have a flag and so by the rule of "finders keepers" Europeans "discovered" it. As the flag bearers had also discovered gunpowder, they were able to "discover" much more of America and build McDonald's restaurants on most of it. (Actually, Columbus never set foot on North America; it's just one of those bits of history that got mixed up along the way and ended up with an annual holiday in the United States celebrating something that didn't technically happen.)

What is extraordinary, and somewhat shocking, about Columbus's discovery of America is that he had almost certainly had source maps that guided his journey. This likely included the Martellus map (see Figure 8.2), which showed that if you kept sailing west from Europe you would

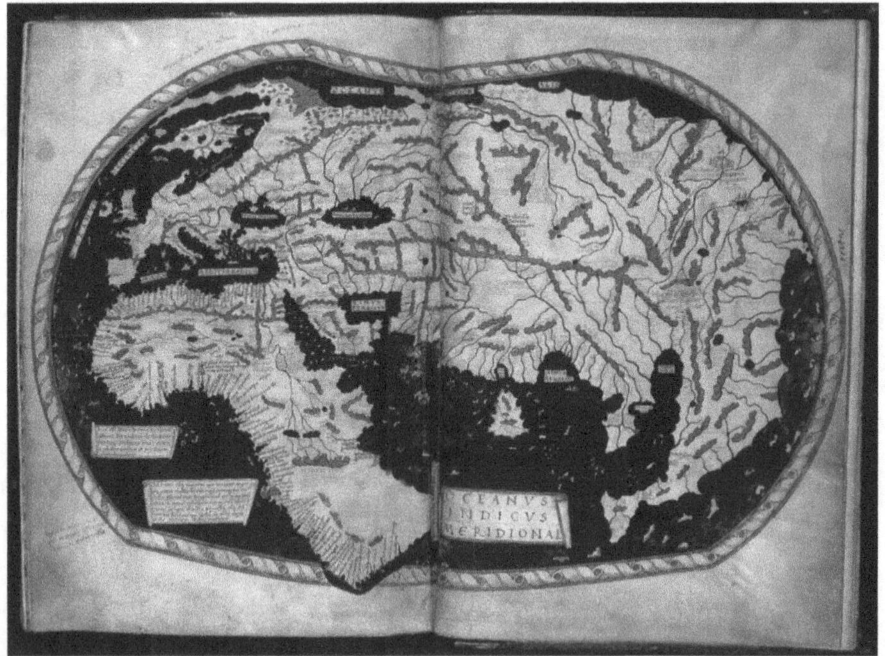

Figure 8.2 Image of the Martellus Map of 1490

bump into China. Of course, this would be correct if the continent of the Americas weren't in the way. When Columbus landed in Cuba, he thought that he was on mainland China and later alighted at Hispaniola, which he thought was Japan. So Columbus discovered a country that had already been discovered and wasn't what he was looking for anyway.

Why is this relevant to a discussion of discovery of evidence related to crimes involving crypto? Because discovery of evidence requires knowing how to look while not being closed-minded as to what you may find. A counterterrorism officer told me once that they were searching a hard drive of a suspect looking for activity related to far-right activity and almost completely missed some innocuous-looking accounts on chat groups that revealed him to be a prolific child groomer. The key is knowing how to look rather than being too narrow-minded as to what you are looking for.

There are several videos that you can find online that demonstrate how easy it is to miss something that you are not expecting to see. Perhaps the most well-known is a video where you are asked to count how many times a ball is thrown between a group of people only to completely miss the person in a gorilla suit who walks through the shot. One example I use in training also has a person leave the group completely and their shirts change color, and unless they have seen it before, no one in the class ever notices. (Search for "the monkey business illusion" and you will find it.) The reason I mention this is not to school you on something you likely already know well, but to highlight the problem we often see where crypto-oriented evidence is missed because it is not being looked for. It could be that you are asked to search a premises of a suspected drug dealer and the briefing officer says that "you are looking for evidence that will support our suspicions that the person is dealing drugs." That mindset has a distinct problem associated with it because it means, like in the video, that you concentrate on counting the balls and miss the gorilla. The briefing creates a sort of investigation bias where you find only what you are looking for.

As we discussed at length in the earlier chapters, crypto use can creep into almost every category of crime and there needs to be an awareness of what crypto evidence looks like and its importance with every person who attends a search or a crime scene or is searching across digital assets such as phones or computers. Often crypto is used as a mechanism for storage of proceeds of crime or for the transmission of criminal funds, and so missing crypto use risks never locating funds for seizure or even not discovering methods by which criminal payments are made. In this chapter we will not attempt to teach the fundamentals of evidential searching and discovery but look at the things that you would be looking for during both premises and digital searches and a few things to look out for that can cause you problems.

Premises Searching: Legal Framework and Search Powers

It is not the place of this book to teach you how to plan and execute a premises search, and certainly laws will differ from country to country and sometimes agency to agency. However, any search of a suspect's environment such as a home or business requires a solid understanding of the applicable legal framework and the process of obtaining the appropriate legal authority. It is an obvious thing to state, but investigators should familiarize themselves with local legislation and consult with legal experts to ensure that their actions are compliant with local or relevant laws.

Whether in a court-ordered search warrant, or by utilization of a legislated search power, it is likely that officers must specify the location to be searched and the items likely to be seized, including any digital assets or physical evidence related to cryptocurrency. The application or authorization for a warrant search power should meet the legal threshold by providing probable cause, demonstrating that there is a reasonable suspicion or belief that evidence of criminal activity can be found at the specified location. This may include a description of the suspected crime, the involvement of cryptocurrency, and any supporting evidence obtained through preliminary investigation.

It is crucial to understand the scope and limitations of a search power warrant. While it may grant investigators the authority to search for specific items related to cryptocurrency, it may not provide unrestricted access to all areas of the premises or devices present therein. Adhering to the scope of the search power warrant is also essential to ensure that any evidence collected is admissible in court and does not violate the rights of the individuals involved in the investigation.

Search Strategies

Handling and Securing Evidence

I'm going to deal with some issues around handling and securing evidence first because it is very important and I always worry that people will not read to the end of the section and miss this bit, because it is a vital couple of paragraphs. We will run through the physical and documentary evidence that you will need to look for in a short while, but you must first stop and think about what it is you are searching for. Much of the evidence related to crypto will give you access to crypto assets, which have a value. Sorry if this is obvious but outside of cash, crypto is the easiest asset to steal and then hide. In fact, we might be able to argue that crypto is easier! If you left a crime scene with $1 million worth of $20 bills stuffed into your coat, someone is going to know about it; if you take a sly photo of a list of seed words with your phone, you now have everything you need to steal the assets quietly when you get home and, if you know what you are doing, have them laundered within the next hour. This has happened on more than one occasion, especially in countries where crypto knowledge may be confined to just a few officers, or even just one, in a department. If you are in an investigative team and find a crypto wallet during a search and your crypto expert tells you that the funds have been moved and the wallet is empty, how are you going to know that they haven't just stolen them? There needs to be protection in place to help prevent this from happening and conversely to protect investigators from false accusations.

We will discuss this more in Chapter 17, "Crypto Seizure," but it is vital for all investigators to understand that seizing a crypto wallet in the form of a private key, seed words, or even a hardware wallet device does not mean that you are the sole owner of those funds. I often equate this to seizing the Porsche car keys from a suspect but leaving the car in the garage, reasoning that you have the keys, and you can pop back tomorrow to get it. What's the problem with this reasoning? Obviously, their girlfriend, husband, lawyer, or anyone else could have a set of keys and by the time you get back to the car you will be faced with an empty garage. This is the same with seizing seed words or a device with a crypto app on it. Just because you have the device or wallet or even a backup seed word list, it doesn't preclude a suspect's collaborator, wife, or dentist from also having been given access and told to move the assets if the police ever arrested them.

This means that you could seize a crypto wallet, head straight back to the lab, engage the help of a financial investigator and/or a cyber expert, and use the seed words that have been found to re-create the wallet. . .only to find that the funds were moved an hour before. This has happened; I've seen it and have had to unpick the issues that resulted. This should not immediately put officers in the crosshairs, suspected of stealing the funds; literally anyone could have done it with access to the same information.

Note: Cryptocurrency cannot be considered to be seized until the funds are moved to an address controlled by the investigator.

In Chapter 17, we will deal in more detail with this risk and consider ways to mitigate it.

Evidence Bags

When you are involved in seizing any evidence small enough to bag and tag, you will put it in an evidence bag, seal it, then write the description, the time, the date, and any investigation-specific information that may be required onto the bag. However, evidence bags are almost always see-through so you can quickly pick them up and ascertain what's inside. This is generally very useful. However, stop and think about seizing a QR code on paper that represents a private key, or a list of seed words that can re-create a wallet. Suddenly, anyone who looks at that evidence bag and can record the information inside can steal the funds. If you are involved in premises searches, just take a moment to stop and think about how many people could see that evidence bag: the person who bagged it, anyone who packs those bags into larger bags or into a vehicle for transportation, and then literally anyone who has access to the evidence locker that it's eventually secured in.

A U.S. law enforcement officer did exactly this and accessed the evidence locker, recorded the seed words on the paper in the evidence bag, and stole the assets. It can and does happen.

The solution is to plan ahead and have access to envelopes that the evidence can be put inside before being put in the see-through bag. It's easy enough to do but requires some forethought.

Body Cameras

If you thought that was a little scary, consider the issues surrounding body cameras. A crime scene or search environment can be full of officers wearing their body cameras, and security of the resulting footage is often not as tight as it could be. A person searching a premises, rifling through paperwork, could pull out a page with a list of seed words printed on the page. Those seed words are now recorded by the camera. He is not sure what the words are and so calls over another officer, who also takes a look and now has also recorded the seed words on her camera. Anyone with access to the footage from either camera can take control of that wallet.

Exactly this sequence of events happened during a routine vehicle stop-and-search by police in the United States. While examining a suspect's wallet, the officer took out a piece of paper and unfolded it to show a list of wallet seed words written on it. All the information needed to steal those assets was clearly recorded on the body camera. Eventually the second officer came over to take a look and suggested that the list of words was "crypto sh*t." The video then went viral on social media (see Figure 8.3).

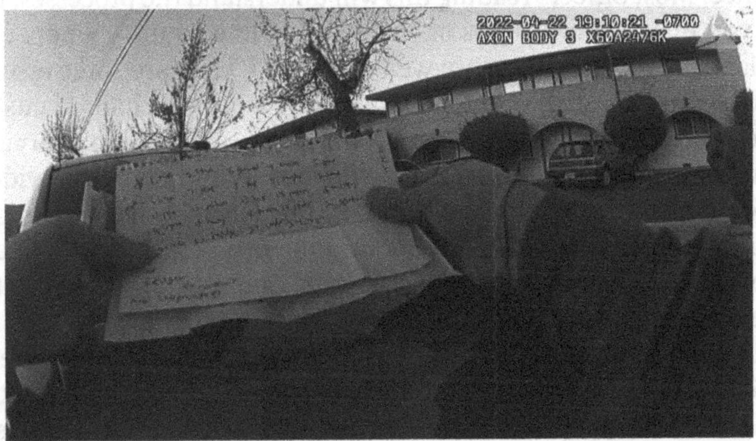

Figure 8.3 Still from the U.S. police stop-and-search that revealed a person's seed words

Photography

Exactly the same issue that we have with body camera footage also relates to on- or off-scene evidence photography. If a search officer or photographer does not understand that what they are putting in an evidence bag and then photographing are details that could possibly be sufficient to steal crypto assets, then problems can ensue. Again, once a picture is taken, perhaps of a list of seed words, who could potentially have access to that image? The picture is on the camera's storage card, which will then be transferred to an evidence folder, likely on the agency's network. What controls are in place to stop anyone on the network from accessing those images? What will happen to that SD card before the images are deleted? Is it deleted securely, as it is a trivial skill to restore deleted files? Your agency will need to consider and resolve these questions, but first and foremost is the training of every person involved in a search to recognize crypto evidence in all its forms.

Chain of Custody

A proper chain of custody in law enforcement is crucial for maintaining the integrity of evidence, and this applies to crypto evidence in exactly the same way as any other type or category of evidence. Ensuring a proper chain of evidence is vital and provides a documented historical record of the custody, control, transfer, analysis, and disposition of the evidence. Most officers reading this will understand the processes; however, you may be new to this or be operating in a country where chain of evidence procedures are not well developed. Here are some essential steps that an officer should follow to ensure a proper chain of custody. I asked a friend of mine to write a few paragraphs with an overview.

First, the officer who collects the evidence should mark the evidence bag for identification with their initials, the date of collection, and the case number. This marking should be done in a way that doesn't compromise the evidence itself. For example, one would not annotate or make any markings on a printed page containing crypto keys or seed words. They should then document in detail where and how the evidence was found, and under what circumstances it was collected.

The collected evidence should be properly packaged and sealed to prevent contamination or tampering. The packaging should be signed and dated by the collecting officer. A mobile phone that is powered on may require sealing in a faraday-screened bag to prevent the phone being wiped or changed remotely.

Next, the evidence must be promptly and securely transported to the police station or evidence storage facility. The evidence should be logged into the evidence management system, noting the date, the time, and the identity of the person submitting the evidence.

Access to the evidence storage area should be strictly controlled and monitored. Only authorized personnel should handle the evidence, and any such handling should be documented, noting the person's identity and the date and purpose of the handling. Each transfer of custody should be signed off by both the person releasing and the person receiving the evidence.

Finally, when the evidence is required for court, it would usually be checked out of the storage area by the officer who will be testifying. The officer should transport the evidence to court and maintain control of it until it is presented in court. The officer should be prepared to testify and demonstrate that the chain of custody was maintained throughout the process.

Following these procedures ensures that the evidence presented in court is exactly as it was when collected, and that it wasn't tampered with or otherwise compromised. This not only helps in the pursuit of justice but also maintains the credibility of the law enforcement agency.

We will discuss in Chapter 17 about crypto asset seizure that it's always best to have "four eyes," another way for describing two people, involved in the seizure process. This ensures that processes are followed and mistakes are minimized and partially protects an officer from accusations of theft should crypto go missing. One could consider that this would also be a useful principle for all of the discovery and evidence acquisition related to crypto.

Okay, with that out of the way, what are we looking for?

Physical Clues

Hardware Wallets

In Chapter 7, "Cryptocurrency Wallets," we covered what a hardware wallet is: essentially a USB device, often with a screen and buttons, that protects the user's crypto private keys. To reiterate, no crypto assets are stored in the hardware wallet, just the private keys for accessing the assets on the blockchain. I had a very nice police officer from the United States attend both my foundation and advanced training where we mention regularly that assets are not stored in wallets, and he still called me a few weeks later and asked how to "get the Bitcoin downloaded" from a Ledger Nano hardware wallet they had found. For my digital forensics friends reading this, as I mentioned previously, you will likely not be able to image (copy) the device without knowing the PIN to unlock it and enable it to be mounted on a computer to be able to copy the contents.

Some researchers have published papers on both hardware wallet imaging and artifacts (a digital artifact refers to any piece of data or digital evidence that can be collected and analyzed to understand activities or events that occurred on a digital device), but I have not tested their findings. Sadly, there have been some exciting projects started at several universities, but the students move on and the projects are not continued.

Some hardware wallets require connecting to a computer to carry out a transaction. Software is installed onto the user's computer and then the hardware device provides the needed private keys, once plugged in, to carry out transactions. Examples include the Trezor and Ledger wallets. There have been several devices launched in recent years that are fully standalone wallets and do not require any software installation on a PC or connecting to any other device. These devices often have a larger screen, and some more comprehensive input buttons. Check out the SafePal S1 hardware wallet as an example. (I am not specifically recommending any of these wallets for use; do your own research.)

A hardware wallet should be treated as a financial asset. Although it will need a PIN to access it, it is no different than a credit card or bank card. Once hardware wallets are seized, cracking them is extremely difficult. Several researchers claim that they have managed to access the PINs and the seed words from some hardware wallets, but this required interfacing directly with the microprocessor and using power glitching (overloading the circuit board to leave it vulnerable) or side-channel/fault injection attacks (fingerprinting power fluctuations while trying different PINs). This type of work will require a specialist lab and some very specific skills outside my wheelhouse and the scope of this book.

In 2022 whitehat hardware hacker Joe Grand, principal engineer at Grand Idea Studio, Inc. posted a YouTube video showing him hacking a hardware wallet and recovering a reported $2 million in crypto. There was some suggestion early on that it was fraudulent until Joe was interviewed by *Wired* magazine at the RSA Conference 2022, which convinced the community that the video was legitimate.

However, if you locate a hardware wallet, all is not lost. Every hardware wallet device comes in a box along with cards for writing the backup seed words on. Time and time again we have found the seed words, written on the provided card, in the original box. Remember, a crypto user will be paranoid about losing their assets and will take steps to ensure that backup seed words are safe. If you find a hardware wallet during a search, keep looking; the seed words will be there somewhere. If, for example, you find a Trezor device and then locate the seed words, simply buy a new Trezor and, when prompted, say that you have seed words during setup. It's very simple indeed, but I recommend playing with the setup and re-creation of wallets ahead of any operation where you could find yourself working on live suspect devices (see Figure 8.4).

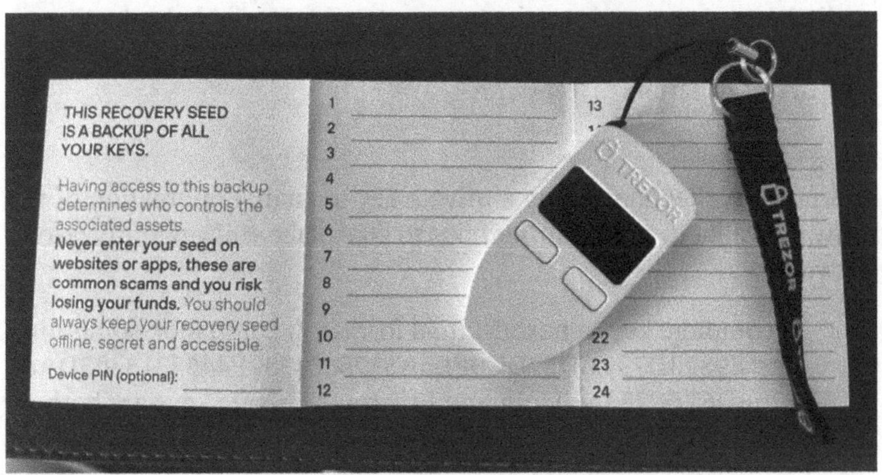

Figure 8.4 A Trezor hardware wallet with backup seed word document

Paper Wallets

I would define a paper wallet as a physical copy or printout of public and/or private keys written in either hexadecimal form or often in the form of a seed word list or QR codes. Although paper wallets are so named because they are generally found on paper (I can't think how else to phrase that without sounding totally obvious), technically it could be made of any material. In fact, there are services and products that will print your keys onto metal and other solid materials.

Search the web for SteelWallet as an example. SteelWallet enables you to add your private key to a steel frame using small metal letters. Although it would technically be classed as "cold storage," I've also heard this type of backup being referred to as a paper wallet even though no paper is involved. Confusing!

Not many people know this. The BIP39 seed word standard used by most wallets has a feature where only the first four letters of a word are needed to uniquely identify the word from the list of 2048 possibilities in the dictionary. So technically, you would only need the first four letters of each word to restore the wallet.

This is important to bear in mind as a search could reveal a list of four-character strings that do not look like a list of seed words from a dictionary, as most investigators are taught. It could also be that a part of the seed words has been torn away or burned, but again just the first four letters are enough.

A paper wallet containing a private key to enable re-creation of the software wallet to allow transactions to take place will generally be one of two types:

- A complete key in hexadecimal format. It could look something like E9873D79C6D87DC0FB6A5778633389F4453213303DA61 F20BD67FC233. Bitcoin and Ethereum private keys are both 64 characters long.

For those of you with an interest in crypto math, we dealt with Bitcoin in more detail in my first book, but a private key is just a random number in the range 1 to $2^{256} - 1$. When written in decimal this is a 78-digit number, which is really, really big. Some reference works will tell you that any random number in the 1 to $2^{256} - 1$ can be used as a private key. This is not strictly true for cryptocurrencies that use elliptic curve cryptography. The mathematical elliptic curve used for finding a matching public key does not encompass all numbers in the 2^{256} range. Bitcoin, Ethereum, and several other systems employ the secp256k1 elliptic curve, which defines a range slightly smaller than 2^{256}. This 78-digit number can be represented as a 256-bit binary number that equates to 32 bytes. Four bits, or ½ byte, known as a "nibble," is required for each hexadecimal character, meaning that a hexadecimal private key will be 64 characters.

(In binary format, numbers represent integers by adding the powers of all bits used (1 rather than a zero). Using 8 bits, we can represent $2^7 + 2^6 + 2^5 + 2^4 + 2^3 + 2^2 + 2^1 + 2^0$, which is 255). Easy!

- Seed word list (sometimes named a mnemonic list but I do not see that term often anymore).

We have already discussed this in some detail but remember that a list of seed words may be split over several lists for security. If a wallet doesn't work when you try to re-create it, consider that the list may be written backward or otherwise obfuscated. Most people do not understand that there is a specific dictionary for seed words and may try to add a word to confuse the list, but these may stand out immediately as non-approved words.

If you find a list with fewer words than you expect, remember that it's generally 12 or 24 words, although it can be a different number; it is trivial to maintain multiple lists that are slightly different or that enable a sort of multisignature protection. Multisig wallets require several parties to approve a transaction. These can be set up in configurations that do not require all parties to approve. This is often written as "multisig 2/3," for example, where there are three signatories to a wallet but only two of the three are needed to generate a transaction. If you head to the website `iancoleman.io/bip39`, you will note that you can generate a new wallet and there is a small tick box titled Show Split Mnemonic Cards. If you give it a try you will see that it splits the seed words up into individual lists, or cards, where only two of the three lists are needed to re-create the whole seed list. An example would be:

CARD 1: cargo legend clerk XXXX urban XXXX husband XXXX XXXX bamboo sail boring tower short select unfair XXXX XXXX credit summer tongue allow XXXX XXXX

CARD 2: XXXX legend XXXX blouse XXXX exhibit husband work lab bamboo sail boring tower XXXX select unfair cigar whip XXXX XXXX XXXX XXXX doll guess

CARD 3: cargo XXXX clerk blouse urban exhibit XXXX work lab XXXX XXXX XXXX XXXX short XXXX XXXX cigar whip credit summer tongue allow doll guess

QR Codes

Although QR codes have been around for a long time it's only been in the past few years that we have begun to see them everywhere to represent links to websites, online services, or values such as a cryptocurrency address or keys. I was in a café in Salcombe, South Devon, in the UK recently and on the table was a QR code; point your phone camera at it and you were taken to the menu where you could order without bothering the wait staff. It seemed a little overkill for a beach café but I always love a bit of tech with my lemon drizzle cake!

QR codes in the crypto world have been around a long time, as manually typing in a Bitcoin or Ethereum address is tiresome and it's easy to make mistakes. Scanning a QR code makes this task much easier. I was involved with a case a few years back where the suspect had the QR code of his private key printed inside a dog tag–shaped locket that he wore around his neck. I won't embarrass my friends in a police force in the Southern Hemisphere any more by naming them, but a senior officer held up a QR code of a suspect on live television while discussing crypto in crime, and the funds had not yet been seized and were subsequently stolen by a sharp-eyed viewer!

Remember that QR codes can be printed on anything, and they should always be treated as a financial evidence item as they could be the key to funds.

Documentation

Although we tend to think about crypto wallets as being an app on a phone or an installed program on a computer, many users do not use local wallets but instead trust their funds to an online exchange or other custodian. Even if a suspect does use a locally installed wallet, it is still very likely that they interact with a crypto service to buy, sell, or convert crypto perhaps into usable fiat currency. This will mean that will likely be both electronic and possibly physical documentation.

This may include such things as printed transaction records, receipts from exchanges for monthly payments or crypto trading, and even printed communication with a service or even with collaborators discussing crypto use. Perhaps the most obvious type of documentation that we routinely seize is bank statements; it can be useful if an investigator notes crypto service company names on the statement to give a financial investigator a heads-up, and they may also encourage active searching for other physical evidence and then, later at the lab, digital evidence.

For these reasons, search personnel should be trained to recognize names and possible names of crypto companies and currencies. This may include names of large exchanges such as Binance, Coinbase, Kraken, Bybit, and others as well as recognition of cryptocurrency names and their abbreviations, as it's often the shortened names that exist on accounts and statements. Some examples of these are:

BCH—Bitcoin Cash

BTC or XBT—Bitcoin

DOGE or XDG—Dogecoin

ETC—Ethereum Classic

ETH—Ethereum

LTC—Litecoin

NEO—Neo

USDC—USD Coin

USDT—Tether

XMR—Monero

XRP—Ripple

ZEC—Zcash

There are of course many, many others, but search officers should note abbreviations on lists, printed spreadsheets, or statements and ensure that they know what they are. Although we focused earlier on finding things like seed word lists, just finding evidence of crypto being used by a suspect can be extremely useful. Finding printed statements related to the purchase, sale, or conversion of crypto will be gold dust to a financial investigator and should never be overlooked. Even just finding a crypto address on a note or printed document can provide a lead for potentially uncovering stored criminal assets or money laundering.

Questioning

Questioning a suspect or witnesses in a case is a specialist skill and we will certainly not be covering it in this book. However, using the old saying "If you don't ask, you don't get," if we neglect to ask a person of interest about their crypto use or their knowledge of others' crypto use, we could easily overlook it.

When questioning a suspect or witness about a crime, the first question should always be something like "Do you use cryptocurrencies?" or in the case of a witness, "In your experience, does the suspect use cryptocurrencies?" From that point on, the questions you ask should aim to gather as much information as possible about the suspect's understanding of cryptocurrencies, their involvement, and the specific details of the alleged crime and how to access any proceeds of crime. Here are some very broad and rather vague questions that you may consider:

General Understanding

- Can you explain how you understand the concept of cryptocurrencies?
- Can you describe how cryptocurrency transactions work?
- Can you explain the concept of blockchain technology and its role in cryptocurrencies?
- Can you explain the use of wallets in cryptocurrency transactions?

Involvement and Knowledge of Cryptocurrencies

- Have you ever used or owned any cryptocurrencies? If yes, which ones?
- Do you use any particular cryptocurrency wallet or exchange? If yes, which ones?
- How long have you been involved with cryptocurrencies?
- Have you ever participated in cryptocurrency mining, trading, DEFI, or similar?
- Do you own any special tokens such as NFTs?
- Do you belong to any online groups, forums, or communities that discuss cryptocurrencies? If so, what are your user names?

Specific Details of the Alleged Crime

- How did you come to possess the cryptocurrencies in question?
- Can you provide the transaction records for the cryptocurrencies in question?
- Are you aware of the crime that was allegedly committed with these cryptocurrencies?
- Were you involved in any way with the transaction or event that is under investigation?
- Did you interact with anyone regarding the cryptocurrencies related to this crime? If so, who?
- Can you explain any suspicious transactions that were made with the cryptocurrencies?
- Are there any witnesses or evidence that can corroborate your version of events?

Technical Details

- Can you provide the private keys for any wallets you own? This would include seed phrases, hardware keys, or passwords.
- Do you know or have you ever interacted with the wallet addresses involved in the crime?
- Have you ever used any cryptocurrency tumblers or mixers (services used to obfuscate the source or destination of a cryptocurrency transaction)?
- Do you use a VPN or other privacy tools when conducting cryptocurrency transactions?

This is in no way an exhaustive list but gives you some idea as to the categories of questions that you may pose or the direction you can head.

Remember that the context of the questioning, the rights of the suspect, and jurisdictional issues could affect how these questions should be asked or whether they can be asked at all. In many jurisdictions, for example, rights may need to have been read or legal counsel would need to be present for this questioning; otherwise it could affect the use of the evidence in an eventual court case.

Searching Digital Assets

I use the term *digital assets* as it is a good descriptive catchall for so many different devices that can be seized during a search. This may include:

- Personal desktop and laptop computers. I was involved in a case in the north of England where the suspect threw his laptop like a Frisbee out of his bedroom window as the police burst in through the front door. It ended up in a pond and none of the officers wanted to get wet!
- Micro-sized computers such as Raspberry Pi and similar.
- Mobile phones. Cell phones just used to be phones; you could make a call and perhaps send a text message. Of course, modern phones are powerful computers in their own right and can contain significant data, history, and applications including cryptocurrency wallets, and care needs to be taken when seizing them. We will discuss this in Chapter 17, but if a phone is unlocked and usable, thought should be given to seizing crypto from any mobile wallets immediately. Applicable laws related to working on a suspect's device directly should be understood and applied.
- Tablets. Same comments as mobile phones.
- External hard drives, USB keys, and storage cards (SD cards, for example). Remember that at the time of writing you can buy a 1TB microSD card, which is very small and easy to hide or even swallow!
- Digital still and video cameras. I worked on a case where the suspect had created an encrypted container on an SD card that was kept in a Canon camera along with thousands of photos. He just plugged in the camera, and it appeared as a drive on his computer; he opened the encrypted container and accessed his wallet software. It's easy to miss a camera when you are looking for a computer.
- Portable gaming devices. Most have onboard storage and often extendable SD card storage.
- Game consoles such as Xbox or PlayStation. Most although not all have accessible internal storage. A colleague told me about a case he worked on where the suspect pushed an SD card through the ventilation slots in a PlayStation 3 when the police knocked on his door to hide his collection of illegal images. Perhaps it's

a good idea to give things a shake, as generally electronic goods shouldn't rattle!

- Servers. Although a server is just a computer running different software, it might be that a suspect has rack-mounted servers or similar. If you suspect that a computer is running as a server, it may be worth having a cyber investigator check if there are remote clients connected to it before disconnecting the power. This could identify other computers that are of interest or even provide intelligence as to co-conspirators. Just using a simple tool to grab the RAM will enable that information to be acquired later by a digital forensics practitioner.
- Networking equipment such as routers, switches, Wi-Fi extenders, and so on. Although most equipment of this type does not have significant data storage, they will often contain log files that that be very helpful.

A friend of mine at the police cyber unit in North Wales worked on a fascinating case where the log files of a Wi-Fi router simultaneously cleared a suspect and identified a murderer. Sadly, a young woman was found murdered, discovered by her boyfriend who had just returned from a short trip. He had gone away overnight for work and when he came back in the morning he reportedly found her body. He struggled to account for his specific location at the time of the murder in the early hours of the morning, and he became the prime suspect. This was until my cyber investigator friend was able to extract the log files from the home Wi-Fi router. As the boyfriend lived at the house, his phone automatically connected to the Wi-Fi when he was close by, and this confirmed that he was in the house at the time the woman was found but critically not at the coroner's estimated time of death. However, another device was discovered to have automatically connected to the Wi-Fi router at two a.m., around the time of the murder. This device was found to belong to the woman's previous partner and the father of her children with whom she was in a custody dispute. This was a brilliant find and it provided strong evidence to pursue.

- Smart speakers. As a general point, remember that smart speakers are often listening for trigger words, and it may be possible to subpoena recordings from the manufacturer.

- Camera devices such as CCTV and video doorbells. CCTV systems almost always used to record to hard drive devices within the premises. It is now common, especially in residential systems, for footage to be uploaded to cloud services. This is true for both the mainstream suppliers such as Ring doorbells and cameras and less-known manufacturers, often from the Far East who run their own cloud storage servers. Internal camera footage may expose a suspect using a computer or device to deal crypto and may offer clues to the investigator.
- Point-of-sale systems such as credit card machines.
- SIM cards.

Legal Framework and Warrants

As mentioned in the brief section on legality in the premises search section, this book does not purport to be a legal document and certainly cannot cover all of the legislative systems that exist around the world for dealing with digital assets.

There are several parts to the examination of digital assets, which will likely all have their own legislative directives. Let's consider two of them:

1. Analysis of copied data, otherwise known as imaging.

Forensic analysis of evidence usually works on the principle of "Do no harm"; in very simple terms, don't taint or change the evidence in any way. A simple example would be not picking up the smoking gun at a crime scene with no gloves on, as you will cover in it in your own fingerprints and possibly eradicate fingerprints that were already there. Worst case, you could put yourself in the frame for the shooting! Most legislative systems have laws or legal principles that govern this process. For many years digital forensic investigations worked on the same principle of "Do no harm"; essentially, do not do anything to the phone or computer that could make any changes to the data on the device. This meant that the device was ostensibly the same as when the suspect last used it, meaning that any evidence extracted from the device could likely be attributed to them. This was often achieved by "hard" powering down the device or computer—for example, pulling the plug out of the wall of a desktop computer. This meant that the hard drive could be extracted and copied, or imaged, without making any changes to it. Analysis was then done on the copy. This is still an accepted process, and it is likely that your legal system will have laws that control this type of practice and you will need to make yourself familiar with these before any seizure of digital equipment and data.

2. Examination or triage of live running systems.

Around 20 years ago I was working with an American investigator named Drew Fahey who had recently left the U.S. Air Force Office of Special Investigations. Air Force OSI, as they were known, had been involved in some really leading-edge cyber investigations and Drew, along with others, had been working on the tools and procedures for grabbing data from live running machines before they were powered down and copied. He built a tool called Helix, which was the default tool for almost a decade for this type of data extraction. The problem was that running any investigation or data extraction tool on a computer made changes to it. These changes were small but nevertheless overwrote some areas of memory and also insignificant amounts of data on hard drives. This was highly controversial and when I presented the concepts at the UK F3 Forensics conference with another great investigator, Jim Gordon, there was a lot of silence in the room accompanied with crossed arms and dissatisfied mumbling. However, as tools improved it became possible to just acquire the RAM of the computer and then investigate the live data once the computer was shut down. Tools such as Volatility (`https://www.volatilityfoundation.org`) completely changed our view of this technique, and over the next few years most agencies switched their best practice processes to include the acquisition of RAM (random access memory) where possible. However, with the emergence of crypto, having laws available to work on a live machine became even more vital. Phones such as the iPhone from Apple or even modern laptops are very secure devices with inbuilt encryption and methods that make cracking passwords or longer PINs very difficult. A suspect may be running wallet apps with access to significant funds from a phone that will likely be protected by a PIN, plus a type of biometric technology, and then the wallet probably has a password too. A wallet on a computer may have two-factor authentication, meaning that gaining access to the wallet requires both the computer password and also the PIN from the second device to access authentication codes. Life as an investigator becomes much easier if you can gain access to the device while it is still live, giving you the chance to move the funds immediately before the device auto-locks.

Working on a live device brings risks; it enables the officer to have complete control of a wallet, and this can result in theft by a dishonest officer (it's happened more than once). Already deleted data can be overwritten, preventing its recovery, and, somewhat critically, many powered devices can be wiped remotely by a co-conspirator.

To mitigate these risks requires sound laws and agreed departmental or national procedures that need to be carefully followed by the officer, and all steps taken must be carefully recorded. We will discuss this later in Chapter 17. This also requires the officer to be well trained and practiced in working on a live device. If the first time you are faced with a live phone with a wallet open with several million dollars' worth of crypto on it is when you are on scene looking at a suspect's device, you are in trouble. Training and repeated practice is absolutely vital. In Chapter 10, we have a contribution from a friend of mine who carried out a crypto seizure on a live device on a moving train surrounded by the public. It's a great read!

I specifically differentiated "agreed departmental or national procedures" in the last paragraph as although the law is the law, the application and procedures agreed upon may differ—for example, from a local police force to a national counterterrorism unit—and a well-written piece of legislation should account for these differences.

Remember that a device that has been used to extract live data or to carry out an on-scene asset seizure should still then be seized, bagged, and tagged, in the proper way. A police officer from the West Coast of the United States told me about the first time he had to seize a very large amount (several million dollars) of Bitcoin using a suspect's computer on scene. He was so stressed that he was literally sweating, and after the funds had been moved he closed the laptop in relief and then left it on the desk. It was only when he was sitting in his vehicle checking his notes that he remembered that the suspect's laptop was still where he left it!

Digital Forensics

There are some good books available about digital forensics and especially live data acquisition and analysis; there are also some decent YouTube videos and other free training. Although these sources can be very good, there is no substitute for peer-tested, commercial training from trusted training companies. If you are going to be using digital forensics software to carry out your investigation, then again, training and certifications can be very important. If a case comes to court and you are asked to verify to the court your experience and abilities, saying that you read a few books and watched a few videos may not be sufficient to satisfy the judge. It is good to have the appropriate certificates from the right companies.

There are a number of primary digital forensics tools available for analyzing computers that have been around for years, such as Encase, FTK, and X-Ways; however, a tool that has found a niche is Axiom from Magnet Forensics. Axiom can be run against computer data such as hard drives or memory dumps and mobile phone data. It focuses on the extraction of both live and deleted digital artifacts and can be a very good tool for triage of large amounts of data. Jad Saliba, the founder of Magnet Forensics, told me that "the tool will automatically extract addresses and transaction IDs, depending on the app. We also support the main Bitcoin client on Windows (along with identifying other crypto clients, but not processing artifacts from them), and then on mobile we support these apps (see Figure 8.5)."

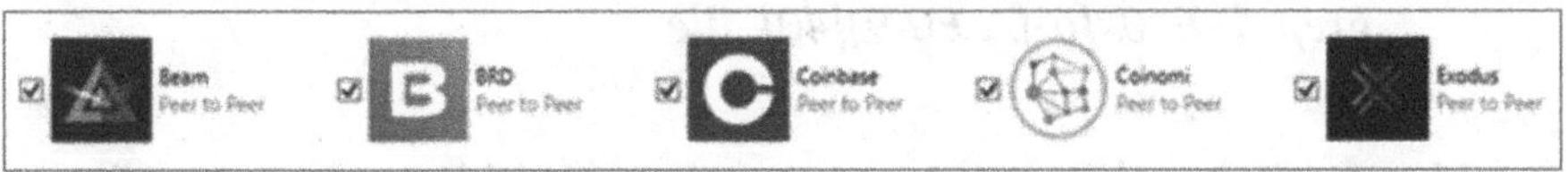

Figure 8.5 Examples of applications supported by Magnet Forensics tools

This is a good tool to start with especially if your lab already has the tool available for use. However, if you are looking for artifacts of other wallets or nonprimary crypto addresses, then you are going to need to do some manual work. This could include writing scripts for software tools such as Encase or building pattern searches, such as grep searches, to identify patterns that could be crypto addresses, private keys, and so on. If you don't know how to write grep searches, there are many resources online to help you.

If you are a little more technical, this box may help you with writing searches. Writing things such as grep searches can be complex, and this can be an area where an AI engine with coding ability can help you.

I tested it with ChatGPT4 at the time of writing and it did a pretty good job. The response was oriented toward a user with a Linux operating system, hence using the BASH shell. I asked:

"Can you write me a grep expression to locate Ethereum addresses, please?" (It's always good to be polite.)

ChatGPT responded:

> *Ethereum addresses are 42 characters long and begin with "0x." Each character after the prefix is a hexadecimal digit (0–9, a–f, or A–F).*
>
> *Here is a basic grep expression that should work:*
>
> *bash*
>
> *grep -E '0x[a-fA-F0-9]{40}' file*
>
> *This command will search a file helpfully named "file" for Ethereum addresses. If you want to search in a different file, simply replace "file" with the path to the file you want to search in.*
>
> *Remember that grep is case sensitive by default. If you want to ignore case, use the "-i" option:*
>
> *```bash*
>
> *grep -i -E '0x[a-fA-F0-9]{40}' file*
>
> *```*

Also note that this regular expression could have false positives if there is other data in the file that matches the pattern but isn't an Ethereum address.

It's also important to note that these grep commands will find Ethereum addresses anywhere in a line. If you specifically want to find Ethereum addresses that stand alone on a line, you can use the beginning-of-line (^) and end-of-line ($) anchors:

> *bash*
>
> *grep -i -E '^0x[a-fA-F0-9]{40}$' file*
>
> *This command will only find lines that consist entirely of an Ethereum address.*

I thought this was a decent response. Of course, Bitcoin addresses are a bit more complex, as they can start with a variety of characters and have different lengths, but I gave it a try anyway.

I next asked, "Please write me a grep search that will find all varieties of Bitcoin addresses."

The reply code used egrep rather than grep (just extended grep) but again looked to be pretty solid.

> *egrep -o -r -i "([13][a-km-zA-HJ-NP-Z1-9]{25,34})|(bc1[a-zA-HJ-NP-Za-z0-9]{25,39})"*
>
> *The first part of the pattern ([13][a-km-zA-HJ-NP-Z1-9]{25,34}) tries to match addresses, which start with 1 or 3 and are followed by 25–34 alphanumeric characters excluding lowercase "l," "I," "O," and "0."*
>
> *The second part (bc1[a-zA-HJ-NP-Za-z0-9]{25,39}) is for Bech32, otherwise known as SegWit addresses, which start with "bc1" followed by 25–39 alphanumeric characters excluding "1," "b," "i," and "o."*

Here's a brief explanation of the egrep command line options used:

-o: Only output the parts of lines that match the pattern.
-r: Read all files under each directory, recursively.
-i: Ignore case distinctions in the pattern and the file.

Remember that grep will only show you if the lines match; it will not validate if it's a correctly created Bitcoin address or not. It's just a simple regex match.

It is possible to check if a Bitcoin address is valid in a variety of ways. If you are happy with tinkering in Python code, then there are two libraries that can be installed from PIP, "bitcoin" and "eth_utils." Both of these can be used to validate if an address is legitimate; obviously the bitcoin library for Bitcoin addresses and the eth_utils for Ethereum style addresses.

Knowing if an address has a balance is vital, of course, as it may represent criminal funds. You can just do a search for an address on a blockchain explorer manually. However, if you would like to automatically check if an address has a balance, then sites such as `blockchain.info` and `blockchair.com` have APIs that can be useful for this. For example, at the time of writing just putting the following into a browser URL bar will check an address for a balance and return a raw text result:

```
https://blockchain.info/q/addressbalance/{address}
```

For example:

```
https://blockchain.info/q/addressbalance/bc1q7cyr
fmck2ffu2ud3rn515a8yv6f0chkp0zpemf
```

Returns:

```
97253917727
```

This value is in satoshis so you will need to count eight decimal places to give you a balance of around 972.5 Bitcoin.

Of course, if you are comfortable writing some code, then it will be straightforward to write a Python script that checks a file for Bitcoin- or Ethereum-style addresses, validates them, and then checks for a balance.

Again, if you are just learning to write code, then you could just ask an AI engine to build something that will extract addresses from a file, validate them, and then check for a balance. Just be aware that the resulting output is unlikely to work "out of the box" and will need some playing with to get right.

There are some excellent commercial tools to help you with this task such as TRM Tactical from TRM Labs, whom I do work with.

Hardware Examination

This section is not going to educate you to be a digital forensics person—that takes years of work and frankly should be the subject of its own book—but we will talk about the basics and make a few suggestions for those of you already working in the area.

Storage Devices

Any hardware storage device should, where possible, be forensically copied before analysis is carried out. This is done using write-blocking technology so the investigating computer does not make any changes to the storage medium. There are also dedicated hardware devices that can do this job for you.

Analysis can be done manually by mounting a file system, but this will miss any deleted or hidden files on the volume. It is recommended that commercial software be used by an investigation lab such as FTK,

Encase, X-Ways, Axiom, or others. All of these tools go some way to locating crypto artifacts, but as previously mentioned, there are no tools at the time of writing dedicated just to extracting crypto addresses and wallet artifacts, so you will need to do your own research and even build your own tools.

Deleted files should always be recovered and scanned for evidence of crypto use; searching for wallet names, grep searching for crypto addresses, and so on can provide evidence of crypto use even if there is limited context from deleted data. It's always worth watching digital forensics forums and speaking to other investigators who may have already done the heavy lifting for you and developed simple tools or scripts to help. Sadly, a quick search for "enscript cryptocurrency artifacts" only found one simple grep-based script and a link to my book from 2018! Some more work in this area by excellent companies such as Magnet Forensics would be much appreciated.

A very useful tool is a script to locate seed word lists. Seed words, as we have learned, are the private key, and finding a list of seed words can be the difference between seizing funds and missing them. A colleague and I wrote a Python program for this a couple of years ago that is now owned by TRM Labs, so I'm unable to share it here. However, it is very useful to be able to do it and we have had significant success against RAM dumps, as wallet software often writes the seed phrase into RAM when the wallet is accessed.

Such a program is surprisingly complex to write, and this breakout box will only interest digital forensics people who can program. Although it is just a list of words, the problem is that a computer hard drive or phone is chock-full of millions of words from the almost infinite number of apps that are available. This is exacerbated if the device is based on the English language, meaning that every word will be in the same language as the seed words. To write a script to locate words from a hard drive, for example, you need to consider the following:

1. Extract all ASCII strings from the binary file.
2. Start searching for words that are in the seed word dictionary or preferably all dictionaries (BIP-39/Electrum, etc.).
3. When you find a word in the dictionary, look for the next word near it in the binary file. Is the next word in the dictionary?

   a. If yes, save the words and their offsets in the file and then go to point 3 until you have a list of 12 or 24 words.
   b. If no, move on to the next word and then go to 3 once you find a hit.
4. Once you have seed word list candidates, usually *many* lists of more than 12 words which exist in the dictionary, consider the offset gap between them and score them as likely connected or not.
5. Candidates where all words appear to be fairly close in the binary file offset have a greater chance of being real lists.
6. Test them, either by manually adding them to a wallet or by automating the task programmatically.

The script that we wrote (and major thumbs-up to my friend Ben Barnes for his code) worked well but was slow. I think that some machine learning would help speed this process up significantly.

If you write something, please let me take a look!

RAM Analysis

As mentioned briefly earlier in the chapter, most cyber and digital forensics practitioners will agree that if a computer is running, the RAM/memory should be acquired before the machine is powered down. The tools available commercially such as FTK and Magnet's Axiom do a fairly good job of being able to carve data from memory, but it is worth looking at Volatility (`https://www.volatilityfoundation.org`) and also a tool by Swedish researcher Ulf Frisk called MemProcFS (`https://github.com/ufrisk/MemProcFS`).

Both tools enable the investigator to extract a vast amount of information, but this could include files that were open on the device at the time of seizure. This could include wallet files, text files from software wallets, web pages connected to crypto exchanges, and emails to co-conspirators; the list is endless. Although you may reason that these files will be on the primary hard disk, that may not be the case. Browsing history may be set to private; files may be encrypted on the disk but were helpfully unpacked in RAM and are fully readable. IP addresses of remote servers and websites might be available; passwords and even encryption keys can be recovered. Live data can also be vital in knowing what the user was running at the time of seizure and also what programs they have run previously; all is available in RAM. Although RAM analysis is a complex task and significant training and experience is needed to do it well, it can be very worthwhile when it comes to crypto artifacts and should be considered. As an aside, for the digital forensics people among you, it is also worth considering the benefits of extracting and analyzing any Pagefile or Hibernation files that may exist.

Volatility is a freely downloadable command line tool; although there are a few aftermarket graphical user interfaces, the software works best in its command-line mode. It can extract a vast amount of data from a memory dump with dozens of commands and third-party plug-ins for most primary operating systems (Windows, Mac, and Linux). It does require some technical capability to run, but the results can be superb.

I recommend using a combination of Volatility 2 and 3; even though version 2 is deprecated, I still find it useful. You need Python installed to run it, but the help files are very useful and building the commands fairly straightforward. I won't go through the setup and use of Volatility, as there are quite a number of steps, and if you are already comfortable in a command shell, then you will work it out fairly easily.

MemProcFS can provide similar data to Volatility from a RAM dump but uniquely can mount the file system just from the memory dump, providing you with a folder structure and recovered files in their right positions in the folder structure. This means that you can browse the file system to the installed location of a crypto software wallet, for example, and locate files and other artifacts related to the wallet. This also means that you can find files under a particular user profile, making the findings more attributable (see Figure 8.6).

Running MemProcFS is very straightforward.

1. Ensure you are running Python 3.6 or later.
2. Download and unzip the latest version from `https://github.com/ufrisk/MemProcFS/releases/latest`.
3. Install the DoAnyKey library from `https://github.com/dokan-dev/dokany/releases`.
4. Run the command **memprocfs.exe -mount s -device c:\temp\win10x64-dump.raw -v**.
5. This will mount the RAM dump called win10x64. . .at drive letter S on your operating system with extra verbosity.

6. Open your file explorer, browse to the S drive, and start your investigation.
7. The file system can be found under the NTFS folder.

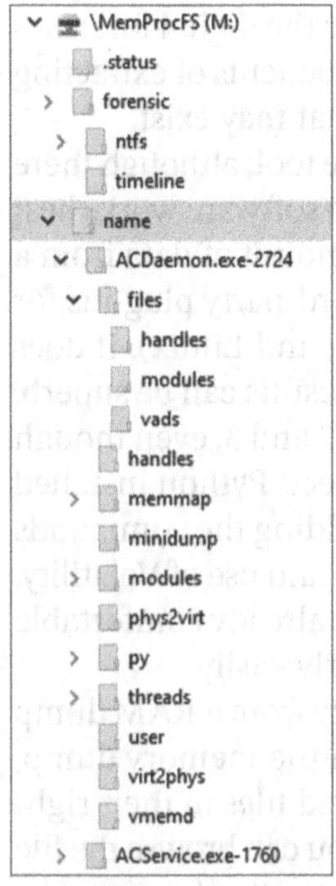

Figure 8.6 File system and other artifacts mounted by memprocfs

What are you looking for?

In simple terms, you are looking anything related to crypto usage. This could be wallet software, crypto addresses; it's a pretty long list, to be honest. Let's look at some of the quick wins:

Wallet applications. Identify wallet software/app names to search for. Just searching Google for "list of cryptocurrency wallets" is a good start. I like the regularly updated list that can be found at `https://cryptoslate.com/products/category/wallets` (see Figure 8.7).

When looking at suspect wallets, remember that a software wallet such as Electrum can support many wallets, each with their own private keys. These are text files found in the folder structure of the Electrum

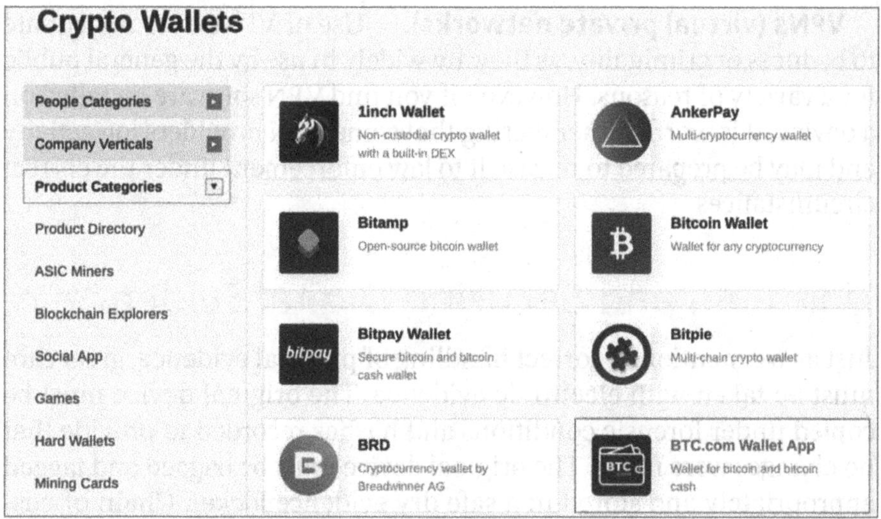

Figure 8.7 List of Wallets Found on the Cryptoslate website

software. If the user has not chosen to encrypt a wallet, then the text file can be completely readable including the private key and seed words.

Cryptocurrency exchange accounts. Internet history and saved bookmarks can reveal use of crypto exchanges, as can the names of plugins for browsers such as the Coinbase or Metamask browser wallets.

Email communication from exchanges can also be a vital source of information, as can social media posts and direct messaging via social media. Remember that computers can also be set up to mirror some messaging apps from mobile devices such as WhatsApp and others, which can reveal everything from deals being done to work with co-conspirators. When investigating crypto frauds, look out for social media "wealth" posts, which may identify real-world assets such as cars and jewelry.

As discussed previously, grep searches for crypto addresses may not provide context or attribution but can be a useful in at least identifying crypto use and perhaps addresses to start looking at to see if they fit with your case. Remember that just because you find a crypto address on a device, perhaps from deleted space, it does not mean it is definitely owned by the suspect. The address could have come from a website or an app or belong to someone else.

Dark web. Evidence of use of dark web browsers should be examined carefully. The browser or memory artifacts may record addresses of dark web sites visited and other hidden dark web activity.

VPNs (virtual private networks). Use of VPNs does not equate to badness or criminality, as they are widely in use by the general public for a variety of reasons. However, if you find VPN software installed on a device, it is worth remembering that some VPN providers log activity and may be prepared to release it to law enforcement under the correct circumstances.

Handling and Securing Digital Evidence

Just as we mentioned correct handling of physical evidence, great care must be taken with electronic evidence. The original device must be copied under forensic conditions and hashes recorded to provide that no changes were made. The original device must be bagged and tagged appropriately and stored in a safe dry evidence locker. Chain of custody must be maintained, and should the other side of an investigation, whether defense or prosecution experts, wish to recopy the device, then this should be done by a qualified individual and under the scrutiny of the device holder. It is always better if the opposing experts agree to work on the existing copy and analyze the chain of custody and copy/image notes rather than to recopy the device.

The Role of Exchanges

The history of cryptocurrency exchanges' cooperation with law enforcement is not one that many of them will be proud of in years to come. With just a couple of notable exceptions, exchanges have routinely accepted funds that they knew full well came from criminality and actively ignored requests for help from law enforcement and in some cases even frustrated investigations into things as important as terrorism funding and child abuse payments. This was all done in the name of privacy and freedom from traditional financial systems but frankly was just profiteering from the very worst of humanity and the suffering of others. There were a few exchanges that interfaced with law enforcement early on and even helped with investigations, but in the early years this was all too rare. As crypto began to be owned and traded by the more mainstream public, some exchanges realized that they needed to clean up their act and start to work for the good of the public, not just their criminal customers. For yet others it took threats of punitive action against the companies and prison terms for directors from government agencies such as the U.S. Department of Justice (DOJ) before any change came about. As I write this chapter we do find ourselves in a better crypto world where an agency can request information about a user or transaction from an exchange and receive information to help an investigation proceed.

The reason that I have included this section in this chapter on discovery is that some of the larger exchanges are now working in line with banking-oriented legislation and producing reports of suspicious behavior. I've decided not to discuss the specifics of the algorithms used to identify a suspicious account or transaction, as I would not want to help criminals evade them. However, if you live in most Western countries and open a bank account and deposit $10 million into it, someone at the bank is going to want to know where the money came from. This is the same with many exchanges, who will not just accept a large deposit without some provenance of the funds.

Some exchanges are now producing what are known as suspicious activity reports (SARs), sometimes termed suspicious transaction reports (STRs). The term *SAR* is used more often, as the *T* in *STR* only relates to transactions, whereas suspicious activity is considered to be related to a broader set of data.

When an account or transaction is flagged as suspicious, the exchange will communicate quite a significant amount of data, including KYC, IP address, and transaction history, to law enforcement. This is a great development and is really appreciated as it can help agencies get ahead of frauds, money laundering, and other activities that they may have otherwise been unaware of.

The challenge for a financial intelligence unit (FIU) can be how they cope with often an avalanche of reports. Good processes are in place for dealing with bank-generated SARs, and similar procedures need to be put in place for crypto exchange SARs. However, this means that more financial investigators need to be trained in crypto investigations to be able to separate the proverbial wheat from the chaff and be able to choose the best and most worthwhile cases to pursue. The ability to triage cases quickly using commercial tools can be a key aspect of this, as they may be able to quickly connect the source or destination of funds to known suspicious addresses, mixers, criminal groups, and so on.

I hope that exchanges and other virtual asset service providers (VASPs) continue to proactively work to discover illegal funds or activity on their platforms and engage with law enforcement to help clean up the crypto space.

Senior Officers/Management

Just a brief word to senior officers or management who may be called upon to plan and implement search and discovery operations. If you are reading this paragraph, I'm hoping this means that you have read this whole chapter and understood its implications.

It is up to you to ensure that front-line officers and search staff are trained and equipped to recognize crypto-oriented evidence and be able to secure it in an appropriate way. It falls to you to understand the legislation that relates to lawful searching and discovery and apply it to searches that may turn up evidence of crypto use.

UK police use the acronym PLAN in relation to searches, and it applies well to any jurisdiction:

P—Proportionality

L—Legality

A—Accountability

N—Necessity

Always ask yourself, does my search fit these four criteria?

Understand the legislative powers available to you. Are they court-ordered or police powers and how can they be applied appropriately and proportionately?

This will be discussed in more detail in Chapter 17.

Summary

To conclude, the discovery phase of an investigation involving crypto is vital; if wallets or addresses are not found, then there is no investigation to be done and evidence, intelligence, and proceeds of crime can be missed.

This chapter has only scratched the surface. It is vital that everyone from front-line officers and investigators through digital forensics and up to senior management understand the need for crypto discovery and implement training into their departments.

Hopefully, new tools and techniques will be developed by law enforcement and private industry to make this task easier in the coming years.

9 The Workings of Bitcoin and Derivatives

It is always difficult when communicating technical information just how deep down the proverbial rabbit hole one should go. We have the same problem when building training, giving a conference speech—and of course writing this book. This problem can be solved by considering your audience, but when publishing a book for a world audience, it is a rather tricky thing to do. In my first book, *Investigating Cryptocurrencies* (Wiley, 2018), I took a very technical approach because, as previously mentioned, I mistakenly thought that all crypto investigations would be done by very technical people. However, this book is aimed at a much broader scope of investigators, from the person just starting out to the person who is already quite familiar with the concepts involved. I'm sure the reviews will let me know if I managed to hit that balance.

This chapter focuses on the workings of Bitcoin and is not technically deep but hopefully reaches a level that is useful to you as an investigator and helps you understand the fundamental concepts. Please don't skip this chapter; having a firm grasp of the underlying workings of, for example, how a transaction works will help you understand the principles of tracking funds, of understanding and identifying change addresses owned by a user, and so on. This will help you to be able to carry out investigations manually, with freely available blockchain viewers, and also help you to visualize what a commercial investigation tool is doing when it builds a graph for you.

The second reason it is important to understand the fundamental workings of a cryptocurrency is to be able to give appropriate evidence in court. If you are cross-examined in court about how you made a particular finding or discovery and your answer is that you clicked a button in your commercial tool and there it was, that's not going to be a popular answer. It is vital that you be able to explain how the evidence was found, how tracking the funds works, how an address could be identified and attributed, and so on. It is also important when the companies that build the commercial tools are disinclined to discuss functions of their software that are confidential and that perhaps contain unique intellectual property. This is not a criticism; anything disclosed in open court is generally public record and this could harm a company's competitive edge. In my experience, courts are usually unwilling to protect this type of disclosure unless it is a covert process, which may harm a law enforcement agency's ability to further deploy a technique or tool. Your legislature may be different, of course.

Bitcoin Is a Blockchain-Based UTXO Cryptocurrency

To understand how to investigate movement on funds on the Bitcoin blockchain, you first need to understand what a blockchain is and what the acronym UTXO means.

We discussed part of this process in Chapter 6, "Mining: The Key to Cryptocurrencies," but let's look at it briefly again and extend that knowledge into understanding a blockchain. Entire books have been written about blockchain technology and the companies that do nothing but build them or convert existing software systems to use them. But if anyone tells you that blockchains are complicated, they are almost certainly selling something, because the underlying concept is simple.

A blockchain is just a ledger. Imagine if you are running a small business and want to keep a list of all transactions with suppliers and customers. You could just record on paper a line for each transaction with fields such as who a payment is from, its destination, and the amount. Very simple indeed. This is fundamentally all the primary fields in the Bitcoin ledger (there are many other fields that enable transactions to take place and be secured). But what differentiates a paper-based or spreadsheet-based ledger from a blockchain?

In the case of Bitcoin, each 10 minutes the list of new transactions are locked into a group called a block (different blockchains have different timings). That block is locked cryptographically through the process of mining or validating, as discussed in Chapter 6. Next, a new block of transactions is started and after 10 minutes this new block is locked. However—and I'm describing this very simplistically—this time we lock the block, including the transactions in all the blocks that came before it. This links the blocks together cryptographically, forming a chain of blocks, or a blockchain. Anyone trying to change transaction data in a block would have to calculate the locks for all the blocks above it in the chain, which after about six blocks is virtually impossible with current computing speeds. The locks on each block use very strong cryptography, like very strong codes, making it virtually impossible for anyone to change the entries in the blockchain ledger. That's it. That's a blockchain.

So, if anyone asks you what a blockchain is, you can just answer "Transactions that are locked into blocks using cryptography and the blocks are linked together in a cryptographic chain. A chain of blocks, a blockchain." They will be very impressed. Actually, in my experience at social events when people find out what I do they will nod politely, smile, and then wander off to speak to someone who does something like art or social media or something interesting like that.

Most cryptocurrencies use blockchains of one flavor or another. But what makes a cryptocurrency a UTXO currency like Bitcoin?

UTXO

UTXO stands for unspent transaction output. What does that mean?

Let's go back to physical money transactions to understand it. Let's say that you want to buy a lemon drizzle cake in your local baker's shop. You have in your wallet or purse two $10 bills. While they are in your wallet, they are unspent outputs from another transaction. They didn't appear in your wallet magically; you maybe went to an ATM and withdrew them from the bank or even carried out a transaction that gave you two $10 bills in change. You buy some cakes and the total you owe the baker is $13. The only way you can pay for the cakes is to hand to the shopkeeper both $10 bills—you cannot tear one of the bills into thirds, so you have to transact the whole note. These are the "inputs" of the transaction. The shopkeeper will hand you change, perhaps a $5 bill and two $1 bills, $7 in total, and will keep the $10 bills as their payment. The bills kept by the shopkeeper and the change given to you are the "outputs" of the transaction.

If you want to know how much money you have, you look in your wallet and add up all the unspent transactions (UTXOs). In this case, you will have the $5 bill and two $1 bills. You add them up and find a balance in your wallet of $7.

In the same way, if the shopkeeper wants to know how much money they have, they will look in the till and add up all their unspent transactions to get a total.

It is almost exactly the same with Bitcoin. If you have received a single payment of 1.2 Bitcoin and you want to buy something for 1 Bitcoin, you have to transact the whole 1.2 and receive the 0.2 (minus fees) as change. You can't split the UTXO in the same way that you can't tear up a dollar bill to pay less than a dollar.

The key difference is that when you "look" in your crypto-wallet for your balance, the funds are not actually in your wallet. They are stored on the blockchain ledger as unspent transaction outputs, which are linked to your private key. The private key in your wallet looks at the blockchain for any UTXOs that it can control, adds them up, and gives you a balance.

In the broadest terms, if you want to know how much Bitcoin there is in total on the blockchain, you would just calculate the sum of all UTXOs in the system, which would represent the total value of all tokens in the system.

In Chapter 11, "The Workings of Ethereum and Derivatives," you will see that it works very differently—more like a bank account, where you can pay any amount you wish from your wallet balance and it simply deducts that payment from the total. The two systems work differently, but the differences and how you follow the flow of funds through the system are critical to an investigator.

EXAMPLES OF UXTO CURRENCIES

Just for reference, here are some examples of UTXO-based cryptocurrencies:

- Bitcoin (BTC): Bitcoin is the UTXO cryptocurrency.
- Litecoin (LTC): Often referred to as the silver to Bitcoin's gold.
- Bitcoin Cash (BCH): This is a fork of Bitcoin that was created with the aim to address scalability issues.
- Bitcoin SV (BSV): This is another fork of Bitcoin, specifically from Bitcoin Cash.

- DigiByte (DGB): DigiByte is a growing, open source blockchain created in late 2013.
- Dogecoin (DOGE): Initially created as a meme cryptocurrency, Dogecoin has gained some popularity and is widely used for tipping content creators online. (A "meme cryptocurrency" refers to a type of cryptocurrency that is created, named, or inspired by internet memes or popular online culture. These cryptocurrencies often use meme-related imagery, branding, or names to capture the attention of a particular online community or audience. While some meme cryptocurrencies may start as a joke or parody, they can gain real-world value and popularity due to the viral nature of memes and online communities' enthusiasm.)

I'm sure that most people reading this book would recognize a cryptocurrency address, but for reference Bitcoin addresses are displayed in alphanumeric format. They do not use a capital O or lowercase i to prevent copy errors. There are four primary Bitcoin address types. The naming conventions can be rather different, depending on who you talk to, but I've stuck to the generally accepted names:

- Legacy addresses, which start with a 1 and are 34 characters long. Sometimes referred to as Pay-to-Public-Key-Hash (P2PKH).
- Legacy SegWit (Segregated Witness) addresses, which start with a 3 and are 34 characters long. Sometimes referred to as Pay-to-Script-Hash (P2SH).
- Native SegWit addresses, which start with bc1q and are 42 characters long. Sometimes referred to as Pay-to-Witness-Public-Key-Hash (P2WPKH).
- Taproot addresses, which start with bc1p and are 62 characters long. Sometimes referred to as Pay-to-Taproot (P2TR). Taproot will be explained in more detail later in this chapter.

If you want to understand the differences between these address types, you'll find many online resources available for you to carry out deeper research. But in simple terms, for an investigator legacy type addresses enable a straight transaction of value, with the transaction code proving that the sender had access to the private key and was authorized to send funds from an address.

Legacy SegWit addresses enable the use of a simple script. They can be used, for example, to set up a multisignature transaction in which a number of users/private keys are needed to carry out the transaction. These are sometimes referred to as multisig operations. The script can be fairly complex and allow a user to set up a wallet, for example, with three other users/private keys that can be involved in a transaction but only two of the three are required for the operation to be approved. This is known as a multisig 2 of 3. This can be useful for an investigator to know as it may indicate that a suspect has co-conspirators. It would also mean that if you were looking to seize crypto assets from a suspect address, other private keys may need to be located to complete the seizure.

Some blockchain explorers will notify you when an address is configured as a multisig address, which might mean you need to be looking for other suspects. `blockchair.com` is a good example of a site that will show you when an address is multisig and how many private keys are included. An example is shown in Figure 9.1.

Figure 9.1: An example of a multisig configured address

The oval shape in the center left tells us that this is a P2SH address and is configured as multisig 3 of 4. This means that three out of four keys must sign the transaction for it to be valid.

It is important to understand that addresses are not always unique to a blockchain and so a single address can have assets on multiple chains. This is especially the case with 0x addresses, which are traditionally associated with Ethereum, but the same public/private key algorithm is used by a very large number of varying blockchains. This is vital for an investigator to comprehend as assets can be missed if all blockchains that support a suspect's address are not checked. Although there are not a large number of blockchains that use the Bitcoin addressing system, they are always worth checking. This would include searching for an address on Bitcoin SV, Bitcoin Cash, and Litecoin chains.

What Does an Transaction Look Like?

Now that you understand the concept of UTXO transactions, let's look at a real example on the Bitcoin blockchain (see Figure 9.2).

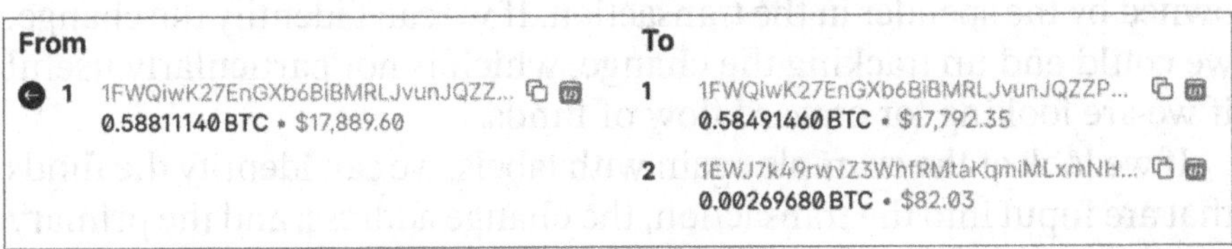

Figure 9.2: Example of a Bitcoin transaction with one input and two outputs

(These screenshots are taken from the blockchain explorer available on the site `http://blockchain.com`. We will talk about different explorers later in this chapter.)

In Figure 9.2, you see a transaction with one input. Although you can equate this to the $10 bill in your wallet, a Bitcoin "note" can be of any amount. Because this user previously received this Bitcoin "note" with a value of 0.588. . .Bitcoin, it cannot be split or "torn in half" and has to be spent whole.

Now look at the two outputs to the transaction. Where you see multiple outputs, one will almost always be change. Why? Let's say you have to pay someone 0.25 of a Bitcoin. You would need UTXOs in your wallet that added up to pay exactly the amount plus the fee, which can vary widely. Calculating this exactly, after the fee, leaving the precise 0.25 Bitcoin payment is very unlikely, so in the vast majority of cases you will have a single output of the intended payment and change. (Since there are 100 million satoshis—the smallest divisible unit of a Bitcoin—the likelihood of having exactly the right value inputs to produce an intended output, including an unknown fee, is essentially 100 million to 1.)

In this example, can you ascertain which address is the payment and which is the change? We will discuss this in more detail in the next chapter, but you will see that (although you can't see the whole address in Figure 9.2) the input address 1FWQ is exactly the same as one of the output addresses. The wallet here is having the change sent back to the input address. (Note that this is not always the case and change addresses are often different from the input address.) This leaves the payment address, the address that the funds are being paid to, as 1EWJ.

Why is this important? If we are following criminal funds, such as a ransomware payment, and we tracked a victim's payment to 1FWQ, we now need to follow the payment of 0.0026 onward to 1EWJ. Often change addresses are different from the input but critically are still owned by the spender in the transaction. If we can't identify the change, we could end up tracking the change, which is not particularly useful if we are looking for onward flow of funds.

If we look at the example again with labels, we can identify the funds that are input into the transaction, the change address, and the primary onward payment (see Figure 9.3).

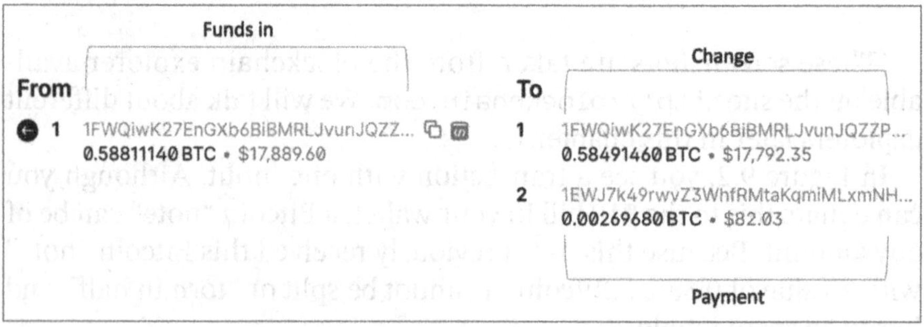

Funds in
From
1 1FWQiwK27EnGXb6BiBMRLJvunJQZZ...
0.58811140 BTC • $17,889.60

Change
To
1 1FWQiwK27EnGXb6BiBMRLJvunJQZZP...
0.58491460 BTC • $17,792.35
2 1EWJ7k49rwyZ3WhfRMtaKqmiMLxmNH...
0.00269680 BTC • $82.03
Payment

Figure 9.3: Elements of the transaction

Let's take a look at another transaction (see Figure 9.4).

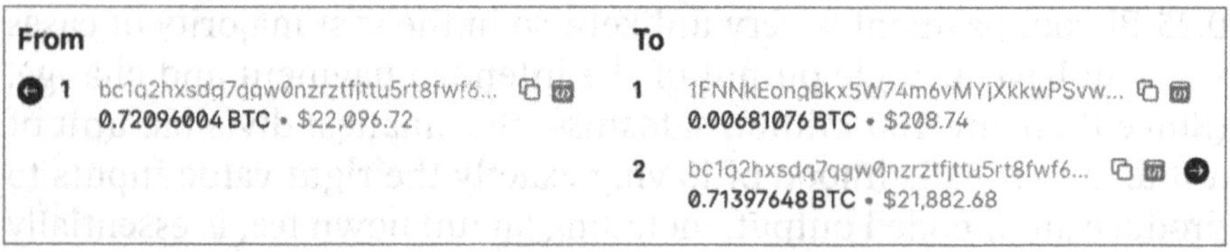

From
1 bc1q2hxsdq7qgw0nzrztfjttu5rt8fwf6...
0.72096004 BTC • $22,096.72

To
1 1FNNkEonqBkx5W74m6vMYjXkkwPSvw...
0.00681076 BTC • $208.74
2 bc1q2hxsdq7qgw0nzrztfjttu5rt8fwf6...
0.71397648 BTC • $21,882.68

Figure 9.4: Example of a transaction

Take a moment and try to identify the three elements. What is:

1. The input payment?
2. The change address?
3. The onward payment?

Hopefully you did not find this too hard.

1. The input payment is the 0.7209. . .Bitcoin from bc1q2h.
2. The change address can be identified several ways. In the outputs, there is, as in the previous example, the same address as the input address, identifying this as the change. However, a bc1 address wallet is fundamentally different from a wallet with addresses starting with 1. Therefore, it would be unusual for change to be returning to a different wallet type. This would also indicate that the bc1 address is the change. We will look at many ways of identifying change in the next chapter.
3. This leaves the 1FNNk address as the onward payment.

Just understanding that a transaction has inputs and outputs, and the concept of an output often being change, is enough to begin to understand how we can trace funds over the Bitcoin blockchain.

In the next chapter, we will discuss in much greater detail the patterns that often exist in transactions and how those "shapes" can help you identify exchanges, mixing, consolidation, coinjoin transactions, and more.

In addition to input and output addresses, a transaction has a unique transaction identifier known as a transaction ID, or simply TXID. A TXID is a long string in hexadecimal format (Base16). This includes the characters 0–9 and A–F. Bitcoin addresses are in Base58, or more specifically Base58Check. Hexadecimal, or hex, does not include any error checking and so is fine for the TXID as it was not really supposed to be revealed to a user. TXIDs are very useful in an investigation, however, as they can be used to uniquely identify a transaction that may include payments to multiple users. Bitcoin addresses are in Base58Check because they include error-checking code.

BASIC BASES

A "base" in mathematics refers to the number of unique digits, including 0, used to represent numbers in a positional numeral system. Let's look at Base10 and Base58 to illustrate this concept.

Base10

Base10, or the decimal system, is the standard system for denoting integers and non-integer numbers. It is called the Base10 system because it is based on 10 symbols: 0, 1, 2, 3, 4, 5, 6, 7, 8, 9. Here's how it works:

- The rightmost digit represents \(10^0\) or ones.
- The next digit to the left represents \(10^1\) or tens.
- The next digit to the left represents \(10^2\) or hundreds.
- And so on.

So, the number 123 in Base10 would be calculated as

\(1 \times 10^2 + 2 \times 10^1 + 3 \times 10^0 = 100 + 20 + 3 = 123\)

Base58

Base58 is more complex because it uses 58 different symbols. It's commonly used in the Bitcoin system and includes the numbers 1–9, the uppercase letters A–Z (except for 0, O, I, and l), and the lowercase letters a–z (without 0, o, i, and l). The exclusion of these characters helps to avoid visual ambiguity when copying, which is very important when you're trying to copy a Bitcoin address accurately.

In Base58, the representation is similar to Base10 but with 58 as the base:

- The rightmost digit represents \(58^0\).
- The next digit to the left represents \(58^1\).
- The next digit to the left represents \(58^2\).
- And so on.

So, if we had a number represented in Base58 as 21, we would calculate it in Base10 as:

\(2 \times 58^1 + 1 \times 58^0 = 116 + 1 = 117\)

So the base of a number system determines the number of unique symbols used in that system and the weight each position has in representing a number. Different bases are used for different applications, and understanding the base is key to interpreting the value of a number in that system.

Transaction IDs are sometimes called Hash IDs or transaction hashes. This is because the TXID is calculated based on the details of the transaction, including the sender and receiver addresses and the value being sent. These and other details are run through a hashing algorithm (called SHA-256) that outputs a 64-character string unique to that transaction.

If you would like to take a moment and type the following TXID into a blockchain explorer, you can view the famous Bitcoin Pizza purchase:

```
Cca7507897abc89628f450e8b1e0c6fca4ec3f7b34ccc
f55f3f531c659ff4d79
```

In May 2010, a hungry Laszlo Hanyecz paid 10,000 Bitcoins (BTC) for two Papa John's pizzas, which were delivered to his home. As of this writing 10,000 Bitcoin is worth $260,000,000. Although everyone throws their hands up and says, "Why did he do it?," the answer is that in May 2010, 10,000 Bitcoin was worth precisely two pizzas!

CAN YOU MISTYPE A BITCOIN ADDRESS?

If a person tells you that they typed in the wrong Bitcoin address when moving funds and don't know where the funds have gone, they are lying. This is because Bitcoin addresses have built-in error-checking code, so any changes to the address will result in the address being invalid and rejected by the Bitcoin network.

A law enforcement officer was attempting to steal crypto funds while supposedly seizing them. They were found out as they used the excuse that they had mistyped. They were lying!

If you are looking at the transaction history of a Bitcoin address in a blockchain viewer and find an interesting movement of funds, just record the TXID to be able to locate it again. The TXIDs can also be useful to record during an investigation as they may relate to multiple movements of coins all in one transaction, and so just quoting the TXID covers all the value movements.

How Does a UTXO Blockchain Help an Investigator?

Because each payment made by a user represents a whole amount that they received, it makes it much easier for us to track individual payments. What do I mean? When I teach this concept, it's often hard for students to understand, but it is super important because it means that we can track, for example, an individual ransomware payment made by a specific victim in a way that we cannot with Ethereum (account-based) blockchains.

We can use the analogy of a bank versus cash to understand this concept, and we will return to it in some depth in the upcoming chapters about Ethereum. Let's assume a fraudster cons 10 victims to each pay $1,000 into their criminal bank account, meaning that the account has a balance of $10,000. The fraudster then transfers $1,000 to an account in the Middle East. Which victim's $1,000 was transferred? It's a bit of a ridiculous question. isn't it? It's impossible to say which $1,000 was moved since it came from an overall balance. As you will learn, this is how Ethereum works, but Bitcoin is different and it can really help us.

If we now think about cash and had some futuristic super-miniature GPS tracker that we could stick to a $100 bill, we would be able to track that specific bill as it was transacted. Say a fraudster again conned 10 people out of $1,000 and each of those people handed over ten $100 bills each. If we had a tracker on a bill from a suspect, we could follow that specific note as it was transacted or laundered, and when we found it, we could return it to that known victim. This is how Bitcoin works. Because each amount received has to be transacted in its entirety, we can track that specific Bitcoin value as it is transacted. How does this help us?

Let's go back to our fraudster who has conned 10 people but make the value 1 Bitcoin instead of dollars. We are contacted by a single victim who provides us with the fraudster's crypto address that they sent their Bitcoin to. Even if all nine other victims sent their 1 Bitcoin to the same address, we are able to see "our" victim's payment specifically. If the criminal then takes some of the Bitcoin and transfers it to a mixer or to an exchange, we can explicitly identify which victims' funds are being moved. This can be very helpful when representing a victim and trying to get funds returned from a service such as an exchange. Because of the UTXO model, we can demonstrate to the exchange the specific transactions from our victim to the exchange at the exclusion of other victims' payments.

When graphing out transactions, we often draw the flow something like the one shown in Figure 9.5. This example shows transactions from various victims flowing into a single address and out to an exchange.

Figure 9.5: Diagram showing victims' payments moving to a fraudster's address and on to an exchange. This diagram better relates to an account-based model such as Ethereum.

Although this diagram makes sense in our heads—all the payments are going to one address and therefore it makes sense to collate them—this diagram better describes an account-based model rather than a UTXO model. In this diagram we see funds flowing from the fraudster's address to an exchange, but which victims' funds? The diagram for a UTXO model such as Bitcoin should really look something like the one shown in Figure 9.6.

Even though in this figure the fraudster's Bitcoin address is still the same, we are able to see exactly whose funds flow onward to the exchange. This is a much better graphical description of what is happening on the Bitcoin blockchain. Remember, there are no "balances" on the Bitcoin chain, just unspent outputs, and each of those outputs can be individually tracked.

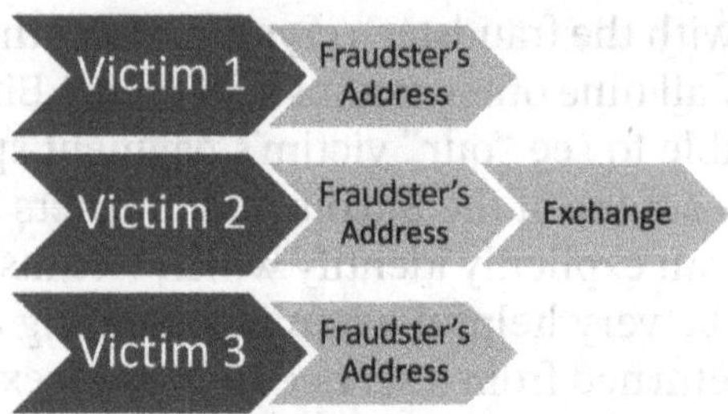

Figure 9.6: Diagram showing victim's funds flowing to a single address, but we can identify which funds move to the exchange

It's a bit tricky to get your head around, and in classes, I often get to this point and am faced with a silent class with lots of crossed arms and students rocking back on the chairs, which is student code for "Eh, say that again?" So I often have to go back and explain it again. If you are finding this hard, head back and reread the section and hopefully it will sink in.

Blockchain Explorers

Although numerous commercial tools can help you track transactions across a blockchain, there are still many free blockchain explorers available with a variety of capabilities and functions. In their simplest form, they will display information extracted from the blockchain in response to a search from a user. This may include the following:

- *Searching for a transaction ID (TXID).* This will return the details of the specific transaction, including the input and output address, the values in Bitcoin, dates and times, the block number that the transaction is mined into, and perhaps any embedded code, known as OP_CODES.
- *Searching for an address.* This will return all the transactions that the address has been involved in, both receiving and sending Bitcoin.

  As mentioned earlier, it's important to note that an address may exist on several blockchains. In Figure 9.7, a search for an address beginning with 1MBR4 returns two possible blockchains, the primary Bitcoin blockchain and the Bitcoin Cash blockchain.

When ascertaining the assets held by a suspect, you must check all the blockchains that an address may exist on. This is especially important with Ethereum-style addresses that begin with 0x because they may exist on a very large number of blockchains. If you just check one chain, you may miss other assets held on other chains. To be clear, the same address on, for example, Bitcoin and Litecoin chains will be owned by the same person as it is generated from the same private key.

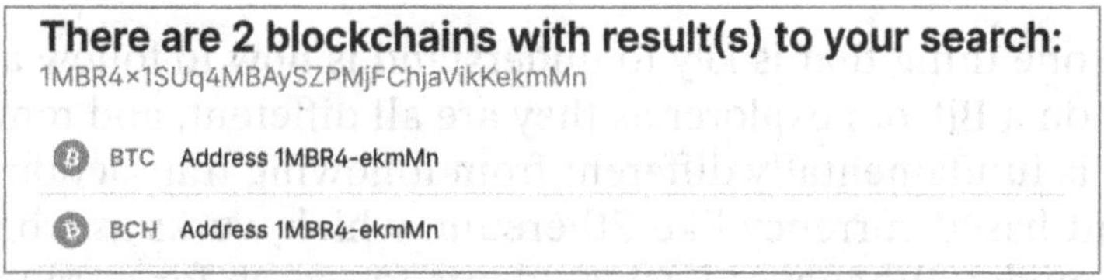

There are 2 blockchains with result(s) to your search:
1MBR4×1SUq4MBAySZPMjFChjaVikKekmMn

BTC Address 1MBR4-ekmMn

BCH Address 1MBR4-ekmMn

Figure 9.7: One address available on two blockchains

- *Searching using a master public key*. This will return all the addresses and possibly the transactions by all addresses controlled by a user's private key. This is read-only and cannot be used to transact values in the user's wallet. A user has to use their private key to generate/view the master public key, and we have often used this to assist with proof of ownership of crypto assets. Note that you should never search using a private key as this could result in funds being stolen.
- *Searching a block number*. This will return all the transactions mined into that block.

During an investigation, you will primarily search for an address to see its transaction history or for a transaction ID to understand how a specific transaction worked and where the funds came from or where they were sent.

There are a great many explorers available, and just doing an Internet search will locate any explorer you may need for a particular currency. A simple search such as **Bitcoin explorer**, **Ethereum explorer**, or **TRON explorer** will reveal a number of options. Explorers do have a tendency to come and go, and more often change the way they look and function, but as mentioned earlier they all tend to display the same information.

My personal favorites for Bitcoin investigations have been around a long time, so hopefully if you try to use them they will still be there:

- `Blockchain.com` covers a large number of currencies in a consistent interface.
- `Blockchair.com` has some good, advanced features if you really need to dig into a transaction.
- `BlockCypher.com` is a simple but effective explorer.

The one thing that is key to understand is how to follow a transaction on a Bitcoin explorer as they are all different, and remember that it is fundamentally different from following transactions in an account-based currency like Ethereum, which works as a balance-based model. Whenever I ask students to search for a transaction ID and then follow the funds, I tend to see most click on an output address. This will just load a list of all the transactions involving that address, not just moving to the subsequent transaction that can be what we are looking for.

In whatever explorer you are using, you need to look for an icon that will enable you to move to the next or previous transaction. In Figure 9.8, an example from `Blockchain.com`, you can see one input address and two output addresses. If you want to see where these exact funds have come from, do not click the address itself. Rather, notice the small black arrow pointing back; if you roll over the arrow, you will see the message "Transaction the funds were received from."

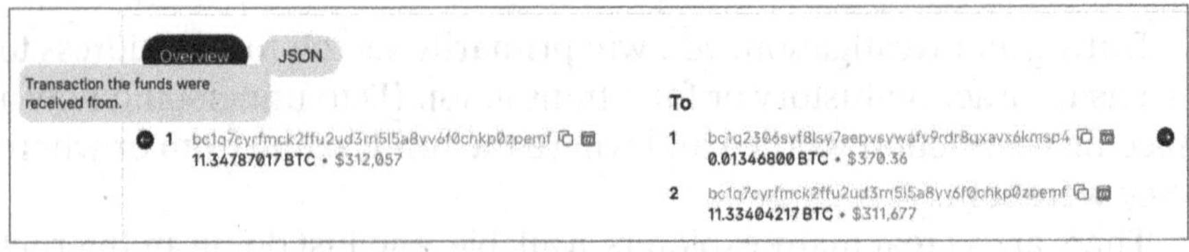

Figure 9.8: The forward and back arrows used to follow the flow of funds

If you click the back-facing arrow, it will load the transaction where this address (bc1q7cyr) was an output and was credited with the

11.34. . .of Bitcoin. The same is true for following the funds forward. In the example, you will note that there is only one arrow for output address bc1q2306. This is because the other address is the same as the input address and therefore is clearly the change to the transaction.

In Figure 9.9 you see a similar transaction in the `Blockchair.com` explorer. Note that there is another arrow icon used and we have the back and forward arrows for the address that Blockchair thinks is likely the change. There is no arrow for the output bc1qvy because it has not been spent, and so there is no forward transaction to browse to (see Figure 9.9).

Figure 9.9: Example of transaction and forward and back arrows in `Blockchair.com`

BlockCypher just uses the hyperlinked words *output* to follow the flow of funds back to the previous transaction and *spent* to browse forward, so as an investigator you need to figure out how to follow funds on your explorer of choice.

It's not wrong to click the address, but you will need to remember that it will load the entire list of transactions that the address has been involved with and that you will need to use dates and times to work out the incoming and outgoing funds that are of interest to you.

Many of the blockchain explorers have APIs that enable you to access blockchain data from your own code. So if you are happy writing your own tools in any language, you will be able to pull block or transaction data via simple API calls. If you are already a coder, then you will not need me to cover this in any detail. `Blockchain.com` has a very straightforward API. For example, the URL command

```
https://blockchain.info/rawaddr/$bitcoin_address
```

will return the transactions for address `$bitcoin_address`. The output taken from an example on the API help site, `www.blockchain.com/explorer/api/blockchain_api`, will look something like Figure 9.10.


```
{
  "hash160": "660d4ef3a743e3e696ad990364e555c271ad504b",
  "address": "1AJbsFZ64EpEfS5UAjAfcUG8pH8Jn3rn1F",
  "n_tx": 17,
  "n_unredeemed": 2,
  "total_received": 1031350000,
  "total_sent": 931250000,
  "final_balance": 100100000,
  "txs": [
    "--Array of Transactions--"
  ]
}
```


Figure 9.10: Example of output from an API call

Some APIs will provide a certain number of calls for free and without any authentication or personal API key, but most will require you to apply for, or even pay for, an API key for the call to function.

TIP You can download the source code for BlockCypher and run the software locally using the API for getting data from the blockchain. It's for expert users only but can be useful. Visit `https://github.com/blockcypher/explorer`.

I'm not going to spend more time talking about explorers since using them is straightforward. Just bear in mind the comments I made earlier about following transactions forward and backward.

What Else Can You Learn in a Transaction?

You have learned that a transaction is named using a transaction ID and that it will contain inputs to the transaction and outputs. You have also seen that most transactions will include change. In the next chapter, you will learn more about calculating a change address as well as patterns of transactions that may not include a change output and what that can mean.

If you see a transaction where the input is named Coinbase, this is not the name of the well-known cryptocurrency exchange but rather the name of the reward transaction given to a miner when they mine a block (see Figure 9.11).

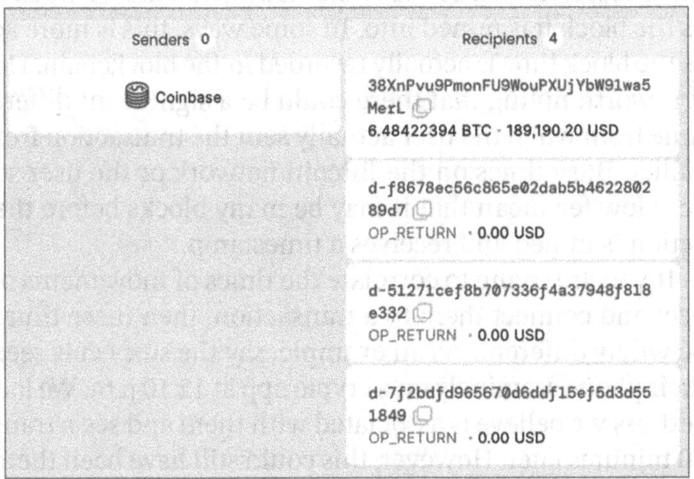

Figure 9.11: A transaction depicted on the Blockchair explorer showing a Coinbase reward input

Times and Dates

Times and dates can be vital to an investigator, but care is needed when recording time data from blockchain explorers. There are actually no times or dates recorded on the blockchain against transactions; however, a time and date stamp is a field added to a mined block. This data is added when the block is mined and is accurate enough, but we have to be cautious when reporting these times in our reports.

Blockchain explorers can report times differently. As they often change, I will not commit in this book to which sites use each way of reporting dates and times, but some simple analysis will help:

- Some explorers show transaction times at the time they first appeared in the blockchain holding area, known as the *mempool*. Transactions are held here until they are mined into a block. These times are only recorded on the explorer and are not on the actual blockchain. Although this time will be closer to the time the sender triggered the transaction, it could take a significant time before the transaction is mined. To determine whether the explorer does this, check all transactions in the block; if all the times are different, then they are the mempool time.

- Most explorers add a time to the transaction that is the same time as the block it is mined into. In some ways, this is more accurate as the block time is actually recorded in the blockchain. However, it is worth noting that there could be a significant difference in time from when the user actually sent the transaction from their wallet. Busy times on the Bitcoin network or the user setting a very low fee mean that it may be many blocks before the transaction is mined and receives a timestamp.

  If you are trying to correlate the times of movements of a suspect and connect them to a transaction, then these times could be wildly different. As an example, say the suspect is seen using their phone seemingly on a crypto app at 12:10 p.m. We look at an address we believe is associated with them and see a transaction 30 minutes later. However, this could still have been them as the transaction could have taken at least three 10-minute blocks to be mined. We had a case in South America where a transaction in a block was timed after the suspect had been taken into custody; however, using another explorer and finding the time the transaction hit the mempool showed that it was actually sent before the suspect was detained.

  To check whether or not an explorer does this, look at the transactions in the block and all the times should be the same as the block time.

- Some explorers localize the time to the time zone of the viewer. This can create major issues with stated times in a report as the times may end up being hours different from the actual time the transaction happened in the area of the world being considered. I find it best to always report all times in Universal Time Code (UTC) and ignore time zones. Some explorers such as `Blockchair.com` have always reported times in UTC, and I can't see that changing. Some explorers will pop up the UTC time when you hover over the stated time. Be really cautious and understand how a blockchain viewer reports times.

Values

Most block explorers will report values of the inputs and outputs in a transaction in both the Bitcoin amounts and a fiat currency amount. The Bitcoin values within a specific transaction are set in the blockchain and will never change. However, when a fiat value is provided, this value is not set in the blockchain and can vary significantly from explorer to explorer or even moment to moment.

There are two ways by which explorers provide fiat currency values for a transaction:

- Calculate the value of Bitcoin at the time the transaction was mined.
- Calculate the value of Bitcoin at the time you as the user are viewing the transaction.

How can you know which value is being presented? Simply refresh the browser displaying the transaction. Figure 9.12 shows a simple transaction with one input and two outputs.

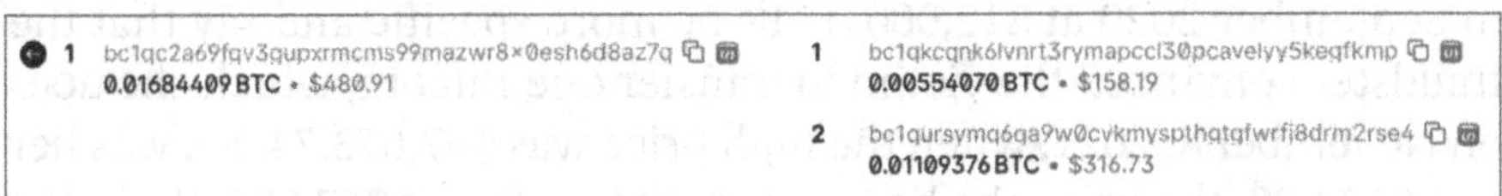

Figure 9.12: An input value of $480.91

You can see that the input dollar value is $480.91. However, if we refresh the browser, forcing it to reload the transaction page, we see the result shown in Figure 9.13.

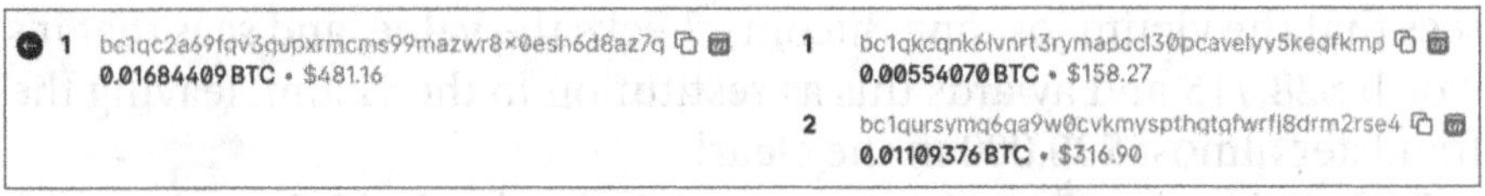

1 bc1qc2a69fqv3gupxrmcms99mazwr8×0esh6d8az7q
0.01684409 BTC • $481.16
1 bc1qkcqnk6lvnrt3rymapccl30pcavelyy5keqfkmp
0.00554070 BTC • $158.27
2 bc1qursymq6qa9w0cvkmyspthqtqfwrfj8drm2rse4
0.01109376 BTC • $316.90

Figure 9.13: An input value of $481.16

As you can see, that input dollar value has changed to $481.16. What has happened? Simply, the Bitcoin-to-dollar exchange value has changed and so the recorded dollar value changes. This explorer is displaying the dollar value at the moment in time that we are looking at the transaction. This would be the case if the transaction was one hour old or one year old. Of course, value fluctuations between Bitcoin and fiat currencies are huge over fairly small amounts of time and so the displayed value to a user today may have no reality to the dollar value of the transaction when it was carried out.

Why is this important? Whenever I carry out an investigation and present a report that includes Bitcoin (or any crypto) transactions, I am almost always asked the same question by senior officers or senior managers: "What is that Bitcoin worth?" As an investigator, you need to be very careful how you answer that question. The value of Bitcoin at the time that a fraud was carried out or money was laundered, which could easily be a year ago or more in a major investigation, will be very different from the value today. So it's vital that whatever tool you are using, whether that be a free online crypto explorer or a commercial investigation tool, you need to know how fiat values are calculated and reported.

Let's illustrate this with a simple example. A victim is defrauded out of one Bitcoin in November 2021. The victim had bought Bitcoin in September 2020 at $12,000. Let's be more specific and say that the fraudster convinced the victim to transfer one Bitcoin, which she does on November 8, 2021, when the high price was $67,673.74. So, was her loss $12,000, the price she bought the Bitcoin for, or $67,000, the value when she sent it to the criminal? It gets worse—the case is investigated, and the fraudster is found. It transpires that they converted the Bitcoin into dollars on November 27, 2021, when the dollar value had dropped to just over $57,000. The fraudster's assets are frozen as part of the investigation, including the $57,000.

Following delays that often come with cases like fraud, the case comes to court two years later, on August 17, 2023, when the judge sees that the victim lost one Bitcoin, checks the value, and sees that it's worth $28,715 and awards this as restitution to the victim, leaving the fraudster almost $30,000 in the clear!

The victim spent $12,000 on an asset; is that her loss? Or perhaps the value of $67,000 the day it was lost? Or is it the $57,000 when it was converted back into fiat by the fraudster? Or is it even the $28,000 value at the time the case came to court? Values are extremely tricky!

I have seen judges award the original asset—in our example, one Bitcoin—reasoning that the exchange values are irrelevant. I've seen awards that represent the crypto at the highest value since the theft, as the victim could have cashed the crypto and taken the profit. It's very hard indeed. It all depends on how local legislation sees virtual assets—as property or as a form of cash. In the UK, it's viewed as property and so a likely return would be the Bitcoin rather than the cash value.

Omni Layer

The Omni Layer, originally called Mastercoin, is a protocol built on top of the Bitcoin blockchain that allows for the creation and then trading of custom tokens and smart contracts. It's one of the earliest efforts to extend the capabilities of Bitcoin beyond simple transactions of its native currency. The Omni Layer is not used extensively, and currently it is primarily used to transact USDT (Tether) and the MaidSafeToken over the Bitcoin blockchain.

Although I have seen very few uses of the Omni Layer to date, you should be aware of it. The key features are:

- *Token creation.* Omni allows users to create and issue their own custom tokens.
- *Bitcoin embedding.* Omni transactions are Bitcoin transactions. The Omni Layer uses a technique called transaction layering, where additional data (related to Omni features) is embedded into Bitcoin transactions. This means that Omni transactions are secured by the Bitcoin network in the same way as any other transaction.
- *Omni assets.* There are native assets like OMNI and TOMNI (Test OMNI for the testnet) that exist on the Omni Layer. OMNI tokens have their own value and can be traded or used to pay for transaction fees on the Omni Layer.
- Since Omni operates on top of Bitcoin, it benefits from the *decentralization, security, and robustness* of the Bitcoin network. Any tool or wallet that can interpret Omni Layer data can decode and interact with Omni transactions, even if they are primarily designed for Bitcoin.

However, it's worth noting that while the Omni Layer was innovative at its inception, the use of other platforms like Ethereum, with its more flexible and robust smart contract capabilities, has greatly overshadowed Omni's popularity. Ethereum allows for even more complex decentralized applications and token implementations, making it a more popular choice for many developers and projects in the crypto space.

For an investigator, keep an eye on a transaction in a blockchain explorer being tagged as OMNI; Blockchair does this especially well. In Figure 9.14, taken from `Blockchair.com`, you can clearly see that the transaction is OMNI and is transacting USDT (Tether) using Bitcoin addresses.

Figure 9.14: Example of an OMNI transaction in `Blockchair.com`

You are able to follow the funds in exactly the same way as Bitcoin, so it shouldn't really be overly complex for you to understand. It's worth noting that there is an OMNI-specific explorer at `OmniExplorer.com`, which will just show OMNI transactions on the blockchain. Although it has some uses such as finding OMNI examples, I tend to use Blockchair for following OMNI transactions.

Taproot

In November 2021, Taproot was introduced to Bitcoin as the most significant upgrade since SegWit in 2017. This also introduced a new address format called Pay-to-Taproot (P2TR). Taproot addresses have certain benefits over standard Bitcoin transactions because they allow for transactions with lower fees and improved privacy, which we will discuss next. Taproot addresses begin with the characters bc1p.

Here's a simplified breakdown of the privacy improvements and possibilities when using Taproot over standard Bitcoin addresses:

Unified Appearance for Transactions One of the primary privacy improvements of Taproot is that it makes different types of transactions look the same on the blockchain. Whether you're making a simple transfer, using a multisignature setup, or employing more complex smart contracts, all these transactions appear the same on the chain. This uniformity makes it difficult to differentiate and hence enhances privacy.

Schnorr Signatures Taproot incorporates Schnorr signatures (digital signatures produced by the Schnorr signature algorithm), replacing Bitcoin's traditional Elliptic Curve Digital Signature Algorithm (ECDSA). While Schnorr signatures have efficiency and scalability benefits, they also allow for signature aggregation. This means that a multisignature transaction (from multiple participants) can be made to appear (and cost) like a regular, single-signature transaction, further enhancing privacy and reducing costs.

Conditional Transactions With Taproot, users can set up complex conditions for a transaction to go through (like needing signatures from two out of three participants), but only the executed condition is revealed on the blockchain. If all participants agree on an outcome, they can cooperate to make the transaction look like a standard one, keeping the other conditions hidden.

Merklized Abstract Syntax Trees (MAST) This is a bit more technical, but essentially, MAST allows for the creation of complex smart contracts where only the parts of the contract that are executed are revealed. This means you could have a contract with 10 possible outcomes, but if only one is executed, only that one is visible on the blockchain, keeping the rest private.

Reduction in Address Distinction With Taproot, there's a reduction in the distinction between types of addresses (like P2PKH, P2SH, P2WPKH). By making different transactions and address types look more similar, it's harder for onlookers to discern user intentions or the type of transaction being made, adding another layer of privacy.

It's worth noting that while Taproot does enhance privacy in many ways, it doesn't make Bitcoin fully private. Transactions are still transparent on the public ledger. However, the methods and structures Taproot introduces make it much more challenging to make accurate assumptions or analyses about those transactions.

What does Taproot mean for the investigator? Whereas with standard Bitcoin transactions we can see the type of transaction it is and exactly what it does, Taproot makes any underlying functionality invisible to the investigator. You will only see the result of a transaction on the blockchain. This uniform appearance of a Taproot transaction makes it challenging for anyone analyzing the blockchain to determine the exact nature or conditions of a transaction. While an investigator can see the outcome of a transaction, they can't see the other possible conditions or outcomes that weren't executed. If all parties involved in a transaction agree on an outcome, they can make the transaction appear like a regular, nonconditional transaction. This makes multisignature transactions appear, and cost, the same as standard transactions, further complicating any transaction analysis.

Let's use a hypothetical example to illustrate how Taproot could potentially make the job of an investigator more challenging. Suppose Alice, Bob, and Charlie are three individuals who frequently engage in joint financial ventures. They've decided that for any expenditure from their joint Bitcoin wallet, at least two of them need to agree and sign the transaction. In the traditional Bitcoin setup, this kind of arrangement is known as a 2-of-3 multisignature (multisig) wallet. Transactions from such wallets have a distinctive appearance on the blockchain, making it obvious to investigators that a multisig setup is being used.

Without Taproot: If an investigator is watching their activities, the investigator can easily spot when the trio uses their multisig wallet. Each time they spend from it, the distinctive multisig "fingerprint" on the blockchain reveals that a multisig condition has been satisfied.

With Taproot: Now, let's say Alice, Bob, and Charlie decide to utilize the features of Taproot. The beauty of Taproot is that it allows them to set up their 2-of-3 multisig condition, but when they all agree on a transaction (let's say Alice and Bob decide to make a purchase), they can use their Taproot-enhanced wallet to make their multisig transaction look just like a standard, single-signature transaction on the blockchain.

To an Investigator: When Alice and Bob jointly agree and make a transaction, the investigator sees a transaction that looks no different from a regular transaction made by a single individual. The multisig nature of their transaction is hidden. If Charlie disagreed and they wanted to enforce the 2-of-3 condition, the Taproot setup would reveal that a multisig condition was met but only the satisfied condition, keeping other transaction details private.

This rather simplified example shows how Taproot can obscure the nature and conditions of transactions, making it harder for external parties to infer the exact agreements or setups participants might have.

The Lightning Network

The easiest way to explain the Bitcoin Lightning Network is with an example. Imagine you and your friend go to a bar often. Instead of paying for each drink immediately and waiting for change, you both decide to open a tab, a running account. You give the bartender $50 as a deposit, and your friend does the same.

Every time you buy a drink, the bartender simply notes it down on your tab. If you buy a drink for your friend, it's also noted. If your friend returns the favor, that's noted too. This way, you both can enjoy several drinks without constantly reaching for your wallets.

At the end of the night, or maybe even after several nights, you both decide to settle the tab. Only then does money get exchanged based on what each of you owes, and you get back any remaining deposit.

The Bitcoin Lightning Network works in a similar way but for Bitcoin transactions. Instead of recording every small transaction on the main Bitcoin ledger (which can be slow and expensive), participants open a "channel" (like the bar tab) and transact as many times as they want within that channel. Only when they decide to close the channel is the net result recorded on the main Bitcoin blockchain.

So, in essence, the Lightning Network allows for faster and cheaper Bitcoin transactions by keeping most of them off the main ledger and only settling the final balances.

Following funds on the Bitcoin Lightning Network is substantially more challenging than following funds on the main Bitcoin blockchain. The Lightning Network is designed to offer faster and cheaper off-chain transactions, and it inherently provides better privacy. However, certain techniques and observations might give investigators some insights:

Node Analysis Each payment on the Lightning Network is routed through multiple nodes. If an investigator is operating several well-connected nodes, they might be able to observe and record payment flows. However, without controlling a significant portion of the network, this method has limitations.

Invoice Information When a payment is initiated on the Lightning Network, it's usually done using an invoice generated by the recipient. If an investigator has access to that invoice (e.g., from a vendor's server or an individual's device), they can derive information about the payment, such as its amount and purpose.

Channel Opening and Closing While the transactions within Lightning Network channels are off-chain and private, the opening and closing of channels are on the chain and publicly visible on the Bitcoin blockchain. Large and frequent channel openings or closings by specific entities might provide clues about their activities.

Timing Analysis If an investigator can correlate the timing of a transaction from one node with the timing of a transaction at another node (e.g., by operating or monitoring these nodes), they might infer that the transactions are part of the same payment route.

Cooperative Entities If an investigator has access to information from cooperative vendors, exchanges, or wallet providers that use the Lightning Network, they might gather data about transactions and payment routes.

Exit Node Monitoring By monitoring frequently used *exit nodes* (nodes where payments often leave the Lightning Network to settle on-chain), an investigator might gather data about the destination of certain funds.

Backup Data Users might create backups of their Lightning Network node data. If an investigator can access these backups, they may obtain transaction histories and other relevant information.

Despite these techniques, it's essential to understand that the Lightning Network provides significantly better transactional privacy than the base Bitcoin layer. Payments on the Lightning Network are routed through multiple hops in a way that nodes only know about their immediate predecessor and successor in the payment route, not the origin or final destination of the funds.

Although it's not impossible for investigators to gain insights into Lightning Network transactions, it's a lot more challenging and requires more sophisticated methods than simply examining the Bitcoin blockchain.

Summary

This chapter has helped you understand how Bitcoin works. In the next chapter, we'll focus on how an investigator can follow transactions, identify change addresses, notice patterns, and many other key skills.

10 Bitcoin: Investigation Methodology

As this section of the book is a little heavy-going, I thought you might like some light relief with a brilliant contribution from a top-notch investigator. This is the firsthand account of a very early seizure of Bitcoin that resulted in an arrest, a conviction, and the return of funds to victims. The case is about a man named Grant West and is told by an officer who was involved from start to finish of the investigation.

Iggy Azad was an officer with the Metropolitan Police (MET Police) Cyber Crime Unit when I first met him back in 2018. I'd built a crypto training course focused on Bitcoin and been invited to teach the very first class to a variety of officers from around London at one of the old police stations owned by the City of London Police (different from the Metropolitan Police). Unbeknownst to me, Iggy was already a bit of a cybercrime rock star at the Metropolitan Police when we met, partly because of the infamous takedown of Grant West. The video of the arrest, which happened on a train, is the stuff of legend, with officers posing as the general public in first class, leaping on the suspect at the perfect moment, a scuffle, a successful detainment, and a round of applause from the passengers in the train car.

I taught the class with a fair amount of nervousness but was pleased with the response from the officers in attendance, many of whom first heard about cryptocurrencies on day one of the course. Having arrived home after the four-day class, I received an email from Iggy. I will never forget it; it contained 20 ways that the course could be improved and every single suggestion was superb. That day I opened my PowerPoint of the course and implemented every single one of his suggestions. They made the course significantly better, and I am forever appreciative of Iggy taking the time to give me specific and practical feedback. Anyway, sit back and enjoy "The Great Train Crypto Robbery."

SEIZURE, STORAGE, AND REALIZATION OF SEIZED CRYPTO ASSETS, OR THE GREAT CRYPTO TRAIN ROBBERY

By Iggy Azad

Intro

I first met Grant West in the car park of the Isle of Sheppey drivers testing center in 2015. After his test, he was arrested for compromising thousands of online food order and delivery platform Just Eat accounts, having phished them. We later learned that he had a successful business online selling compromised accounts from banks, online merchants, and services. He used the name of Courvoisier within dark net markets as a brand for his goods, and he made hundreds of thousands of dollars. His crime spree came to an end in the first-class train car of the 1350 Rhyl to Euston, when he was arrested (again).

Background

The story began in 2015 when Just Eat reported that many of their accounts had been compromised. Just Eat encountered repeated attempts to access online accounts—hundreds of thousands of automated attempts to log into accounts. Some were successful, but most were not.

I was working in the Metropolitan Police Cyber Crime unit with Helen, who was the case officer. She is now doing very well for herself at Accenture.

As we would normally do, we followed the lines of inquiry that Just Eat provided us with from IP address logs, device identifiers, emails, and telephone numbers. Unfortunately for West, he had used one of the compromised accounts to order a delivery to his home. He had also used his home IP to launch the attempts to access the accounts, as well as that of his girlfriend in sunny Rhyl.

It was surprising to discover that he lived on a holiday camp on the Isle of Sheppey in a trailer with no broadband. British network operator and ISP EE, to their credit, had installed a huge cell tower outside the holiday camp, which gave West a very good 4G signal and therefore excellent Internet connectivity. Extremely helpful for using account crackers and running multiple servers.

Back to the arrest. As the police normally do, we seized everything electronic and documentary in his trailer and from his family, who were in another trailer farther down the lane. This included several paper Bitcoin wallets, hidden behind a picture frame.

West was interviewed and later released on bail. There was nothing to hold him on, and we needed more evidence about his involvement in the compromise of Just Eat accounts.

We returned to the police station late at night and put away the exhibits, ready to examine them the next day.

The next day, the laptops, phones, and digital storage were all submitted for analysis while Helen and I dug through the other documents. The paper Bitcoin wallets revealed a balance of 226 Bitcoins, which, funnily enough, had all been withdrawn hours after his release from custody.

Even though all the electronics had been taken from him and from his family's home, he had still been able to access and withdraw the BTC. At the time, the value was about $60,000.

First lesson: Always seize and safeguard any digital asset. At the time the law had not caught up with Bitcoin, so there were no provisions to seize and withdraw the funds to a police wallet, and there were no police facilities at the time for storing BTC. It was gutting, but no one suspected that the price would skyrocket in later years.

In any case, the investigation into his activities continued. Helen did an amazing job tying West to the Just Eat compromise, but then she found something even more interesting. On his devices were digital artifacts linking him to the online username of Courvoisier.

Courvoisier was very active on AlphaBay, a dark net market (later taken down by an international police investigation). He was a busy chap on the market, selling compromised online accounts for all major retailers worldwide, although his customer service did leave a little to be desired. Payments were all in BTC, funnily enough.

I could not believe that West, who lived on the Isle of Sheppey, was this one-man online crime wave. I was later proven very wrong: West was indeed Courvoisier. He had earned over 1,500 worth of BTC in his time on AlphaBay and other sites. Investigations sometimes take a turn, and this was no different. Just Eat was just the latest in a long line of companies West had targeted.

We learned that West was almost entirely self-taught and extremely capable at using many tools available to criminals to commit crime online. YouTube was his university; it was free and offered a wide variety of courses to the budding student of cybercrime. It is probably a testament to EE's services that he committed all his online activity via 4G.

As the investigation gathered pace, we learned that West used a virtual private server (VPS) service to host all his crime software tools, including Sentry MBA. Sentry MBA is a credential stuffing tool, the idea being that you load it with a combination of passwords and associated usernames (combo lists) and a script with instructions (also known as a configuration file) on how to log in using the combo list, and then aim it at a merchant's login page. Click Go and it will automatically try to log into any associated accounts using the password and username combos. Any accounts found would then be returned with a positive result. At the time many online retailers would not use proper two-factor authentication to protect accounts.

Combo lists are aggregated from the many breaches of personal information that have occurred over the past years. Because people will reuse or not change their passwords over time, such account holders are vulnerable to credential stuffing tools.

Using a combination of proxies and virtual private networks (VPNs), West would try to crack as many accounts as his Internet connection would allow.

He also had another side hustle; he would phish banking customers. He would set up a phishing site posing as a mobile phone company. The domain name would be very similar to the legitimate company, and West would pay Google to ensure his site was at the top of the search results. Of course, he paid with stolen credit card details.

The phishing sites would be constructed by others he would pay, again in BTC. When users went to the website, they would enter their login details for the legitimate business and then be prompted to enter their banking credentials. West captured this and then either sold it on AlphaBay or tried to monetize it himself by conducting account takeovers. How would he get people to access his phishing site? Well, he would buy Short Message Service (SMS) spamming services and "smish" a whole list of numbers. At some point, someone would click the link and access the site, enter their bank details, and later get "pwned."

The investigation went for a year or so, obtaining more and more evidence of his activities online. Near to the time he was arrested, in September 2017, we had full knowledge and visibility of his daily activities, including all his cryptocurrency holdings.

In the video of his arrest, you will notice that his laptop is swiftly taken away. We were not going to make the same mistake twice.

How Much Did He Earn and Where Did It Go?

With any type of investigation there are different parallel streams. In the West case, there was the intelligence case, the evidential one, and of course the financial one. We won't talk about the intelligence one as the Metropolitan Police may get annoyed.

This was a first for a financial investigation as we quickly discovered that West had no bank accounts in his name. I suppose there was no need as he was happy to simply use other people's.

After his arrest and bail, someone was able to withdraw the 226 BTC from wallets that we had recovered. The person who did this must have had access to both the public and private key, backed up somewhere. So where did the BTC go, and more importantly, where did it come from?

And this is the crux of a financial investigation: to find out how much someone has earned from their criminal activity and what they have now to seize. So armed with the BTC addresses that we had on the paper wallets, the cryptocurrency artifacts on his devices, and what we knew of his traditional financial accounts, I set about trying to find out (1) where the BTC went, (2) how much money West had, and (3) where he got it from.

At the time, the criminal use of cryptocurrency was basic, compared to today. Now we have bridges, swaps, and mixers on Ethereum virtual machines (EVMs) and multiple chains. Back then, obfuscation tools were limited to mixers, and they were expensive. Many criminals simply transferred their ill-gotten gains to exchanges, where they cashed out. However, the number of exchanges where one could cash out was limited.

Using cryptocurrency analysis tools, I was able to track West's assets to Poloniex and Bittrex. The ongoing investigation had remote access to his activity online, and we knew how much he had in his wallets and where he was storing those wallets.

Inquiries to those exchanges revealed how much had passed through his accounts. Some 480 BTC in total had been passed through the accounts, and 55 BTC remained. The difficulty with the accounts was that both companies were based in America.

It is very fortunate that we were friendly with U.S. federal agencies located in the U.K., who were able to help us secure those funds and ensure that they could not be dissipated. Another lesson here is to make friends with foreign law enforcement so that they can help you freeze funds.

As soon as I had identified assets in the United States, we engaged with the Crown Prosecution Service (CPS) so that the lengthy paperwork could be completed in preparation for any arrest. Early engagement with prosecutors is key to any recovery of assets in the U.K. or elsewhere.

Other BTC addresses ended up being a dead end, with no assets to identify. Not a lot remained from the 226 BTC we first saw, and from what had passed through the accounts at Poloniex and Bittrex. I had sent requests to all other major exchanges and hadn't found any other accounts.

From his online activity, we saw that West was still selling fullz on AlphaBay. AlphaBay was very helpful in allowing the user to view the number of sales and what each vendor was selling, plus the price. So, a rough estimate as to the earnings and therefore "criminal benefit" could be made.

However, the FBI took down AlphaBay in July 2017. Not to be deterred, West moved his operations to Dream Market. However, police shut down that market as well, and he was forced to move his business to a lesser-known market, TradeRoute.

I now knew the entirety of his financial holdings from the ongoing investigation and from the information being received by us on a near daily basis. He had assets in exchanges and in wallets contained on his devices. Some 82 BTC (about $750,000) was up for seizure if we could get our hands on it.

To Seize or Not to Seize

The first problem I encountered was how to legally seize the cryptocurrency he had contained in his wallets. The crypto held in different exchange accounts was straightforward; obtain a restraint order in the U.K. and then ask the CPS to politely ask the U.S. Department of Justice (DoJ) to seize and freeze the crypto held in his accounts. Sounds simple, but international judicial assistance is never quick and involves a lot of paperwork.

Seizing crypto from a self-hosted wallet was problematic as there was no case law or clear process. Luckily a relatively new piece of legislation had come into effect in the U.K.: section 47C-F of the Proceeds of Crime Act (POCA). This allowed certain officers to seize property or assets that could be used to satisfy a confiscation order should a person be found guilty of a relevant offense and be shown to have benefited from their criminal conduct. Importantly, we could seek to obtain judicial authority prior to an arrest so that the police could be armed with all the authorizations and powers that were required.

In this circumstance, we were fast approaching the time when we wanted to arrest West. We had all the evidence from the ongoing investigation, and we knew his comings and goings. All that had to be decided was when.

"When" was dependent on a lot of other factors: resources, support from prosecutors, authorizations, and West's movements as well.

A rough plan was drawn up to arrest him while he had access to his laptop and was logged on. This would negate lengthy forensic examination and provide immediate evidence, attribution to the devices under his control, and highly relevant access to his wallets.

There were several requirements to use the power under Section 47 legislation:

- You had to be suitably trained.
- There had to be an investigation into a relevant offense.
- Someone had to be arrested or was to be arrested.
- Realizable property had to be present.
- Seizure is necessary to prevent its dissipation.

There were several other conditions, but those were the main ones. The decision to exercise the power is at the discretion of the police. But this was a new power that had not been used to seize crypto, so I sought out our legal services. I obtained the assistance of a very good lawyer, Kevin Barry, to help draft the application to obtain judicial preauthorization—essentially a court order allowing me to seize and transfer assets under his control to us, the police.

We drafted an application explaining what West had been doing online—that is, using credential stuffing, phishing sites, and all sorts of other badness. The next part to the application was to explain what crypto was, how it fell into the definition of property, and why it was realizable.

Another thing that had to be explained was how the Metropolitan Police were going to store the crypto. There was nothing in the way of corporate storage facilities for crypto, not in the Metropolitan Police stations or anywhere in the U.K. I looked at our two options: self-hosted or with a service.

With self-storage, there were several questions to be answered: where would we store the wallet or seed phrase, how would we protect it from potential theft, what wallet would we use, who would have access, what were our backup options, what insurance could we get against theft or loss, which method of storage (online/physical) would we use, what software would we use, what were the device requirements, whether we should use air gapping, and how would we secure our safes.

The other option was to use an established exchange to create an account and store the crypto with them, using their own insurance as a hedge against any loss due to a hack. Remember at the time that many exchanges were being exploited by various groups. Crypto prices were pumping but still volatile (which isn't very different to today).

With an exchange account, we could institute levels of authority and keep the account locked, and this option had the added benefit of allowing us to quickly realize any crypto.

Using an exchange is similar to existing cash seizure rules; you seize, and you then bank it as soon as possible. Mirroring this process with crypto would be more palatable to senior officers who had to sign off and remove the headache of storing crypto in a safe in a police station, with all the risk assessments and authorities required to store assets worth nearly $1 million.

Luckily common sense was in abundant supply within the Metropolitan Police, and we opened an exchange account.

All these concepts may be simple now, but back in 2017 crypto was still very new and the judiciary was not used to it. Diagrams, slide decks, and appendices were all used in a hearing to obtain the order. Every single point of the case had to be explained, including how we would store the crypto and what we would do with it.

It is important to note that the assets were not the property of the Metropolitan Police. The purpose of the application was to seize assets and safeguard them for use in satisfying any eventual order against West to pay back his criminal earnings. The police are custodians in the process, but because of this and the ongoing volatility, I felt that if they were successful in seizing crypto from West, he should be given regular and meaningful opportunities to deal with any assets seized.

Any confiscation order would require him to pay. As we were hoping to seize assets for that order, I felt West should be asked whether he wanted any of it sold to preserve its fiat value while proceedings took place. Criminal cases and financial confiscation take a long time, and the value of what a defendant has earned because of their crimes is only determined and settled on once they have been convicted. Therefore, working out the value could take years. In some instances, the whole case could take three to five years. Therefore, we must take a long view on a case and plan for what might happen in two to four years' time.

So, I decided that any responsibility for selling seized crypto should fall to West and that he must pay any order so he can decide when to sell. If he let it ride, he ran the risk of the assets falling in value; conversely, they could appreciate, though it does not follow that he would get any crypto back if it increased in value spectacularly because he earned it through crime.

This is a different approach to that of the Dutch, who seize and then immediately sell the crypto to preserve its value at the time of the seizure, or close to it.

The Robbery/Seizure

Grant West continued to be watched. Then the opportunity arose to arrest him and take control of his devices. The arrest was going to take place on a train from Rhyl to London Euston. West had helpfully bought himself a first-class ticket (using someone else's bank account, of course), so the team also had to be in the same train car. One of the officers had followed him all the way from Rhyl. GW decided to open his laptop and get to work hacking accounts, which was very fortunate for us and in plain sight of the team.

Oblivious to the swarm of officers surrounding him, West proceeded to log into various parts of his infrastructure. At the time he was arrested, an officer distracted him while everyone else (in the finest traditions of British policing) tactically jumped on him. A brief melee ensued; on the video you can see one of the forensic team squirrel the laptop and phone away.

West was handcuffed, dusted down, and made to sit while applause broke out from the rest of first class. It began to slowly dawn on him that this was going to be a long train ride.

The forensic team had exited quickly to begin the slow and meticulous process of examining the laptop for evidence, recovering compromised data to safeguard victims' data, and locking down any VPSs or servers.

Once the team arrived at Euston, West was taken to the police station so that he could be booked and later interviewed. Searches took place of his trailer, storage units, and other premises. Cash and drugs were found, adding more evidence to the case.

The seizure order had already been obtained, and once all the searches were completed and all devices had been reviewed, I could start the painstaking process of seizing and transferring his crypto. Remember, this was all new to me and everyone else, so I made sure to copy as much as possible what we'd normally do with cash:

- Documenting and recording everything—screenshots, notes, timestamps, and so forth. The blockchain helps with public records.
- Ensuring sterile working environments.
- Using clean stand-alone devices, fresh installations of wallet software, and deposit addresses at our exchange account.

As I had all of West's wallet credentials, I re-created his wallets in new installations of wallet software on a new machine and then sent the BTC and other crypto to our exchange account. That account was locked down and could only receive funds.

Sounds simple, but it took a lot of coffee and hours to accomplish, recording every step and transaction. Once completed, I had drained all his wallets and sent word to our friends in the United States that we had arrested West. The covert part of the investigation was over, and we had secured a significant portion of money that could be used to pay back his victims.

On to the interview. At Charing Cross police station I had the pleasure of speaking to West again. He didn't say much, but I gave him the seizure order and the opportunity to sell his seized crypto. All the transaction IDs were given to him and his representatives so that they could independently verify the seizures. He was later charged and sent up to the court.

Court proceedings take a long time in the U.K. Because West was in custody, there were certain timeframes that had to be met in terms of serving evidence on his defense and the courts. After he was charged, a lot of work still had to be done to complete the case and submit the file to the prosecutors, to finalize the repatriation of assets to the U.K., and of course to deal with other crypto assets found on other devices after his arrest.

Lots of smaller amounts kept cropping up from storage media and older laptops, and each of these had to be seized and documented in the same manner as the first lot. On each occasion the courts, as well as West, had to be updated as to the status. He was again offered the opportunity to sell to safeguard the values. After we seized the crypto, it was sent to the same exchange to sit with the rest of the assets.

An interesting point to note is that before his arrest, a fork, or split, of Bitcoin took place. Some developers of Bitcoin wanted to institute changes in the base protocol that were not universally accepted. Because there was this impasse, a new chain was born in August 2017 called Bitcoin Cash (BCH). Everyone who held BTC at the time of the fork in a self-hosted wallet also had the equivalent amount of BCH.

I had to sweep his wallets not only for BTC but also BCH, which meant more assets to sell to pay back the victims. So always be mindful of this when conducting seizures. There may be other "hidden" assets that can be seized. Researching the chain and assets will provide you with the necessary information to make such an assessment.

The End

The criminal case rumbled on with numerous hearings and deadlines to meet. Eventually he pleaded guilty to the charges, and we had the fun and games of the sentencing hearing. It started with Kevin Barry getting email bombed. (This is when you receive a flood of emails that can be used to hide an account takeover—or simply to annoy the hell out of someone. . .Can't imagine who may have been responsible for this!)

It concluded with the summing up from the judge, who to the journalists' delight kept referring to the Just Eat credential stuffing attack as a "hack" and, once hearing all the criminal offenses West had committed, focused on one, saying, "If you, Grant West, are capable of attacking a fine establishment like British Airways, it makes me wonder what depths you are truly capable of."

West was sentenced to 10 years and 8 months. That was a very long sentence for cybercrime at the time in the U.K. Now the process of determining his earnings from his criminal activity could begin.

West had been active on AlphaBay for a long time. The U.S. authorities had seized the servers that hosted AlphaBay and were able to provide us with all his activity on that market. I could see that he had made over 1,500 BTC in sales of compromised details on that site. This may sound a lot given the current value of BTC, but at the time of his activity it was not.

Each sale on each dark net market had to be converted to the U.K. sterling equivalent to prove his earnings. This was a very laborious task.

During the various court hearings, the price of crypto was a hot topic of conversation between all parties as adoption and popularity soared. I would go so far as to say that most of the lawyers were "bitten by the Bitcoin bug" and would gleefully discuss the latest goings-on in crypto.

A calculation of West's earnings was duly provided, as well as an accounting of what had been seized, what had been seen in 2015, and an overview of his crypto accounts.

The courts decided on an amount of $600,000 that West had to pay back, and an order was issued.

Because we had an exchange account, all the crypto could be sold for cash and sent to the court's service bank account. No middlemen taking an administration fee and no auctions adding 20 percent on top. Using an exchange meant accessing highly liquid markets at low fees, using "white-glove" services such as an Over the Counter (OTC) desk or personalized trading services usually reserved for high-net-worth individuals or institutions.

In addition to this, we knew that many agencies (especially in the United States, where agencies were further ahead in their crypto journey) were also using this exchange because of their reputation in assisting law enforcement, maintaining an effective Anti-money Laundering (AML) compliance program, and registering with Financial Intelligence Units (FIUs) and regulators. All of this helps when deciding on the risks; you aren't going to use an exchange that is constantly under fire for being a bit shady, are you? But you *are* going to use one that many other agencies and corporations use daily for executing trades, that has many different fiat payment methods, and that is generally trusted in the financial community.

At the conclusion of the case, $600,000 was given back to the victims and the courts, West went to prison, and I left the police.

Check out these sites to learn more:

Adapted from `https://www.dailymail.co.uk/video/news/video-1681014/Video-Moment-officers-storm-train-carriage-arrest-Grant-West.html`

`https://www.theguardian.com/technology/2019/aug/23/bitcoin-seized-hacker-grant-west-uk-compensate-victims`

Terrific account, Iggy, and thank you for sharing it with us.

Building an Investigation in Bitcoin

Bitcoin was the first cryptocurrency that utilized a public blockchain. As we have discussed in previous chapters, Bitcoin became a bastion of criminality quite early on, and the investigative community has become quite adept at scrutinizing crimes involving it. Often when running training I have been asked for *the* accepted methodology or process for working a Bitcoin- or other crypto-oriented case. The problem that we are faced with is that crimes involving crypto do not all start in the same place or proceed in the same way, or even to the same destination. That sounds quite cryptic, so let's dive into that a bit.

When students attend a class or when I'm talking at a conference about investigating crypto crime, many assume that I'm talking about tracking and tracing assets over the blockchain. Of course, that will often be part of a crypto case, but not always. One of my earliest cases involved a man who had lost his $300,000 pension pot to a crypto theft. The funds had moved from his address to an address he didn't control. Seven years later, those stolen funds were still in that address. There were no clues in the tracing, as the address appeared to be owned by a personal crypto wallet with no attribution available in crypto intelligence tools. The thief stole the funds and maybe got cold feet or lost the "private key" to the wallet they moved the funds to. So, in this case, although it was a crypto theft and everyone assumed that the first step would be to jump into our expensive tracing tool, actually it was not helpful and other more physical clues had to be considered. In this case the victim kept their seed words in their physical wallet and left the wallet in their jacket in the staff room at work. To add to this, the victim had told one or two people to keep an eye on the jacket because his Bitcoin seed words were in there, representing his whole pension pot. (This would be a good place for a "face-palm" emoji if I was allowed to use them!) This case required traditional questioning of suspects, nondigital forensics, and CCTV, building a case around those physical clues.

If you are dealing with a case such as a murder, they tend to start with a body and end with the identification and hopefully prosecution of a murderer. Although there are many twists and turns, most cases head in a similar direction and process. This would involve forensics, pathology, CCTV, digital forensics, timelining, suspect identification, and so on. However, with crypto you may face a crypto theft or fraud, or the case could just involve crypto in that a drug dealer was using it to store funds or crypto was being used to pay people in an otherwise traditional criminal enterprise. Hence, a forensic methodology written on an FBI-style, bullet-pointed, laminated sheet is very difficult to define.

The tracking and tracing of funds as they move through a public blockchain such as Bitcoin is the mainstay of crypto investigations, but there are a number of areas that an investigator should be aware of. Although it's possible to track funds using open source tools, the reality is that if you are planning to carry out investigations that are likely to be used to prosecute, defend, or otherwise depend on accuracy of interpretation, then a commercial blockchain intelligence tool will be important. You might need more than one tool if your budget can stretch that far. However, even if you have access to these tools, it's still important to be able to recognize patterns in transactions and also understand what the tool is doing behind the scenes.

Almost the entire *Investigating Cryptocurrencies* book that I published in 2018 was about understanding and investigating Bitcoin as Ethereum and other EVM-style blockchains had not yet become popular in the criminal community. Although some of the tools and techniques that worked back in 2018 may no longer work, the fundamental details and concepts of understanding the investigative process on the Bitcoin blockchain have not changed. So if you want to understand Bitcoin at a technical level, I strongly suggest reading that book. In the remainder of this chapter, we'll look at key investigative concepts.

Let's begin with clustering!

Address Clustering

The concept of crypto address clustering is simple. A *cluster* of crypto addresses refers to a group of cryptocurrency addresses that are believed to be controlled by the same entity or individual. This grouping is typically inferred through various heuristics and analytical techniques that examine patterns of transactions, shared usage, and other blockchain metadata. In this section, I'll show you some of these methods.

Clustering was developed to help investigators and analysts understand the relationship between multiple addresses, to track the flow of funds, and to identify the activities and ownership behind seemingly disparate wallet addresses. By identifying clusters, you can often uncover larger networks of transactions and gain insights into the behaviors and connections within the blockchain ecosystem. As a basic example, say you find a crypto address being used by a suspect during a search of a digital device. Clustering techniques may help you identify other addresses used by the suspect that can help extend your investigation.

When a Bitcoin investigator talks about clustering, it is important to understand what they mean, since there are a number of ways by which clusters can be used. This breaks down into two primary uses:

Ownership Clusters. Most blockchain intelligence tools use ownership clustering in their databases. This is the action of grouping addresses under a single entity/owner using various heuristic and analytical methods. This, for example, enables all addresses identified as being owned by an exchange such as Binance to be stored together. This facilitates metadata such as the throughput of funds to be aggregated for the entire scope of addresses owned, giving you a better idea of the value of an investigation. Although this is not terribly useful when looking at a cluster owned by an exchange, it is very helpful when you find a suspect's address and the cluster provides other addresses and aggregates the total number of transactions, as well as funds received, spent, and held by the suspect. This metadata is sometimes missed by investigators, who can become rather fixated with tracing the movement of funds rather than focusing on what can be learned by the transaction metadata.

For example, if you search any of the primary blockchain intelligence tools for an address owned by suspected (as of this writing) Botnet 911 S5 admin Yunhe Wang, you will find that there are another 60-plus addresses in the cluster. Some of the individual addresses associated with Yunhe Wang had as little as $900 received, but the entire cluster showed earnings just shy of $130 million. If you only had the one small address, you could potentially miss the fact that this is a major criminal enterprise. Because of this, clustering addresses is vital for the investigator.

Cluster-Level Tracing. Some commercial tools, such as Chainalysis, graph address tracing results using cluster-level entities. This means that if you search for a single address—let's use an address alleged to have been owned by Yunhe Wang as an example again—instead of just plotting that single address, the tool will by default plot an entity to the screen that represents the entire cluster of 60-plus addresses. Other tools such as ones from TRM Labs work the opposite way and will plot just the address you have asked for while still providing the cluster metadata if requested. Such tools enable you to plot by cluster or by single address, but as of this writing their default settings are different.

Cluster-level tracing can be extremely useful in getting a high-level view of a case and can help keep potentially massive graphs to a manageable size. However, many courts prefer the evidence to be in the form of specific address-level tracing. The reason for this was explained to me by a financial crime investigator at the Metropolitan Police in the U.K. She used the example of bank accounts and told me that they would often aggregate the value of bank holdings or throughput so that they could say, "This suspect has a total bank held cash value of. . ." But when presenting movement of funds, the court requires that the data put into evidence focus on the specific bank account and even more specific transaction with its more granular metadata, rather than a generic statement that *X* amount left a bank account. This can relate to blockchain transactions. Instead of stating that a certain amount of Bitcoin left the cluster, you need a transaction ID from and to specific crypto addresses.

If you are buying a commercial tool, you will need to do your own research and consider how you work to decide on the right tool for you. The next section will deal with ownership clusters.

How Are Clusters Defined?

Clusters can be built using a variety of methods. I will outline just the key techniques, but keep in mind there are more complex and protected methods used by blockchain intelligence companies.

Co-spend Heuristic

A Bitcoin wallet can contain many used and unused addresses. To pay an amount of Bitcoin, a user may have to use a number of addresses with individual values in order to make the payment. For example, say a user has three addresses with one Bitcoin, two Bitcoin, and four Bitcoin in them. He wants to spend 6.5 Bitcoin. This means that all three addresses will be needed to carry out the transaction and generate change. All of the addresses on the input side of a transaction, by definition, have to be owned by the same entity. Although this statement breaks with CoinJoin transactions, they are easy to identify, and to ignore, when building a cluster.

Let's assume that you've found an address, 35GHbYHRaDFgG7Rey WP3L6d7PgqgB1itV2. (It is worth noting that a Bitcoin address may also exist on forked chains such as Bitcoin Cash.) If you look at the metadata around this address, you see that (as of this writing) it has been involved in 52 transactions and has received 1.131 . . .Bitcoin. However, if you look at the transactions such as TXID 46ed5f6da0f2c04d61e718b2d14c87661d1d1f12dec67fd56bcd0140c4decebe, you see that the address is input with five other addresses:

```
Input (6)1.51725076 BTC
        3FwYUzmNYYAEWg644EiYrJUG3pTCcGzZHw
        35GHbYHRaDFgG7ReyWP3L6d7PgqgB1itV2 (Address we searched for)
        3HGkVo45HqhpGrMBaLNhR6AL4zvVAqLZxz
        3GS9UJBfgh1zaau7mXR3FCGC9qY7Lsn61v
        3KpUH5vht9pvGtAuye6onviBedJe51ztn9
        3MU2j7BEzmHyRKcMshGLVUoHu7GUo5UatK
```

You can think of all these addresses as owned by the same entity, person, or service that owns the original address you searched for: 35GHbYH. Now imagine that you add these addresses to a spreadsheet and then work through all the other transactions that include 35GHbYH and add all those addresses. The next step you need to think about. Take all of the new addresses you've found and look at all the other transactions they are involved in, and then extract all the other input addresses, and so on and so on. If you are feeling like you have nothing else to do today, try clustering all the addresses you can from this start address. Actually, don't try that—it's a terrible idea. If you cheat and look at the cluster in a commercial tool, you will find that it's owned by the exchange OKX and that there are nearly 13 million addresses in the cluster. There are other grouping methods, but this one is the primary process.

Change Analysis

It is important to be able to identify the output address that contains the change being returned to the person who triggered the transaction. There are two primary reasons for this:

- If we are building a cluster of addresses, then the change address becomes part of that cluster.
- If we are following a suspect's money and tracing funds, if we don't know what the change address is, then we can end up tracing the change funds around in circles, thinking that we are following the coins to other users rather than back into the suspect's wallet.

There are a number of ways to identify a change address, and some block explorers such as Blockchair and commercial blockchain intelligence tools will attempt to identify the change address for you. It's important, though, that you are familiar with the methods that can be used to do it manually. We will look at four primary ways of working out the change address in the transaction:

- A method that is known by various names—simple spend, nominal spend, or optimal change
- Address type analysis
- Multisig analysis
- Round number payments

Bear in mind that all these methods provide an indication of the change address, but they can be wrong because they rely on inferred conclusions. It is useful when you get several of these heuristics that support each other.

Nominal Spend

The concept of finding a change address is pretty simple but often causes all manner of confusion when we teach the process in class. Bitcoin transactions all charge a fee, and the larger the transaction size in bytes, the more expensive the fee. For each address referenced, this increases the size of the transaction; therefore, it's more expensive. To deal with this, wallet software will build a transaction as efficiently as possible to keep the fee as low as possible. Hence, when a user triggers a transaction, the wallet will look at all the addresses available with funds to be able to cover the required spend. As I mentioned in Chapter 9, "The Workings of Bitcoin and Derivatives," because there are 100 million satoshis (the smallest divisible unit) in a Bitcoin, the odds of having exactly the right value inputs to produce an intended output, including an unknown fee, is essentially 100 million to 1. Even if you wanted to spend exactly one Bitcoin and had an address with one Bitcoin available from a previous transaction, this would not allow for the fee and therefore another previous incoming transaction would need to be included to cover the fee. So, sending a third party exactly the right amount plus the fee and for it to be correct to the 100 millionth satoshi is highly improbable, so change will almost always be part of a transaction unless a wallet is just moving funds, perhaps to another wallet they own.

Nominal spend works by taking into account that the wallet will use the minimum number of inputs, so if we compare each input value with the output amounts, we can predict what the change is. We can ask the simple question, "Are all the inputs needed to pay the highest output?" Confused? A real-world example can be found at TXID ac7e855d06a7a1d1b0fe4000bf11feea6e1fee44e18675549ec696e766581244.

Here we see a transaction with three inputs and two outputs:

Inputs

```
bc1qqjew4scj0ywlpapx...zxu8ljkqd5lrym4zvf40    0.03183296
bc1qqjew4scj0ywlpapx...zxu8ljkqd5lrym4zvf40    0.00304770
bc1qqjew4scj0ywlpapx...zxu8ljkqd5lrym4zvf40    0.49107418
```

Outputs

```
3PtJ3KRdnNz9TuH3D4AiLBEerPJxnAjgJf             0.51884135
bc1qsy74gfue39f5amnp...7l8a7dtpghk4zh28srr2    0.00642224
```

If we look at the inputs, we see that they are all the same address. Why? Because, as you learned in Chapter 9 you can only spend whole individual inputs, so the address bc1qqjew has received these three amounts (0.03183296, 0.00304770, and 0.49107418) in previous individual transactions.

If we now look at the outputs, were all three inputs required to pay for the output bc1qsy7 0.0064222? No, two of the three inputs could have paid the 0.0064222 without the need for the others. What about the 3PtJ3KR 0.51884135? We can see that all three inputs were needed to pay this amount, including the fee, so this is the payment in the transaction and bc1qsy7 is the change.

If you understand, well done and move on, but if you are still struggling with the concept, take a look at TXID 03ba36a19bb7cb3ede88dd4cca78a9bed380524c8995a6a910e98f944ee91053. I am a bit attached to this example as I have used it in training for many years, and it's quite easy to figure out the payment address and change address. Take a look at the transaction and see if you can figure it out.

Inputs

1FkRsNmsacihn4iH5eFLEzogX55hEGkate.	1.00000000 BTC	$67,087.65
16SFxoGe4K4vkctJ4Y2mAFYoiUkTwKY4yc	0.99951167 BTC	$67,054.89
1C3NQAvQmoqNF7Ppw6wio6i3yH5kWr7qet.	0.78960600 BTC	$52,972.81

Outputs

19GmggChQdakj3fb66ecrk53EkmJQ4e7Vj	0.78856700 BTC	$52,903.11
1PsKxKtARw9fU6mA6m7L4zM7W241uWGRwD.	2.00000000 BTC	$134,175.00

Take a minute to look at this carefully and it becomes quite obvious what the change is. All of the individual inputs could have paid the 0.78856700 BTC from the 19Gmgg output (with the fee 1C3NQA it would have been close but not quite enough). However, all three payments were needed to pay the output of 2 BTC for 1PsKxKt. Therefore, 1PsKxKt is the primary payment and 19Gmgg must be the change.

What does this mean in reality? Two things. First, we can cluster 19Gmgg back into the inputs as an address belonging to our suspect. Second, we can be confident in following the money onwards rather than going around in circles.

Address Type Analysis

When you set up a wallet, it will follow the BIP standard that you specify. This could result in Bitcoin addresses that start with a 1, a 3, or a bc1. This means that change addresses generated by the wallet will follow the same address protocol. So, if the input addresses are "1" addresses, then the change addresses will also almost certainly be "1" addresses.

Let's return to the first example from the previous section to see a good example of this:

Inputs

bc1qqjew4scj0ywlpapx...zxu8ljkqd5lrym4zvf40.	0.03183296
bc1qqjew4scj0ywlpapx...zxu8ljkqd5lrym4zvf40.	0.00304770
bc1qqjew4scj0ywlpapx...zxu8ljkqd5lrym4zvf40.	0.49107418

Outputs

```
3PtJ3KRdnNz9TuH3D4AiLBEerPJxnAjgJf                0.51884135
bc1qsy74gfue39f5amnp...718a7dtpghk4zh28srr2.     0.00642224
```

Note that the outputs are a "3" address and a "bc1" address. As the input wallet contains all "bc1" addresses, we would expect the change to also be a "bc1" address—and this is what we see. Is it possible that they had configured wallets to generate change back to a different wallet with a different address type? That's possible, although it's hard to do. However, the nominal spend calculation identified that the "bc1" address was the spend and the payment was the "3" address, so the address type analysis simply confirms this for us. When we have two analysis types confirming payment and address, this can help increase the confidence we have in which payment to follow and can be useful when outlining evidence for court. One heuristic can be quite easily challenged, but when it is confirmed by other heuristics it helps prove the conclusion you've made.

Multisig Analysis

Bitcoin wallets can be configured to require multiple users with their individual private key signatures to sign any transaction before it can be sent. These are called multisignature, or multisig, wallets. When the wallet is set up, the user defines how many signatures are involved in the use of the wallet and how many are required to sign a transaction. For example, a wallet can be set up with four users' keys, and it can be specified that only two of the four are required to sign a transaction. It would be very rare to see four of four required because if a user lost their key or was hit by a proverbial (or real) bus, then the wallet would be locked forever.

If we see that inputs to a transaction are from a wallet defined as being for three users but only two are required to sign, we would call that a multisig two-of-three wallet, often written as *multisig 2/3*. In the outputs, if we saw multisig 3/4 and multisig 2/3, then it is most likely that the 2/3 wallet is the change as it comes from the same wallet type. Let's look at an example. If you are looking at the TXIDs on the blockchain, then I recommend using `www.blockchair.com` for the example shown in Figure 10.1.

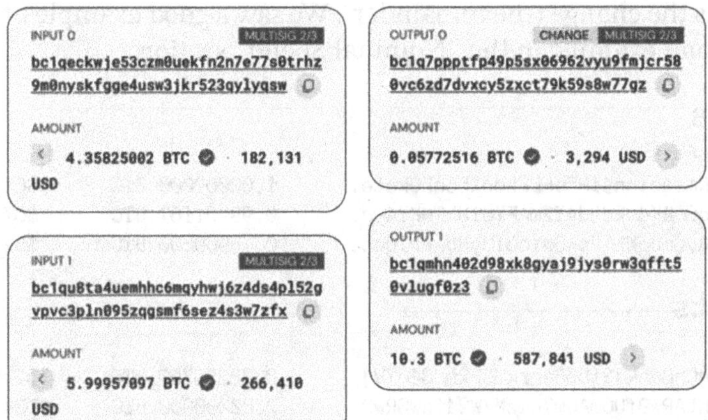

Figure 10.1: Multisig transaction from a 2/3 wallet

It was easier to use an image for this example, as the display on Blockchair.com uses these terrific little notification headers, which can be very useful. On the input side, we see that the addresses are from a multisig 2/3 wallet. The outputs are other "bc1" addresses, so we couldn't use address type analysis, but we see one address that is also multisig 2/3, indicating that it is likely the change. Blockchair helpfully also tags the address with the header "Change," confirming our analysis.

Is there another heuristic we could use to confirm that bc1q7ppp is the change? Yes; if we look at the values, both inputs are required to pay bc1qmhn, but either would have been sufficient to pay bc1q7ppp.

Round Number Payments

This is a really easy one. You ask, "Is one of the payments a round number?" Because there are 100 million satoshis in one Bitcoin, the odds of a payment and a fee leaving a change amount of, for example, 1 exact Bitcoin is literally 100 million to 1. However, humans tend to think in round numbers and will often pay using nice, easy-to-remember numbers. For example, a scammer is unlikely to ask for 0.24736589 BTC in their scam email or ransomware alert. They will ask for 0.3, 0.1, 1 or generally a nice, easy number. When we see this, it provides us with a quick heuristic to define which is the payment (the round number) and which is the change (the remainder). We saw a good example of this in the second example in the "Nominal Spend" section:

Inputs

```
1FkRsNmsacihn4iH5eFLEzogX55hEGkate.       1.00000000 BTC      $67,087.65
16SFxoGe4K4vkctJ4Y2mAFYoiUkTwKY4yc.       0.99951167 BTC      $67,054.89
1C3NQAvQmoqNF7Ppw6wio6i3yH5kWr7qet.       0.78960600 BTC      $52,972.81
```

Outputs

```
19GmggChQdakj3fb66ecrk53EkmJQ4e7Vj        0.78856700 BTC      $52,903.11
1PsKxKtARw9fU6mA6m7L4zM7W241uWGRwD.       2.00000000 BTC     $134,175.00
```

Notice that the address we identified as the primary payment using the payment amount heuristic is also a payment for exactly 2 BTC. This leaves change of 0.78856700 BTC. The odds of the 0.78856700 BTC leaving precisely 2 BTC, as I mentioned, is 100 million to 1.

Some Other Things to Note

There are some other clues that can help you identify the payment and change address, but they are pretty obvious and don't require any detail. For example, some wallets use the same input address as the change address; this can be easy to miss so watch out for it. Some addresses are set up as "vanity" addresses, which contain a clue as to the owner such as:

```
1N1CKFVvXjJ538y3rgY6HUptdDHspEHyYK
```

Some blockchain explorers such as Blockchair.com will attempt to identify a change address for us; the same is true of many commercial blockchain intelligence tools. However, I always recommend spending time to confirm the identity of the payment and change yourself if you are able to. I mentioned court evidence earlier; if you presented evidence that a particular address was payment and the other was the change based purely on a tool output, you could be open to criticism. Therefore, it is wise to manually confirm these things when you can.

Change of Ownership

Identifying when funds move from one owner to another can be a valuable skill when investigating movement of funds on the Bitcoin blockchain. Many of the clustering and change analysis skills that we have discussed can be useful to ascertain when funds move from one owner to another, but please remember that this can only ever be an educated guess unless we can get resulting hard ownership information from an exchange or other service that can provide know-your-customer (KYC) data.

Change of Wallet

As discussed earlier, if we see funds moving from a "1" wallet to a "3" wallet, this may lead us to conclude that funds have moved ownership. But it's possible that the user simply moved funds to another wallet that they own, so how can we extend our investigation to provide a higher level of confidence in our conclusion?

Look at the Amounts

Users tend to think in round numbers, and so if a user is spreading funds between wallets, then often round numbers are used—for example, sending 0.3 BTC rather than 0.35676523 BTC. If a user is moving all their funds to a new wallet, then we could tend to see inputs of a list of addresses to a single output address with no change. Why? Well, if they clear a wallet to another address, all the funds will move from the wallet, including from all change addresses, and the fee will be paid. No change is required as all funds are moving.

This transaction is a good example of a user simply moving all their funds, likely to a new wallet that they control (note there's no change):

Inputs

```
bc1q34lqcua8wh7lvue8...6zej0jt7f3zdy4n8gc00.   0.00557547
bc1q34lqcua8wh7lvue8...6zej0jt7f3zdy4n8gc00.   0.00191348
bc1qkp9u9uwptkjwkfdw...5wv0p2tsnu2jpsyygfyf.   0.00063892
bc1q34lqcua8wh7lvue8...6zej0jt7f3zdy4n8gc00.   0.00232593
bc1qkp9u9uwptkjwkfdw...5wv0p2tsnu2jpsyygfyf.   0.00031369
bc1qkp9u9uwptkjwkfdw...5wv0p2tsnu2jpsyygfyf.   0.00063812
bc1qkp9u9uwptkjwkfdw...5wv0p2tsnu2jpsyygfyf.   0.00046871
```

Output

```
bc1qnxq0vegmsc5wj34g...ngatfszp07uuf2zclpcn.   0.01084202
```

It can be easy to look at a transaction and just assume a change of ownership, but examples such as this one are more likely to be movements within wallets controlled by the same person. Note that I said *more likely*. There are reasons why someone would move their entire wallet; being scammed is a good example.

Other patterns help us conclude change of ownership, such as movement of funds to an exchange. When you move funds to an exchange, you request a deposit address, which the exchange provides, and you then move funds to the deposit address. This will look like a standard transaction almost certainly with change. However, if you identify the payment address and follow that to the next transaction, it will generally be the exchange consolidating a large number of deposits into a single address, usually a hot, or live, wallet controlled by the exchange.

A good example would be TXID 0fef4aae322eeb271882b5e 2200ef4593e617244de4b4797e5272ce416b347f2, which shows 60 inputs to 1 output. It's too big to print here, but take a look in a block explorer. If you have a blockchain intelligence tool, you will see that the output address is owned by Binance in this case, confirming that the funds are moving into an exchange. (Remember that you cannot track through centralized exchanges; you can sometimes trace through decentralized exchanges, and I'll cover this in Chapter 12, "Ethereum: Investigation Methodology.")

The converse is also true when you see a transaction with a single input address and a large number of output addresses. This is often funds leaving an exchange or service bound for many different users. You can see an example of this at TXID 27b3360e96c7785a901161f7e 7090294429a4ede02925cb4da9d2cf15bcc3773. In this case, a single address sends a variety of sums to 20 addresses of differing wallet types. Again the input address is attributed to Binance in a blockchain intelligence tool.

It's very important to be able to discern change of ownership if you can, and this leads us to the next point: How many blind transaction hops should you take before you stop? What I mean by this is that if you are examining a transaction that you know relates to your suspect, you identify the primary payment or payments and follow the money on. Is this next wallet owned by your suspect or has it changed hands? You use the techniques we've discussed, but you still cannot discern who this belongs to. So, you then open up your blockchain intelligence tool, and it doesn't have any attribution for it either. If it's not in the cluster with the original addresses, then you can be fairly comfortable that it's changed hands but not with a high level of confidence. How much further do you go? I've always had a three-hop rule. If I have followed the funds for three transaction hops and I still don't know the owner or haven't clearly identified a change of ownership, then I stop and try another route.

The exception to this rule is when the transactions seem to enter a mixer. We will talk a little more about mixers later in the book, but mixers tend to work on patterns. These patterns can be something like combining coins, splitting coins into an onward chain, taking the rest as change, and then repeating many times to obfuscate the original coins. Following a mixing chain is an advanced technique and won't be covered in this book.

As you will learn in Chapter 14, "Applying What You Have Learned to New Cryptocurrencies," mixers are sometimes referred to as "peel chains." To be technically accurate, mixers entwine funds from multiple users whereas peel chains tend to look like a small amount (often low value) of BTC being sent to an exchange or other service and the remainder returned as change and then repeated many, many times.

Address Triage

I wrote extensively in *Investigating Cryptocurrencies* about the risk of seeing crypto-oriented investigations as just about following the money, tracing from one transaction to the next. The blockchain enables you to follow funds continuously until they hit a service such as an exchange, but just because you can doesn't mean you should. In fact, some of the worst reports and tracing graphs that I have seen are the ones that look the "coolest"! Lines going everywhere, splits and combines, bridges and coin conversions—generally, graphs like that are fundamentally meaningless and do not add anything to a report. I have to admit to once submitting a graph with over 700 transactions on it, but that was demonstrating a complex mixing of funds. I think the best transaction graph I ever submitted had only two transactions on it. The scammer had received funds from a victim and moved them straight to an exchange in Asia. When it comes to crypto reports, *simple* should be the watchword. Trying to look clever when submitting a complex report will only make you look foolish when you realize that no one else understands it and then it becomes useless as evidence.

In the previous section, I discussed generally not tracing more than three hops if we do not have a meaningful reason for the funds moving or any reliable attribution. The reality is that once we have an address that we know is owned by a suspect and then apply clustering heuristics to find other addresses, either manually or via our blockchain intelligence tool, there are other things we can do to help the investigation.

If you are given or locate an address from a suspect, take time to triage the address before immediately heading down the tracing rabbit hole. Triage can include looking at the patterns of dates and times. When did an address first appear on the blockchain? When was it last used? These questions can help you understand the timeframe of a scam or see whether the address use fits in with other details of your investigation. The same type of questions can be asked about the values. Do the values appear to be the same as the ones the suspect was asking victims for in a ransomware or "pig butchering" scam? The number of inbound transactions can help us understand the likely number of victims in a scam investigation. Then, clustering addresses helps us extend the investigation and perhaps locate more victims.

If you have a commercial blockchain intelligence tool, you will usually find many graphs showing the flow of funds over time for an address or a cluster, or the total and average values of inbound and outbound coins. Don't ignore this data; it can help you identify or confirm patterns of use or perhaps suspected timeframes.

If you do not have access to a commercial tool, there are ways of getting raw data from blockchain explorers. You can use an application programming interface (API), which requires some technical knowledge, or you can use an export feature to get at raw JavaScript Object Notation (JSON) or comma-separated values (CSV) files. I covered API calls fairly extensively in *Investigating Cryptocurrencies* but that information has not stood the test of time very well—explorers changed their APIs, removed them, or put them behind a paywall. Currently, my favorite API is provided by Blockchair and allows direct access to 14 blockchains. For the number of times that an investigator would use it, it only costs about $1 each time. You can find the documentation at `https://blockchair.com/api/docs`.

The other method of extracting raw data is via the export functions of blockchain explorers. Again, in the past few years many sites have either removed this ability or made it pay only. As of this writing Blockchair still has a free export feature. Although you can export this data into a spreadsheet such as Microsoft Excel, more recently I've been using ChatGPT to help me with analysis. You can choose to do this even if you're not a programmer. ChatGPT will look at a CSV file and format it appropriately and then generate code, such as Python code, to carry out analysis and generate graphs. I appreciate that many investigators are not programmers, but I'm a big fan of a tool called PyCharm that enables you to copy and paste code straight from ChatGPT and then run it without needing to know any command lines or anything overly technical.

I used Blockchair to export the transaction records for a random Bitcoin address. Then, as an example, I used the following ChatGPT prompt:

> *I'd like you to do some data analysis for me. I'm uploading an Excel spreadsheet that contains all the data related to Bitcoin address 1La7LPC9U9WSRL2nhKC MmU2nUFb65YMGGj and all the transactions that include this address. I need analysis done on the following categories: date analysis, time analysis, value analysis, and any other insights you think would be useful to me as an investigator. Please graph everything you think is useful in an appropriate graphing format.*

ChatGPT then provided some fairly simple Python code that output a series of useful graphs such as Transaction Counts over Time and Distribution of Transactions by Hour of Day. I did have to reformat the log data a little, removing quotation marks and changing semicolons to commas (see Figure 10.2 and Figure 10.3).

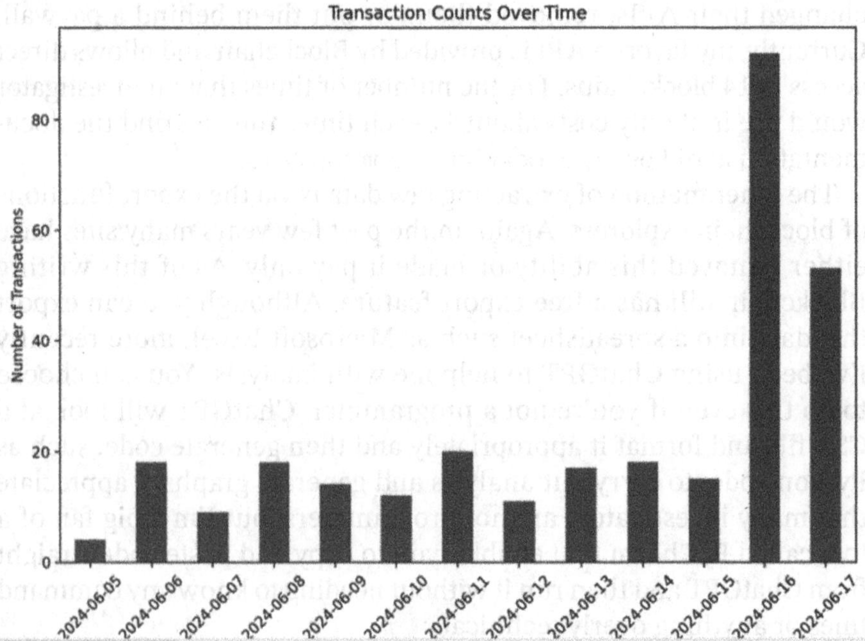

Figure 10.2: Graph showing transaction counts over time

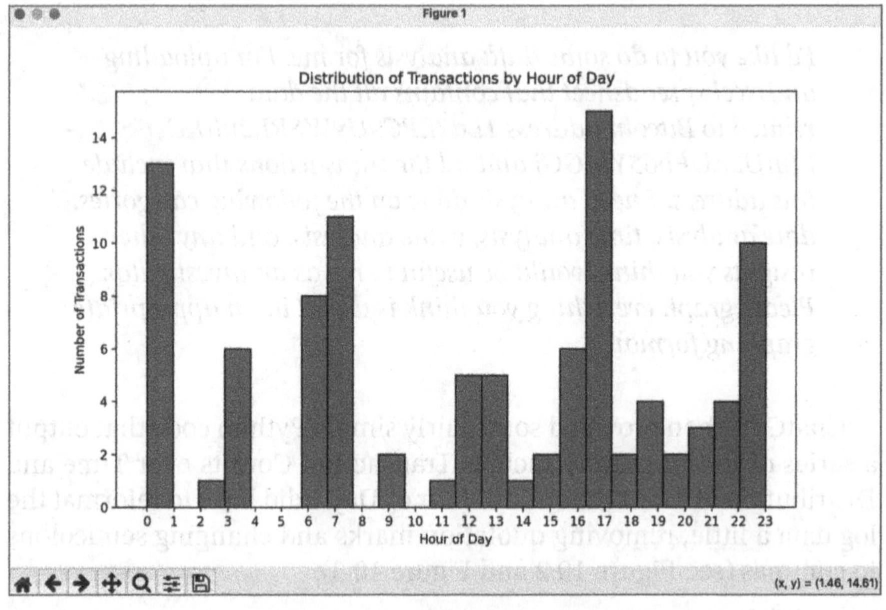

Figure 10.3: Graph showing distribution of transactions by hour of day

The code generated by ChatGPT was as follows:

```
import pandas as pd
from io import StringIO
import matplotlib.pyplot as plt
import seaborn as sns

# Sample data as provided by the user
data = """
Transactions number,Affected address/xpub,Effect,Ticker,Amount
fiat (USD),Asset rate (USD),Date/Time,Transaction hash
1,1La7LPC9U9WSRL2nhKCMmU2nUFb65YMGGj,0.00666645,BTC,441.22,
66185.21,2024-06-17 21:36:07,a31a28e53b6b09f2d0db02d3d4
609876ba0bacc3603b93b4b3acf2ea006645b7
2,1La7LPC9U9WSRL2nhKCMmU2nUFb65YMGGj,0.0001929,BTC,12.77,
66185.21,2024-06-17 21:26:20,93880d1ff731a2f8f9bf3ad7a8b
56be5522a5fe49d5a90ecf3aa924bd765a1b9
3,1La7LPC9U9WSRL2nhKCMmU2nUFb65YMGGj,0.00105143,BTC,69.59,
66185.21,2024-06-17 21:26:20,43a673d6158489b793d697487fa3b
619b0b268f8111955d53c2a8df0588527ab
4,1La7LPC9U9WSRL2nhKCMmU2nUFb65YMGGj,0.00378036,BTC,250.20,
66185.21,2024-06-17 20:16:20,63e7012ee96c72946e6d162a2ceff
30c390ea90dca4d59902155e23f7bfb6c7d
5,1La7LPC9U9WSRL2nhKCMmU2nUFb65YMGGj,0.00008311,BTC,5.50,
66185.21,2024-06-17 19:38:10,b9d1619309ab553492f7e0b2a189
ec8b51164958937a004d97042dcbbbc1533c
"""

# Read the sample data into a DataFrame
df = pd.read_csv(StringIO(data))

# Convert Date/Time to datetime
df['Date/Time'] = pd.to_datetime(df['Date/Time'])

# Create additional columns for analysis
df['Date'] = df['Date/Time'].dt.date
df['Time'] = df['Date/Time'].dt.time
df['Hour'] = df['Date/Time'].dt.hour

# Plot transaction counts over time
plt.figure(figsize=(10, 6))
df.groupby('Date').size().plot(kind='bar', title='Transaction
Counts Over Time')
plt.xlabel('Date')
plt.ylabel('Number of Transactions')
plt.xticks(rotation=45)
# plt.show()
```

```
# Plot distribution of transactions by time of day
plt.figure(figsize=(10, 6))
sns.histplot(df['Hour'], bins=24, kde=False)
plt.title('Distribution of Transactions by Hour of Day')
plt.xlabel('Hour of Day')
plt.ylabel('Number of Transactions')
plt.xticks(range(0, 24))
# plt.show()

# Plot value of transactions in BTC
plt.figure(figsize=(10, 6))
df.plot(kind='bar', x='Date/Time', y='Effect', title='Value of
Transactions in BTC', color='blue')
plt.xlabel('Date/Time')
plt.ylabel('Value (BTC)')
plt.xticks(rotation=45)
# plt.show()

# Plot value of transactions in USD
plt.figure(figsize=(10, 6))
df.plot(kind='bar', x='Date/Time', y='Amount fiat (USD)',
title='Value of Transactions in USD', color='green')
plt.xlabel('Date/Time')
plt.ylabel('Value (USD)')
plt.xticks(rotation=45)
# plt.show()

# Adjust layout to prevent overlap
plt.tight_layout()
plt.show()

# Display summary statistics for additional insights
summary_stats = df.describe()
summary_stats
```

I've included five lines of raw data from a Blockchair output, but my testing of this was with over 500 lines of transaction logs. You'll need to install the dependencies Pandas, Matplotlib, and Seaborn. If you don't know how to do that, ask ChatGPT or use a tool like PyCharm.

If you want to get a little more advanced, you can connect the code to an API call to extract the data directly from a blockchain explorer and produce the graphs. I'll leave that up to you.

The purpose of this code is not to just produce pretty graphs but to triage an address to understand any patterns that may help with your analysis.

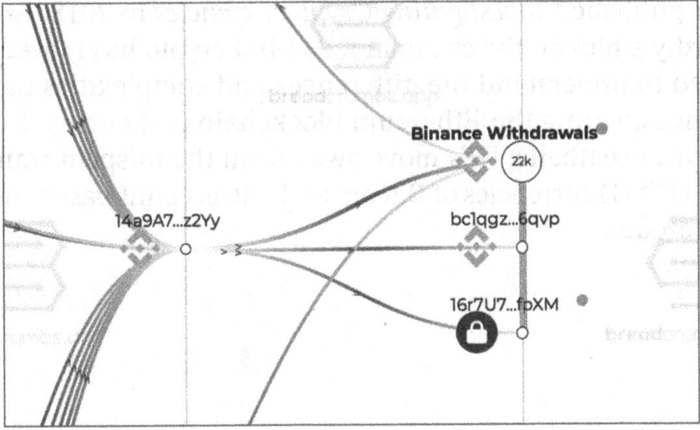

Figure 10.4: Graph from `Breadcrumbs.app` showing attribution

Attribution

One of the primary reasons for buying a commercial blockchain intelligence tool such as TRM, Chainalysis, or Elliptic is to get access to their attribution database. These companies spend millions of dollars clustering addresses and working to identify likely attribution from those clusters. This is achieved in many ways, such as test spends, open source information, court and government records, and many other heuristics that are confidential to each company. If you do not have access to any of these tools, there are a few free or low-cost options such as Wallet Explorer (`http://walletexplorer.com`). An excellent choice is Breadcrumbs (`http://breadcrumbs.app`), which has a significant database of attributed addresses and, as of this writing, has a free option (see Figure 10.4).

Investigating Bitcoin

What stands out from this chapter and Chapter 9 is not the words that you have just read on the subject of Bitcoin investigation, but rather just how much is missing. As I mentioned at the start of this chapter, almost my entire *Investigating Cryptocurrencies* book was about Bitcoin and that was four times the length of these two chapters. These two chapters have given you enough information to understand how Bitcoin works and how you can use the blockchain to investigate malevolent behavior.

When I published *Investigating Cryptocurrencies* in 2018, Ethereum was hardly a blip on the criminal radar, but crypto has moved on and you need to understand the differences and complexities that come when investigating the Ethereum blockchain and currencies like it. Fasten your seatbelts; let's move away from the unspent transaction output (UTXO) currencies of Bitcoin and into account-based currencies like Ethereum.

11 The Workings of Ethereum and Derivatives

In this chapter, we will provide sample Ethereum addresses, and we encourage you to get out a computing device so that you can look at the examples in a blockchain viewer yourself. You will learn a lot more if you get involved.

However, we know it's a pain typing in the addresses by hand and it's easy to make mistakes. If you have a smartphone available (we're using an iPhone), open the camera and point it at the book, Kindle, or whatever device you are reading on. You can press the text icon (number 1 in Figure 11.1), and it will extract any text in the yellow chevrons. Next you can use your finger to highlight the address, as in Figure 11.1. The iPhone will recognize this as a Ethereum address, and you can press the link (number 2 on the image) to browse straight to the block explorer recommended—in this case, Etherscan.io. Alternatively, you can copy the address and paste it manually into your notes or whatever you wish.

The history of criminal crypto use is dominated by Bitcoin, and we have discussed it at length. However, the majority of investigations I have been involved with in the past four years has been on the Ethereum network, and it is vital that investigators understand the fundamental differences between the two currencies. Because my book *Investigating Cryptocurrencies: Understanding, Extracting, and Analyzing Blockchain Evidence* (Wiley, 2018) went into significant detail about the workings of Bitcoin, you can still use the book as a reference. However, that book did not deal with Ethereum in any detail, and so we will cover it more extensively in the next few chapters.

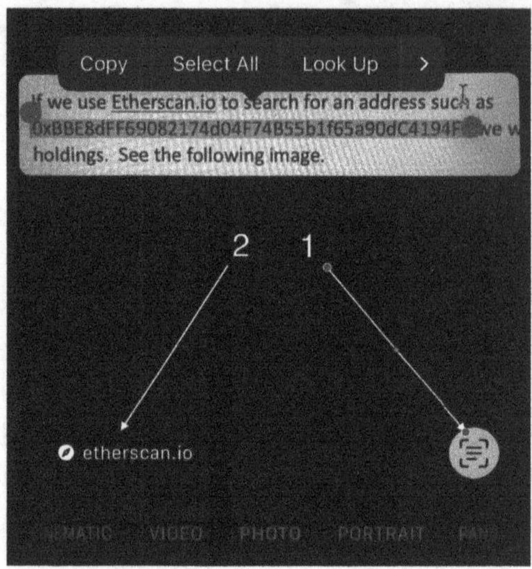

Figure 11.1: iPhone highlight text feature

In this chapter, you will learn about the history of the Ethereum cryptocurrency, the workings of the blockchain, and how smart contracts work to enable the creation of tokens and other contracts. Finally, this chapter examines how we follow both the transactions for its primary coin, ETH, and complex contract transactions.

Much of what you will learn in this chapter will translate to investigating funds on blockchains that use a similar codebase, such as TRON and Binance Smart Chain.

History of the Ethereum Cryptocurrency

Ethereum stands as a pivotal cryptocurrency with a profound influence on the development of blockchain technology and decentralized applications otherwise known as dApps. Its inception in 2015 marked a significant moment in the evolution of digital currencies.

The foundation of Ethereum can be attributed to visionary programmer Vitalik Buterin. In late 2013, Buterin introduced the Ethereum whitepaper, outlining his ambition to create a novel blockchain platform capable of accommodating smart contracts and dApps. He recognized the limitations of Bitcoin's scripting language and aspired to establish a more versatile framework.

Ethereum's journey was initiated through a public crowd sale in July 2014, amassing an impressive $18 million in funding.

NOTE In 2021, I did an investigation for a man who had bought 3,000 ETH during the initial sale at around $1 per ETH with money he borrowed from his mother. At the time of the investigation, his rather risky investment was worth over $10 million!

This significant financial backing laid the foundation for the realization of Buterin's vision. Ethereum's development was characterized by its open source nature, which quickly attracted a community of developers who actively contributed to its progress.

On July 30, 2015, Ethereum transitioned from its developmental phase to its initial release, known as Frontier, bringing to the live blockchain the concept of the Ethereum virtual machine (EVM), an innovation that facilitated the execution of smart contracts and dApps.

Since its inception, Ethereum has undergone a series of substantial upgrades aimed at enhancing its scalability, security, and functionality, each introducing improvements to Ethereum's consensus mechanism, reduction of block rewards, and the incorporation of new features.

This culminated in major changes in what was, for a long time, called Ethereum 2.0. Those not in the "know" still talk about Ethereum 2.0, but once it was implemented in September 2022 it was accepted by users and miners alike and simply became Ethereum. This update was eagerly anticipated by the Ethereum community, as it represented a vital upgrade designed to address the network's scalability challenges and facilitate a transition from the proof-of-work (PoW) to the proof-of-stake (PoS) consensus mechanism. In addition, it encompassed heightened transaction throughput and reduced energy consumption, thus fostering a more sustainable network.

The significance of Ethereum extends far beyond the realm of cryptocurrency. Its pioneering smart contract capabilities have catalyzed innovation across diverse industries, including finance, supply chain management, gaming, and decentralized finance (DeFi). DeFi, in particular, has witnessed exponential growth on the Ethereum network, affording users access to financial services without intermediaries.

Ethereum Fundamentals

The differences between Bitcoin and Ethereum are significant, and it's vital that an investigator be able to transition from one currency to the next. To be honest, having waded through the last two chapters about Bitcoin, the best place for you to begin is to suspend what you know about Bitcoin and start again!

The primary Ethereum currency is Ether, or ETH. Addresses start with 0x—that's a zero, not a letter O—and are 42 characters long. If you are interested in the technical bit, 0x just signifies that the following string is made up of hexadecimal characters and is used as a standard signifier, not just for Ethereum addresses. The 0x is followed by 40 characters, which are made from the last 20 bytes of the public key. Eight bits make up a byte, and four bits are required to define each character. That's a bit of information you will probably never need again!

0^{40}

When you start browsing the Ethereum blockchain and reading contracts you will sometimes see an all-zero address, which looks like this: 0x0000000000000000000000000000000000000000.

This is called the Genesis address, otherwise known as Black Hole, Null address, or simply 0^{40}.

If you send coins to this address, you will never get them back as there is (apparently) no private key, and so this address is often used to "burn" coins. More on this later, but some tokens or bridges between cryptocurrencies use a system known as Mint and Burn. For example, if you want to send a token to a different currency over a crypto-bridge, some will function by burning the crypto on one side of the bridge and minting the correct value on the other side.

As of this writing there was over $13 million worth of ETH and $143 million worth of other tokens in the Genesis address (see Figure 11.2).

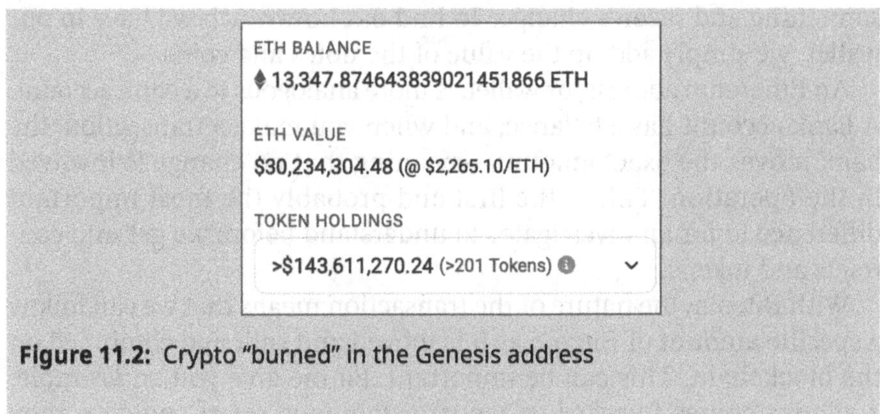

Figure 11.2: Crypto "burned" in the Genesis address

If you would like to generate an ETH address with a prefix and suffix of your choosing, known as a *vanity address*, you can use the site `https://vanity-eth.tk`. You can decide to have an address that starts and ends with hexadecimal characters of your choosing, 1–9 and A–F. By using numbers to replace letters, you can generate personalized addresses (see Figure 11.3). (If you are planning to actually use one of these vanity-style addresses, I highly recommend downloading the code from their GitHub site and running it offline.)

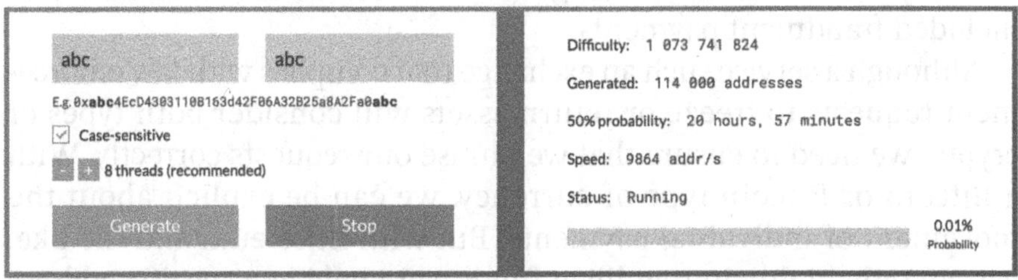

Figure 11.3: Using the vanity address generator to produce an address starting and ending with ABC

One of the largest differences between Ethereum and Bitcoin for an investigator is that an Ethereum address has a balance and a transaction generates no change. With Bitcoin, we spoke at length about how an address does not have a balance; rather it's just a sum of its inputs and outputs and when a transaction is generated it will almost always have a change amount as an output. We used the example of a standard wallet with paper money and having to use a whole note to purchase something and receive change. To find out how much we have in our wallet, we simply add up the value of the notes and coins.

An Ethereum address, or wallet, is more analogous to a bank account. A bank account has a balance, and when you make a transaction, the bank moves the exact amount—meaning that no change is involved in the operation. This is the first and probably the most important difference to for an investigator to understand before we get into contracts and tokens.

With Bitcoin, the nature of the transaction means that we can follow a specific amount of Bitcoin as it is moved and split and combined on the blockchain. This can be important; let me give you an example. A victim comes forward to report a romance scam and says they have paid 0.2BTC to the scammer. Even though there may be many payments to the scammer from multiple victims, we can follow our victim's specific payment to the scammer and then continue to follow that specific payment on to an exchange, for example. However, if the victim pays the scammer in ETH, let's say 0.2ETH, then the scammer's address is simply credited with the amount, adding 0.2ETH to their balance. When the scammer attempts to cash out their ill-gotten gains by moving 0.2ETH to an exchange, then the value is just deducted from the balance. We are unable to precisely follow the victim's funds; we can only assert that the exchange received funds from an address that included fraudulent payments.

Although a service such an exchange that complies with law enforcement requests to freeze or return assets will consider both types of crypto, we need to ensure that we phrase our requests correctly. With a Bitcoin or Bitcoin type of currency, we can be explicit about the movement of individual payments. But with Ethereum and the like, we can only highlight that illicit funds were held at a specific address and that our victim's funds were part of the balance. A service provider may be hesitant to freeze an address, especially if there is significant evidence of legal activity at the address. Just because an address receives criminal funds does not mean that the owner of the address is complicit.

HOW TO MAKE AN INNOCENT PERSON LOOK LIKE A CRIMINAL

A good example of how an address can be criminalized in error came when the mixer Tornado Cash was sanctioned by the U.S. government's Office of Foreign Asset Control (OFAC) in summer 2022.

The sanctions included any address receiving funds from the banned mixer. Pranksters then set about channeling funds through the mixer and sending the output to celebrities such as Jimmy Fallon, Shaquille O'Neal, and, rather embarrassingly for him, the CEO of the exchange giant Coinbase, Brian Armstrong, in an attempt to get their wallets banned under the new OFAC sanction rules.

Ethereum runs on a blockchain, but unlike Bitcoin, where blocks are mined every 10 minutes or so, Ethereum blocks are mined using a process called proof-of-stake (see Chapter 6, "Mining: The Key to Cryptocurrencies") about every 12 seconds. You can check the current block time here: `https://ycharts.com/indicators/ethereum_average_block_time`.

Ethereum operates on a blockchain-based platform that is fundamentally different from Bitcoin's due to its coding system, which can build code blocks known as *contracts*. These contracts enable developers to create and deploy various decentralized applications (dApps) and digital assets on the Ethereum chain.

Types of Tokens

In the crypto ecosystem, we use the term *tokens* as a catchall term for crypto systems built on an existing cryptocurrency platform, usually using smart contract code. We tend not to call Bitcoin or ETH a token even though there is no semantic reason not to. To understand the difference in the phrasing, generally tokens cannot be traded without a primary cryptocurrency coin to pay the transaction fee. You cannot trade Tether on the Bitcoin network without Bitcoin to pay the fee, and you cannot trade a token such as stETH (staked ETH) on the Ethereum blockchain without ETH to pay the fees.

Ethereum bases its standard around Ethereum request for comments, or ERC, a nomenclature akin to Bitcoin's BIP (Bitcoin Improvement Protocol), highlighting Ethereum's community-driven approach to protocol development. Ethereum continues to evolve with numerous other standards and proposals aimed at enhancing its functionality and enabling innovative blockchain-based applications. To explore these standards in more detail, you can refer to the Ethereum Improvement Proposals (EIPs) documentation available at `https://eips.ethereum.org/erc`.

The primary standard within Ethereum is the ERC-20 type token, which is the basic standard used for creating the thousands of digital currencies and utility tokens. Additionally, Ethereum introduced ERC-721, a standard dedicated to nonfungible tokens (NFTs), primarily used for the representation and ownership of unique digital assets, such as collectibles, gaming, and digital art. An enhancement of ERC-20 is ERC-1155, which combines aspects of both ERC-20 and ERC-721, offering versatility and efficiency in managing multiple types of assets.

The ERCs that you will come across most often are as follows:

- ERC-20: A set supply of tokens that can usually be traded.
- ERC-721: Each token is unique and can only be held by one person.
- ERC-1155: A reduced supply of a token available to a set number of holders. Similar to a limited run of numbered prints by an artist.

These are the standards that you will see most often as an investigator, but there are many others, such as the following:

- ERC-777: This token standard extends ERC-20 with additional features, including hooks for token transfers, allowing for more complex interactions and customization of token behavior.
- ERC-1400: This standard is designed for security tokens, which represent ownership of real-world assets such as stocks, bonds, and real estate. ERC-1400 includes features for regulatory compliance and investor protections.
- ERC-223: Similar to ERC-20 but with improved security features. ERC-223 tokens prevent tokens from being accidentally sent to smart contracts that cannot handle them, reducing the risk of token loss.
- ERC-621: This standard extends ERC-20 by adding the ability to increase or decrease the token's total supply through smart contract functions, making it more flexible for projects that require supply adjustments.
- ERC-827: An extension of ERC-20 that allows token transfers to include data payloads, enabling more complex transactions and interactions between tokens and smart contracts.

- ERC-1404: This standard is designed for tokens that need to comply with regulatory requirements, providing features for token transfer restrictions based on specific rules and permissions.

A NOTE ON VALUES AND TIMES

As mentioned at the start of the chapter, the primary Ethereum currency is Ether, or ETH. People commonly mention amounts such as 1 ETH or 0.1 ETH to quantify their transactions and holdings. However, beneath this Ether-centric perspective lies a fundamental unit known as Wei, which shares similarities with Bitcoin's satoshis. One Ether is equivalent to a staggering one quintillion Wei, specifically 1,000,000,000,000,000,000 Wei (10^{18}). In essence, a single Wei represents one quintillionth of an Ether, a little like a penny is 1/100th of a dollar, highlighting the granularity of Ethereum's smallest unit. When it comes to measuring transaction fees within the Ethereum network, it is customary to express them in Gwei, which equates to 1 million Wei. This system allows for precise and scalable quantification.

The dollar value of an ETH fluctuates based on market forces and has traditionally followed Bitcoin in its value trajectory. Although 1 ETH is worth significantly less than 1 Bitcoin, the value graphs tend to follow each other quite closely. Although I do not place significant importance on dollar values when investigating crypto, the investigator needs to keep one eye on fiat values as senior officers, management, and even the courts will often demand to know how much something is worth.

Values of tokens, apart from stable coins, which follow a fiat currency, are a complex area. There have been many fraudulent tokens that have used social media, celebrity endorsement, or technical measures to inflate the dollar value of the token only for the criminals to cash out and crash the token. A good example of this was the SQUID coin that we mentioned in Chapter 3, "Understanding the Criminal Opportunities: Theft," where the scammers built a token reflecting the popularity of a game show only to take all the funds once it had gained value purely through demand.

In Ethereum, transaction times are determined by the block mined time, much like in the case of Bitcoin where individual transactions do not have times, only the block time is recorded. In the same way,

Ethereum transactions do not possess their own distinct timestamps. Instead, they rely on the timestamp of the block in which they are included. These block timestamps are recorded in UNIX time (representing the number of seconds that have elapsed since January 1, 1970). Whereas Bitcoin block explorers often switch between reporting block times for transactions and the time the transaction hit the Mempool, because Ethereum block times are so short all transactions in the block will always be the time the block was mined. This standardized time measurement ensures consistency across the blockchain network.

Just a small technical point: The timestamp can be influenced by miners to some degree. The current block timestamp must be larger than the timestamp of the last block, but the only guarantee is that it will be somewhere between the timestamps of two consecutive blocks in the canonical chain.

Ethereum Transaction Types

Although it could be argued that in the broadest sense there are thousands of different transaction types on the Ethereum blockchain, it actually all boils down to just two main types:

- Ether (Eth) transactions
- Contract transactions (These are sometimes inaccurately called token transactions, but not every contract moves tokens.)

ETH can be thought of as the fuel that powers the Ethereum ecosystem. All transactions, no matter their type, have the transaction fee paid in ETH. This is a key piece of information for an investigator. This means that no matter what a suspect is doing with contracts and tokens, they will always have to own ETH to pay for transactions and the ETH would have to have been acquired from somewhere, providing a trail, possibly back to a service such as an exchange (which may be able to help us with know-your-customer [KYC] information).

ETH is not a token. In fact, to trade ETH as a token, you have to convert it into a tokenized form called Wrapped ETH (WETH). You will see this conversion of ETH to WETH many times when doing investigations, and we will look at examples later in Chapter 12, "Ethereum: Investigation Methodology."

MAKE SURE YOU HAVE ETH!

This is such an important point that I will likely mention it again later. When you are engaged in seizing crypto from a suspect on the Ethereum blockchain, you will often be faced with a variety of tokens held in their wallet. Often the value is in the held ETH, and so the natural reaction is to seize the ETH first. This is a bad idea, as it means that you have no ETH to pay the fees required to move the tokens. Always seize the tokens first and then the ETH.

I have seen officers, having made this mistake, have to send ETH to the suspect's wallet to be able to seize the tokens. Incredibly, I've seen criminals do the same. I was working on an investigation where a hacker had gained access to a victim's wallet. They drained all the ETH and then realized that they could not steal the tokens and so transferred funds back into the victim's wallet to be able to steal the rest.

I tend to call ETH-to-ETH transactions *primary* transactions in that they are using the default or "primary" coin to move a value. Everything else is a contract transaction, and within this category there are almost limitless types. However, it's worth getting clear in your head that these are just triggering code and that the underlying transaction is always on the primary blockchain. (Some transactions leave the primary blockchain to be processed on what is known as Layer 2 systems. More on that later in the section "A User's Address Can Be the Same on Other Blockchains.")

At the heart of Ethereum transactions lies the concept of contracts. These smart contracts serve as autonomous agents, capable of executing code when triggered by a transaction. This mechanism opens the door to a wide array of possibilities, from simple token transfers to complex decentralized applications. The following are just a few examples:

- Nonfungible tokens (NFTs) are based primarily on the ERC-20 and 1155 standards. This contract type enables the creation of unique tokens or limited-edition tokens. You can think of it like owning an original artwork (ERC-20) or a limited-edition print (ERC-1155). These were extremely popular for a few years but have rather lost their luster in recent times. However, they are still widely used in blockchain-based gaming.

- Decentralized gambling platforms, where trustless interactions and transparent outcomes "redefine the concept of fair play"—or at least that is what the gambling websites claim. This is an interesting area where placing bets on games and receiving winnings are based on transactions happening on the blockchain and so are immutable and unarguable.
- Decentralized exchanges (DEXs) and decentralized finance (DeFi) protocols are at the forefront of Ethereum's success, offering users the ability to trade assets and access financial services without the need for intermediaries. To once again quote a company that sells these services, "These platforms empower individuals with unprecedented control over their finances, paving the way for a more inclusive and accessible financial system." While it is true that these systems offer a potential way to provide financial services for those not able to access traditional banking, we are certainly not seeing that in the marketplace at the moment. Tracing funds through DEXs and other DeFi type contracts can be very complex for an investigator, and so we will be covering this in more detail in Chapter 12.

Standard Ethereum user addresses are properly referred to as externally owned accounts (EOAs). These serve as the entry points for users to interact with the Ethereum blockchain. These addresses, generated by users, have a paired private key that grants access to any assets held under that EOA.

Standard Ethereum transactions are EOA transactions, facilitating the transfer of ETH and execution of contracts on the blockchain. To simplify, when an EOA initiates a transaction, it signals the movement of Ethereum's native currency (ETH) or the execution of smart contract functions. As mentioned before, the fee will always be in ETH.

EOA-to-EOA transactions represent the standard Ethereum transaction method, producing the straightforward transfer of ETH value from one external address (EOA) to another. This fundamental transaction type forms the backbone of Ethereum's peer-to-peer payment system, enabling users to send and receive ETH across the network. This is the simplest of transaction types and is straightforward for an investigator to follow.

INTERNAL TRANSACTIONS

There is technically another type of transaction, but these are never triggered directly by a user, have no unique signature, and are not recorded on the blockchain. They are called *internal transactions.*

It is usually the result of a contract initiating a value transfer, or calling another contract, typically using the CALL OpCode.

Standard token transfers are always related to a smart contract and are triggered by an EOA transaction, and they always exist as an entry on the blockchain. We will look at examples of this later in the chapter, so don't worry if this is all a bit bewildering.

A few more things to know: Stable coins are just another type of token usually based on ERC-20, but their values are pegged to a fiat currency. In simple terms, one stable coin should equate exactly to the fiat currency it is pegged to. This is almost always the U.S. dollar; therefore, one token of the stable coin should be one dollar. This is different from the values of other tokens, which tend to fluctuate based on supply and demand.

Stable coins can be traced in the same way as normal tokens. Examples include:

- USDT—Tether (also available on the Bitcoin blockchain using OMNI)
- USDC—Circle and Coinbase
- DAI (stabilized by MakerDAO)
- BUSD—Binance stable coin

The name *stable coin* or *pegged value coin* makes it sound more trustworthy somehow compared with the vagaries of value fluctuations of other types of token, but this should be viewed with caution. The guaranteed pegged value is generally based on real-world assets held that should correlate with the tokens available in the smart contract. There have been questions asked about whether some of these tokens really have the real-world assets to support the tokens' value. We have seen massive failures such as the crash of the Terra (UST and Luna coins) project. This token lost $45 billion (or 99.9 percent of its value) in just 72 hours in May 2022. You can read a good explanation of stable coins and how they can fail here: `www.richmondfed.org/publications/research/economic_brief/2022/eb_22-24`.

One Address for All Tokens

A single Ethereum wallet address can hold ETH as well as any tokens on the blockchain. This means that when we look at a wallet we need to check both the ETH holdings—remember that they have to have at least some ETH to carry out transactions—and any tokens that are being held. This step can be very easy to miss but, even worse, makes valuation of the wallet very complex.

I recommend the block explorer Etherscan.io for any Ethereum investigations. Even where I have access to a commercial investigation tool, I still like to see the "raw" data that I can obtain from Etherscan. (I use the term *raw* to mean a text-based interpretation of the blockchain code rather than graphs. I would normally associate raw data with JSON-style data, which can be obtained via API calls, but we will not be delving into that topic that deeply in this book.)

NOTE Please note that functionality on sites such as Etherscan will change over time. Screenshots used in this book may not reflect what you see at a later time. However, it is unlikely that functionality is removed, so look to see where a button or option may have moved to. Other sites such as `blockchair.com` can also be used for Ethereum investigations. Please also note that unless explicitly mentioned, I am not ascribing any wrongdoing to the example addresses that are used.

If we use Etherscan.io to search for an address such as 0xBBE8dFF69082174d04F74B55b1f65a90dC4194FE, we will see a summary of the address holdings, as shown in Figure 11.4.

Figure 11.4: Overview of ETH and token holdings in this wallet address

We can clearly see that they are holding 0.007ETH in this wallet address with a value of $16.51. However, we can see that one token is being held with a value of $491.23. So the value in this wallet is very much in the token. If we click the drop-down box, we can see the token name, as shown in Figure 11.5.

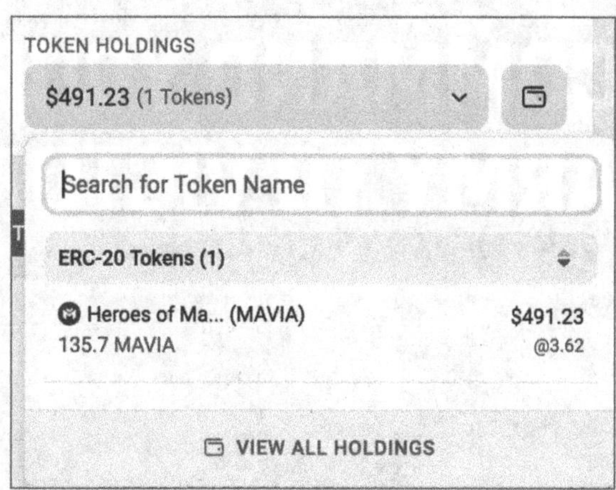

Figure 11.5: Token being stored in the address

Here we can see that they are holding a token called Heroes of Ma— but with a token name of MAVIA. A quick Google search shows that this is related to a gaming site called Heroes of Mavia (see Figure 11.6), which uses tokens for trading and governance. As an aside, we will get into this type of thinking in Chapter 12, but if an address is holding a suspicious token, do not immediately suspect wrongdoing. A token can be sent to anyone without their knowledge. Although I have no reason to doubt the veracity of this gaming site and token, we would need to do a little more research to see what it's all about and whether this user purchased the token or received it free of charge.

So, you have learned that a user address (EOA) can hold both ETH and tokens, but it goes further than that.

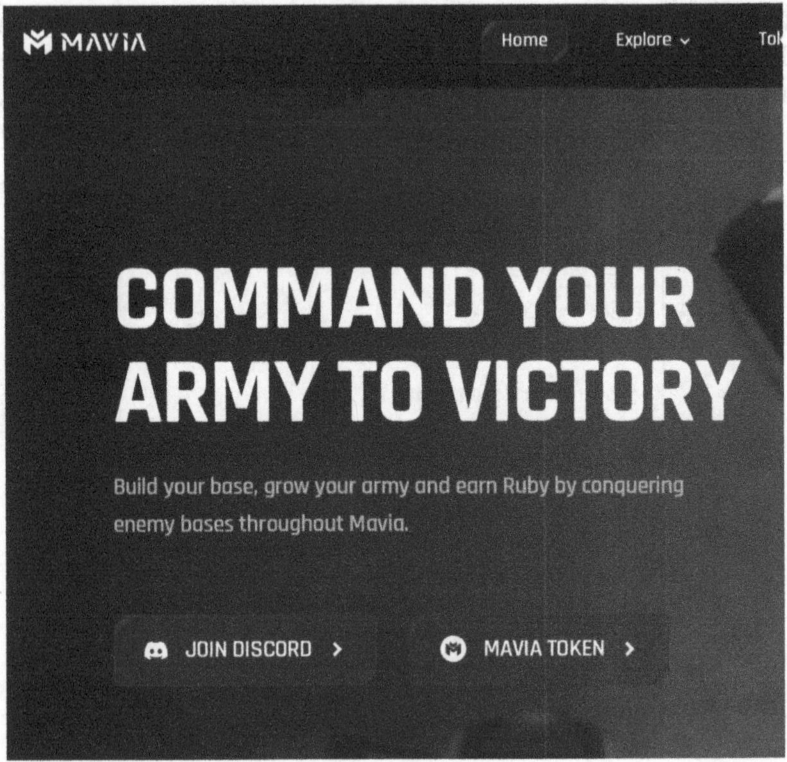

Figure 11.6: Heroes of MAVIA home page

A User's Address Can Be the Same on Other Blockchains

Yes, you read that title correctly. If a user owns an Ethereum address—and of course that means they have the private key to control the funds—then the same address on other blockchains will be owned by the same person. I'm actually going to repeat that point although I'm guessing the editors will not like it:

The same address on other blockchains will be owned by the same person.

This is massively important to understand; otherwise, we risk missing assets to account for to extend our investigation or to potentially seize proceeds of crime.

If you take a look at address 0x3a194c54985D77896b02Ac608D6223F 96bec279A on Etherscan.io, you will see that this user has a small amount of ETH and five different tokens on the Ethereum chain. However, just below the summary is the Multichain Portfolio button. If you click this button, you will see that there are other chains where this user owns funds. One of these is Base. You can research this if you wish, but Base, which was primarily developed by the exchange Coinbase, is known as a Layer 2 service, which enables transactions to be handled more quickly and less expensively than on the prime Ethereum chain.

We can browse to the Base explorer at `http://basescan.org` (you will see similarities with Etherscan.io) and enter the same address as previously. You will see that the user owns a small amount of ETH (as of this writing) and seven tokens. This is different from the holdings on the primary Ethereum chain and would need to be taken into account or seized separately. This knowledge can massively extend an investigation (Figure 11.7 shows the holdings on basescan at the time of writing).

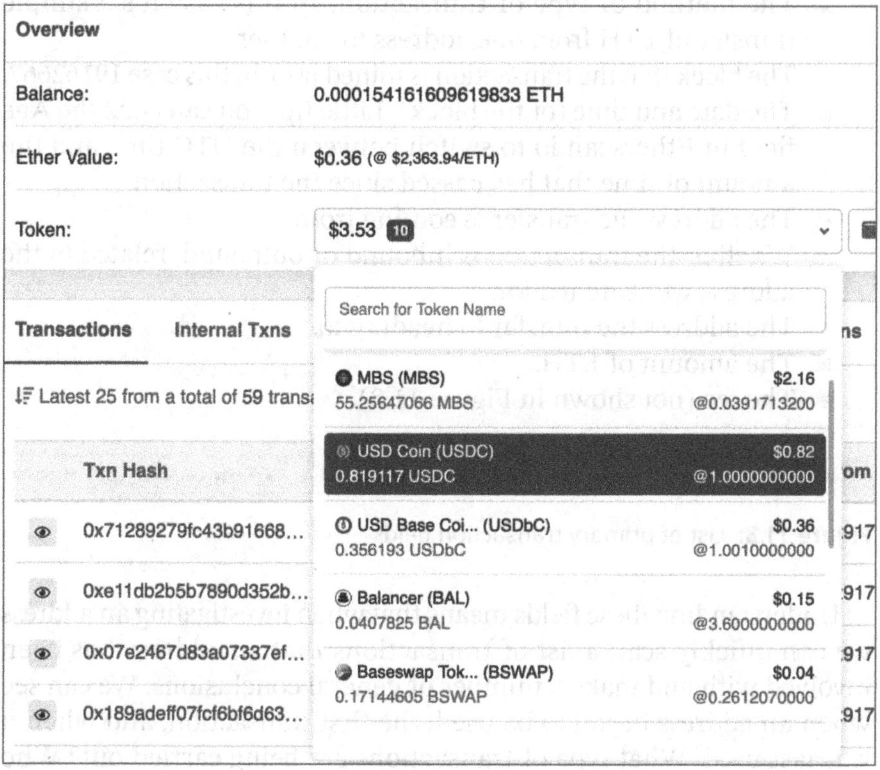

Figure 11.7: Holdings on the Base Layer 2 chain

Whenever you are looking at an Ethereum address, it is vital to check all other primary chains, including Binance Smart Chain, Base, and many others for other funds. The Multichain Portfolio button in Etherscan or your commercial tool can help you with this.

Reading Basic Transactions

If we search for an address on a blockchain explorer such as Etherscan .io, it will display a list of all the transactions and the primary fields associated with those transactions. For example, in Figure 11.8, we see the following fields:

- The type of transaction this is. In this case it is simply a transfer of ETH. We will look at this field in more detail later.
- The Transaction Identified, or TXID. This is a unique value to identify the transaction.
- The method or type of transaction. In this case it's a simple transfer of ETH from one address to another.
- The block that the transaction is mined into, in this case 19162667.
- The date and time (of the block). Little tip: You can click the Age field in Etherscan.io to switch between the UTC time and the amount of time that has passed since the transaction.
- The address the transfer is coming from.
- Whether the transaction is inbound or outbound, related to the address we searched for.
- The address the transfer to heading to.
- The amount of ETH.
- The fee (not shown in Figure 11.8).

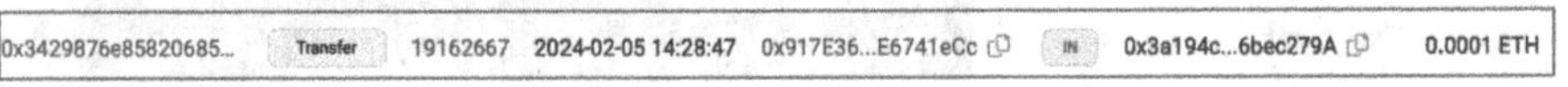

Figure 11.8: List of primary transaction fields

Understanding these fields means that when investigating an address we can quickly scan a list of transactions that an address has been involved with and make a number of general conclusions. We can see when an address began to be used, the first transaction, and when it was last used. What type of transactions are being carried out? Who are they trading with?

Transaction Methods

We saw in the last example that the transaction method was simply Transfer. This is helpful as it tells us that this is a straight transfer of ETH. However, there are a vast number of methods that you will see, and there is no directory to tell you what they are. The methods are simply the function name in the transaction code. This means that a programmer can use a useful, explanatory method name or something meaningless, or indeed nothing at all, and we just get a function code.

Take a look at the list of methods in Figure 11.9, which was taken from a series of transactions mined into block 19176763.

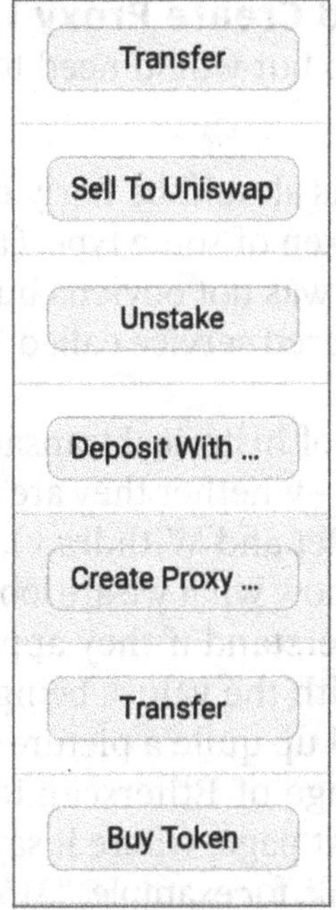

Figure 11.9: A variety of transaction methods

What do all these mean?

Transfer We know what Transfer is, as you saw that earlier, and it relates to an ETH-to-ETH transaction.

Sell To Uniswap This seems pretty self-explanatory. Uniswap is a service to swap between tokens. However, a quick Internet search tells us that a user can set up investment positions and create Buy and Sell positions on Uniswap related to token pairs. This could be related to this, or perhaps it's just selling one token to swap to another. We would need to look at the transaction specifically to know, but just at a glance we might conclude that this user is swapping or investing tokens, which may be of interest to us.

Unstake Staking is related to crypto investing and can be involved in validation via proof-of-stake, as we discussed in Chapter 6. Therefore, unstaking is the process of withdrawing or unlocking the staked funds. So we can quickly ascertain that this user is involved in crypto investing.

Deposit With. . .and Create Proxy I can take a guess at what these two functions do but would need to dig into the transaction to find out more.

Buy Token Again this should be fairly obvious. This transaction is the purchase of a token of some type. (I had to dig a little on this one as the transaction was not obvious but was related to a presale for a new Ethereum-based service called Mollars.)

A quick look at the list of historical transaction methods can tell us quite a bit about this user—whether they are trading, involved in gaming (methods like Place Bet and Withdraw), staking, and so on. This information can help us know what we are looking at related to our user and can also help us understand if they appear to be an experienced crypto user. Tie that in with the values being held, dates, tokens, and so forth, and we can build up quite a picture of the person.

Browse to the front page of Etherscan.io and click on the latest block number. On the next page, where it says Transactions, click the <number> transactions link, for example, "315 transactions." Take a look at the different methods and see if you can figure out what they mean.

GOING ATOMIC!

You will sometimes see the method "atomic match." This typically refers to a type of transaction where multiple transactions are executed simultaneously, ensuring that either all transactions are successfully completed, or none of them are.

For example, in a decentralized exchange (DEX) scenario, when a user wants to swap one token for another, an atomic swap ensures that either the entire exchange occurs successfully, with both parties receiving their intended tokens, or the exchange fails and reverts to its initial state. This prevents scenarios where one party receives their tokens but the other does not, which could potentially lead to unfair or incomplete transactions.

The term *atomic* in this context derives from the idea of atomicity in computer science, which refers to a property of transactions where they are indivisible and either fully complete or fully undone. In the case of an atomic match, all transactions involved are treated as a single atomic unit, ensuring consistency and reliability in the exchange process.

Transaction and Address Types

There are two types of address on the blockchain:

- Externally owned accounts (EOAs): We referred to these earlier; they are addresses generated from a private key and owned by a user. These addresses can contain ETH and multiple token types.
- Contract addresses (accounts): These addresses store and execute code only when prompted by a transaction from an EOA. A contract cannot execute itself but can only be triggered by an EOA transaction or another contract, but somewhere up the chain there needs to be an EOA-prompted transaction.

There are four user-generated transaction types on the Ethereum chain:

- EOA sending Ether to another EOA: This is simply an Ether-to-Ether transaction.
- EOA creating a contract: There is no ETH transacted apart from the fee.
- EOA sending a transaction to a contract: This could be transacting a token, carrying out a token swap, placing a bet on a gambling site, or a myriad of other things.
- Transferring between ERC standard coins.

Each of these transaction types will be examined in much more detail in the next chapter. If you already are involved with Ethereum investigations and have access to a commercial tool, these transaction types should be clearly displayed, usually as ETH-to-ETH or ETH-to-contract transactions, and should provide some information about that trade. However, it is worth noting that if you are planning to use Etherscan as your primary investigation tool, there are a couple of things you should be aware of:

- Etherscan does a pretty good job of naming exchange addresses and naming the owner of contract addresses, which can be very helpful.
- The Transactions tab displays all types of transactions occurring on the Ethereum blockchain, with the exception of straight ERC-20 token transactions. The ERC-20 tab specifically filters and displays transactions related to ERC-20 tokens, offering a more focused view for users interested in tracking token-related activity. When other token types are present, new tabs will appear, for example, for NFTs.

What Are These Contracts We Keep Mentioning?

An Ethereum contract is a digital agreement or program that runs on the blockchain. It's written in a programming language called Solidity. Solidity is known as a Turing-complete language, which means it can express any computation that can be computed, making it capable of implementing a wide range of complex functionalities and algorithms within smart contracts. That's all a bit dry, so here's the interesting bit: These contracts aren't just about boring stuff like legal agreements (though they can do that, too); they're also about making clever things happen automatically, without any intermediaries or central authority.

Let's say you're into gaming. With an Ethereum contract, you could create a virtual marketplace where players can trade in game items or characters securely and transparently, without worrying about scams or fraud. The contract would handle all the transactions automatically, ensuring that everyone gets what they're promised.

Or maybe you're passionate about social causes. You could create a contract that collects donations for charity and automatically distributes the funds to verified organizations, cutting out the need for intermediaries and ensuring that your contributions reach the right hands.

The beauty of Ethereum contracts is that they're versatile and can be customized to do pretty much anything you can imagine. They're like the building blocks of a new digital economy, where trust is built into the code and power is in the hands of the programmer.

In a nutshell, an Ethereum contract is a programmable digital agreement that runs on the Ethereum blockchain, enabling automated and trustless interactions for all kinds of purposes, from gaming and finance to social impact, or whatever you can dream up.

We must not make the mistake of assuming that because something is written "on the blockchain" that it's automatically secure. Just like any code, bugs or exploits can exist, which can be found by bad actors who can steal funds or otherwise do bad things.

Reading these contracts can be complex, but in the next chapter you'll learn a simple way of trying to understand what a contract does.

Identifying Contract Transactions

An ETH-to-ETH (EOA-to-EOA) transaction will always carry an ETH value, and the input and output address will be user (EOA) addresses. When a contract is involved in the transaction, then the value of the transaction may or may not have an ETH value. I've heard trainers say that a contract address will always have a null ETH value (except the fee), but in situations such as converting ETH to Wrapped ETH, for example, there will be an ETH value. Contract addresses are formatted identically to EOA addresses and so can't be identified by the way they look. The only way to check that an input or output address is a contract is by either checking manually or looking for tags in your favorite block explorer.

Take a look at the two transaction examples in Figure 11.10.

Transfer	18656761	72 days 23 hrs ago	Binance 20	IN	0x754B77...D8684b6a	0.0262857 ETH
Approve	18654437	73 days 7 hrs ago	0x754B77...D8684b6a	OUT	Contract 0x133218...C61094E4	0 ETH

Figure 11.10: Examples of an inbound and an outbound transaction

We can see that the first transaction in the list has a Transfer method, and you have learned that this is an ETH-to-ETH transaction. In fact, Etherscan tells us that the sending address belongs to Binance. But look at the second transaction. This is an Approval method, which allows a token holder to grant permission to another address to transfer a specified number of tokens; it's often related to DEXs and other decentralized finance products. If we look at the Out address, we see a little icon of a page. Hover over it, and you will see a pop-up that identifies it as a contract. How we follow this transaction and even read the contract will be covered in the next chapter.

Contracts are a massive subject, and I could write a book on this topic alone, but there is a limited amount that most investigators need to know that doesn't require understanding Solidity, and so we will dig deeper in the next chapter.

Conclusion

This chapter has provided you with the primary knowledge that you need to understand how Ethereum works and the types of transactions that can be carried out. The next step is using this knowledge to read transactions and follow funds. How can you read contracts and find funds that have been swapped for other tokens or moved to DeFi services? Go and get a coffee as the next chapter will start to help you actively investigate on the Ethereum blockchain.

12 Ethereum: Investigation Methodology

Chapter 11, "The Workings of Ethereum and Derivatives," helped you understand transactions, contracts, how the Ethereum blockchain works, and how it all hangs together. In this chapter you'll get your hands dirty and learn how to follow the money, both through standard transactions and, critically, through contracts. We'll look at ETH-to-ETH, ETH-to-contract, and token-to-token transactions. I'll provide specific examples such as decentralized exchanges and decentralized finance contracts and show you how to track funds. Even if you are not technical, please do not skip this chapter; having an understanding of flows on the Ethereum blockchain—and especially through contracts—is a vital skill if you are involved with crypto at all, and will translate to other cryptocurrencies such as TRON and Binance Smart Chain.

Let's start off with the easiest of Ethereum transactions, ETH to ETH.

Following ETH-to-ETH Transactions

You know that ETH is the primary coin of Ethereum and is required to pay the fees for any transaction. ETH is not a token. Well, it is, in that any entity that can be used for a transaction could be termed a token. A dollar could be called a token, as could a euro because they represent a nominal value. Because currencies such as ETH or Bitcoin are the primary fuel for their blockchain ecosystems, they are generally termed *coins*, and any contract-based entity is called a *token*. Online you will see these terms used interchangeably, but in the next few chapters if I refer to a *coin* I will mean the primary currency and *token* will relate to a contract-based currency. Clear as mud? Let's get started.

ETH-to-ETH transactions are similar to a Bitcoin transaction in that there is an input address and value and an output address and value. As we've previously discussed, there is no change as an Ethereum address is more akin to a bank account with specific values able to be transacted without generating change. This makes the transactions very easy to read.

Let's look at this example from transaction ID (TXID) 0xf714d916443435ca229b389e46fe45d779c8e64a6ecd4ffce71753850a2667d7 (see Figure 12.1).

From:	0x754B77a3073A6DD535f6F12FCdcE9304D8684b6a
To:	0xf070cA4cfCFb1ab8c5dF3139CEB8fD06b84b19b0
Value:	♦ 0.099759565831320712 ETH $242.24
Transaction Fee:	0.000817846641234 ETH $1.99
Gas Price:	38.945078154 Gwei (0.000000038945078154 ETH)

Figure 12.1: Example of an ETH-to-ETH transaction

This screenshot is from `Etherscan.io` (as are all the screenshots in this chapter). Please copy the TXID (remember the iPhone trick from the start of Chapter 11?) and take a look at it yourself.

It is pretty straightforward to read. Funds were sent from the address starting with 0x754B to the address starting with 0xf070c. The value was 0.0997. . .ETH and the fee a little over 0.0008 ETH. Like the example of a bank account, 0x754B had its balance reduce by 0.0997 plus the fee and 0xf070c had its balance increase by 0.0997.

Notably, in `Etherscan.io` it shows the dollar price of the ETH. If you hover your mouse over the dollar price it will show Displaying Current Value. This is the value of this input at the time you are viewing it. This is fine, but it is often useful to understand what the transaction was worth in dollars at the time of the transaction. If you click the dollar value, it will change to Estimated Value On Day Of Txn. I use this very often. For example, I know that a scammer was asking for $300 worth of ETH in a ransomware scam. I may be investigating the case six months later and the current value of a transaction I'm viewing may be $400. However, when I click and check the value at the time, I see that it was worth $300, or close to it, which may help to confirm that this could likely be a ransom payment. I'm simplifying but you get the idea (see Figure 12.2).

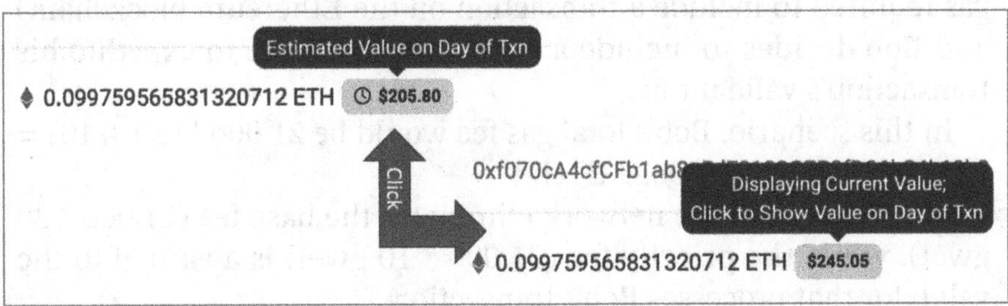

Figure 12.2: Changing from the current value to the value on the day of the transaction

The transaction fee is calculated from the gas price, analogous to the price per gallon of fuel when you fill up your car.

ETHEREUM FEES

Fees are not usually very useful for an investigator, so I don't focus on them. The only reason that fees are of interest is because ETH is needed to fund any type of transaction and so a user will always need to have ETH in their wallet. Also, ETH is easier to trace. If you are interested in fees, here is the lowdown.

After the update to Ethereum in August 2021 called the London upgrade, a new method for calculating gas fees was introduced through EIP-1559. This method uses a fixed base fee per block and an adjustable block size to address network congestion issues.

The upgrade aimed to eliminate the uncertainty surrounding gas fees, which previously forced users to engage in a bidding war over gas prices, inadvertently driving the fees up.

Under the new system, gas fees are determined using the following formula:

$$\text{Gas fee} = \text{Gas units}\left(\text{limit}\right) * \left(\text{base fee} + \text{priority fee}\right)$$

Consider an example where Bob wishes to transfer 3 ETH to Alice. If the gas limit is the standard 21,000, the base fee at that moment is 30 gwei (the base fee refers to the minimum amount of gas required to include a transaction on the Ethereum blockchain) and Bob decides to include a 10-gwei priority fee to expedite his transaction's validation.

In this scenario, Bob's total gas fee would be 21,000 * (30 + 10) = 840,000 gwei, or 0.000839 ETH.

In this process, the network eliminates the base fee (21,000 * 30 gwei), while the priority fee (21,000 * 10 gwei) is awarded to the validator that processes Bob's transaction.

I should also mention ERC-4337. ERC-4337 is a proposed standard for Ethereum that introduces a significant shift in how users can interact with the Ethereum blockchain by enabling account abstraction. This concept, often discussed within the Ethereum community, aims to enhance the usability and flexibility of user accounts on the blockchain.

Understanding Account Abstraction

Traditionally, Ethereum accounts are divided into two types: externally owned accounts (EOAs), which are controlled by private keys, and contract accounts, which are controlled by their contract code. This dichotomy can complicate user interactions, especially for those unfamiliar with blockchain technology.

Account abstraction seeks to simplify this by treating all accounts more like contract accounts, thereby abstracting away some of the complexities associated with transaction initiations and management. Under this model, an account can pay fees in tokens other than ETH, and smart contracts can automate transaction responses, enhancing usability for average users.

Key Features

Let's look at the chief characteristics of ERC-4337:

- **User Operation (UserOp):** ERC-4337 introduces a concept called User Operation (UserOp), which represents a bundle of information describing an action a user wants to execute. This includes the target contract, the call data, the gas limit, and the fee payment details, among other parameters.

- **Sponsored Transactions:** With ERC-4337, transactions can be sponsored, meaning that the gas fees for executing transactions can be paid by someone other than the account initiating the transaction. This opens the door to new use cases, such as allowing decentralized application (dApp) developers to subsidize transaction costs for their users to encourage adoption.
- **Entry Point Contracts:** The standard specifies a mechanism for having "entry point" contracts on the blockchain that act as routers. These entry points manage the execution of UserOps, ensuring they're carried out correctly and efficiently. They are responsible for validating the user's signature, paying the miner's fee, and enforcing the transaction's execution rules.
- **Enhanced Security and Flexibility:** By allowing users to define conditions under which transactions are executed (via smart contracts), ERC-4337 can potentially offer enhanced security features, such as recovery options and limits on transaction types or volumes, which aren't possible with traditional EOAs.

Implications and Impact

ERC-4337 could drastically improve user experience on Ethereum by allowing more people to interact with the blockchain in a way that feels familiar and integrated into applications. It lowers barriers to entry for nontechnical users and could lead to broader adoption of Ethereum-based applications. Moreover, by enabling transactions to be paid in tokens other than ETH and allowing others to sponsor transaction fees, ERC-4337 could foster a more versatile economic environment within the Ethereum ecosystem.

This proposal is part of a broader movement within the Ethereum community to make blockchain technology more accessible and efficient, continuing Ethereum's evolution toward a more user-friendly platform.

I hope that satisfies any fee type questions.

This transaction seems very simple, but the issue comes when we want to track that transaction to its destination and onward. A Bitcoin explorer provides a button that when clicked enables us to follow the exact transaction to the destination address, which then enables us to follow it again, and so on. But because Ethereum wallets are like a bank account, the transaction is recorded on the blockchain and is added to the balance. To find the exact transaction, we need to search through all the transactions in the destination address to locate it. The easiest way to do this is to take note of the date and time of the transaction.

If you still have the previous transaction open, you will note that the UTC date and time is November 26, 2023, at 06:05:47 PM UTC (see Figure 12.3).

73 days 18 hrs ago (Nov-26-2023 06:05:47 PM +UTC)

Figure 12.3: Recorded time and date of the transaction

If we click the destination address, 0xf070c. . . , it will load all the transactions that this address has been involved with. As of this writing, there were 67 transactions. (In `Etherscan.io` you can click the word Age at the top of the column to switch between time passed since the transaction and the actual date and time. The column header will switch to Date Time [UTC]). We then need to scroll down through the transactions until we find the right date and time and the corresponding correct value. We can also verify that it's the right incoming transaction by checking the TXID. In this case, it was just 3 from the top, as in Figure 12.4.

Transaction Hash	Method	Block	Date Time (UTC)	From		To	Value
0x11699146b11a9377...	Transfer	19176930	2024-02-07 14:32:23	0x754B77...D8684b6a	IN	0xf070cA...b84b19b0	0.00262952 ETH
0x7595f4d903e275c91...	Transfer	19042323	2024-01-19 17:12:23	0x754B77...D8684b6a	IN	0xf070cA...b84b19b0	0.05185632 ETH
0xf714d916443435ca2...	Transfer	18657517	2023-11-26 18:05:47	0x754B77...D8684b6a	IN	0xf070cA...b84b19b0	0.09975956 ETH

Figure 12.4: List of transactions for the destination address

In this example, at the time we're looking at the wallet, there are no outbound transactions after the transaction of interest, just the transaction we have followed and two more incoming transfers. This means that the value we're following is currently part of the balance.

But what about this situation in the next figure? A victim has paid 0.27 ETH to this suspect's address. You can see the 0.27 ETH arrive. Following, another incoming payment arrives of 0.02. . .ETH. Next the suspect moves 0.3. . .ETH to Binance (see Figure 12.5).

0xf070cA...b84b19b0	OUT	Binance 14	0.30075645 ETH
0x754B77...D8684b6a	IN	0xf070cA...b84b19b0	0.02384254 ETH
0x754B77...D8684b6a	IN	0xf070cA...b84b19b0	0.27 ETH

Figure 12.5: Example of in- and outbound transactions (note, read from bottom to top)

This is all very convenient as our victim's 0.27 ETH added to the 0.02 basically adds up to the 0.3 ETH moved to Binance, and so we can approach Binance and demonstrate the movement of the victim's funds to them, even though we don't know who the 0.02 belongs to. Easy! But what about the situation in Figure 12.6?

0x853f16...d0646244	OUT	0xDf8DD5...fE602Cb3	0.00937388 ETH
0x8610C2...640a5C1a	IN	0x853f16...d0646244	0.01100101 ETH

Figure 12.6: Whose funds have moved?

We are following a victim's payment of 0.011. . .ETH into the suspect's address 0x853. The wallet already had a balance of 1.1 ETH before the deposit we are interested in was added to the balance. Next the suspect moves 0.009. . .ETH out to the address 0xDf8. Whose funds have moved? Is it our victim's funds or funds the suspect already owned? This highlights exactly the problem with Ethereum; we simply have no way of knowing. With Bitcoin's unspent transaction output (UTXO) model, we could follow the victim's funds through a series of transactions, but with our suspect's account-based Ethereum wallet we are working from a balance and so the 0.009. . .ETH moved cannot be attributed to any one input.

Although it's a subtle difference, it is a difference, and it may change the way we pursue freezing or having funds reclaimed for a victim.

So ETH-to-ETH transactions are very simple. We just need to focus on the from, to, date/time, and value fields to be able to follow payments across the blockchain—sort of. The account-based system means we are really just following from address to address rather than transaction to transaction.

Although you will come across a large number of pure ETH transactions during investigations, the vast majority will be contract-based transactions. We covered the meaning of a contract briefly in the previous chapter, but we now need to look deeper and cover some more advanced ground before we can start deconstructing contract transactions.

Smart Contracts Deep Dive

If you have taken my Ethereum-based training (currently named TRM Labs Advanced Crypto Investigator [ACI]), you may recognize my definition of a smart contract:

> *Self-executing contract with the terms of the agreement between buyer and seller being directly written into lines of code.*

A smart contract permits trusted transactions and agreements to be carried out among disparate, anonymous parties without the need for a central authority, legal system, or external enforcement mechanism.

The problem is I couldn't remember if I explicitly wrote this definition or found it elsewhere, so I Googled it and found that these exact two sentences are used on numerous sites but all dated after my course was written in 2019. So maybe it was me?

To see if there was a better definition available, I asked ChatGPT 4 to "Define a smart contract in 1 paragraph." Guess how it responded?

> *Self-executing contract with the terms of the agreement between buyer and seller being directly written into lines of code.*
>
> *A smart contract permits trusted transactions . . .*

It would seem to be a good definition.

The concept of self-executing code can be a bit overwhelming for an investigator whose skills may be financial or perhaps computer crime, but although it's not vital for an investigator to be able to write Solidity code, we will look at how a nonprogrammer can try to figure out what a contract is doing. It can be useful to have access to a programmer with these skills either on the team or as a consultant.

Why can this be useful? If a fraudster is using malevolent contracts in order to defraud, or a hacker has exploited a contract to steal funds, or a poorly written contract is losing funds, or indeed a wide range of possibilities, it can be very helpful to be able to look at a contract and ascertain what it's designed to do. If you are not a programmer, you will always be limited, but we will show you some tricks to help you get a head start before picking up the phone to your Solidity consultant.

Contracts can be created by a user or by another contract. However, even if you find a contract created by another contract, at the top of that tree will also be a user, a primary contract created by an EOA address.

Address 0x881D40237659C251811CEC9c364ef91dC08D300C is a contract. If you search it on Etherscan, it will be tagged at the top of the page as a contract. In the More Info pane, the creator of the contract will be listed and the TXID where it was made. See Figure 12.7.

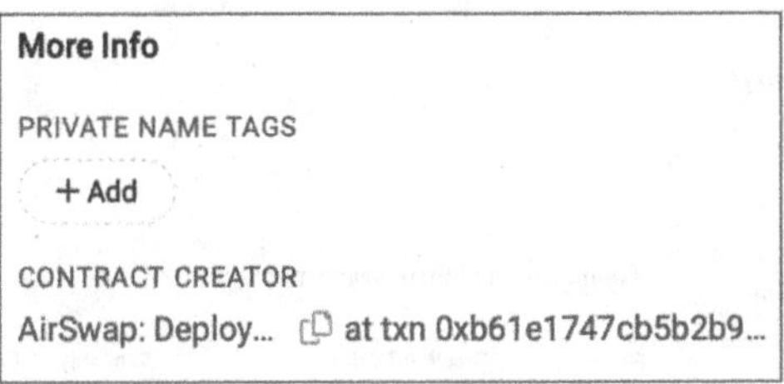

Figure 12.7: Image showing the contract creator

We can clearly see that the contract was created by an address that is tagged as Airswap: Deploy. . .at TXID starting with 0xb61. Following the link to the creating transaction will provide us with the date that the contract was created. Why is this data important? Because so often fraudulent contracts are deployed at the start of a fraud and are usually very recent. We use the same technique when checking Internet domain names. For example, you find a fraudulent investment company with a shiny website and grand claims, but when you check the domain name registration history it's only two months old. Metadata like this can help us to put pieces together and start to draw conclusions about a case.

Another extremely useful capability that Etherscan has is the ability to find similar contracts or indeed contracts that are identical. When scammers run fraudulent contracts, it's rarely the first time and they may have a number of similar scams running simultaneously. Obviously, rather than writing new code each time, they will often reuse the smart contract code; if we can find these contracts, it can help extend our investigation, find more criminal funds, and even locate more victims.

At this point, search for the contract address 0x1c479675ad559DC151F6Ec7ed3FbF8ceE79582B6. To be clear, this contract is related to the Arbitrum service and there is nothing suspicious about it. In the Overview and More Info panels are a row of buttons, including Contract with a tick next to it to demonstrate that it's a verified contract. Click Contract to view details about the contract and the raw code. We will be looking at this page in more detail in a moment, but as of this writing, on the right of the page is the More Options drop-down list, which has the option Similar. Clicking this will load any contracts where the code is similar or exact. As you can see in Figure 12.8, there are 59 contracts that are exactly the same.

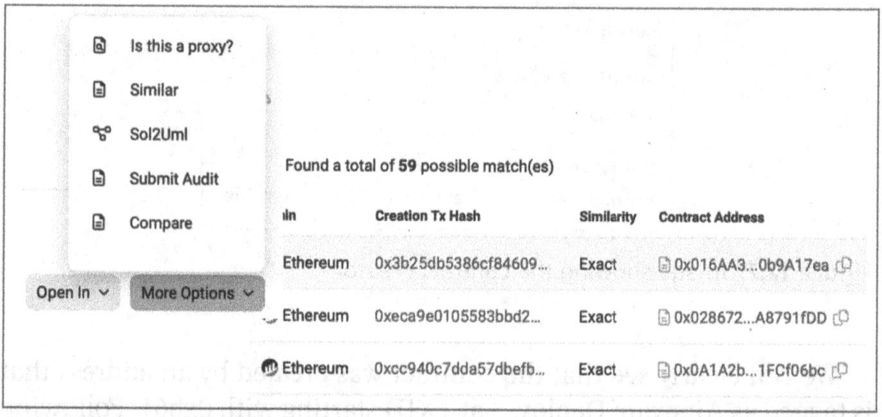

Figure 12.8: Image showing similar/exact contracts

As mentioned, this can be hugely helpful in extending your investigation. On a case of mine two years ago, it led to an identification of the suspect. Having identified the fraudulent token contract, we looked for similar contracts. It led to three exact matches, one of which had not been actively used. The address that generated the contract had previously sent funds to an exchange, and we were able to apply to the exchange for details, which provided a suspect identification.

Methods, Functions, and Events

Let's look at some contracts and learn how to discern their purpose without having to read the code.

Toward the end of the previous chapter, I briefly discussed how the method listed for a transaction could be useful, and we considered the methods Transfer, Stake, Withdraw, and so on. In smart contracts, these methods are a function defined in the code and can frankly be anything. The primary function of a transaction will be listed with the transaction, but there are many more under the surface that we can find by looking at the code to understand the role of the contract.

There are no required functions. but you will find some quite common examples such as the following:

`Name` Name of the token

`totalSupply` Returns the total supply of the token

`balanceof(address _owner)` Returns the account balance of the address

`transferFrom(address from, address to, value)` Transfers the `value` amount of tokens from the address `from` to the address `to` and is used by contracts allowed to transfer tokens on behalf of the user

`approve(address spender, value)` Allows the owner of the address `spender` to withdraw tokens from your account, up to the `value` amount

(For the programmers among you, the value field is `uint_256`).

You will also come across function names that can be useful in locating the suspect. Some contracts have an `owner` function that lists the EOA address that owns the contract, or a `Mint` or `MasterMint` address that provides the address that can mint, or create, new tokens.

Always be suspicious of a contract that has few or no defined function names, as these are needed to help check and validate the contract.

A contract can also have *events*, which log what the contract is doing. There are no universally "required" events that must be included in every smart contract. However, events are important for logging information and communicating from smart contracts to external applications. They are used extensively to signal when significant actions occur within a contract.

Events in Solidity allow smart contracts to emit logs, which are then stored on the Ethereum blockchain. These logs are accessible to external applications and can be used to inform users about transactions, changes, or any other notable activities that happen within the contract. While not required by the syntax or functionality of the language itself, including events is considered best practice in many cases for the following reasons:

- **Transparency:** Events help in making the contract's operations transparent, allowing users and external applications to see what actions have been performed.
- **Efficiency:** Reading events is often more gas-efficient than storing and retrieving values directly from the contract's state, especially for off-chain applications.
- **Interactivity:** Events are essential for dApps that interact with smart contracts, providing a way to listen for and react to contract events in real time.

Examples of commonly used events include the following:

Transfer Events In token contracts (e.g., ERC-20, ERC-721), a `Transfer` event is emitted whenever tokens are transferred from one account to another. This is part of the standard interface for these token types.

Approval Events Also in token contracts, an `Approval` event is emitted to log that a token owner has approved another account to spend a specific amount of tokens on their behalf.

Custom Events Contracts can define custom events to signal specific actions unique to the contract's logic, such as voting, staking, or executing a particular contract function.

While the Ethereum virtual machine (EVM) and the Solidity language do not enforce the use of events, the design of a smart contract might require them for the effective operation and interaction with the contract. Therefore, while not strictly *required* in a technical sense, events play a critical role in the practical deployment and usability of smart contracts.

This means that if you see a contract with limited or no logging, this would again be a possible red flag that this contract is hiding what it is doing or that the developer has no interest in transparency.

How can you see these functions and events? Etherscan has a useful capability that enables you to see the functions of a contract and view the logs generated by a transaction. Let's start with contract functions.

In Etherscan, as previously mentioned, when you see a contract address in a transaction it will have a little page icon next to it. A double page icon indicates a new contract address. Examples can be seen in Figure 12.9.

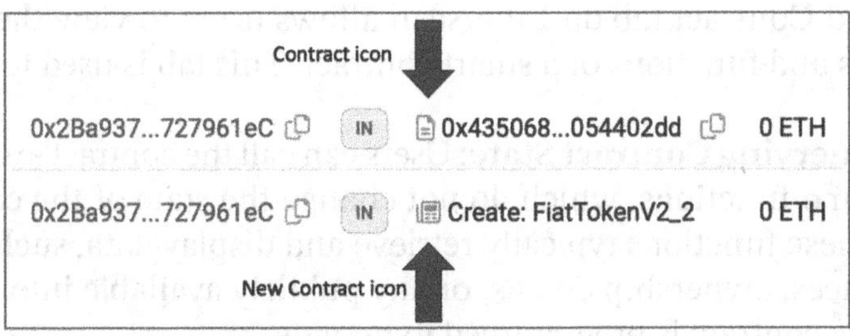

Figure 12.9: Examples of contract icons

When you click a contract address, in the Overview and More Info panes will be a Contract button. Click this button to access information about the contract. We accessed an example contract page when we looked for similar contracts a few paragraphs ago.

On the Contract page, you will see three buttons: Code, Write Contract, and Read Contract. We will look at what each button provides and then consider how they are useful to an investigator.

Code

The Code button enables you to see the raw public code written in Solidity. If you are a programmer, read the code and please explain it to the rest of us. If you are not a programmer but there is a senior officer or manager in the room, then look at the code and just point at it and nod in a knowing way and say something like "That's exactly what I was expecting." This will look impressive and may result in pay rises and promotion. Although I would not rely on it completely in an investigation, you can paste the code into an AI engine such as ChatGPT and it will attempt to explain the code.

If we find Solidity code for a contract on Etherscan or equivalent, that's because a user has uploaded their code and had it verified by Etherscan. The raw byte code on the blockchain is compared with the submitted Solidity code to see if it matches. If it does, then it is flagged as verified.

If you find that the contract code in Etherscan is just a block of hexadecimal numbers, it simply means the code hasn't been validated yet.

Read Contract

The Read Contract tab on Etherscan allows users to view the public variables and functions of a smart contract. This tab is used for:

- **Querying Contract State:** Users can call the contract's `view` and `pure` functions, which do not change the state of the contract. These functions typically retrieve and display data, such as balances, ownership details, or any publicly available information the contract is programmed to provide.
- **No Transaction Required:** Reading from a contract does not require a transaction or consume any gas since it does not alter the blockchain's state.
- **Public Accessibility:** Only functions that are marked as `public` or `external` and are `view` or `pure` can be accessed through the Read Contract tab.

Write Contract

The Write Contract tab, on the other hand, is used for interacting with the contract in a way that can alter its state. This tab is used for:

- **Executing Contract Function:** Users can execute functions that write to the blockchain, such as transferring tokens, altering permissions, or any other function that changes the contract's state. It is unlikely that an investigator will make use of these functions unless they are actively involved in seizing funds since writing to the contract will add a transaction to the blockchain.

- **Transaction Required:** Writing to a contract requires a transaction to be sent and processed by the Ethereum network. This consumes gas, and therefore requires the user to have Ethereum in their wallet to cover transaction fees. This also means that to write to a contract, users need to connect their Ethereum wallet to Etherscan. This is necessary to sign and authorize the transaction.

  Since the write actions can have real effects (like transferring tokens or changing ownership rights), investigators need to be very cautious and ensure they understand the function they are executing.

PROXY CONTRACTS

Sometimes these buttons will say Read As Proxy or Write As Proxy. The Ethereum blockchain is immutable, meaning once a smart contract is deployed, its code cannot be changed. This poses challenges for fixing bugs or upgrading features. Proxy contracts provide a solution by separating the contract's logic (implementation contract) from its state and interface (proxy contract). A proxy contract delegates calls to an implementation contract. The implementation contract contains the actual logic. When there's a need to upgrade the contract, the proxy's reference to the implementation contract is updated to point to a new version, while the state remains in the proxy contract.

This enables the contract to be updated or fixed without deploying a completely new contract and, in the case of a token contract, transferring all the token holders assets to the new contract.

How are these capabilities useful to an investigator? Simply, the function names in the Read and Write lists can help us to understand what a contract is designed to do. For example, browse to 0x1844b21593262668B7248d0f57a220CaaBA46ab9, which is an interesting example. This contract is quite famous as it was related to the Oyster Pearl token. I won't go through the details here, but a lot of crypto was stolen and the founder went to prison. If you were passed this contract address in an investigation with no context, how could you get an idea of what it does? If you have browsed to it, click Contract and then Read Contract. You can see the first nine functions in Figure 12.10.

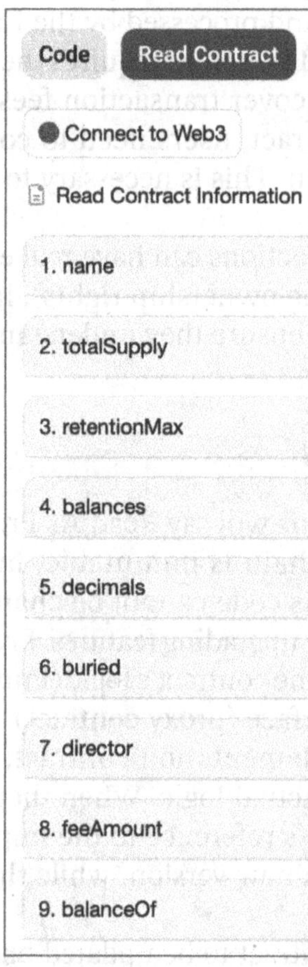

Figure 12.10: Functions from the contract

What can we learn from these functions? If you click the `Name` function, it will return the name of the contract, Oyster Pearl. That can be immediately useful. Second, we have total supply and balances. This would lead us to consider that this is likely a token contract as it will (almost) always have a total amount of token supply in the system and the ability to check the balance of the token being held at an address. If you click Balances, you can enter the Ethereum address of a user and click Query, and it will return their balance of the Oyster Pearl token. You are interacting with the contract but without writing to it.

If you clicked `totalSupply`, you might have been surprised to see a massive number—as of this writing, 104223796797303340986343938. That's a really big number! However, if you click the `Decimals` function it will tell you how many decimal places are used for the token; it's usually 18 but can be different. In this case it returns 18 as normal. To get the actual supply, you count 18 decimal places from the right. User balances have to be calculated in the same way, but it's easier to just search on a user address and see the holdings of a token in the Token Holdings drop-down list.

If you click the Write Contract button, again you'll see functions that are relevant to this being a token contract: `openSale`, `transferFrom`, `withdrawFunds`, and so on. If it's not obvious why this would relate to tokens, then I suggest spending some time browsing different known token contracts and looking at the functions to see what looks "normal." You can do this to understand different types. Try looking at 0xBC4CA0EdA7647A8aB7C2061c2E118A18a936f13D. The following are some of the function calls in the Write Contract screen; can you figure out what they may relate to?

```
mintApe

reserveApes

safeTransferFrom

transferOwnership
```

Any ideas? This contract relates to the Bored Ape Yacht Club NFT collection. What about 0x881D40237659C251811CEC9c364ef91dC08D300C?

Some of the functions from the Write Contract are:

```
pauseSwaps

swap

transferOwnership
```

Any ideas? The word *swap* should be the clue. This would seem to be a contract for swapping between tokens. Indeed, Etherscan identifies this contract as being the Metamask Swap router.

Let's try a trickier one. Browse to the contract page at 0xC2e9F25B e6257c210d7Adf0D4Cd6E3E881ba25f8. You'll see:

```
liquidity

burn

mint

swap
```

Thoughts? If you click `swap`, note that the functions are well annotated and state `Swap token0 for token1, or token1 for token0.` This is clearly a contract for swapping between two tokens. We will discuss later in the chapter that swap contracts also have liquidity of each token to facilitate the swap, hence the liquidity function. Etherscan identifies this contract as a Uniswap V3 DAI swap contract.

Using the function names can really help a nonprogrammer to identify what a contract may be doing. Even if a contract has no function names or virtually no names, this can still tell you something about the programmer. I will often view this with some suspicion although it may just mean that it's a poorly written and annotated contract.

Logs

An Ethereum transaction will also generate logs. These are a little complex to read, and to be honest I can only think of one or two occasions where I used them during an investigation—for example, when tracing across bridges. The logs outline all the movements of funds that are triggered by a transaction. Although this is very straightforward in an ETH-to-ETH transaction, they can be quite complex when contracts are involved. They will be easier to understand once you have completed this chapter as we will be looking at the multiple steps that contract transactions often go through.

Browse on Etherscan to TXID 0x9ffa9c9e4b39a818e7081f86db3fbe 54d32e2325c468d33ede7224f1ad260afb. This transaction is a straight ETH-to-contract transaction.

As of this writing, there are three buttons near the top left of the screen: Overview, Logs, and State. (Sometimes you will see an Internal

TXNs button for more complex interactions.) If you click Logs, you will see the following:

```
Address - Lido: Execution Layer Rewards Vault
Name - ETHReceived (uint256 amount)
Topics - 0 0x27f12abfe35860a9a927b465bb3d4a9c23c8428174b
83f278fe45ed7b4da2662
Data amount : 205154322788559076
```

This is the only log generated by this contract transaction. It breaks down as:

- **Address:** The receiving address of the funds. In this case it is an Ethereum Name Service (ENS) representation of the address; roll over the name for the full 0x address.
- **Name:** This is the function name and the type of data it accepts (Unsigned 256bit integer).
- **Topics:** This is a hash of some parts of the transaction data.
- **Data Amount:** This is the value transacted. It uses a decimal count of 18 again and translates as 0.205154322788559076 ETH.

This is a very simple example, and as mentioned, I don't use the Logs feature a lot, but what it will often do is provide each step in a complex contract transaction and enable you to break down what each part of a transaction does. This will be much clearer as we look at the different transaction types in the upcoming paragraphs. However, what I do use regularly is the State button.

The button next to Logs is named State. Click it (it will format better on your screen than I can replicate here) and you will see the following data (see Figure 12.11; I had to clip off the addresses in the image for the rest of the data to be visible).

Before	After	State Difference
241.903673239965530517 Eth	242.108827562754089593 Eth	▲ 0.205154322788559076
196.019107373218487434 Eth Nonce: 201895	195.813573895784471325 Eth Nonce: 201896	▼ 0.205533477434016109

Figure 12.11: State logs

The State log provides data on how each address in the transaction was affected. Critically it shows the balance of each address before and after the transaction has completed. The first line is related to the Lido address and shows that the balance in the address went up by 0.205. . .ETH. But it also shows us the balance before the transaction of 241.903. . . . This can be very useful indeed to understand the balance of an address before a transaction of interest was made. This may not seem important but it's almost impossible to do this with Bitcoin. If you want to know the balance of an address at a point in the past with Bitcoin, you would have to manually add up all the incoming transactions (TXs) from the start of the wallet's life until the point in time we are interested in and deduct all the outgoing TXs to get a value. However, with the `State` function we can just find the closest transaction to the date we want to know the balance of the address, and see the balance as it was at that time.

For example, a suspect during their interview says that at a certain time in question their Ethereum wallet had a balance of only 2 ETH. By finding a transaction near to the time of interest, we can ascertain the true balance at that time. You'll find this technique really useful.

ETH-to-Contract Transactions

There are many times when you will see a contract transaction where ETH is transacted to a contract. This might involve purchasing an NFT, buying a token, converting funds, laying a bet on a gaming site, and many other situations.

An ETH-to-contract transaction will always have an ETH value and be triggered by a user (EOA) address. As always, the fee will also be paid in ETH. The destination address will be a contract address. When we looked at an ETH-to-ETH transaction, you saw it was easy to trace the funds—there was a source address and a destination address; thus it was straightforward to trace the funds from one address to the other. However, when a destination address is a contract, it is very rare that the contract address is the destination address. The contract will either have the destination address as a variable or as a hard-coded address. Sometimes, in the event of a purchase of a token, the destination of the funds will actually be the source address. The ETH is paid into the contract, swapped, and the third-party token is sent back to the same wallet address. In an ETH-to-contract transaction, the flow looks like Figure 12.12.

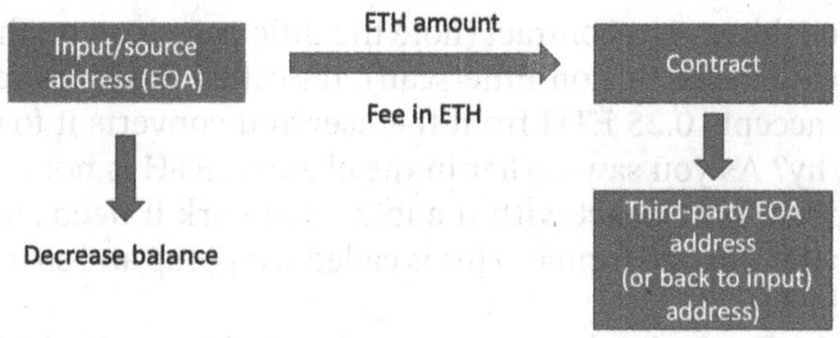

Figure 12.12: Flow of funds in an ETH-to-contract transaction

Let's look at an example of this type of transaction. We'll take a look at TXID 0xb892ad91b112cbd2181c42d1fefea54e19dd1714fff481684fae29f55bdb1c7c.

As usual we will use Etherscan as our viewer. The first useful data is always the time and date. I came from a digital forensics background and we live on timestamps! The next is something Etherscan calls Transaction Action. This is a description of what Etherscan thinks is basically happening in this transaction. It reads:

```
Swap 0.25ETH For 2,895,602.647723909 DEGEN On Uniswap V2
```

What does this mean? Well, it's pretty self-explanatory: The transaction swaps 0.25 ETH for almost 3 million of a token called DEGEN and uses the swapping service Uniswap V2 to do it. This is very useful in helping us understand the fundamental purpose of the transaction and it may be all you care about, but there is more to it than this if you really want to understand what the transaction is doing.

If you scroll down, you will find From and To:

```
From: 0xDF62F7CB774fDE2c519523F697e0850D309DaBb1

To: 0x80a64c6D7f12C47B7c66c5B4E20E72bc1FCd5d9e
(Maestro: Router 2)

Transfer 0.25 ETH From Maestro: Router 2 To
Wrapped Ether
```

What's going on here? There's no sign of the DEGEN token. This is just the initial part of the transaction from the user to the contract.

The From address is the user's EOA address. They have triggered the transaction.

The To address is a contract (note the little page icon on the page if you are able to see this on Etherscan). It's called the Maestro: Router 2, and it accepts 0.25 ETH from the user and converts it to wrapped Ether. Why? As you saw earlier in the chapter, ETH is not an ERC-20 token and so to interact with the token network it needs to be converted to the ERC-20 format. This is called wrapping and so it becomes wrapped ETH.

To understand what happens next, you need to scroll a little farther down the page to the section ERC-20 Tokens Transferred. This is what you'll see:

```
From Maestro: Router 2 To 0x6eBAde. . .c4BDF89C
For 0.25($662.89) Wrapped Ethe. . .(WETH. . .)

From 0x6eBAde. . .c4BDF89C To 0xDF62F7. . .309Da
Bb1F or 2,895,602.647723909 Degen Coin. . .
(DEGEN. . .)
```

The From/To section already told us that the ETH was converted into wrapped ETH, and this section details what happens next. The Maestro Router address moved the wrapped ETH to the address starting with 0x6eBA. The Maestro: Router 2 refers to a component of a cryptocurrency trading bot system used on the Telegram messenger app, known as MaestroBots. The next line tells us that the 0x6eBA address then moves 2.8 million of the DEGEN token to the address starting with 0xDF62. Now, if you are eagle-eyed you will recognize this address; look back at the original From address. This is the address of the transaction originator, so this is a swap of ETH to DEGEN and the new tokens are sent back to the original address.

This seems fairly self-explanatory, but where in this process was the wrapped ETH converted into the DEGEN token? To understand this properly, let's get a bit more technical! Maybe go and grab a coffee first.

Scroll down the page a little more and you will see a More Details section with a link that reads +Click To Show More. Click this link to view details about the ETH price at the time of the transaction and also gas price information. We are interested in the scary-looking section Input Data. I won't display all of it here, but if you are not following along online, then it's important that you see it. There is a box of raw data that looks like this:

```
Function: swapExactETHForTokensSupportingFeeOn
TransferTokens(uint256 amountOutMin, address[]
path, address to, uint256 deadline) *
MethodID: 0xb6f9de95

[0]:
0000000000000000000000000000000000000000000000
000041d6a02e42c9b
[1]:
0000000000000000000000000000000000000000000000
0000000000000080

[2]:
000000000000000000000000df62f7cb774fde2c51952
3f697e0850d309dabb1
```

The first win for us is that we can see the primary function that this transaction was designed to complete. To break up the function into plain English, it reads Swap Exact ETH For Tokens Supporting Fee On Transfer Tokens. This confirms that this transaction was to swap ETH for a token. We already knew this from the Transaction Action data we saw previously. But what about the rest of the data? Underneath the box of raw data is a Decode Input Data button. Give it a click, and the display will change to an interpretation of the raw code that reads:

#	Name	Type	Data
0	amountOutMin	uint256	1158241059089563
1	path	address[]	0xC02aaA39b223FE8D0A0e 5C4F27eAD9083C756Cc20x b27b907C2De4A2bf 87C14Fe503cf7eA4388451D5
2	to	address	0xDF62F7CB774fDE2c519523F 697e0850D309DaBb1
3	deadline	uint256	1707825420

Row 0 provides the minimum output amount of the swapped token; in this case, we know it to be DEGEN. It's a minimum (min) amount since the swap value can change quickly with crypto and so this sets the minimum amount that will be output. It's generally termed Slippage Protection. Slippage occurs when there is a difference between the expected price of a trade and the executed price. By setting an amountOutMin, the user specifies the minimum acceptable amount they are willing to receive for their trade to go through.

Row 1, path, is the row we are really interested in to understand how the transaction is working. Please feel free to check the addresses, or you can just take my word for it. If we check the address starting with 0xC02aa (just click it if you are following along with the book), we find that it belongs to wrapped ETH. We have already learned that this was the first part of the transaction. However, when we check the second address starting with 0xb27b, it is tagged in the More Info pane as belonging to Degen Coin (DEGEN).

If we look at the transactions for the Degen Coin address, you will note that they are almost all `Approve` functions rather than transfers of their coin as you might expect. The primary purpose of the `Approve` function is to enable a third party (like a smart contract or another user) to spend tokens on behalf of the token holder under certain conditions. So this address approves other contracts such as the Maestro Router that is involved in this swap to move tokens from DEGEN to the receiving address. Here's how it works:

1. Delegation of spending authority: The `Approve` function allows a token owner to give permission to another address (which could be a user or a contract) to transfer a specific amount of tokens. This is useful in scenarios where the token owner wants to allow a smart contract to interact with their tokens without giving up their ownership.
2. Function parameters: Typically, the `Approve` function takes two parameters: the address of the spender and the amount of tokens they are allowed to spend.
3. Row 2 is the To address, or the recipient address. Sometimes this is the only place that we can see the output address in a contract transaction and so can be very useful indeed.
4. Lastly, row 3 is the Deadline. This specifies a time limit for the transaction to be executed. If you are a digital forensics

professional you may recognize the date/time format used as UNIX time. UNIX time is calculated as the number of seconds since January 1, 1970. If you take the value 1707825420 and enter it into any UNIX time calculator online, it will provide a date and time of Tuesday February 13, 2024, 11:57:00 GMT. If you check, the deadline is only a second or two after the transaction timestamp.

By checking this data, we are able to get a better view of the path that the transaction took and the addresses and contracts that were triggered by it. This is all pretty complicated the first time, but the more examples you look at the easier it becomes to read. Why do we care about this? Once we saw that it was a token swap, and checked that the recipient was the same as the originator, why do we need to see the rest of the path of the transaction? Simply, you don't every time; you often just see the input, what it was and where it went, and that is sufficient. However, in other investigations where we are looking at suspected fraudulent contracts, it is vital to be able to follow the path and track where all the funds go.

There is one oddity in Etherscan that I just want to point out before we summarize this example, and that's the way that Etherscan links addresses. In the From/To section of the transaction, we saw two movements of funds that looked like this:

```
From Maestro: Router 2 To 0x6eBAde. . .c4BDF89C
For 0.25($662.89) Wrapped Ethe. . .(WETH. . .)
From 0x6eBAde. . .c4BDF89C To 0xDF62F7. . .
309DaBb1F or 2,895,602.647723909 Degen Coin. . .
(DEGEN. . .)
```

Highlighted in bold, we see two entries of the same address. The Maestro Router moves funds to 0x62BA and then in the second part we see 0x62BA move the DEGEN coins to the user's address. So if we click either the first or second address entities, we would expect to see the same result, but we don't. Clicking the address in the top line appears to take us to wrapped ETH, and clicking the bottom address takes us to Degen Coin. So, who owns 0x62BA, wrapped ETH or DEGEN? Neither. Confused? This is why I wanted to cover this with you as it can be very confusing and can result in misidentifying addresses.

A clue can be obtained by looking at the links underlying each address:

First address: 0x6eBA

`https://etherscan.io/token/`**`0xc02a`**`aa39b223fe8d0a0e5c4f27ead9083c756cc2?a=`**`0x6eba`**`de7ea56b6efc2106549c047d1faec4bdf89c`

This link takes us to the address 0xc02a, which is the wrapped ETH address, but filters for any transactions that include 0x6eb.

Second address: 0x6eBA

`https://etherscan.io/token/`**`0xb27b`**`907c2de4a2bf87c14fe503cf7ea4388451d5?a=`**`0x6eba`**`de7ea56b6efc2106549c047d1faec4bdf89c`

This link takes us to the address 0xb27b, which is owned by DEGEN, but again filters for any transactions that include 0x6eba.

So, who owns 0x6eba? If we copy and paste the address into Etherscan, the address is tagged as belonging to Uniswap V2. This makes sense as the original Transaction Action section told us that:

Swap 0.25ETH For 2,895,602.647723909 DEGEN On Uniswap V2

We have now found the Uniswap address, which enables us to plot out exactly what has happened in this transaction.

You have to be very careful when you click addresses in Etherscan that you check the destination and see if it is a filtered view or a direct list of the address transactions. Watch out for the page stating Filtered By Token Holder (see Figure 12.13).

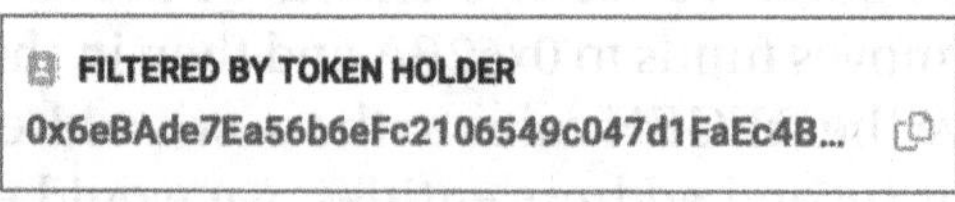

Figure 12.13: Filtered By Token Holder

We now have enough information to sketch out this transaction and see exactly what happened:

1. User 0xDF62F sends 0.25 ETH to the Maestro Router 2, which converts it to wrapped ETH.
2. The wrapped ETH is sent to Uniswap V2.
3. DEGEN approves for Uniswap to transfer DEGEN coins.
4. Uniswap converts it to DEGEN coin. (It doesn't actually change it, of course; it just gives the ETH to the ETH side of the swap contract and retrieves the DEGEN coin—more on this later in the chapter).
5. The DEGEN coin is sent back to the user 0xDF62F.

Is that clear enough? If you fancy a little challenge, what can you learn about the user who owns 0xDF62F? Can you track back and see where their funds came from and when?

Being able to read the flow of funds through the contracts in the transaction also helps us to understand what we see in our commercial tool. If you have a decent blockchain intelligence tool and search on this transaction, you should see something that looks like Figure 12.14.

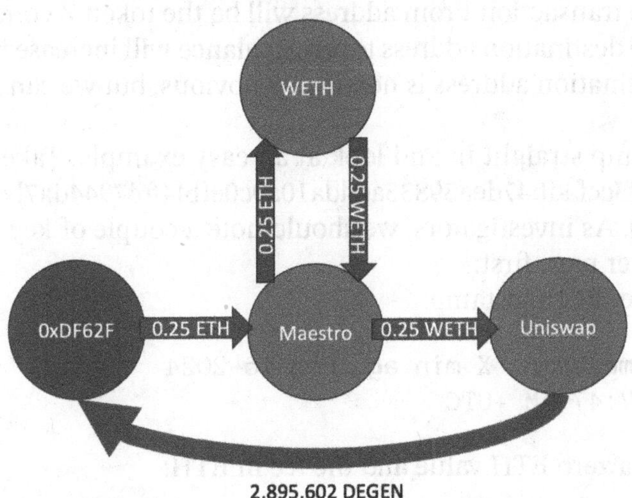

Figure 12.14: Graph of transaction flow

I would hope that your expensive commercial investigation tool would generate a rather better-looking graph than the rather blocky attempt I made, but the flow should be the same. Understanding the contract flow and the fact that there were actually three contracts triggered helps us to follow the funds correctly and be able to explain the transaction fully in a report or if having to give evidence.

Token-to-Token Transactions

Having gone through the pain of learning ETH-to-token transactions, you should find that token-to-token transactions are slightly easier. By a token-to-token transfer, we mean that we are looking at a transaction that has no ETH component but is a transfer via a contract for tokens built using an ERC standard. This could be ERC-20 tokens or an NFT-style ERC-721 token and many others that we covered in the previous chapter.

Say a person owns a token we will call Z, and they want to send 10 Z tokens to another address. This is how it works:

- There is no ETH value in the transaction; it will always be 0.
- ETH is still needed to pay the fee.
- The user's token Z balance reduces by 10.
- The transaction From address will be the token Z contract.
- The destination address token X balance will increase by 10. The destination address is not always obvious, but we can find it.

Let's jump straight in and look at an easy example. Take a look at TXID 0x7f3ccfadb47dea39835a0dda10a0c0efbf4f6f7944da7bdf6c3b02cca7fde6d0. As investigators, we should note a couple of key things on the explorer page first:

We have the timestamp:

```
    Timestamp: X min ago Feb-16-2024
  09:07:47 AM +UTC
```

We see a zero ETH value and the fee in ETH:

```
Value: 0 ETH ($0.00)
Transaction Fee: 0.0012835278726216 ETH ($3.61)
```

We can then look at the Transaction Action to get an idea of what the transaction is doing. In this case it is very straightforward:

```
Transaction Action: Transfer 6,000,000 VRA
To 0x974026. . .702Ac35C
```

Okay, this seems clear; this is just a transfer of 6 million VRA coins to the destination address starting 0x9740. Whenever I come across a token I haven't had any experience with, I do a couple of things.

I first do a quick bit of Internet research to find what the token is and what it's designed to do. My go-to site as of this writing is `CoinMarketCap.com`. CoinMarketCap indicates that VRA is the VERA coin and it helpfully states that:

> *Vera is the leading decentralized protocol that enables NFT sharing, renting/leasing, and financing/mortgaging. Founded in 2021, Vera's mission is simple: To build open, secure, and powerful NFT financial products that are equally available to everyone everywhere.*

Good for them; I wish them all success! (I'm just using this token as an example and there is no suggestion of any wrongdoing.)

Next, I check how long the coin has been trading. CoinMarketCap has a graph showing the price of the coin against the dollar, and you can select All time. This shows me that the VERA token has been trading since September 2021, and although I'm not always interested in the dollar price, I can see that the coin topped out at around $0.60 in December 2021 and has since settled at around the $0.21 mark. Understanding the fluctuation of pricing can help you to see whether a coin has been artificially "pumped" to increase its price and then "dumped" when the scammers remove all the liquidity, for example. In the same way, knowing if a token starts trading perhaps a couple of days before the first scam reports were made is not dissimilar to a company domain name being brand-new in an investment scam. Your commercial crypto investigation may be able to provide you with similar data, but there are sites that can help if you don't have access to one (see Figure 12.15).

We have learned something about the token involved in this transaction, but let's dig deeper into how the transaction is working.

If you are working along, head back to the transaction in Etherscan and scroll down to the From/To section. You will see this description:

```
From: 0xBFCd86e36D947A9103A7D4a95d178A432723d6aD

Interacted With (To): 0xF411903cbC70a74d22900a5
DE66A2dda66507255 (Verasity: VRA Token)
```

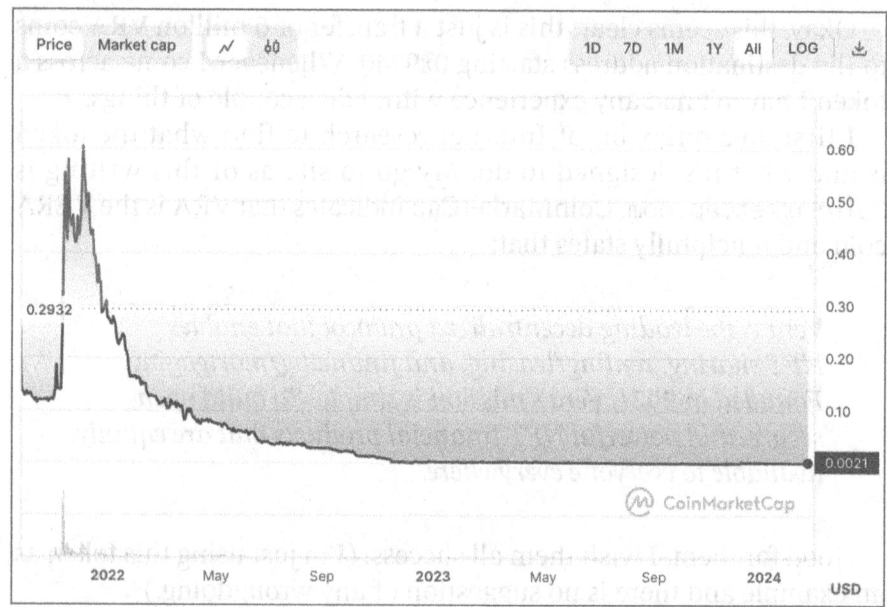

Figure 12.15: Graph from `CoinMarketCap.com` showing all the time it has been traded the price fluctuation of the VERA token

At first glance this would seem clear—funds are being sent from 0xBFC to the address 0xF411. However, this is where mistakes happen all the time by investigators who don't understand the difference between a straight transaction and a contract transaction. The To address here is the contract address for the VERA token, *not* the destination address. It is possible for the contract address to be the destination address in a transaction, but this is rare when moving tokens. You do see it sometimes with gaming where a user places a bet, for example, and the funds move into a contract address, but generally with token-to-token transactions the contract is not the final destination.

What are we seeing here? The user's address, To, triggers the From contract address, and the contract address now triggers code functions to carry out a series of instructions. What does the contract do in this transaction?

Look in the From/To section and you will find a section called ERC-20 Tokens Transferred. The data looks like this:

```
ERC-20 Tokens Transferred: From 0xBFCd86. . .
2723d6aD To 0x974026. . .702Ac35C For 6,000,000
($45,205.51) (VRA).
```

Putting it all together in plain language, user address 0xBFC asks contract 0xF411 to move 6,000,000 VRA tokens to end-user address 0x9740.

In some transactions, the contract will move the funds through several other contracts and may even take an internal fee for the transaction, and sometimes it's not obvious where the funds end up. In this case you can use the More Details section at the bottom of the transaction. If we look at the raw data in this transaction it states:

```
Function: transfer(address recipient,
uint256 amount)

MethodID: 0xa9059cbb

[0]:
000000000000000000000000974026e01660d11b5b5f
08394806b619702ac35c

[1]:
000000000000000000000000000000000000000004f68
ca6d8cd91c6000000
```

The function here confirms for us that this is a straight transfer of funds but also states that the variables in the function will be the recipient address and also the amount. If we now click the Decode Input Data button, it decodes the data into the following:

#	Name	Type	Data
0	recipient	address	0x974026E01660D11B5b5F 08394806b619702Ac35C
1	amount	uint256	6000000000000000000000000

This provides us with the final destination address that the funds have been sent to and also the amount of VERA coins moved. Remember that tokens normally use a decimal count of 18, and so if you count 18 zeros from the right you will be left with 6,000,000, as we saw in the summary at the start of this section.

You can see an example of funds terminating at the contract address at this transaction. Can you tell what's going on? Take a look at TXID 0xa00d6d3384c371e45930dfedb26e1193a5b41017701a8f f08ac67d2228c284c5.

I won't break that transaction down in detail as it's pretty simple, but we see Tether tokens withdrawn from Exchange Bitrex into the primary Tether contract. (The Tether contract starts with 0xDAC. You will see this address all the time, and you will look very impressive if you can point at an address and know by heart that it's Tether. It's like wrapped Bitcoin, which starts with 0x2260, and wrapped ETH, which starts with 0xC02aaa. Once you recognize them, you can spot them quickly in a transaction.

There is a useful tool available in Etherscan. As of this writing it is available at `https://etherscan.io/balancecheck-tool`.

The check tool enables you to verify whether a user address was a holder of a particular token or of ETH at a specific time. This information can be very useful in an investigation. A victim says that they paid a scammer in USDT on a certain date, but the scammer says that they have never traded any USDT. Perhaps if we look at the scammer's address today we see no USDT, but we are able to use the balance check tool to see if their address had a USDT balance on the day the victim says they transferred their funds. Although we could look back at the history and try to add up all the USDT inputs and subtract all the outputs, this is a quick way to get a balance on a certain day.

It's straightforward to use; you can choose ETH from the drop-down menu and provide the user's EOA address and the date you are interested in, and this will provide a balance of the user's ETH at that time. Otherwise, you can choose Token from the drop-down list; enter the token contract address, the user's address, and the date of interest; and again it will provide a balance of that token on that date.

For example, using the Balance Check tool we can find out how many DONALD TRUMP 2024 tokens (token address – 0xa41f7ED 89D86258bB8fdeF8e77e91F43c28AB74C) were held by the user address 0xa53F88280931Cd4e27Ee C00E45DB57A07EB957F9 on the 19th February 2024. If we enter the details into the balance checker, we get results shown in Figure 12.16 and Figure 12.17.

This can be a very useful tool and worth bookmarking. Can you have a look at this user's address and find out what their ETH balance was on the same day?

Token-to-token transactions are generally pretty simple to follow but can get more complex when we look at decentralized exchanges, decentralized finance (DeFi), and NFTs. Let's have a look at some trickier transactions.

Figure 12.16: Search for Donald Trump 2024 tokens on February 19, 2024 for the user address starting with 0XA53F8

Token Balance for Account Address: 0xa53F88280931Cd4e27EeC00E45DB57A07EB957F9

SNAPSHOT DATE	BLOCK	TOKEN QUANTITY
2/19/2024	19262653	170,410,772,852.471141294

Figure 12.17: Results for Donald Trump 2024 tokens on February 19, 2024 for the user address starting with 0XA53F8

NFTs

An NFT, or nonfungible token, is a type of digital token that represents ownership or proof of authenticity of a unique piece of content, such as a gaming card, artwork, music, and more. Unlike cryptocurrencies like Bitcoin or traditional ERC-20 tokens such as the tokens we have looked at already in this chapter, which are fungible (meaning each token is identical to and interchangeable with every other token), NFTs are unique. This uniqueness and indivisibility make them ideal for certifying the ownership of digital and sometimes physical assets in a secure, immutable manner.

NFTs reached the peak of their trading with around $17 billion in trading volume in January 2022, but the hype was short-lived and the

NFT market collapsed by 97 percent in September 2022 (see `https://coinmarketcap.com/academy/article/8728797c-3d26-4864-ad19-b35ba777fc81`). However, although many NFTs were wildly overpriced (in my humble opinion), the technology is sound and they are still widely used in online gaming where assets such as gaming cards (characters, skills, weapons, etc.) can be won, bought, and traded on the blockchain. Because the NFT provides an actual usable asset within the gaming environment, they are still popular and would seem to be the majority of NFT-type transactions that we see at the moment.

It is worth being aware of NFT transactions when looking at a suspect's wallets as they can easily be used for money-laundering purposes due to the unregulated valuations of "art" and other online assets.

Although an NFT is just another token transaction, they are often more complex to read than other token transactions since there are often more elements and functions that the contract triggers. For example, a typical NFT transaction through a broker such as OpenSea would have the following elements:

- User/buyer
- OpenSea contract
- OpenSea fee address
- User/seller address
- Blockchain fee

These elements in the transaction mean that the buyer of the NFT has funds flowing "from" them to buy the asset and has the NFT asset flowing "to" them, the seller also receives funds from OpenSea, and the OpenSea contract sends the NFT, receives the funds, sends the funds to the seller, and keeps some for itself. Confused? Let's look at an example.

On Etherscan search for TXID0x66276114032a34cc8c547049e4ce498f7194b49bd2c48d1e415d51463f30fab2. As before, we can look at the Transaction Action that just tells us:

Sale: 1 NFT For 0.8499 ETH On OpenSea via Seaport

At least we now know that this transaction is an NFT sale and that it was handled by the OpenSea company. (Seaport is the system that handles all the OpenSea transactions). However, in this case the Transaction Action doesn't tell us who bought the NFT, what the NFT is, or who it was bought from. Let's see if we can break it down:

The first section we see gives us this data:

```
From: 0x3D1ff3F071CfaF83407e73666744412F113CEEF6

Interacted With (To): 0x0000000000000ADc04C56B-
f30aC9d3c0aAF14dC (Seaport 1.5)

Transfer 0.0042495 ETH From Seaport 1.5 To Open-
Sea: Fees 3

Transfer 0.8456505 ETH From Seaport 1.5 To
0x35F4bf. . .53514Cfa
```

The From address here is the user who triggered the transaction. This represents the buyer of the NFT. The user interacts with the Seaport 1.5 contract that will handle the sale. The actions represented in this section are the movement of the ETH that the user has injected into the contract to buy the NFT. We see that 0.0042495 is paid to the OpenSea Fees address and the remainder is sent to the address starting with 0x35F4. This address is the seller of the NFT. But where is the transfer of the NFT to the buyer?

We now know that the two key addresses are:

```
0x3D1f: Buyer

0x35F4: Seller
```

If we now look at the section ERC-721 Tokens Transferred, we see the transaction of the NFT:

```
ERC-721 Tokens Transferred:

ERC-721 Token ID [658] Mavia Land. . .(LAND)
From 0x35F4bf. . .53514CfaTo 0x3D1ff3. . .113CEEF6
```

We learn from this that the NFT is transferred from the seller to the buyer and that the NFT is from a collection called Mavia Land and has an ID of 658.

If we click on the Token ID [658] link, it will take us to a page that will display the NFT (although not always), some details about the NFT such as any collection that it's part of, and critically for an investigator, the history of this NFT from when it was originally minted (created) through any intermediary transactions to its current owner (see Figure 12.18).

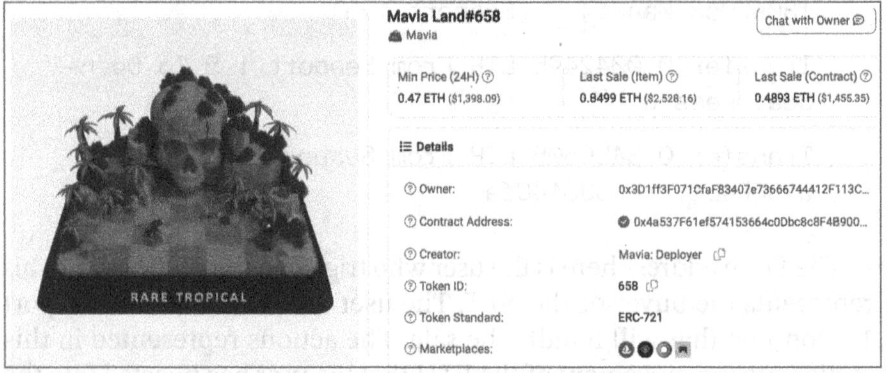

Figure 12.18: Details of NFT #658

The Details pane can be very useful to the investigator as it provides the current owner and the last sale value. Scrolling down the page, you will find the history of the NFT, and this includes the values. If you were, for example, to see an NFT minted and then immediately sold for 10 ETH and then later sold for 1 ETH, you could just be seeing fluctuation or you could be witnessing money laundering or a scam sale. I can't replicate the whole history, but the portion of the page in Figure 12.19 shows the date, function, and value.

Browse to this page and you will also see the buyer and seller addresses, which can be useful as you will see in a moment. The history of the NFT is easy to read. It was minted, transferred twice without a value, sold for 1.3899 ETH, transferred again, and then sold twice more for 0.7739 ETH and 0.8499 ETH, respectively. For the eagle-eyed among you, the NFT was bought and sold for a $200 profit in just over an hour on February 20, 2024.

NFT SCAMS

I am not suggesting any wrongdoing in this example, but at the height of the NFT boom, scammers were minting a picture of their pet rabbit (or anything really) then selling it to "themselves" for thousands of dollars and then selling it on at a "price" to investors.

The investor could see that the NFT had sold for $20,000 and so the asking price of $10,000 for a "quick sale" appeared to be a sound investment. In reality, it was worth nothing.

Date Time (UTC)	Action	Price
2024-02-20 13:28:47	Sale	0.8499 ETH ($2,528.16)
2024-02-20 12:08:59	Sale	0.7739 WETH ($2,302.09)
2024-02-19 23:01:59	Transfer	
2024-01-28 4:02:23	Sale	1.3899500001 ETH ($3,136.56)
2024-01-28 2:45:47	Transfer	
2022-04-10 4:09:10	Transfer	
2022-03-04 15:11:24	Mint	

Figure 12.19: Transaction history of NFT #658

Most NFTs are traded on sites like OpenSea, LooksRare, and Rarible, among others. Most of these sites do not use traditional authentication like a username and password but rather enable you to connect your browser-based wallet; you are then anonymously authenticated with your public/private key pair. This provides a very useful tool for investigators as you are able to search on the NFT site for the user's Ethereum address and it will list all the NFTs owned by this user. If you can, give this a try on `OpenSea.io`, `rarible.com`, and `looksrare.org`. The owner of the NFT we have been looking at is 0x3D1ff3F071CfaF83407e73666744412F113CEEF6. Just enter the user's address in the search bar of any of these sites and it will list the NFTs owned, how many were bought and sold, the value, and other analytics (see Figure 12.20 and Figure 12.21).

Sometimes accounts on these sites are also associated with user profiles and aliases. These aliases often exist elsewhere on the Internet and can help us make an identification.

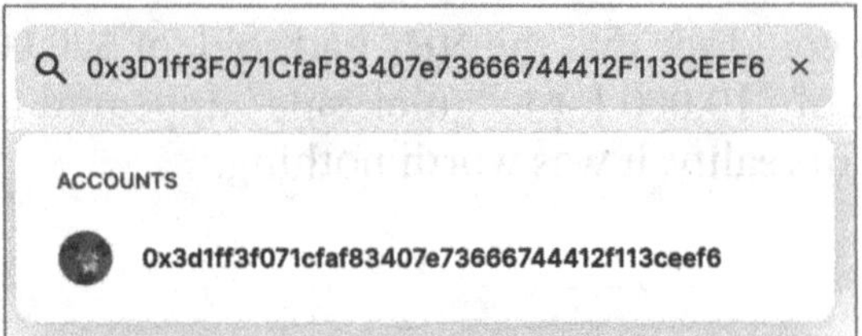

Figure 12.20: Searching for the buyer's Ethereum address on OpenSea

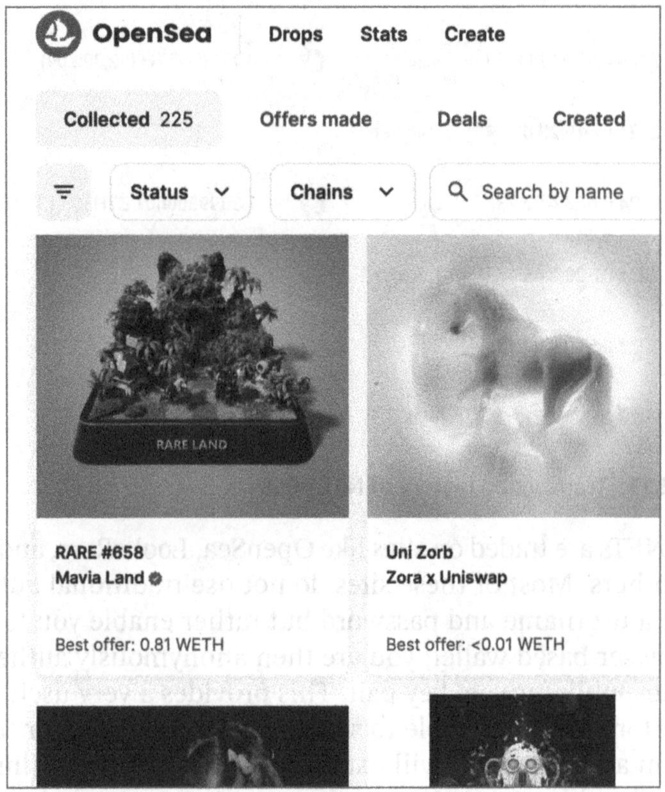

Figure 12.21: Results of search on OpenSea showing other owned NFTs

For example, in the NFT transaction we have been looking at, the NFT was purchased from an address starting with 0x35F4. If we search for the seller's address on OpenSea, we find that the address has a username of NFTinitcom_CheckBlur. If we Google NFTinitcom, we find that there is an X account and a website `NFTinit.com`, which may relate to our seller (see Figure 12.22 and Figure 12.23).

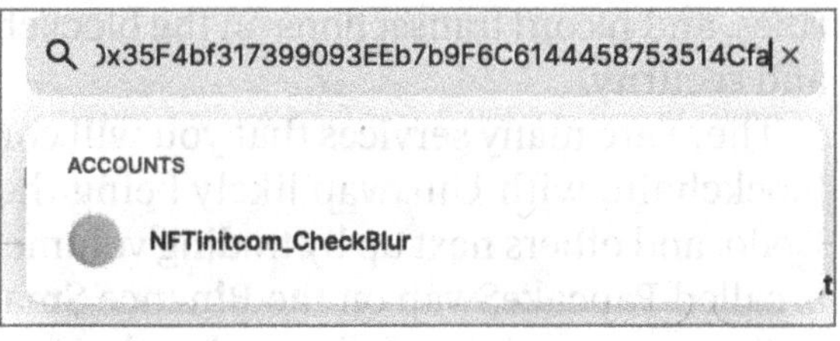

Figure 12.22: Finding an alias when searching on OpenSea for the seller's address

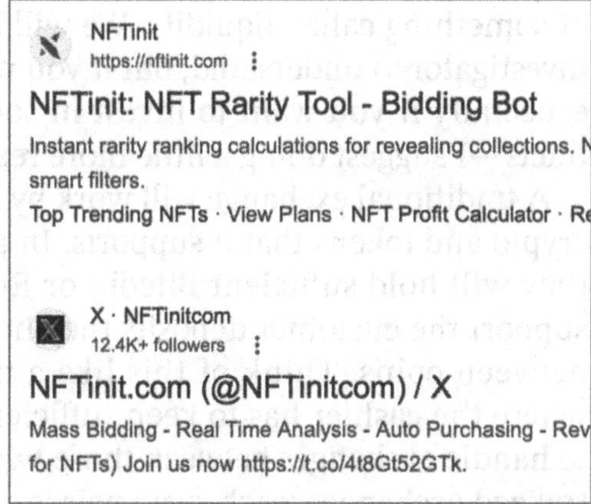

Figure 12.23: Google search for alias

I'm always delighted when I see that a suspect address has traded or owns NFTs as it often opens up many other open source lines of inquiry. We will expand on this technique in Chapter 15, "Open Source Intelligence and the Blockchain."

In the meantime, if you would like to look at other NFT transactions, go to the home page of Etherscan and select the NFTs menu and choose Latest Trades. That will give you an almost infinite amount of NFT transactions to read and learn from.

Decentralized Exchanges

A decentralized exchange (DEX) is an online platform that enables users to trade cryptocurrencies directly with one another without the need for an intermediary or central authority to facilitate the trades. Unlike traditional exchanges, which are operated by a centralized organization (like a company), DEXs operate on a blockchain such as Ethereum using the smart contract system we have been discussing. These smart contracts automate the exchange process, enforce trading rules, and record transactions on the blockchain, ensuring transparency and security.

There are many services that you will come across on the Ethereum blockchain, with Uniswap likely being the most obvious and Curve, Dodo, and others next up by trading volume as of this writing. Uniswap is called PancakeSwap on the Binance Smart Chain blockchain.

Before we get into reading and understanding real-world DEX transactions, you need to understand how exchanges work and the role of something called liquidity. We will be covering just enough for an investigator to understand, but if you want to use these services—and especially if you want to invest in some of the liquidity swap contracts—I suggest doing a little more reading and research.

A traditional exchange will work by holding its own liquidity in the crypto and tokens that it supports. In practical terms this means that they will hold sufficient Bitcoin or Ether or Tether, for example, to support the customer deposits they hold and also to carry out swaps between coins. Think of this like a traditional currency exchange where the cashier has to keep sufficient dollars and euros to be able to handle exchanges between those two currencies. With most decentralized exchanges, each swap pair is a contract and that contract will hold sufficient liquidity in each token to manage user swaps. As users swap between tokens, each side of the liquidity pool will rise and fall according to demand, which will affect the exchange rate.

As a user, you can add liquidity to a swap contract and then benefit from a portion of the fees paid. This is a simple form of crypto investment. If you see a suspect making deposits into a swap contract, then they will likely be paid some benefit on those deposited funds. This can be a quick way of making some money on criminal funds, so it's worth keeping an eye out for it (see Figure 12.24).

UNDERSTANDING LIQUIDITY 101

At the heart of a swap contract is the *liquidity pool*, a smart contract that holds reserves of two or more tokens. Users can trade against the liquidity available in the pool, with the swap contract automatically determining the exchange rate based on the relative supply of the tokens in the pool.

Users, often referred to as *liquidity providers (LPs)*, deposit an equivalent value of two tokens into the pool to provide liquidity.

In return, they receive liquidity tokens or pool shares that represent their stake in the pool. These liquidity tokens can later be redeemed for the original tokens plus a portion of the trading fees generated by the pool.

High liquidity in a pool means that larger trades can be executed without significantly impacting the price of the tokens involved. This is beneficial for users who wish to execute large trades without experiencing high slippage, which is the difference between the expected price of a trade and the price at which the trade is executed.

If a liquidity pool has low liquidity, it can lead to high slippage, making it costly for users to perform trades. Additionally, low liquidity can make a pool more susceptible to price manipulation.

To encourage users to provide liquidity, DeFi platforms often offer incentives such as a share of the transaction fees or distribution of governance tokens. These incentives help to ensure that there is sufficient liquidity in the pool to facilitate trades smoothly.

One of the risks faced by liquidity providers is impermanent loss, which occurs when the price of tokens in the pool changes compared to when they were deposited. This can lead to a scenario where the dollar value of the tokens withdrawn is less than if the LP had simply held on to the tokens outside the pool, although fees earned can offset this loss.

We will not look in detail at deposited funds, but we'll talk more about this in the next section related to DeFi. To be clear, providing funds to a swap contract is a type of DeFi, but I wanted to differentiate between the two for the subject of investigations. Investigating a user swapping funds to obfuscate them is quite different from a suspect investing funds into a swap contract liquidity pool.

The flow for the swap of funds is in general quite simple. The user deposits funds into the swap contract. The swap contract will check to see if an initial swap needs to happen—most often swapping ETH to wrapped ETH so that it can swap for another token—and then will often look at the cheapest route to make the conversion. The deposited funds will stay in the contract and the funds swapped are sent to the user.

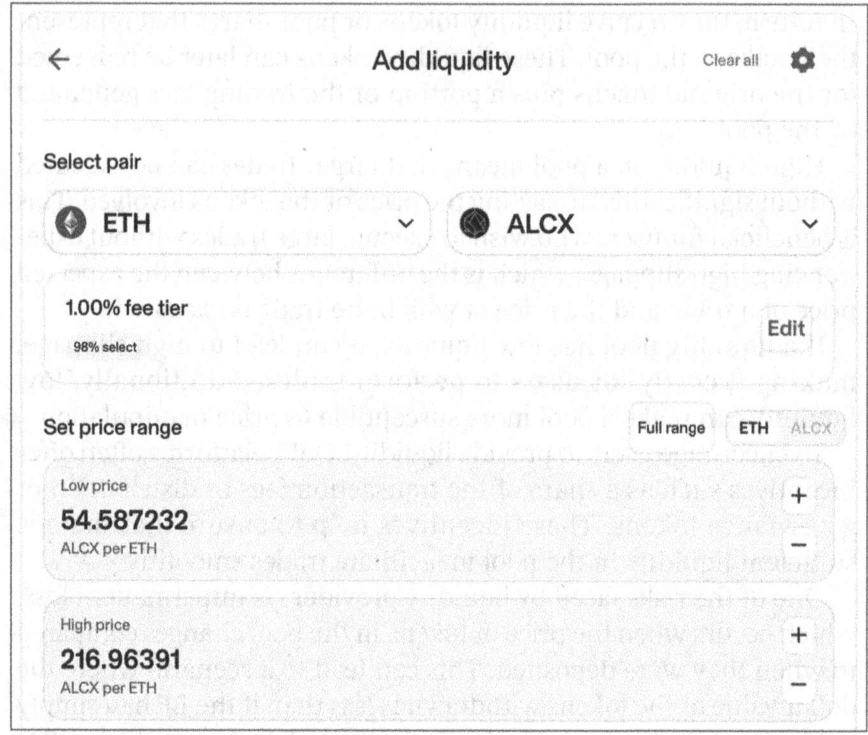

Figure 12.24: Uniswap Add Liquidity screen

As we have already looked at some contract transactions, we will jump straight into a more complex swap, I think you can handle it! Take a look at the following transaction in Etherscan:

```
0xb46f35d20c4e2b94e7db1da6879a1c39977e256898
6d92162fbd509b412f1749
```

The first thing you might notice is that the Transaction Action information is not very helpful at all; it states:

```
Call Swap Function by 0x94dF40. . .Ff8b9D58 on
1Inch V5 Aggregation Router
```

At least this tells us that this is a swap function, and its originator is the user address 0x94df, but we don't know what tokens are being swapped or indeed any other information about the transaction other than it's using the 1inch contracts. (`Gemini.com` describes 1inch as "an exchange aggregator that scans decentralized exchanges to find the lowest cryptocurrency prices for traders, and is powered by its 1INCH utility and governance token.") Because 1inch looks for the cheapest way to do a swap, the contracts can be tricky to interpret. What can we learn? If we look further down the screen from the Transaction Action to the From/To information, it only gives us the same information:

```
From: 0x94dF40e816276357Fc4a269D4f4670FBFf8b9D58
Interacted With (To):
0x1111111254EEB25477B68fb85Ed929f73A960582
(1inch v5: Aggregation Router)
```

To learn what's going on, we must look at the series of transactions that happen within the 1inch swap contract. I'll split them up a little bit and number them to make the lines a bit clearer so we can just refer to line numbers when working out what the transaction does

1. From 0x94dF40. . .Ff8b9D58 To 0x5F515F. . .2e9904EC For 113.27660691 ($335.30) dYdX. . . (DYDX. . .)
2. From 0x5F515F. . .2e9904EC To 0xd17a89. . .3Ddc11d8 For 1.076127765645 ($3.19) dYdX. . .(DYDX. . .)
3. From 0xbAd9AD. . .712a6Ee1 To 1inch v5: Aggregation Router For 332.108918 ($331.41)
   USDC. . . (USDC. . .)
4. From 0x5F515F. . .2e9904EC To 0xbAd9AD. . .712a6Ee1 For 112.200479144355 ($332.11) dYdX. . . (DYDX. . .)
5. From 1inch v5: Aggregation Router To 0x94dF40. . .Ff8b9D58 For 332.108918 ($331.41) USDC. . . (USDC. . .)

What we are looking at are five movements of funds carried out by the contract to enable the swap that this transaction is designed to do. (Something very important that you need to understand is that these coin movements are rarely listed in order; you must figure out what order they are in and then follow the flow.)

As we already know the user's address, we just need to find the From 0x94dF line. This is line 1 in the list. We see about 113 DYDX coins move to the address 0x5F515. We now know the input token as DYDX. If you are online and browse to the address 0x5F515, you will see that it's related to the DYDX token. What happens next? We need to look for funds flowing from 0x5F515. Can you find them?

You will note that I said "them." If you look carefully, you will see that lines 2 and 4 have funds flowing from 0x5F515. Line 2 is for just over 1 DYDX and line 4 for the remaining 112 DYDX. What do you think the smaller one is for? We can guess that this is a fee being sent to DYDX. The smaller amount goes to the address 0xd17a8 and there are no other movements of funds out from this address in this transaction.

This leads us to focus on line 4. We see 112 DYDX move to the address 0xbAd9. If we search this address on Etherscan, we can see that it's a contract related to USDC. To confirm this, we can find 0xbAd9 as an input at line 3 and take a look at what flows out: around 332 UDSC. So 0xbAd9 was the address that handled the DYDX-to-USDC swap. Line 3 mostly moves these funds to the 1inch v5: Aggregation Router, which, at line 6, moves the USDC back to the user's address.

That is much easier to show in a classroom than it is in a book! If we were to graph this transaction, it would look something like Figure 12.25.

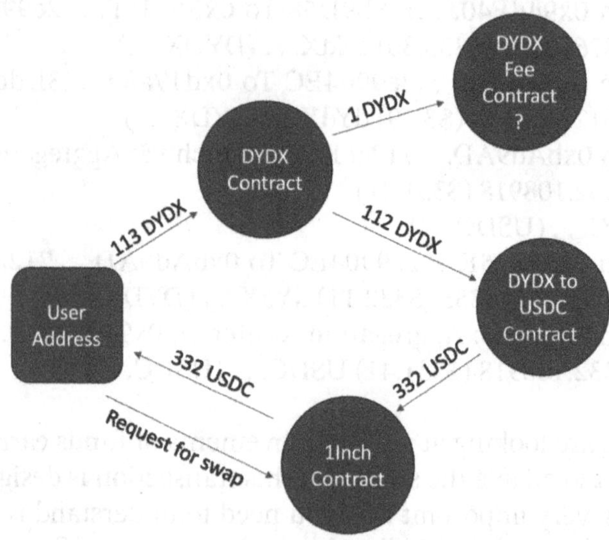

Figure 12.25: Movement of funds in a contract

Apologies for the quality of the graphic; I'm no designer, but if you have access to a commercial tool, then the graph should look something like this. I often find that investigators still struggle to interpret what a graph like this means, and so it's very important that you can break down the contract functions and movements of funds to see where the funds came from, where they were sent, and what happened during the transaction.

If that description was difficult for you, don't hesitate to go back and reread the breakdown of this transaction.

Let's have a look at one more, I'm hoping it should be fairly straightforward. Please take a look at this transaction and figure it out before reading the breakdown. The next transaction is 0x368cca1c0a7b7ffd4c9f8c219cf51db76108e3f88832320c599e890a99e00c06.

Take a look at the data from the transaction and answer the following questions:

1. What is the user's address?
2. What is the first service used to carry out the swap?
3. Are other services used to do the swap?
4. What is swapped?

```
Transaction Action: Swap 0.11895 ETH For
46,201.254751832695912721 EJS On Uniswap V2

From: 0x7F575039E3313236e2D1Dc
c6e7994F8f30390B62

To: 0x881D40237659C251811CEC
9c364ef91dC08D300C (Metamask: Swap Router)

Transfer 0.12 ETH From Metamask: Swap Router
To 0x74de5d4F. . . .794016631

Transfer 0.11895 ETH From 0x74de5d4F. . .
794016631 To 1inch v5: Aggregation Router

Transfer 0.11895 ETH From 1inch v5:
Aggregation Router To Wrapped Ether

Transfer 0.00105 ETH From 0x74de5d4F. . .
794016631 To MetaMask: DS Proxy

From 1inch v5: Aggregation Router To Uniswap
V2: EJS 2 For 0.11895 ($409.) Wrapped Ether
```

```
From Uniswap V2: EJS2 To 0x74de5d4F. . .
794016631 For 46,201.254751832695912721
($409.14) Enjinstarter(EJS)

From 0x74de5d4F. . .794016631 To
0x7F575039. . .f30390B62 For 46,201.
254751832695912721 ($409.14) Enjinstarter(EJS)

Value:
0.12 ETH($413.11)
```

There's a lot going on in this transaction, but let's work through and answer the questions.

1. The From field gives us the user address 0x7F575039E3313236e2D1Dcc6e7994F8f30390B62.
2. The To field shows that the Metamask: Swap Router is called to carry out the swap. This would indicate that the user is likely using the Metamask wallet.
3. As you have learned, ETH needs to be converted to wrapped ETH (WETH) before it can be swapped for other tokens, and this is what we see here. Metamask sends funds to the 1inch v5: Aggregation Router to swap into WETH. Next the WETH is moved through the Uniswap V2: EJS2 contract to convert the WETH to EJS2.
4. ETH is swapped for EJS tokens.

Again, if that's not completely clear, just go back and work it through again.

If you want to practice this skill—and I strongly suggest that you do—browse to Etherscan and to the Tokens-Token Transfers menu. Look for transactions in the list with the Swap function and see if you can work through them to understand what they are doing.

Reading Decentralized Finance Contracts

An entire book could be written about DeFi and the ways that DeFi contracts can be used by criminals. I advise liaising with a financial investigator if you have someone available, as they will understand some of the tricks and methods that are used in FIAT currency scams and, in line with the title of this book, these often translate to crypto; the scams don't change, just the payment mechanism. It is worth noting that some crypto-oriented crimes are against financial services, which may not record all of the transactions on the blockchain. An example would be crypto derivatives trading where an investor bets on the price of a crypto asset at some point in the future. On some online systems the derivative contract that supports the position is handled by the company's systems and not on the blockchain. It is only at the point that a contract matures and the crypto is purchased that the entry may be visible on the blockchain. In this case, an investigator will need to request the logs of the internal systems from the service provider as well as the blockchain transactions. Other systems work purely on the blockchain and utilize smart contracts to connect investors who are betting on opposite positions.

The key when investigating DeFi investments made by a suspect is that there will be a two-way relationship with a contract. Funds will be deposited or transferred into a contract, and then we will likely see withdrawals from that contract or service at a later date. By looking at the values of the funds transferred in, the balance in the investment contract, and lastly funds withdrawn, we can begin to understand the value of gains or losses on their trading position. Again, at times, position balances may only be available by approaching the company providing the trading platform. This is very important to figure out as criminal funds may be used to invest in DeFi and profits could be locked up in a service, which also need to be frozen or seized.

Other simple investment DeFi opportunities are related to adding funds to liquidity pools in swap contracts. Uniswap is a good example of a service that enables this. A user is able to add funds to the liquidity pool that supports the swap contracts and then benefit from a portion of the fees charged when people swap between those currencies proportionate to the investment made. In a contract swapping between what may be considered "safe" tokens, the financial reward is fairly small, but the developer of a new token will want to attract liquidity and so will often add very attractive rates. It is very straightforward to set up a new token and then add the Uniswap contract to enable swapping between ETH and the new token.

JELLY BEANS AND M&MS

The concept of liquidity pools and swap contracts can be a little hard to wrap your head around, but in a classroom it can be illustrated simply; I'll do my best to be clear here. Imagine you have a cup of jelly beans and a cup of Peanut M&Ms, and there are an equal amount in each cup. You have three jelly beans in your hand and would like some jelly beans to eat instead. A display is connected to the two cups and knows how many sweets are in each one and provides you with an exchange rate. Currently the display tells you that it is one jelly bean for one M&M. You add your three M&Ms to the cup and take three jelly beans from the other cup. (We will assume that we are not worried about germs!)

The display now sees that the jelly beans are in demand and are rarer than the M&Ms and so the exchange rate jumps to one jelly bean to two M&Ms. More people come and add M&Ms and take jelly beans, and as the jelly beans become rarer, they also become much more valuable—many more M&Ms are needed to buy just one jelly bean.

Now imagine that you are the person who made the jelly beans in the first place and you have a stock of beans. Your jelly beans have just become much more valuable, and you can swap your beans for many more M&Ms than you could before because of the perceived popularity and rarity of the beans. It might sound crazy, but this is a very close simile to a swap liquidity contract.

Let's add a little extra to the picture. The owner of the jelly beans doesn't want the bean cup to run dry or no one can trade for them anymore. So he allows people who own beans to add them to the cup, and every time a swap is done, the contributors earn a little bit of the sweets. This is how you invest in a swap contract.

Let's now switch away from sweets as I feel rather driven to pop down the road to the local store and grab some jelly beans! Our pretend cups now have ETH in one cup and the awesome NickCoin token in the other (my original book talked a lot about the fictitious NickCoin, so I'm resurrecting it!). I am the creator of NickCoin, so I set up the swap contract on Uniswap, add some NickCoin to the cup, and hope that someone comes along with some ETH and swaps for my coin. ETH has a value set by the community and other market forces, but NickCoin is worth a big fat zero. Hence, until some ETH exists in the other cup, on the other side of the swap contract, the NickCoin has no value other than the nominal exchange rate that I set. So I say that 0.1 ETH will give you 10,000 NickCoins.

Next, I get on social media and make posts and videos about how totally awesome NickCoin is and how it's going to save the polar bears and end nuclear weapon proliferation by changing the world and forcing governments to be nice to each other. (I've literally seen sales pitches for new tokens that were more outlandish than that.) I might even pay an influencer, or a celebrity who was on *Love Island* once, to post about it, too. This will drive people to want NickCoin and they will come along, put ETH in one pot, and take NickCoin from the other. As the NickCoin becomes more popular, the exchange rate will change and more ETH will be added to the contract. This gives NickCoin a verifiable, inherent value as the exchange rate from NickCoin to ETH provides an exchange level, quite similar to the way fiat exchanges are often related to the U.S. dollar.

As an aside, if I am criminally minded and I set up a malevolent contract, I can "pump" interest in NickCoin and then when the exchange rate between NickCoin and ETH is at its peak I "dump" all the coins I personally own on the contract and take all the ETH and retire to Mexico. This is the classic "pump and dump" scheme, and when done cleverly, it technically hasn't always broken any laws. Regulators in the EU, the UK, and the United States have been working hard on this issue over the past few years to ensure that these schemes are classified as fraud.

Hopefully you now understand swap contracts and liquidity pools a little better.

Investing in swap contracts and similar is often termed *yield farming*. Proof of investment is sometimes provided by tokens given to the user. These are sometimes LP (liquidity pool) tokens and/or governance tokens. Here's a few notes about what governance tokens are and what they provide a holder:

Voting Rights Governance tokens grant holders the right to vote on proposals concerning a protocol's development, changes, or upgrades. This can include decisions on modifying parameters, introducing new features, or allocating resources and funds within the ecosystem.

Proposal Submission Typically, holders of governance tokens can propose changes or new initiatives within the platform. The threshold of tokens required to submit a proposal ensures that only serious and potentially impactful suggestions are considered.

Incentivization By distributing governance tokens, a project can incentivize users to participate actively in the ecosystem, fostering a sense of ownership.

Decentralized Decision Making Through these tokens, the power to make significant decisions is distributed among users of the service, preventing centralized points of failure and ensuring that the platform remains aligned with the interests of its active users.

Economic Stake Holding governance tokens often correlates with having a vested economic interest in the platform. This connection is designed to motivate token holders to vote in ways that they believe will increase the platform's value and success.

It is entirely feasible to combine liquidity farming and yield farming to optimize earnings in the DeFi space. For instance, you can deposit DAI tokens into Curve's crypto liquidity pool, where your DAI will start earning interest and fees. Upon depositing, you receive LP tokens, which represent your share in the pool. These LP tokens can then be deposited into Curve's staking pool, where you begin to earn CRV tokens as a reward for staking your LP tokens. This strategy allows you to benefit simultaneously from the interest and fees earned on your DAI in the liquidity pool and from the CRV tokens you accrue as rewards for staking the LP tokens, effectively maximizing your returns from two different yield-generating activities within the same platform.

One of the challenges in locating a suspect's assets is that held funds may not all be in their wallet but may be tied up in investment contracts. The only way to know is to look at the tokens they own and see if they are holding governance tokens or LP tokens, for example, as that would be a clue as to them having investment assets. We can also look at the list of all their transactions and see if there are function calls that are indicative of DeFi use. One of the challenges is the sheer number of function calls that are used that may relate to DeFi deposits and withdrawals. Let's look at what they might include:

Deposit-Related Functions

`deposit()`: A generic function to deposit assets into a smart contract

`addLiquidity()`: Often used in liquidity pool contracts to deposit tokens in exchange for liquidity provider (LP) tokens

`stake()`: Common in staking contracts; allows users to lock their tokens to participate in protocol security or to earn rewards

`enter()`: Used in some contracts for entering a staking pool or a farming opportunity

`mint()`: Can be used in the context of depositing assets and minting new tokens or LP tokens in return

`invest()`: Sometimes used to deposit funds into a yield aggregator or an investment pool

Withdrawal-Related Functions

`withdraw()`: A basic function to withdraw funds from a contract

`removeLiquidity()`: Used in liquidity pools to withdraw deposited tokens by burning LP tokens

`unstake()`: Used to retrieve tokens that were previously staked in a contract

`exit()`: Used for withdrawing from a system or contract, often also claiming any earned rewards

`burn()`: In some contexts, used to burn LP tokens and withdraw the underlying liquidity

`harvest()`: Common in yield farming; used to collect earned rewards, sometimes also withdrawing the principal

`claimRewards()`: Specifically for claiming accrued rewards, often without touching the principal deposit

Generic Functions with Context-Specific Meanings

`transfer()`: While a standard ERC-20 function, in the context of DeFi, it can be used to transfer tokens into or out of a contract `approve()`: Necessary for allowing a contract to access your tokens, a prerequisite for depositing tokens in many DeFi applications

Please don't think that these examples represent all the function calls that may be related to DeFi, but they are certainly the ones I see most often. Each DeFi environment will likely have its unique function calls, or none at all, but these function names offer a glimpse into the common functions that I see in many investigations.

It may be that we are not looking for assets but investigating a hacker who has exploited or undermined a smart contract with the result of stealing funds. This can be complex, and I recommend having a Solidity programmer available to help you understand the vulnerabilities in exploited code.

Let's take a look at an example of a DeFi contract. They are not always terribly complicated, but we will consider an example that has a few complications for us to figure out. Browse on Etherscan to TXID 0xadc1b92dc6477b229999274465984l049d0599f43a9a4f ecf1d44812a997f392.

I'm hoping that you are not reading this chapter in one sitting (life is frankly too short) and are spending some time looking at, and learning from, other transactions. With a bit of practice under your belt, this transaction should be within your grasp. I will paste all the primary data first in its individual sections for you to look through and then we will step through it. Remember everything you have learned about wrapped ETH, liquidity pool tokens, and the like.

Transaction Action

```
Remove 71.975634137177351328 DAI And 0.027040075544690143
ETH Liquidity From SushiSwap

From/To section

From: 0x1F14bE60172b40dAc0aD9cD72F6f0f2C245992e8

Interacted With (To): 0xd9e1cE17f2641f24aE83637ab66a2c
ca9C378B9F (SushiSwap: Router)

Transfer 0.027040075544690143 ETH From Wrapped Ether
To SushiSwap: Router
```

```
Transfer 0.027040075544690143 ETH From SushiSwap:Router
To 0x1F14bE60. . .C245992e8
```

ERC-20 Tokens Transferred (Line numbers are added by me)

1. From 0x1F14bE60. . .C245992e8 To SushiSwap: DAI For 0.89074597($103.52) SushiSwap LP. . .(SLP)
2. From Null: 0x000. . .000 To SushiSwap: WethMaker For 1.066517691214385553 ($123.94) SushiSwap LP. . .(SLP)
3. From SushiSwap: DAI To Null: 0x000. . .000 For 0.89074597 ($103.52)SushiSwap LP. . .(SLP)
4. From SushiSwap: DAI To SushiSwap: Router For 71.975634137177351328$72.05 Dai Stableco. . .(DAI)
5. From SushiSwap: DAI To SushiSwap: Router For 0.027040075544690143 ($93.98) Wrapped Ethe. . .(WETH)
6. From SushiSwap: Router To 0x1F14bE60. . .C245992e8 For 71.975634137177351328$72.05 Dai Stableco. . .(DAI)

Input Data (Raw)

Function: removeLiquidityETH(address token, uint256 liquidity, uint256 amountTokenMin, uint256 amountETHMin, address to, uint256 deadline)

Have you figured out what this transaction is doing? The Transaction Action description is only partly helpful; it just tells us that some DAI and some ETH are being removed from a SushiSwap liquidity pool. At this point, as the description is not clear, you can scroll to the bottom of the page and take a look at the function call in the Input Data section, which states `removeLiquidityETH`. This confirms that this function is removing liquidity and includes some ETH.

Removal of liquidity will be triggered by a user (it's always worth clicking an input address and checking if it's tagged as being owned by a known service or just a user) and the From/To section gives us the user's address starting with 0x1F14b and that it is interacting with a contract identified as a SushiSwap router. Remember that the From/

To section gives us any actions taken by the contract, which include ETH. In this case we see two actions:

```
Transfer 0.027040075544690143 ETH From Wrapped
Ether To SushiSwap: Router

Transfer 0.027040075544690143 ETH From
SushiSwap:Router To 0x1F14bE60. . .C245992e8
```

This is pretty simple. 0.02 WETH is sent to the SushiSwap router and is converted (or unwrapped) into ETH. The 0.02 ETH is then sent to the user at the address 0x1F14b. This was the ETH liquidity deposited into the contract. So far, so good, but what happens with the DAI?

For this we need to look at the ERC-20 Tokens Transferred section. We have six lines of internal transfers carried out in this transaction. As we discussed previously, these are rarely in a seemingly logical order, so we need to get the order straight before we understand what's happening. The first thing to do is check whether the input or output of any of the transfers are the user address 0x1F14b. We see the user input in line 1 and the output in line 6. Let's look at each line in turn.

Line 1: From 0x1F14bE60. . .C245992e8 To SushiSwap: DAI For 0.89074597($103.52) SushiSwap LP. . .(SLP)

The user address sends SushiSwap LP tokens to the SushiSwap:DAI contract. The LP tokens are the proof that the user had deposited funds into the contract and so when removing the liquidity the LP tokens have to be returned.

Line 2: The SushiSwap WETH contract mints (creates) 1.066 liquidity pool tokens from the Null Address.

Line 3: The SushiSwap DAI contract burns (destroys) 0.89 DAI by sending it to the Null Address. (Remember the illustration of the two cups; line 2 and 3 are playing a part in balancing the liquidity pool.)

Line 4: 71.97 DAI is sent to the SushiSwap:Router.

Line 5: 0.02 ETH is sent to the SushiSwap:Router.

Line 6: 71.97 DAI, the DAI liquidity, is sent back to the user.

To put all of this in a simple paragraph: The user wishes to remove liquidity from the SushiSwap DAI:ETH liquidity pool. They send their proof, the LP tokens, back and the deposited ETH and DAI are returned. LP tokens are internally minted and destroyed to balance the liquidity pool.

That's it! I appreciate that this is a fairly complex transaction, but if you just work through the internal transfers and understand some of the standard rules such as ETH needing to be wrapped ETH or burning or minting coins from and to the Genesis address (Null), then you can start to work out what the transaction is doing.

Use a block explorer like Etherscan to find some transactions that appear to relate to DeFi and see if you can interpret them. You will find that once you are quick and experienced at reading them, it can be easier to see these complex transactions in a blockchain viewer rather than a commercial tool. Although the commercial tool will do a better job of graphing it out, most do not provide the primary function call, which is essential in properly interpreting the reason for the transaction.

The Approve Transaction

We have mentioned approve transactions a few times but I haven't really explained them properly. They are vital in understanding how a contract can be allowed to transfer tokens on behalf of a token holder. This is a common scenario in DeFi applications, where users often need to allow smart contracts to interact with their tokens.

Here's an overview of how an Approve transaction works:

1. **The token holder initiates the approval.** The token holder initiates an Approve transaction by calling the `Approve` function of the token contract. This function requires two arguments: the spender (the address that is being allowed to spend the tokens) and the amount (the number of tokens that the spender is allowed to transfer).

2. **An allowance is set.** When the `Approve` function is executed, it sets an allowance, which is the maximum number of tokens the spender is allowed to transfer from the token holder's account. This allowance is recorded in the token contract and is associated with the token holder's and the spender's addresses.

3. The third-party transfers tokens. Once the approval is granted, the spender—which could be an individual address or a smart contract—can transfer an amount of the token holder's tokens up to the approved amount. This transfer is typically executed by calling the `transferFrom` function in the contract, specifying the token holder's address, the destination address, and the amount to be transferred.

In practice, Approve transactions are a common requirement in DeFi applications. For example, before you can trade tokens on a decentralized exchange, provide liquidity to a pool, or engage in yield farming, you must approve the DeFi protocol to access your tokens. Although it seems odd to provide approval for a third party to transfer your tokens, the token holder can limit the amount accessible to the third party and can revoke the approval at any time by setting the allowance to 0. It also prevents the need to hand over your tokens to a third party, reducing the risk of loss or theft.

Often when you see an Approve transaction you will see an Execute or AddLiquidity transaction or similar in the next or subsequent transactions. In Figure 12.26, you can see several Approve transactions followed by Execute transactions. If you were to look at these transactions you would see approval for a token to transfer tokens followed by execution of the transfer.

0xddf26371c77...	Approve
0x7666198807...	Execute
0x5dec885524...	Execute
0x0e3a19b45c...	Approve

Figure 12.26: Example of Approve transactions followed by an Execute transaction

Take a look at the following two transactions. They happen one after the other and show approval to trade the Link token on Uniswap and then the Execute transaction.

```
0x0e3a19b45c5a184076b2a936eebd8b50513d95815074820bcb
b55526e88b065a
```

'Approved LINK For Trade On Uniswap Protocol: Permit1'

```
0x5dec8855247694c74f025aa9df25361dd4b3cdac573864d11e02b
1d9bebe1ba4
```

'Swap 10 LINK for on Uniswap'

Summary

This was a really tricky chapter to write. Some of the concepts are much easier to demonstrate in a classroom than they are to write about in a book with limited imagery. The practical explanation and interpretation of Ethereum and token transactions could consume a book in itself. However, I hope that what we have covered has given you as an investigator enough knowledge to be able to look at a transaction, follow the funds, and potentially interpret what the transaction is doing.

You will also understand that there is a lot I have not written about. Just as a law enforcement officer can buy and read this book, so can a scammer. (If this is you, please know that I have great respect for your intelligence and creativity, but please consider using your powers for good. When you look back on your life in your twilight years, do you want to remember all the people you have hurt or the people you have helped?) Because of this, I have had to limit descriptions of some of the tricks that can tip the balance in an investigation. Please engage with professional trainers, law enforcement subject-matter experts, commercial software companies, and their professional services—all of these folks will be able to expand your knowledge in a safe and secure environment.

In the next chapter, you'll see how your new knowledge can be transferred into another blockchain such as the popular Binance Chain and Smart Chain, which by the time you read this will likely be merged into BNB Chain.

13 Investigating Binance Smart Chain

This short chapter will look at the Binance Smart Chain and will consider the similarities with Ethereum. We will apply the same investigative processes to this blockchain, demonstrating that we don't always need to learn something completely new to be able to investigate chains we haven't worked with before.

What is Binance Smart Chain?

In the evolving world of blockchain technology, the emergence of Binance Smart Chain (BSC) represented a significant milestone. The story begins with Binance Chain, which was launched in 2019. The BNB token on which it was based had actually been around since 2017 on the Ethereum platform. Despite its efficiency in transactions, the chain's limited scope in programmability and smart contract integration was far behind Ethereum. To bring the fight to Ethereum, Binance created BSC in September 2020. I am writing this chapter in mid-2024 and BNB is due to be merged with Binance Smart Chain to create a unified BNB Smart Chain during the course of this year.

BSC wasn't merely an addition; it was a strategic extension running, at the time, alongside Binance Chain. This dual-chain model allowed for seamless asset transfers, providing users with a robust trading infrastructure on Binance Chain while allowing decentralized applications on BSC. By integrating Ethereum virtual machine (EVM) compatibility, BSC extended an obvious new platform for Ethereum developers but with a less expensive fee mechanism, faster transactions, and proof-of-stake mining, which Ethereum didn't catch up with for several more years. There were those who felt that the relatively small number of validators meant that the chain was not truly decentralized, a claim that was strongly repudiated by Binance. As of this writing, BSC has just 56 live validators approving transactions. Also, as of this writing, Ethereum has a validator pool of just under 1 million validators. You can take a look at the list of current validators here: `https://bscscan.com/validators`.

Despite its success, BSC encountered challenges, particularly around security vulnerabilities and the aforementioned centralization debates. These issues highlighted the ongoing need for robust security measures and sparked discussions on finding the right balance between scalability, cost, and decentralization.

It would stand to reason that just as we have had to discuss the significant differences investigating transactions on the Bitcoin and Ethereum networks that we would need to fundamentally start again for Binance Smart Chain. However, what is now called BNB Smart Chain (BSC) is a hard fork of the Go Ethereum (Geth) protocol and, as such, shares many similarities with the Ethereum blockchain. In fact, for the investigator there are so many similarities that you can sometimes forget what blockchain you are looking at. To make life easier, Etherscan built an explorer for BSC that looks almost identical to its Ethereum cousin; it's called BscScan rather than Etherscan. You can find it at `BSCscan.com` (see Figure 13.1).

This means that instead of starting again we will find that there are significant similarities, which means that BSC should not be scary at all for an investigator, and this will be a much shorter chapter than the marathon that was Chapter 12, "Ethereum: Investigation Methodology."

Because BSC is based on the EVM and is based on the Geth protocol, many decentralized applications (dApps) on BSC are essentially code forks of their Ethereum counterparts. An example is PancakeSwap, which is a derivative of Uniswap that we considered in Chapter 12. Just to consider the semantics of *forking*, whereas PancakeSwap's initial implementation may have been inspired by Uniswap's code (which is open source and allows for such forks), PancakeSwap has evolved to become its own entity with unique features and a distinct community. The term *hard fork* is more commonly associated with blockchains rather than dApps, referring to a split in the blockchain itself, not the application built on top. In the context of dApps like PancakeSwap and Uniswap, it's more accurate to describe PancakeSwap as a project that made use of Uniswap's code rather than a hard fork of Uniswap.

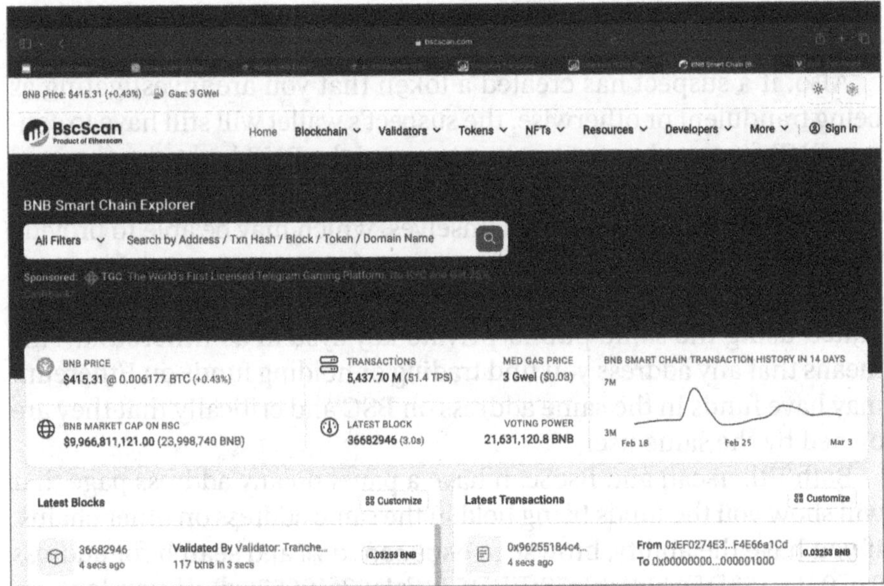

Figure 13.1: BscScan looks almost identical to Etherscan.

BSC tends to follow the same token protocols of Ethereum. ERC-20 in Ethereum is BEP-20 in BSC for standard token creation. The same is true for BEP-721 instead of ERC-721, the NFT protocol, and BEP-1155 rather than ERC-1155 for the creation of limited-edition tokens.

Both platforms host a vast array of dApps and smart contracts, but Ethereum's ecosystem is larger and more diverse due to its longer history. BSC has seen significant growth in this area, with numerous projects choosing it for its efficiency and lower costs.

Investigating Funds on Binance Smart Chain

Whereas the primary coin for Ethereum is ETH, the primary BSC coin is BNB. This works in the same way as ETH and so we need to remember similar principles. For example, all fees are payable in BNB; this means that a user's wallet must contain BNB to be able to transfer any other type of token. For the investigator, this means that when seizing funds from a suspect's wallet they must ensure that tokens are seized first before the BNB. As with ETH, if you seize the BNB first, then there will be nothing to pay the fees.

Also, if a suspect has created a token that you are investigating as being fraudulent or otherwise, the suspect's wallet will still have to contain BNB for carrying out transactions and the BNB had to be obtained from somewhere. The trail of the BNB may take you back to a service provider, often Binance themselves, which may be able to provide know-your-customer (KYC) information about your person of interest.

The other key principle to remember is that user addresses are generated using the same public/private key system as Ethereum. This means that any address you find trading or holding funds on Ethereum may have funds in the same address on BSC and critically that they are owned by the same user.

Both Etherscan and BscScan have a panel on any address page that will show you the funds being held in the same address on other chains. If you have the ability, browse to `bscscan.com` and search for address 0xC03F6a53DFc434DbD78fFED528FcDd3f406576a0. If you look on the right-hand side you will see the Multichain Info pane. As of this writing, it states that there is $4772 (Multichain portfolio) in funds in a variety of chains. Clicking this link provides a list of all the chains that contain funds for this address (see Figure 13.2).

Ethereum (9) $3,291 (69%)	Scroll (2) $605 (13%)
Arbitrum One (11) $116 (2%)	Base (4) $77 (2%)
Arbitrum Nova (1) $41 (1%)	Linea (4) $39 (1%)
Polygon (6) $20 (<1%)	Avax C-Chain (3) $6 (<1%)

Figure 13.2: Some of the funds held in various chains for address 0xC03F6a53DFc434DbD78fFED528FcDd3f406576a0

In my experience, users of BSC often—and by often I mean over 80 percent—also have funds on other chains, especially Ethereum. In fact, I can't think of a recent investigation where at least some of the addresses in an investigation that had funds on BSC did not also had funds on Ethereum. Finding other chains provides other investigative strings to pull on, which might have been missed by a suspect when they were hiding their activity.

A good example of this was a scammer who was carrying out successful targeted romance scams against primarily wealthy women in California. All of the identified Ethereum addresses were carefully managed by the perpetrator to ensure that it was hard for us to get any clue as to an identification through any service providers; it was very frustrating. However, we found the scammer's Ethereum address on the BSC network that had been used to buy an NFT on one of the mainstream NFT reseller sites. This address led to a unique alias on the site, and that unusual alias was the same as the Twitter (X) handle of a person who was living in the Midwest. Previous tweets led to a Google Drive they used, and a subsequent request to Google provided several unprotected IP addresses and, as we say in the UK, "Bob's your uncle"—essentially, we got him. Well, sort of got him. In this case, the alias similarity was not considered sufficient to go and kick in the guy's door and have a firm word with him. He was invited to attend an interview, which he refused, and as if by magic the several running scams against women who had come forward went quiet. What an odd coincidence!

Anyway, back to investigating funds on BSC. If you look at an example of a BNB transfer, you will immediately see the similarities with Ethereum. If you are able take a look at TXID 0xe99ea2e2aee935c8f4a2cc8ab5060923d127692dfd4411752e33c44c74559070 on `bscscan.com`, the data will be instantly familiar to you (unless you totally ignored Chapter 12!)

```
Transaction action:
Transfer 0.003360550442197827 BNB To 0x8b8C61...3BbdFB8B

From/To:

From: 0xF8C3F0a461e1303C738eF48917FbC33173d7f096

To: 0x8b8C61ff363575c33b3B51283E1191573BbdFB8B

Value: 0.003360550442197827 BNB $1.37

Transaction Fee: 0.000021 BNB $0.01
```

I'm hoping that you can quickly understand this transaction. It's a transfer of 0.003. . .BNB to an address starting with 0x8b8C from address 0xF8C3. Easy!

Now let's consider something related to a contract transaction. As with Ethereum, these transactions can be more complex, and I find that there are often differences in function names, which is interesting. Take a look at TXID 0x6e3cbfc9a497dcca983d3fbf503463ed4445fcbc6b1f9678cf935704116b5af6 if you are able. Actually, if you are fortunate enough to have a shiny and expensive commercial crypto investigations tool, pop the TXID in there and see how it helps—or doesn't help. Here is the primary data:

```
Transaction action:

Transfer 388 PLAY To 0x4d5bE2...1AE8473A

From:
0x4d5bE2147362679619Cb57E82e3C20C21AE8473A

Interacted With (To):
 0xa30dC51Ff59a83384B6FFbD61E2caEf3337AEc04 (XCAD Network: PLAY
Claim)

BEP-20 Tokens Transferred:

From Null: 0x000...000 To 0x4d5bE214...21AE8473A For 388
$0.91 PLAY
```

This is an interesting one; the address triggering the transaction starts 0x4d5b but if we look at the transaction action we see that 0x4d5b is also the recipient. Is this a swap? What's going on here? This is an occasion where it's good to look at the raw function call in the More Details – Input Data section. It provides the function call:

```
Function: claim(address _to,uint256 _nonce,address _token,
uint256 _amount,bytes _signature)
```

The function is called `claim` and there is a field called `uint256_amount` and another called `address_token`. This would indicate that an amount of tokens are being claimed by 0x4d5b. But claimed from where? If we look at the name associated with the contract 0xa30d, we see that it's tagged XCAD Network: PLAY Claim. A quick Internet search for XCAD provides a large number of links, but an overview of XCAD on `dappradar.com` states:

> *XCAD Network is a dapp on BNB Chain that has introduced a Watch2Earn platform, connecting with YouTube. The decentralized application, or dapp, allows users to earn rewards from watching certain content directly on YouTube. You could say that XCAD Network curates content based on earning potential for Web3 video enthusiasts.*
>
> `https://dappradar.com/blog/what-is-xcad-network-how-earn-watching-youtube#`

This is very helpful and assists us in understanding that this user is watching social media content curated by XCAD and is earning tokens based on their activity. A little more reading tells you how to "claim" earned tokens. This transaction is clearly a user claiming or extracting earned tokens from XCAD.

We also see that 388 PLAY tokens comes from the Genesis (Null) address, and you learned in Chapter 12 that this is a minting of new coins. How much of that did you figure out on your own?

I cannot emphasize enough how important it is to be able to do this external open source research and use contract tags to help you understand a transaction. I checked this transaction in several commercial tools, and in basic form, the graphed result looked like the one in Figure 13.3.

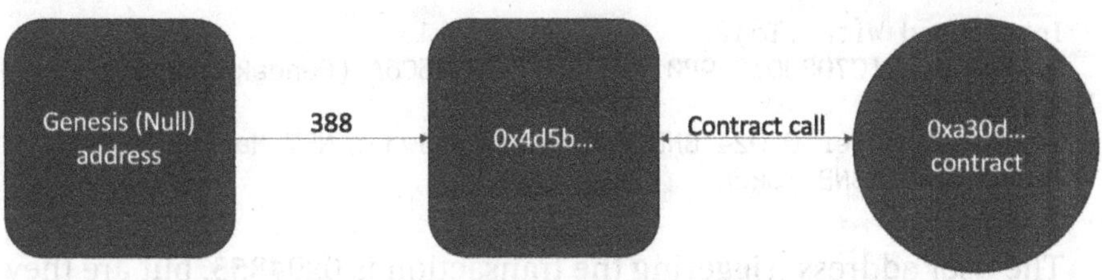

Figure 13.3: Example diagram from commercial tools of transaction

That's all the detail the tools provided! Although there is nothing factually wrong with the diagram, it simply doesn't tell you what the transaction is for or what it is doing. We can guess that the funds from the Null address are a minting of new coins, but nowhere can we discern that this is a claiming of coins from a pay-per-view contract system, and that information is really important. Commercial tools are amazing, but I still have Etherscan or BscScan and others open at the same time as my paid tool along with my favorite search engine.

So, by now you should be realizing that if you become experienced in understanding and investigating Ethereum tokens you also become proficient in BSC. In the next chapter, you will see how this knowledge translates to other crypto coins too, which may on the surface appear quite different but in reality follow the same fundamental rules.

Let's take a look at another good example. Again, if you have the ability, browse to `bscscan.com` and search for TXID 0xffdcf57310f5aa336edb8dc2b4a61cb05c40dfb34464c7c2cd57fe394a189ff4. Can you figure out what is happening here? You may look at the transaction action and state with confidence that it is the sale of an NFT from PancakeSwap for 0.024 BNB.

```
Transaction Action:

Sale:1 NFT For 0.024 BNB On PancakeSwap
```

You would be right but who sold it and who bought it? Let's take a look at the From/To section:

```
From: 0x94853d7d09c94cc425C951b22F794D5D7175B9d1

Interacted With (To):
0x17539cCa21C7933Df5c980172d22659B8C345C5A (PancakeSwap: NFT
Market V1)
      Transfer 0.024 BNB From PancakeSwap: NFT Market V1 To
BNB Chain: WBNB Token
```

The user address triggering the transaction is 0x94853, but are they the buyer or the seller of the NFT from PancakeSwap NFT Market? The transaction action says it's a sale, but if you scroll to the bottom of the transaction page and look at the More Details – Input Data function call, you will see that it says:

```
Function: buyTokenUsingBNB(address _collection,
uint256 _tokenId)
```

This tells us that 0x94853 is triggering a buy action and so they are the one purchasing the NFT. Great, but there is a lot more going on here. There are three sections of transactions happening. Let's look at all of them and see what's going on. In addition to the transaction action already pasted here, we have two more sections:

```
BEP-20 Tokens Transferred:

From PancakeSwap: NFT Market V1 To sledge1313.bnb For 0.0216
($9.34) Wrapped BNB(WBNB)

BEP-721 Tokens Transferred:

BEP-721 Token ID [7175]
BinanceBullS...(Binanc...) From PancakeSwap: NFT Market V1
To 0x94853d7d...D7175B9d1
```

We can see that we have movement by the PancakeSwap contract of both BEP-20 tokens and the BEP-721 token. If we look at the BEP-721 transaction, we can see that simply the NFT ID 7175 from collection BinanceBullSoc is transferred from the PancakeSwap NFT Market to the buyer, user 0x9485.

But why are BEP-20 tokens transferred as well, if this is an NFT transaction? If we look at the BEP-20 section, we see that 0.0216 WBNB is transferred to sledge1313.bnb. Who is sledge1313.bnb? This is a name registered against an address starting with 0x4688a; this is a similar system to the Ethereum Naming System (ENS) on the Ethereum chain. If you are looking at this transaction online, then just rolling your mouse over the sledge1313 name will expose the 0x address. This user receives the majority of the funds and so is clearly the seller of the NFT.

If you are super eagle-eyed and are not watching this at 11 p.m. after a few glasses of your favorite liquor, you may have noticed that something is not quite right. The transaction action says that the sale was for 0.024 BNB, but the seller is only paid 0.0216 WBNB (Wrapped BNB). What's happened to the amount and to the original unwrapped BNB? If we look back at the From/To section, we see that the user injects 0.024 BNB into the transaction (this is confirmed in the Value line near the bottom of the transaction page if you are online). However, just as with ETH needing to be converted into Wrapped ETH to transact with tokens, it is the same with BNB. 0.024 BNB is input into the transaction and next the coin is converted to WBNB:

```
Transfer 0.024 BNB From PancakeSwap: NFT Market V1 To BNB
Chain: WBNB Token
```

This step has a fee associated with it so that when we see the funds transferred to the seller, it has reduced to 0.0216 WBNB. Interestingly, there does not appear to be a specific fee from PancakeSwap for the sale of the NFT itself, like we saw on Ethereum where the contract had a specific payment to a fee address. However, if we do a little math, we will see that PancakeSwap does take a fee.

If we add the 0.0216 BNB sent to the seller to the fee for the transaction (0.000590511 BNB), it comes out to just over 0.022 BNB. The remainder has been held by the PancakeSwap contract as a transaction fee.

As before, if this seems a little complex, read back over it and try to understand how the transaction is working.

As BSC fees are cheaper than Ethereum, it's been used extensively for DeFi dApps. Thankfully the transactions look pretty similar, so once again if you are confident with Ethereum, then you are going to be okay with BSC DeFi transactions.

What Have You Learned?

This is the shortest chapter in the book, but I believe that it's an important transition chapter as next we will be looking at cryptocurrencies that at first look do not appear to be the same as Ethereum but when you dig deeper you can find significant similarities. As I mentioned at the end of Chapter 12 about Ethereum, I recommend that you find time to browse around `bscscan.com` and look at some transfers, contract transactions, and the like and just become aware of the subtle differences between the two chains. You will quickly become comfortable with the currency and the vagaries of the chain compared with Ethereum.

Although most commercial investigation tools now support BSC and should report any multichain assets on the same address, as you saw with the example in Figure 13.3, they often miss some data that can be very useful. This includes the function calls, open source data, and identifying what a service is designed to do. This is not just BSC, as similar problems exist with Ethereum in commercial tools; most do not report the primary function call or broader open source data about the service.

In the next chapter we are going to look at some other currencies that you will likely encounter on your investigative journey and how you apply your newly acquired knowledge to these other coins.

14 Applying What You Have Learned to New Cryptocurrencies

You should now have Bitcoin, Ethereum, and Binance Smart Chain (BSC) knowledge in your proverbial investigative kit bag. However, many other blockchains have become popular and in the future there undoubtedly will be many more. The point of this book is not just to get you comfortable with the concepts around crypto-oriented crime and specific currencies but to show you that the principles learned around the major coins relate to most other chains that exist or will exist in the future. You rarely have to relearn from the start when faced with a new cryptocurrency.

For example, cryptocurrencies that use the Ethereum virtual machine (EVM) or are compatible with it extend beyond Ethereum and BSC, as you learned in Chapter 13, "Investigating Binance Smart Chain." Many other blockchain platforms have adopted or adapted the EVM because of its robust smart contract capabilities, allowing for EVM compatibility. These include but are no way limited to the following:

Polygon (MATIC) Originally known as Matic Network, Polygon is a scaling solution for Ethereum that provides an EVM-compatible sidechain, otherwise known as a Layer 2 protocol, enhancing speed and reducing costs while maintaining compatibility with Ethereum's existing ecosystem. It has an explorer that looks very similar indeed to Etherscan (`https://polygonscan.com/txs`). Just a reminder that a Layer 2 chain is designed to enhance Ethereum's capabilities through an increase in speed, throughput, or other factors.

Avalanche (AVAX) The Avalanche C-Chain (Contract Chain) is EVM-compatible, allowing developers to deploy Ethereum-based dApps on the Avalanche network, benefiting from its high throughput. You can find the primary Explorer at `https://subnets.avax.network/c-chain`.

Fantom (FTM) Fantom offers an EVM-compatible chain, allowing for the creation and execution of smart contracts and dApps with the benefits of Fantom's high-speed consensus mechanism. There are several explorers but my favorite is found at `https://ftmscan.com`.

Ethereum Classic (ETC) After the Ethereum network underwent a hard fork following the DAO incident (see Chapter 1, "A History of Cryptocurrencies and Crime"), the original chain continued as Ethereum Classic. It maintains compatibility with the EVM and supports smart contracts and dApps. Again there are several explorers but the one I use is found at `https://etcerscan.com`.

Tron (TRX) Although Tron initially focused on digital content sharing, it has expanded its functionality to support smart contracts and dApps, offering an EVM-compatible layer. Find the explorer at `https://tronscan.org/#`. This looks quite different from Ethereum; we will look at Tron specifically in this chapter.

Harmony (ONE) Harmony's blockchain features an EVM-compatible shard that allows developers to deploy Ethereum dApps and Ethereum-based assets on its network. Find the explorer at `https://explorer.harmony.one`.

I've chosen a selection of examples, but there are many more, including many Layer 2 chains such as Optimism and Arbitrum and even Layer 2 chains such as Immutable oriented toward gaming. All will have explorers if you do a quick Internet search, and most will "feel" very similar to Ethereum in their transaction construction.

We will look at examples of transactions in some of these chains later in the chapter, but first of all it is important that we look at a key currency and why it's important to an investigator.

Stable Coins Such as USDT, USDC, and Paxos

There are quite a number of stable coins, so called because they are nominally pegged 1:1 to the U.S. dollar (USD). They are designed to be pegged to the U.S. dollar to combine the flexibility of cryptocurrencies with the stable value of the USD. I used the word *nominally* because stable coins are only "stable" if the organization that controls them has the same value of dollars as issued crypto. There have been questions about the value of the stabilizing assets held by some companies.

Tether (USDT) is one of the most widely used stable coins, as previously mentioned, designed to be pegged to the U.S. dollar. USDT is issued on multiple blockchains to ensure broad accessibility and interoperability. Some of the key blockchains that support USDT are:

- Ethereum (ETH)
- Bitcoin (Omni Layer)
- Tron (TRX)
- Binance Smart Chain (BSC)
- Algorand (ALGO)
- Solana (SOL)
- EOSIO (EOS)
- Polygon (Matic)
- Avalanche (AVAX)
- Liquid Network
- Tezos (XTZ)

By issuing USDT on these diverse blockchains, Tether aims to provide stability and liquidity across various segments of the crypto market. Users and investors leverage USDT for trading, hedging, and maintaining value across different platforms, benefiting from the unique advantages each blockchain offers.

Why is this of interest to an investigator? Like most of the other stable cryptocurrencies, USDT does not have a predefined issuance limit like some cryptocurrencies (e.g., Bitcoin's 21 million cap). The supply of USDT is designed to be flexible, expanding and contracting in response to market demand.

In simple terms here's how the process works:

Issuance Tether Limited, the company behind USDT, issues new tokens based on demand. When a user or an entity wants to acquire USDT, they can send USD to Tether's bank account, and Tether issues an equivalent amount of USDT to the user's address.

Redemption Conversely, when someone wants to convert their USDT back to USD, they can send the USDT to Tether Limited, which will then remove the equivalent USDT from circulation and transfer USD to the user's bank account.

As mentioned earlier, the amount of USDT in circulation is thus theoretically backed by an equivalent amount of USD (or sometimes other assets) held by Tether in their reserves. This mechanism is meant to ensure that USDT maintains a stable value relative to the U.S. dollar.

QUESTION MARKS ABOUT TETHER

The exact composition of Tether's reserves and the transparency around its issuance process have been subjects of scrutiny and controversy. Financial investigators, users, and regulators have expressed concerns about whether Tether's reserves are fully backing the USDT in circulation, an issue that has led to legal challenges.

In summary, USDT does not have a hard-coded cap or limit. Its supply is dynamically adjusted by Tether based on demand and the redemption process, aiming to ensure that each USDT token remains closely pegged to the U.S. dollar. This all matters to an investigator because Tether owns and controls its crypto assets. This is fundamentally different from fully decentralized currencies such as Bitcoin or Ethereum where no central agency has any control over the assets. Tether is able to burn and mint coins if they wish, and this opens opportunities to law enforcement. If we are able to trace funds into USDT, it may be possible for Tether to burn the funds, depriving the criminals of their assets, and then mint new tokens to be given to law enforcement or to provide restitution to victims.

USDC, or USD Coin, operates on a similar principle to USDT in that its supply is not capped and it is designed to be elastic, adjusting based on demand. However, there are key differences in how USDC is managed and issued, particularly regarding transparency and regulatory compliance.

Issuance USDC is issued by regulated financial institutions. When a user wants to acquire USDC, they send USD to the issuer's bank account, and the issuer provides an equivalent amount of USDC. This process is overseen by a consortium co-founded by Circle and Coinbase, which sets standards for issuing and redeeming USDC.

Redemption Users can redeem USDC for USD by sending their USDC to the issuer, which then removes the corresponding USDC from circulation and transfers USD to the user's bank account.

Transparency One of the key distinctions of USDC is its commitment to transparency. Issuers of USDC are required to provide monthly attestations of reserve balances, conducted by independent accounting firms. These attestations are published to provide assurance that each USDC is backed by an equivalent amount of USD held in reserve.

Regulatory Compliance USDC issuers are subject to U.S. financial regulations, and the reserves are held in regulated financial institutions. This regulatory framework is intended to provide users with a higher degree of trust in the stability and backing of USDC.

Like USDT, USDC is also available on multiple blockchains, including Ethereum (as an ERC-20 token), Algorand, Solana, Stellar, and others, enhancing its interoperability within the crypto ecosystem.

Both USDC and USDT are stable coins pegged to the U.S. dollar and have flexible supplies based on demand. USDC distinguishes itself with a strong emphasis on transparency and compliance with U.S. financial regulations. These aspects are crucial for users, investors, and financial investigators to consider when comparing the two stable coins.

In a similar vein, Paxos (USDP) states on its website that (caps theirs):

> *ANY USD STABLECOINS OR FIAT CURRENCY UNDERLYING USD STABLECOINS THAT ARE SUBJECT TO FREEZE, SEIZURE, FORFEITURE OR SIMILAR LIMITATION ON THEIR USE IMPOSED BY LAW MAY BECOME WHOLLY AND PERMANENTLY UNRECOVERABLE AND UNUSABLE, AND IN APPROPRIATE CIRCUMSTANCES, MAY BE DESTROYED.*
>
> `https://paxos.com/stablecoin-terms-conditions`

Investigators should be aware that any criminal funds found on the primary blockchains are locked and cannot be accessed without access to the private keys or through an appropriate request by the courts if stored with an exchange or other service. However, any funds traced to the stable coins described earlier may be both freezable and returnable in the right circumstances.

Tron

I wanted to include Tron in this book because at first look it can appear very different from Ethereum and we could back away from it, feeling that it would take too much time to learn. Although there are some significant differences, it is compatible with the Ethereum EVM and so reading the transactions is not as difficult as it may first appear. While Tron might have drawn inspiration from Ethereum and aimed to improve upon its perceived limitations, it is an independent blockchain with its own network, cryptocurrency (TRX), and technical infrastructure. Tron's founder, Justin Sun, positioned the platform as a competitor to Ethereum, intending to address issues like scalability and cost that have challenged the Ethereum network. For example, Ethereum originally validated transactions at the rate of about 30 per second and Tron boasted upward of 2,000 transactions per second, which was a huge benefit. However, Ethereum 2.0 will eventually scale to around 100,000 transactions per second.

Tron Fee Structure

The Tron network's transaction fees are structured quite differently from Bitcoin and Ethereum. Tron uses a combination of energy and bandwidth to calculate costs. Users receive free bandwidth points daily, which cover most standard transactions. If these points are insufficient, users can freeze TRX to obtain more or pay a fee in TRX.

Smart contract transactions on Tron consume energy and bandwidth. The bandwidth costs are the same as regular transactions, but the energy costs vary based on the contract's complexity. Query transactions, however, are free, not requiring energy or bandwidth.

Overall, Tron's fee structure is designed to encourage usage with low costs for standard transactions, whereas smart contract interactions may incur higher fees depending on their complexity.

What Transactions Look Like

Let's dive straight in and have a look at the explorer, which you can find at `https://tronscan.org`. Pause for a moment and go take a look at the explorer.

At first glance the home page looks horribly confusing, but if you break it down visually you will see that the first strip of data is just some overview statistics, below that are the latest blocks, and next a rapidly updating pane of the latest transactions. So far, so good, but the page keeps scrolling. Below the transactions is a panel of data that we don't see in the Ethereum explorer, its data tagged as TVL. TVL stands for Total Value Locked and provides the figure of the amount of TRX locked in DeFi contracts on the chain. In fact, it provides two figures, the total value locked in all DeFi contracts and the amount locked in the TRX staking governance contract (see Figure 14.1).

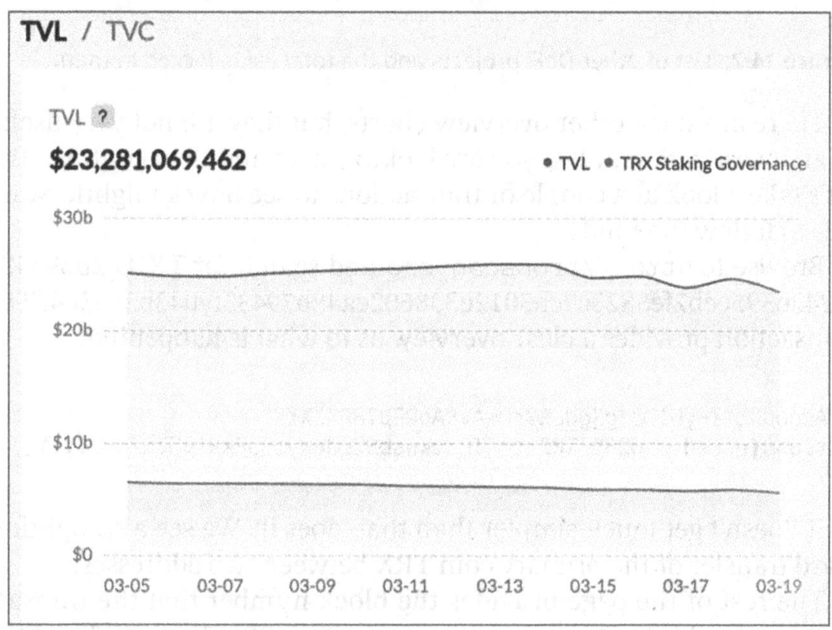

Figure 14.1: Chart showing total value locked in DeFi projects and amount in the TRX staking governance contract

TVC often stands for Total Value Created on blockchains and refers to such things as rewards or interest paid to investors, but on Tron it stands for Total Value on and provides a value of all chain assets with a trading volume greater than $1 million in the previous 24 hours.

The pane next to it shows the other DeFi projects and the TVL in those contracts (see Figure 14.2).

Project	Category	TVL	Change (24h)
JustLend DAO	Lending Staking	$7,443,657,582	-3.96%
Just Cryptos	Cross Chain	$7,373,627,783	-2.77%
TRX Staking Governance	Governance	$5,387,186,616	-5.03%
JustStable	Stablecoin Lending	$1,380,118,099	-4.37%
Staked USDT	RWA Staking Yield	$1,247,872,171	0.00%
SUN.io	DEX Stablecoin Farm	$445,735,798	-3.34%

Figure 14.2: List of other DeFi projects and the total value locked in them

There are some other overview charts, but they are not very useful in an investigation unless you are looking at a fraudulent contract. But let's take a look at a couple of transactions to see how straightforward it is to follow the funds.

Browse to `http://tronscan.org` and search for TXID 2b393483bef42e395eeb2fe8823c7cb3012e338602ea48b79433f9043b353364. The transaction provides a clear overview as to what is happening:

```
Account TFy61DS7gXgJLE2rDwAVRApDEB7HPXXXXX
transferred 0.0285 TRX to TEZukwsbSZDdeWyo5uFkRivGYmXHAYYYYY
```

It doesn't get much simpler than that, does it? We see a straightforward transfer of the primary coin TRX between two addresses.

The rest of the page provides the block number that the transaction is mined into, the super representatives (SRs) that validated the transaction, and the time and date in UTC. The Overview tab then provides us with the same information as the opening summary. Just as with Ethereum or BSC, we simply browse to the receiving address to follow the funds. Locate them by date and then see what happened afterward. So although it is a very different blockchain at its core, for an investigator this is easy to follow.

The same is true of contract transactions. Take a look at TXID f65bf 889c78136a067b17c85d6006e2f7702000df9594cfe2149a682779b0e9a:

```
Account TAzsQ9Gx8eqFNFSKbeXrbi45CuVPHzA8wr
(Binance-Hot 5) transferred 735.893 Tether USD USDT to
TJneUGrpat5shQbb5Wyc3mFD9HzmRNvGK8
```

Once again, this couldn't be easier. We see USDT moved from a user TAzsQ9 to TJneUG. The sending address is also tagged for us as belonging to a Binance hot wallet. If we want to understand what is happening in detail, we can look at the Overview tab, which outlines the transaction to the contract address as we would see in Ethereum:

```
Owner Address:
TAzsQ9Gx8eqFNFSKbeXrbi45CuVPHzA8wr (Binance-Hot 5)
Send Tokens to:
Contract Address:
TR7NHqjeKQxGTCi8q8ZY4pL8otSzgjLj6t (USDT Token)
```

We even have a raw function, which we can look at if there is any doubt as to what the transaction is doing. In this case, it reads:

Transfer(address _to, uint256 _value)

#	Name	Type	Data
0	_to	address	TJneUGrpat5shQbb5Wyc3mFD9HzmRNvGK8
1	_value	uint256	735893000

Once again, this reads nearly identically to an Ethereum function. It describes the Transfer function having two variables, the address being sent to, and the value of the transaction in uint256 format. Note that you need to count six decimal places to get the actual value of USDT transacted.

One of the unique aspects of Tron is that it offers its own internal staking program that enables users to have voting rights and also to earn a share of block rewards in relation to their ratio of staking. This works by staking TRX by freezing the funds, which earns you Tron Power tokens, which can be used to vote for SRs and get rewards. By providing a vote to a particular SR, you will get a reward of varying value. This isn't an investment tutorial, but if you see funds flowing back into an address using function terms such as "Reclaim resources," then this is an example of TRX being unstaked and rewards claimed.

Take a look at TXID c73fb4aae0f30c6c1166dc5adc7ebec9f8a367c59cbc39a26c566ea58ade721f. The transaction overview reads:

```
Account TZ3mMDaZP7rnh8qC1MPzAMeHWJq4hTkAse reclaimed
TXVteQquA4g1dCrCmvLrwozeSAfdzUvAjg 161,547.52 Energy
(This figure will vary with time.)
```

The user TZ3mM withdraws their stake and earns 161,547.52 Energy, but if we look further down the page, we see that:

Staked Asset Released: 12,000 TRX

If we look at the user's address, TZ3mM, it is very interesting from an investigator's perspective. Please note that I picked this address at random and there is no suggestion of wrongdoing. Let's pretend that we have traced the victim's funds into Tron and into this address. Figure 14.3 is an overview of the address as of this writing.

We can see at the top of the page that there are over $1.6 million worth of assets in the address, but the little wheel to the right indicates that 93.48 percent of those assets are Portfolio, meaning that they are staked or deposited in DeFi contracts. We see underneath the totals that 5,000,000 TRX are staked. This is important for you to consider—if you wish to seize these assets, you cannot simply transfer the funds out. These funds would first need to be "unstaked," and, once confirmed as a balance in the wallet, can then be transferred.

There is another interesting field: Claimable Voting Rewards. This tells us that over 1,567 TRX are available to claim from the voting rewards contract. Again, if you were detailing the assets of a suspect or wanting to seize the funds, then these would have to be claimed back from Tron. This would require generating a *claim* type transaction and then transferring the assets to a wallet controlled by you.

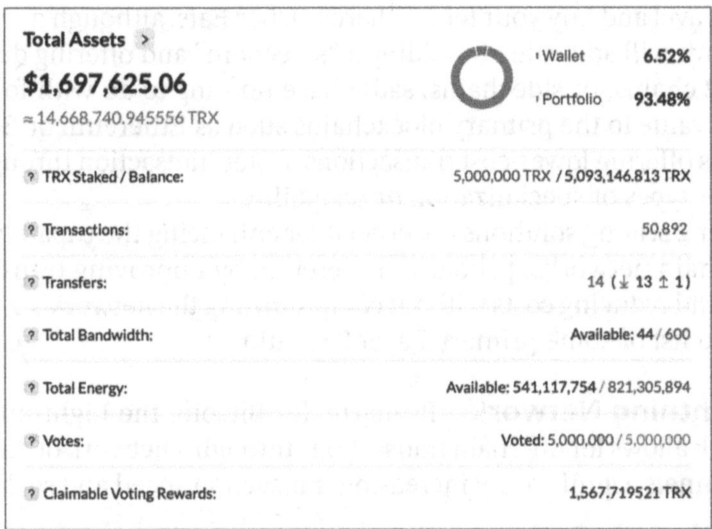

Figure 14.3: Overview of Tron address TZ3mMDaZP7rnh8qC1MPzAMeHWJq4hTkAse

This short section is not designed to be a Tron investigative tutorial; rather, it demonstrates that principles learned on the Ethereum and BSC chains are directly translatable to chains such as this.

Just one more useful detail before we move on is the ability, as with other explorers such as Etherscan and BSCscan, to export CSV files of lists of transactions from Tronscan. Browse to `http://tronscan.org` and search for TZ3mMDaZP7rnh8qC1MPzAMeHWJq4hTkAse again. Then scroll to the bottom left of the list of transactions and you will find a small link that reads Download CSV File. Clicking this link will give you a CSV file of the last 10,000 transactions, which is generally more than enough when investigating most addresses.

Another blockchain that proports to be very different from Ethereum is Solana. Take a look at the explorer, `http://solscan.io/txs`, and you will see that things are very similar. A bit of poking around and perhaps some Googling will enable you to start an investigation with little trouble.

Layer 2 Chains

Layer 2 chains are fairly easy to understand. Think of them this way: Your local Indian restaurant may be great, but you have to get in your car to travel and buy your food, whereas Uber Eats, although a separate company, will add value by adding a "sidechain" and offering delivery. Layer 2 chains, or sidechains, sadly have nothing to do with food but do add value to the primary blockchains such as Ethereum or Bitcoin, perhaps offering lower-cost transactions, faster transaction throughput, or other types of specialization or scalability.

Layer 2 scaling solutions are crucial for enhancing the capabilities of blockchain networks, primarily Ethereum, by improving transaction speed and reducing costs without compromising the network's security. Here's a list of some primary Layer 2 solutions:

Lightning Network Primarily for Bitcoin, the Lightning Network allows for off-chain transactions through a network of payment channels, significantly increasing transaction speed and scalability.

Optimistic Rollups These are Layer 2 solutions that execute transactions outside the main Ethereum chain but post transaction data on it. They assume transactions are valid by default and only run computations in the event of a dispute. Examples include Optimism and Arbitrum.

zk-Rollups This Layer 2 technology also moves computation and state storage off-chain but uses zero-knowledge proofs to maintain data integrity. Examples include zkSync and Loopring.

Plasma A framework proposed by Vitalik Buterin and Joseph Poon, Plasma creates child blockchains linked to the main Ethereum chain, enabling more efficient processing of transactions. Matic Network (now Polygon) initially used a version of Plasma.

Some services, such as Polygon, extend beyond traditional Layer 2 solutions like rollups or state channels. Polygon aims to be an Internet of Blockchains for Ethereum, supporting various types of infrastructure such as stand-alone chains, sidechains, and other Layer 2 solutions, all of which can interconnect and provide a versatile platform for developers. It can be daunting for an investigator faced with Layer 2 chains, especially as many Layer 2 chains are not supported by most commercial investigation tools, but again the principles dictated by the primary chains still hold true. I'm not going to go into significant details about the workings of Layer 2 chains since my goal is to be as nontechnical as possible, but once again we can look at a Layer 2 chain explorer and quickly understand what we are looking at. We'll take a look at tracing assets between chains, such as a Layer 1 chain like Ethereum and a Layer 2 chain such as Polygon in the next section, but first you need to understand how to trace assets once they are on a Layer 2 platform.

Let's use the Immutable blockchain as an example. As a Web3 gaming platform, Immutable X (IMX) has established itself as a popular choice for powering NFTs and in-game transactions, attracting titles like Gods Unchained and Guild of Guardians. With its dedicated focus on the gaming and NFT sectors, Immutable X has successfully drawn in projects that were initially based on different chains, underscoring its appeal and specialization in the gaming domain. You might think that this is a specialist chain and that tracking assets on it would be difficult, but you simply need to apply what you have already learned and perhaps do some searching online to fill in gaps.

Immutable has its own explorer at `http://explorer.immutable.com`. The explorer follows the same general pattern as other explorers, with the home page displaying some graphs representing activity on the chain as well as recent blocks and transactions.

As with other chains, you can search for TXIDs or user addresses. This time let's start off by looking at a user's address (correct as of this writing). Browse to `http://explorer.immutable.com` and search for address 0x277e9d30d965eEbE0e30b989fE35aab2Aa6b6A3c. The screen you are presented with is quite busy, but if you break it down all the familiar elements are there:

Balance: 435.79760494 IMX ($1,303.03)
Tokens: 1
Transactions: 9
Transfers: 11
Gas used: 892,443

This isn't so different from Ethereum. We see a balance of the primary coin, which in Immutable is IMX, which is used to pay fees and so forth. We see that they own one token type (not just one token) and that they have done nine transactions, which are different from the 11 transfers of tokens.

Below the summary information there is a list of buttons: Transactions, Token Transfers, Tokens, Internal Txns, and Coin Balance History.

If you click Tokens and then the NFT button, remembering that Immutable is based around gaming NFTs, you can see a graphical list of all the NFTs owned. As of this writing, this looked like Figure 14.4.

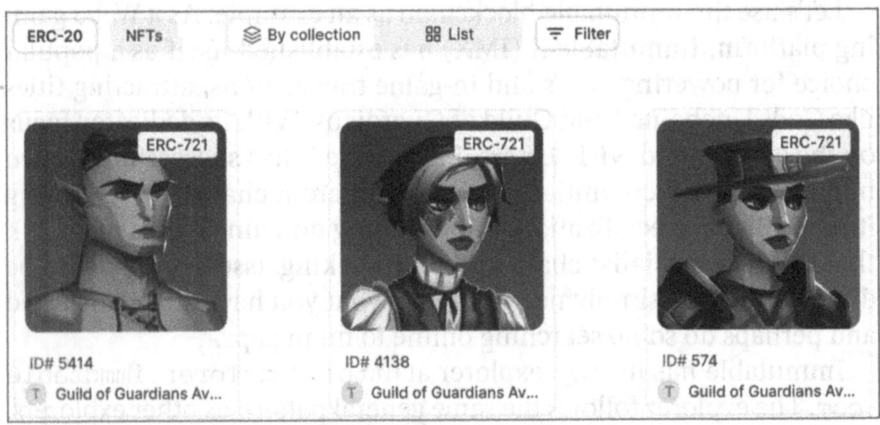

Figure 14.4: List of NFT tokens owned by 0x277e9d30d965eEbE0e30b989fE35aab2Aa6b6A3c

Click the Token Transfers button and you will see the transactions representing the buying and selling of NFT tokens. An example, as of this writing, is TXID 0x8f8e2ccd51ba3f8957a3f8a68bb397801ff766faea1d2f7e5b13b3d07212b9a7. Take a look if you can.

If you have been able to browse to the TXID, you'll see that the data isn't too scary and follows the basic rules of other transactions we have looked at. The important data looks like this:

```
From: 0x277e9d30d965eEbE0e30b989fE35aab2Aa6b6A3c
Interacted with contract: ImmutableSeaport
Tokens transferred: 0xd4. . .0639 to 0x27. . .6A3c
for token ID 4138 of Guild of Guardians Avatar (GOGA)
     Value: 861 IMX ($2,574.39)
```

I'm hoping that you can read this data quite easily now, even though this is on a nonfamiliar blockchain. The user we are looking at with the address starting with 0x277e9 triggers the transaction with the ImmutableSeaport contract. The contract transfers Token ID 4138 from the address starting with 0xd4 to our user for 861 IMX. So what is happening? Our user is buying token 4138 from 0xd4. The data tells us that the token is related to the Guild of Guardians and is an avatar. This would tell us that this is almost certainly an NFT related to this Guild of Guardians game. A bit of Googling would tell us all about it. The Immutable explorer links the token ID, so if we click it we see the NFT and its buy and sell history since it was minted (see Figure 14.5).

Figure 14.5: The NFT bought in TXID

Why would an investigator end up looking at gaming NFTs? Money laundering. NFTs can be bought, traded, even lost in a battle. As NFTs can change hands for quite significant funds (the one we just looked at was bought for $2,574.39), it doesn't take much imagination to think about how parties wanting to launder money could make use of these assets. Use criminal crypto to buy several NFT gaming equipment cards, lose them in a battle to a known third party or another account owned by you, sell the NFTs on the gaming market place. Easy!

On Layer 2 gaming marketplaces, you will see a lot of minting and burning of assets. A good example can be seen at this TXID on Immutable, 0x68863452efe9c3e3de0331292ef985ce3b6ee79a38698f1cafc1cdd1ecf59f39. Take a look if you can. I will not break this down in detail but here's the primary data:

```
Transaction action:
Burn 1 of GOGO
Mint 1 of GOGH
```

```
From: 0x630BDCf2d3f387309304F60D7de98561F0C0e326
Interacted with contract: MultiCallDeploy
Tokens minted: 0x00. . .0000 to 0xC2. . .e810
for token ID 20692467714500873103637140394366215 21 of Guild
of Guardians Heroes (GOGH)
Tokens burnt: 0xC2. . .e810 to 0x00. . .0000 for token ID
20692086967666458775543371470206878 21 of Guild of Guardians
Other(GOGO)
```

This transaction triggered by user address 0x630B burns an NFT token and mints a new NFT token. We see the 0x00000. . .address used again to burn the old token and mint a new one.

Now, we don't need to know much about how Guild of Guardians works, but if we look at the two NFTs referenced here we can pretty much work out what is happening. If we click the token IDs, we find that the burned token looks like Figure 14.6.

Figure 14.6: Burned NFT

This NFT has the name Rare Prayer. The history of the NFT shows it being created and sent to our user address and then the next transaction is burned. If we look at the NFT that is minted when this is burned, we see the image in Figure 14.7.

Again, if we look at this NFT, we learn that it's a "Rare" avatar named Okubo. I suspect that the user/gamer bought or was gifted the Rare Prayer token in the game and when they trigger the "prayer" it gifts them an avatar. Hence, the "prayer" is burned so it can't be used again and the avatar is minted for the player.

Figure 14.7: NFT that is minted

I hope you are beginning to believe that once you have some solid knowledge of the Ethereum blockchain, reading other chains such as Layer 2 chains becomes fairly easy. You may have to do a bit of research on the specific chain you are investigating to understand any unique or unusual uses or terms.

Bridges

Having looked briefly at Layer 2 chains, we need to pose the obvious question as to how funds from Ethereum, for example, are able to be transferred to a completely different chain. The same question exists for someone who owns Bitcoin and wishes to convert the funds to ETH; they are on completely different chains and work in completely different ways. The answer is a bridge that connects the two chains together and enables conversion between the two currencies. Actually, the use of the word *connects* is rather misleading as the two bridged blockchains are not actually linked. When assets are transferred from one blockchain to another using a bridge, the assets on the source blockchain are typically locked in a smart contract or, in some cases, burned (permanently removed from circulation). This step ensures that the same assets cannot be used simultaneously on both chains, preserving the integrity of each blockchain's ledger.

Corresponding to the locked or burned assets, an equivalent amount of assets or a representative token is minted or released on the destination blockchain. This new token acts as a stand-in for the original asset on the new blockchain, allowing users to interact with it within that blockchain's ecosystem. Most bridges use smart contracts to automate the locking/burning, issuance/minting, and transfer processes, ensuring that the bridge operates efficiently.

I tend to visualize this as similar to the matter transporter as depicted on *Star Trek*. Even if you are not a Trekker, I'm sure you all know the phrase "Beam me up, Scotty" attributed to, but never actually said, by Captain Kirk in the original *Star Trek* series. When a human is "beamed" or sent from the starship to the planet, there is no physical bridge that connects that person to the destination. Rather, the person is separated into their atoms (the asset is burned) and the information is read and then sent to the destination and re-created from new atoms. The person who materializes on the planet surface is actually a completely new person built from the information sent. This is the same as sending, for example, USDT from the Ethereum chain to the Polygon chain. The original USDT isn't sent; it's burned and the information about the burn is sent electronically to Polygon, which mints new USDT. Confused? Let's look at an example to confuse you even more.

It is very important to recognize transactions that transfer funds over bridges, as it's a good way to launder money by carrying out movements between chains, which seem on first glance hard to follow. In an investigation, you may be considering a suspect's crypto assets on the Ethereum chain when you see a transaction that seems to go nowhere. Take a look on Etherscan at TXID 0x01e6bd613ba1d591d b78257bbb35b6a13039e4f3361b3759ec04025e7c9aa7c2. Here is the core data for you:

```
Transaction Action: Transfer 730.534136 USDT To
(Polygon (Matic): zkEVM Bridge)
```

The clue here is in the tag—it tells us that the contract address that the USDT is sent to is a bridge owned by the Polygon chain. Where do the funds go? If we look further down the page, we will find the following:

```
From: 0x8F95d981D515FB58cF07cCbbE98DB4AE118c800D
Interacted With (To): 0x2a3DD3EB832aF982e
c71669E178424b10Dca2EDe (Polygon (Matic): zkEVM Bridge)
```

```
ERC-20 Tokens Transferred:
From 0x8F95d981. . .E118c800D To Polygon (Matic):
zkEVM Bridge For 730.534136 ($731.26) Tether USD (USDT)
```

Well, that's not very helpful, is it? It seems that the funds have disappeared into the bridge, never to be seen again—but all is not lost.

At the bottom of the page we have the More Details, Click To Show More button. Clicking that button reveals the function call and the variables in the function. It reads:

```
Function: bridgeAsset(uint32 destinationNetwork,address
destinationAddress,uint256 amount,address token,bool
forceUpdateGlobalExitRoot,bytes permitData)
```

I've put in bold the variables that are of use to us. The destinationNetwork will tell us what chain the funds are heading to, the destinationAddress is the address that the funds will be transferred to on that chain, and the address token will tell us what token is being transferred. If you are browsing with me, click the Decode Input Data button below the function box. This is what we see decoded:

#	Name	Data
0	destinationNetwork	1
1	destinationAddress	0x8F95d981D515FB58cF07cCbbE98DB4AE118c800D
2	amount	730534136
3	token	0xdAC17F958D2ee523a2206206994597C13D831ec7

For reference, destinationNetwork 0 is Ethereum and 1 is the Polygon chain. We see 1 here, meaning that the funds are headed for the Polygon chain; we could've figured that out from the name of the contract, of course. Next, we get a destinationAddress, which is 0x8F95d981D515FB58cF07cCbbE98DB4AE118c800D. We have the amount, which was reflected in the summary data, 730.534136 (when the six decimal points are taken into account), and then lastly the token address. USDT is easy to recognize as it starts with 0xdAC17. Not sure why that's easy to recognize, but it seems to stick in my brain.

So, how do we follow the funds? Take note of the date and time; we should find an incoming transaction from the bridge on the Polygon network a little after this transaction. This transaction was Mar-25-2024 09:31:59 PM +UTC. Don't expect it to be immediate; I've often waited more than 20–30 minutes for the transaction to appear on the other chain. We need a Polygon chain explorer—remember that this was sent using the zkEVM bridge, so Google for the Polygon zkEVM explorer. My favorite is at `http://zkevm.polygonscan.com`.

Search for the destination address on the Polygon explorer (0x8F95 . . .) and you will find the address with all its historical transactions. We know that this is a transfer of USDT, so we need to click the Token Transfers button. We will see an incoming transaction Mar-25-2024 21:45:21 UTC. This is about 14 minutes after the transaction on the Ethereum side and so would seem like a good candidate to be receiving the USDT (see Figure 14.8).

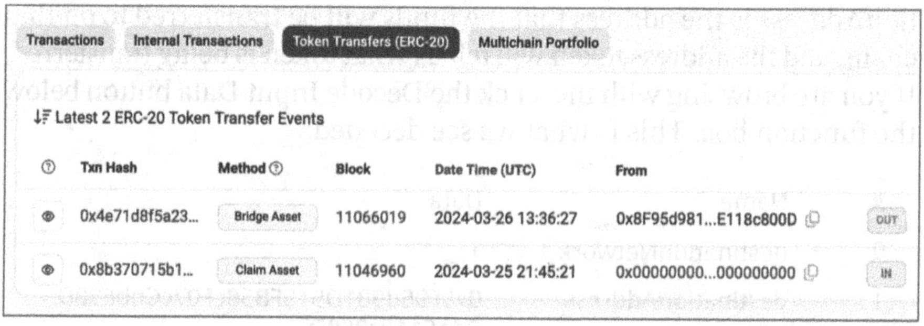

Transactions | Internal Transactions | Token Transfers (ERC-20) | Multichain Portfolio

Latest 2 ERC-20 Token Transfer Events

	Txn Hash	Method	Block	Date Time (UTC)	From	
	0x4e71d8f5a23...	Bridge Asset	11066019	2024-03-26 13:36:27	0x8F95d981...E118c800D	OUT
	0x8b370715b1...	Claim Asset	11046960	2024-03-25 21:45:21	0x00000000...000000000	IN

Figure 14.8: List of token transfers for address 0x8f95d. . .on the Polygon chain

We can also see that the function/method name is Claim Asset, which also sounds like it could be right. Click the TXID, which is 0x8b370715b1e625256ed9d083b6cf6d90d351a7e858635bc7355a01a1c65e62ca, if you want to search for it specifically. Here is the primary data we see:

```
Timestamp: Mar-25-2024 09:45:21 PM +UTC)
Transaction Action: Transfer 730.534136 USDT To
0x8F95d981. . .E118c800D
```

This is the right amount of USDT sent from Ethereum, but if we look at the From address, there is something odd about it:

```
From: 0x4ca25C4E560FB5aDC3Ff43eB0AD82EE0cD84aAce
(Zenland: Deployer)
Interacted With (To): 0x2a3DD3EB832aF982ec71669E178424b10Dca2EDe
(Polygon Hermez: Bridge)
ERC-20 Tokens Transferred:
From 0x00000000. . .000000000
To 0x8F95d981. . .E118c800D
For 730.534136 ($730.14) Tether USD (USDT)
```

What's going on here? We see the transaction triggered by an address tagged as the Zenland:Deployer, but the tokens are transferred by the 0x000. . .genesis address? Essentially, this transaction has to be triggered by a user address, and because it is coming out of a bridge it can't be the originating Ethereum address. So, a third-party address (Zenland) triggers the Polygon Hermez: Bridge contract and then the USDT is minted (created) "from" the genesis address and sent to the end user.

That's fundamentally how bridges work, although different bridges have slightly different ways of working. What I have missed in this brief example is the validation key that is passed between chains to prove that coins have been burned on one side and minted on the other, but this is quite complex and an investigator will be primarily concerned with following the funds.

WORMHOLE BREACH

As we mentioned in Chapter 2, "Understanding the Criminal Opportunities: Money Laundering," the Wormhole bridge, a prominent cryptocurrency bridge connecting Ethereum and Solana, experienced a significant security breach in February 2022. This attack resulted in the loss of over $300 million worth of cryptocurrency, marking one of the largest exploits in DeFi history at the time. Here's how the attack unfolded.

The attacker identified and exploited a vulnerability in the Wormhole bridge's smart contracts. Specifically, the flaw was in the bridge's token validation process; this is the key sharing I just mentioned that confirms that assets were burned on one side of the bridge, enabling the generation of new coins on the other side. However, the attacker found a way to trick the system into minting assets on the destination blockchain without burning the equivalent assets on the source blockchain.

Utilizing this vulnerability, the attacker executed a sophisticated series of transactions. They submitted a fraudulent proof to the Wormhole network, claiming that a certain amount of Ethereum had been locked on the Ethereum side of the bridge. The network, failing to validate this claim properly due to the exploited vulnerability, accepted the fraudulent proof as legitimate. Relying on this false proof, the Wormhole bridge incorrectly minted a large number of tokens on the Solana blockchain, which the attacker then quickly transferred out of the bridge's control. This action essentially created new assets out of thin air, diluting the value of legitimately minted tokens.

The Wormhole bridge attack underscores the intricate security challenges facing cross-chain bridges and the broader DeFi ecosystem. It highlights the necessity for rigorous security practices, including comprehensive audits and monitoring, to safeguard user assets in this rapidly evolving space.

Being able to identify and read a bridge transaction on chain explorers can be very important, as many commercial tools still struggle with tracing across bridges and into Layer 2 chains. Bridges are a large and complex subject, but I hope that my example and explanation can at least give you a head start in learning about tracing funds across chains.

Mixers

Mixers are, as their name suggests, services that attempt to mix, or obfuscate, the ownership of crypto assets. In the simplest terms, a user injects funds into the mixer, and when the funds eventually exit the mixer service, they should be difficult or impossible to trace to the original owner of the funds. The issue facing mixers is that any transaction on the blockchain is public and immutable, making true anonymous mixing very difficult.

I should state up front that although I will talk through the basics of how some mixers work, I will not be covering how funds can be traced through them. Specialist investigators and many law enforcement teams have techniques that enable tracing through most mixers with a high level of confidence, but we will not be exposing them in this book. If you are working within law enforcement and need assistance in this area, I suggest contacting your preferred commercial tracing tool supplier, as most have departments dedicated to mixer exploitation.

Although mixers are just an algorithmic series of transactions that obey blockchain transaction "rules," it's important to note that the legality and ethicality of using mixers have been the subject of considerable debate. In some jurisdictions, using a mixer is considered a form of money laundering, given that it can be used to obscure illegal funds' origins. However, others point out that mixers can be used by people living in countries where they may be at risk because of social, religious, or ethnic persecution and mixers enable them to make financial transactions without government oversight. Of course, this capability could be used legitimately, but it also provides a useful tool for those who wish to obfuscate movement of funds for criminal purposes and so are viewed negatively. The U.S. government has taken the lead in this thinking; the U.S. Treasury Department's Office of Foreign Assets Control (OFAC) sanctioned the Ethereum mixer Tornado Cash on August 8, 2022 and the takedown of Bitcoin Fog in April 2021. The U.S. Department of Justice (DoJ) arrested Roman Sterlingov, a Russian-Swedish national, accusing him of operating the Bitcoin Fog mixer, which allegedly laundered over 1.2 million Bitcoin. (Sterlingov was found guilty in the United States in March 2024; see `www.justice.gov/usao-dc/pr/jury-finds-russian-swedish-operator-bitcoin-fog-guilty-running-darknet-cryptocurrency`.)

Bitcoin Mixing

You've seen how the Bitcoin blockchain functions; every transaction is recorded to the ledger and is immutable and cannot be changed. (Well, for the purists among you, technically recent blocks could be changed if you have epic levels of computing power, but doing so would be very hard indeed and is only theoretically feasible.) Transactions are written to the ledger, and we can trace each Bitcoin or fragment of Bitcoin from address to address, including funds going to change addresses. This should mean that any funds can be traced no matter what you do, but it is possible for a mixer to make it very difficult indeed. Sometimes mixers are termed "tumblers," but this would technically only refer to Bitcoin-type mixers rather than Ethereum-style mixers since they work in very different ways. The other phrase sometimes used is *peel chains*. This refers to the original input of crypto "peeled" by being split up and transferred on.

Bitcoin mixer services work in a variety of ways but generally operate on the principle of breaking down users' deposits into smaller amounts and pushing them through a series of random transactions, each at a random time with "change" going to new unused addresses, which is again split and so on. Although the parts are still individually traceable through the blockchain, the disconnect between the users' funds start address and then breaking apart and heading through a number of other transactions just obfuscates the chain. For an investigator, it can be difficult to discern if these transactions are legitimate moving of funds between addresses, maybe payments or otherwise, or whether they are being obfuscated. This is tricky enough, but a true mixer also includes funds from other users or funds they already own. User funds are combined in transactions with third-party coins and then split again and combined and split before users are paid their initial deposit minus fees. This is where we get the term "tumblers" from, as user funds are tumbled with other funds. This process makes tracing through mixers very challenging.

As mentioned, I will not be discussing the more detailed methods for unpicking these types of tumblers, but there are some logical processes that are in the public domain. The first is that many mixers use a distinct algorithmic pattern to carry out the splitting and combining of coins. In the past I've used pen and paper to manually and painstakingly draw out transactions and eventually see a pattern appear. With some mixers you can get so good at recognizing the pattern that you can predict what the next transaction will be.

Another method we can apply to find the mixed funds headed to our suspect is a reuse of addresses post-mix that are attributable to them. A mixer will eventually output funds to an address provided by the user; it is always recommended that the address be a new unused address. However, users will sometimes simply transfer the funds back into their original pre-mix wallet or transfer coins to colleagues or services that they have used before. This can be a direct identification or at least narrow down the likely candidates from a list of mixed outputs. You might think that this is such an obvious mistake that no one would do it, but I have seen it many, many times. I think the problem for a user is that they likely have a crypto infrastructure where they receive and pay coins from, or they have a series of addresses used as scam deposit addresses but post-mix want to bring it into their primary wallet or exchange service to convert or extract FIAT currency. By nature, this means that suspects often reuse addresses.

In Figure 14.9, we see a high-level example of a peel chain splitting funds many times but the final output ends up at a Kraken address that the suspect had used previously. In Figure 14.9, the same primary set of funds also flows through a mixer where an output always goes to a Binance address.

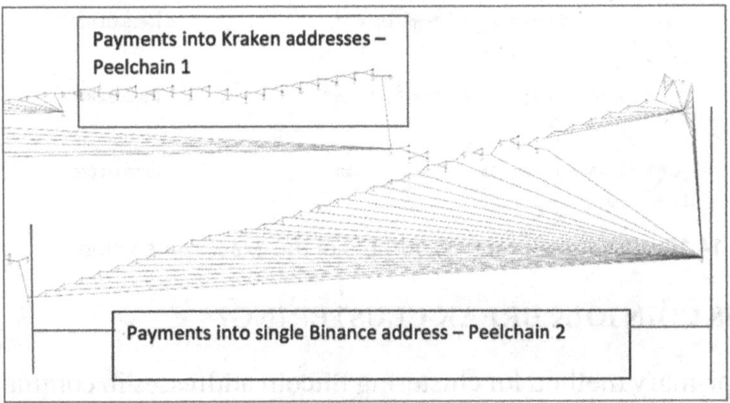

Figure 14.9: Example of multiple mixing chains returning to exchange addresses via a large number of transactions

There are other types of mixing like CoinJoin transactions, the system used by the popular Wasabi wallet until they deprecated the CoinJoin capability in June 2024 after pressure from the U.S. government. In very simple terms, several users who wish to make transactions agree to combine their funds into a single Bitcoin transaction. Each participant inputs the amount of Bitcoin they want to send, and the output amounts are constructed to make it difficult to connect the input to the output. You would think that when a user inputs, for example, 0.5 Bitcoin, we would be able to see the 0.5 Bitcoin coming out the other side.

By having many inputs, some of the same size, and obfuscating the output amounts, it becomes hard for an investigator to unravel (see Figure 14.10).

#33 bc1qgdr6uajlmmf9ngy0funmhxlj9kwjj33phmnpuf	0.10890321 BTC
#34 bc1qwfjdsf5l7yqt5fkjtzdhmgaxzypqpflnx0rgy6	0.10890321 BTC
#35 bc1qgctpazcmjm2rfrglzge4amsrvzn6vdnuapedmv	0.10890321 BTC
#36 bc1q0p4zvqnkt8qklkr5f895zam8ha0us6tx6e8tpt	0.10890321 BTC
#37 bc1qqplrtzh5f63nqs3tlsyulh3xswcfuee2ch297j	0.10890321 BTC
#38 bc1qpp72uw2d5wlsplll0yje0dsv0c9pste7fdz8p7	0.10890321 BTC
#39 bc1qyrz8gsv6w8qr9f24m2a6jx036m954yq995fz87	0.10890321 BTC
#40 bc1q3x40mygnqze4gex23nqjlrwxrsfac708x22jt0	0.10890321 BTC

Figure 14.10: Just some of the 96 outputs of the exact same value

DOES COINJOIN BREAK CLUSTERING?

The primary method for clustering Bitcoin addresses in commercial investigation tools is to group input addresses from transactions, as you learned in Chapter 10, "Bitcoin: Investigation Methodology." Some investigators have questioned the veracity of this method as it is broken by CoinJoin transactions where the inputs are not all owned by the same person. However, it is very easy to recognize CoinJoin transactions. For example, Wasabi CoinJoin transactions have a very large number of inputs combined with a large number of outputs with blocks of the same output amounts. There is a good example here: `https://blockstream.info/tx/16a7c04139883d33997ed475918afcc4f54355478cb1737076cbb8b97c208316`.

In this transaction we find 78 inputs and 96 outputs, many of which are for exactly the same amount, which would strike an investigator as an unusual transaction. Figure 14.10 shows just some of the 96 outputs of exactly the same value. In fact, the Blockstream explorer even tags this transaction as "Possibly a CoinJoin transaction."

As previously mentioned, there are techniques for tracking through CoinJoin transactions, but I will not be discussing them here. To be honest, I'm not an expert on this topic, but I have colleagues who seem to revel in the math and algorithms and who can do some real unmixing magic in many circumstances.

Ethereum Mixing

As you learned in Chapter 11, "The Workings of Ethereum and Derivatives," Ethereum-style cryptocurrencies do not make use of change addresses (UTXO), and whereas Bitcoin can be described as partly synonymous with physical cash transactions, an Ethereum transaction is more closely related to a bank account, where there is a balance, and payments in and out of an address are the total amount with no change. This makes mixing rather tricky. You could take input coins and send small amounts to a range of addresses and then split them and send to more addresses, and so on and so on, but doing so is difficult and time consuming. The most successful mixer for Ethereum was/is Tornado Cash. I wrote "was/is" because it was successful until the U.S. Treasury sanctioned it in 2022, but as of this writing it's still functioning and appears to be in regular use. Usage seems to be shifting to an incumbent called RailGun, which states that it's not actually a mixer but fundamentally still obfuscates funds from input to output.

Let's look at Tornado Cash as an example. To be honest, Tornado Cash works on a very simple premise, which is that you can only input certain amounts of coins. For example, if you want to mix ETH, then you can only input 0.1, 1, 10, or 100 ETH. If you want to input 25 ETH, then you would have to deposit 2 × 10 ETH and 5 × 1 ETH. Tornado Cash then puts the amounts into an address that contains all the same amounts. So the 2 × 10 ETH deposits would be put in the 10 ETH address and the 5 × 1 ETH would be put in the 1 ETH address. The user waits however long they wish and then withdraw the deposits to an unused address. If you were the only user of the mixer, then it would be useless, as an observer would see the 25 ETH be deposited and then see the only coins in the system withdrawn and so would be able to connect the input and output addresses. However, if there were a large number of users, then it becomes increasingly difficult to connect the inputs and outputs (see Figure 14.11).

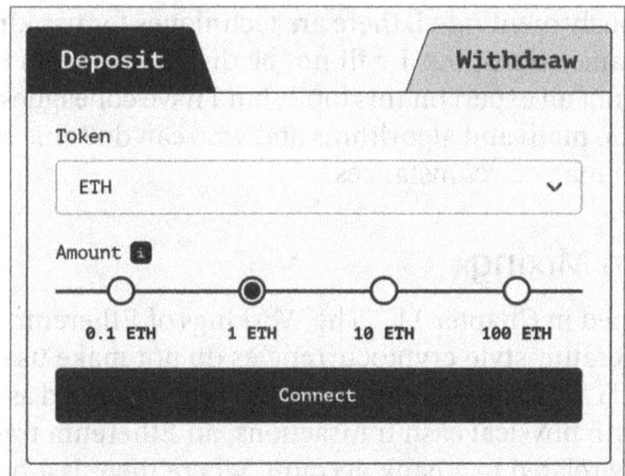

Figure 14.11: The deposit screen for Tornado Cash

Think of an example where we are tracing the 25 ETH from a known scam address. We see the funds deposited into Tornado Cash, but on the same day another 10 users deposit funds into the 10 and 1 addresses. Over the subsequent days funds are withdrawn. We can see where all the funds go, but which user withdrawing is our scammer? It's very hard to know.

Tornado Cash provides an encryption key known as a *deposit note* for each deposit to the user that identifies how much the mixer owes them after fees and enables them to withdraw the right amount. This is worth knowing. If we found a key during a premises search, it would enable an investigator to extract any funds still in the mixer.

I like to think of this as bowls of M&Ms labeled with colors. If you had two red and five yellow M&Ms, you put them into the right color bowls. Later you come and take them out. If they were the only M&Ms in the bowls, identification of the owner would be easy—you could "trace" them in and out of the bowls. However, if there were a queue of people with M&Ms all putting their red and yellow candy into the right bowls, and then later coming back and taking the right number out, "tracking" the candy in and then out of the bowl to a specific end user becomes almost impossible.

A more detailed description of the workings of Tornado Cash can be found here: `https://www.coincenter.org/education/advanced-topics/how-does-tornado-cash-work`.

There are a number of techniques that can be applied to tracing funds through services like Tornado Cash, but I'm not going to discuss them here as this would be useful to those trying to hide criminal funds. If your team does not have this capability, please reach out to your chosen commercial tracing tool company and they will have specialists who can help you.

Privacy Coins

I feel the need to apologize. I was planning to write a whole chapter about privacy coins, but it has become a bit of a proverbial "hot potato" with tools and investigators doing remote digital battle. Privacy-oriented cryptocurrencies have carved out a niche by prioritizing the anonymity and confidentiality of transactions. Unlike traditional cryptocurrencies such as Bitcoin, which offer pseudonymity, privacy coins go several steps further to ensure that the details of a transaction and its participants remain obscured. The primary blockchain intelligence companies continue to work hard to develop methods for tracing through privacy coins, and it is a constantly changing landscape. If I included too much detail in this book, it would be out of date by the time it was published. Also, it could be useful to those who would use the information to circumvent current law enforcement techniques. Because of those reasons I'm going to keep this relatively short. However, as with mixing, if you are a government investigator, then a conversation with your friendly neighborhood blockchain intelligence company would be useful for you. I am in no way suggesting that the primary privacy coins are broken or completely exploitable, as that would be misleading, but there are techniques that can assist you in an investigation that includes privacy coins.

It is also disingenuous to conclude that the developers of privacy coins all have criminal motives any more so than developers such as Phil Zimmermann (who wrote the encryption program Pretty Good Privacy) were when the U.S. government investigated him for illegal "munitions export" back in 1993. Most are just very clever people who desire privacy in their communications and financial transactions. The rights or wrongs of this thinking are well outside the scope of this book, but privacy is not always a bad thing.

Apologies again if this section is a little dry, but we'll look at some examples of privacy coins and their investigative challenges. Let's start with Monero.

Monero (XMR): The Vanguard of Privacy Coins

Overview and Mechanisms Monero arguably stands at the forefront of privacy-focused cryptocurrencies, distinguished by its robust anonymizing features. It employs stealth addresses to create onetime-use addresses for each transaction, effectively masking the recipient's real address. Ring signatures blend the digital signature of the actual sender with those of nonparticipating signers, thereby diluting the traceability of the transaction. Furthermore, Ring Confidential Transactions (RingCT) conceal the amount transferred, adding another layer of privacy.

Investigation Challenges The combination of stealth addresses, ring signatures, and RingCT makes Monero arguably the most private cryptocurrency, complicating efforts to trace transactions. Traditional blockchain intelligence tools that track transaction flows on more transparent ledgers like Bitcoin do not have built-in capability for Monero as of this writing. Investigators must rely on sophisticated pattern recognition, metadata analysis, and potential network vulnerabilities to glean any useful information, often requiring significant resources with no guarantee of success.

Zcash (ZEC): Selective Transparency

Overview and Mechanisms Zcash offers users the choice between transparent and shielded transactions, facilitated by zk-SNARKs, cryptographic proofs that allow for the validation of transactions without revealing any sensitive information. This dual approach enables users to enjoy the benefits of blockchain technology without compromising on privacy for transactions they wish to keep shielded.

Investigation Challenges Zcash's dual transaction model presents a unique set of investigative hurdles. While transparent transactions can be analyzed in a similar way to Bitcoin, shielded transactions are cryptographically protected, hiding the sender, receiver, and amount. The selective transparency requires investigators to identify patterns or relationships between the transparent and shielded ecosystems within Zcash, a task that demands deep cryptographic knowledge and advanced analytical tools.

Dash (DASH): Privacy as an Option

Overview and Mechanisms Initially launched as XCoin, later rebranded to Dash, this cryptocurrency introduced PrivateSend, an optional privacy feature based on the CoinJoin mixing technique. By combining multiple inputs from several users into a single transaction with several outputs, PrivateSend makes it challenging to link any input to its corresponding output, thereby obfuscating the transaction trail. PrivateSend also utilizes multiple rounds of mixing to further obfuscate the inputs from the outputs.

Investigation Challenges Despite its privacy features, Dash's implementation of PrivateSend offers a weaker form of anonymity compared to Monero and Zcash, primarily because it is not a default setting. This aspect somewhat simplifies the investigative process, as transactions not utilizing PrivateSend remain transparent. Nonetheless, when PrivateSend is activated, it requires advanced tracing techniques and a comprehensive understanding of the mixing process to potentially de-anonymize transactions.

Horizen (ZEN): Extended Privacy with Sidechains

Overview and Mechanisms Horizen extends privacy beyond simple transactions through the use of a sidechain platform, Zendoo, allowing for the creation of privacy-focused applications. By leveraging zk-SNARKs within its sidechain ecosystem, Horizen offers both scalability and privacy, providing developers with the tools to build applications that inherit these features.

Investigation Challenges The complexity of investigating Horizen transactions lies in the sidechain architecture. Each application or sidechain can have its own privacy rules and mechanisms, requiring investigators to adapt their methods for each case. Analyzing transactions across multiple sidechains necessitates a customized approach, blending cryptographic expertise with an understanding of each sidechain's unique implementation of privacy-enhancing technologies.

Grin and Beam: Mimblewimble Protocol

Overview and Mechanisms Both Grin and Beam use the Mimblewimble protocol, which compacts blockchain size and enhances privacy by allowing for the aggregation of transactions. This protocol removes the need for most transaction data, leaving no trace of transaction histories. Grin focuses on minimalism and scalability, whereas Beam adds additional features like confidential assets and opt-in auditability.

Investigation Challenges The Mimblewimble protocol presents a paradigm shift in how transaction data is treated, significantly limiting the effectiveness of conventional blockchain analysis techniques. The compacted transaction data and lack of explicit addresses require investigators to develop new methodologies for tracking the flow of funds. This might involve analyzing transaction kernels, the only permanent, verifiable record of transactions, though these provide minimal data.

To sum up. Privacy coins represent a significant evolution in the digital currency space, prioritizing user anonymity and transaction confidentiality. While they serve legitimate needs for privacy, they also pose substantial challenges for financial regulation, law enforcement, and investigation. The ongoing development of investigative techniques and tools, alongside advancements in privacy technology, underscores the dynamic and contested nature of privacy in crypto space. As privacy coins continue to evolve, so too will the strategies for their analysis and investigation, reflecting broader debates over privacy, security, and regulation in the digital economy.

What Have You Learned?

This chapter has helped you understand that you do not need to relearn techniques for every new blockchain you come across. Most work on similar principles to the primary currencies Bitcoin and Ethereum, and even where there are different approaches used, similarities tend to still exist. Once you can read a contract, tracing through bridges and coin swaps becomes a logical process that most investigators should be able to work through.

As with almost any investigative technique, practice, ongoing learning, and hands-on practical experience will enable you to work through most new currencies that cross your desk.

15 Open Source Intelligence and the Blockchain

This chapter was written by my good friend and colleague Luke Russell. Luke has investigated crypto crime to the tune of millions of dollars across a wide scope of criminality. He has a particular interest in open source investigations and so was perfect to write this section. Although you could write a book on this subject alone, hopefully this will give you a practical overview of how freely available information can help in a crypto-related investigation. You will find this chapter a little more technical than previous chapters but hopefully still accessible to you.

For several years now I have had the privilege of teaching investigators around the world techniques that can be used to leverage open source data and technologies to conduct detailed and successful investigations.

When asked what open source really means, I always go back to what Nick and I refer to as "Emma's rule." Years before I began working with Nick, a particularly gifted investigator asked the simple question "What really is open source?" After what I can only assume was some time of discussion around the room, Emma simply said "Okay, so it's open source if you go from point A to B and the data you are looking for is there." And that was it—Emma's rule was born. Although a simple statement, that really is a great definition of open source.

For example, the code to Apple's macOS is closed source. As a user I cannot move from point A, my MacBook, and travel to point B to view the underlying proprietary code that belongs to Apple. In contrast, if I so desired, I could go and find the open source code to build my own Linux distribution. That is open source: information or data shared openly and without restriction.

By their very nature, most cryptocurrencies are open source. There is no central data center hosting the code; the blockchain on which the transactional data is stored is decentralized. There is no central authority that makes overarching decisions about the direction of the technology. Typically these decisions are made by the consensus of the community.

Therefore, any investigation into cryptocurrencies will inevitably involve open source intelligence (OSINT). When using OSINT to investigate cryptocurrencies, there are two categories of data: on-chain and off-chain data. On-chain data is any information that exists on the blockchain; transaction data, address information and micro messages all constitute on-chain information. On-chain data is vital to investigate cryptocurrency-enabled crime—Nick will be covering this in significant detail throughout the rest of the book. But in this chapter, we will focus on how we can gather off-chain data, and how that data can work to support on-chain intelligence. (We define off-chain data as any data that is not resident on a blockchain.)

Mindset

One of the first things you should consider when delving into the depths of OSINT is how to cultivate the right mindset. Although a plethora of online tools, scripts, and techniques that allow for the relatively easy access of online data are available, the key to conducting successful and impactful OSINT investigations is to cultivate an investigative mindset. The UK College of Policing states that an investigator with this type of mindset will apply a "systematic approach to the gathering and the assessing of material."

When conducting OSINT research on your case/suspect, you will at times encounter piles of information. This data may seem irrelevant and perhaps have no bearing on your investigative task. However, someone who cultivates an investigative mindset will apply their ABCs when sifting through the gathered data:

- A – Assume Nothing
- B – Believe Nothing
- C – Challenge Everything

In order to expedite your investigation, it may be tempting to discard assumingly irrelevant information. You may wish to believe the data to be true because it supports the investigative narrative you have been provided. It is vital to challenge everything you uncover in your investigation, essentially leaving no stone unturned.

At times you may feel that you have unearthed a mountain of rubbish, digital trash that is seemingly irrelevant to your case. When I am overwhelmed by the amount of data gathered, I like to remind myself of the art installation by Tim Noble and Sue Webster titled *Dirty White Trash (With Gulls)*, 1998 (see Figure 15.1).

Figure 15.1: A pile of sculpted trash casting a shadow depicting a man and woman drinking and smoking

Source: Album / Alamy Stock Photo

It reminds me that when isolated, each piece of data I collect may appear to be trash, seemingly unimpactful or irrelevant to my case, but when combined they can create a clear digital shadow of my suspect's activity. Within the context of a cryptocurrency investigation, where on-chain data is often unattributed, off-chain information can be overlaid to create a clear digital outline of the suspect's activity.

A book could be written on both how to cultivate a mindset that is conducive to an OSINT investigation and how to use the many online tools available for OSINT extraction. (On this I strongly recommend Michael Bazzell's *Open Source Intelligence Techniques* [independently published, 2019).) In this chapter, though, we will focus on some practical examples that demonstrate how OSINT can be used to support your on-chain investigations.

As cryptocurrencies are open source, it means that literally anyone can control a crypto address—provided they follow the rules laid out by the protocol and the consensus of the community. As such, attributing addresses to specific users and entities can be somewhat of a challenge.

Blockchain intelligence companies, such as TRM Labs and Chainalysis, do an excellent job of identifying addresses and attributing them to known entities and actors in the blockchain ecosystem. Although this information is incredibly invaluable, investigators' need to feel confident in being able to attribute addresses to actors and entities themselves without relying solely on these tools is vital.

The processes by which investigators attribute addresses can vary in complexity. Our goal when attributing addresses remains simple: connect on-chain data with off-chain intelligence.

Just "Search Engine" It

The first thing I do with cryptocurrency data is rather unceremonious; I simply plug my addresses of interest into a search engine to see if anything sticks. This will often indicate where you should do some further digging. For me, using a search engine is always the first, but never the only, step. You should not assume or believe that the search engine is giving you the full picture; the results should be challenged and verified.

First, a warning when using search engines. Be cautious of "search engine bias." This is when, for whatever reason, different search engines will show you different results. It may be because of the way the tool indexes particular sites, or because it is trying to be clever in showing you only what it thinks you want. So, when searching on an address of interest, limiting yourself to a single search engine could limit the amount of data you collect.

Interestingly, during one of the first child sexual abuse material (CSAM) cases I worked, we found a Bitcoin (BTC) address on the payment page of the dark web site we were investigating. The site itself was an example of a CSAM scam, supposedly selling access to a database of indecent images for a small amount of cryptocurrency, in this case around $40 worth of Bitcoin. Searching on the payment address revealed a clear web proxy of the dark web site that had been indexed by Google. Other than that, there was no additional off-chain data that connected the address to illicit activity.

The payment page on which the address appeared was a simple HTML-constructed web page. It was rather unsophisticated but contained several artifacts that would allow for further investigation (see Figure 15.2).

Notice the references to "PayLink Generator 3.0" and "CoinGate." These payment services typically work by providing a unique payment link to each site visitor to pay the desired amount of crypto. Therefore, it was highly unusual to see a static Bitcoin address displayed in this way. An analysis of the web page's source code revealed that the logos for these services were simple embedded JPEG files, rather than any hyperlinked services as you might expect.

I suspected that these logos were provided to give the appearance of legitimacy, but rather than making that assumption, it was easily challenged by reaching out to these services directly and researching their modus operandi. CoinGate confirmed that they indeed had no affiliation with this crypto address, nor do they operate in this manner. PayLink Generator also established that they do not deal in cryptocurrencies.

Considering the simple build of the web page, I wondered if there were other sites online that were built in a similar way. When I searched on specific text strings that appeared on the web page, Google revealed four new sites that were almost identical to the original site. Running the same search on Bing revealed three additional sites not indexed by Google. In total, this provided seven new and unique addresses that seemed to be connected to our suspect. Of course, Bing and Google are not the only search engines available, but these two were the ones that provided the best results in this case.

PayLink 3.0 Generator

Small girls -★★★★★ (100%)

Invoice # 71938- CoinGate Order ID # 362180547.

The link generated.

Membership-Download Login Details

http://nh7zph33i3hkuurc.onion/download/login_details_links_507821.txt

To activate the links send 0.003725 BTC to address:

16sDWLJnVj3826xTvZqzX54ChHhnkFpG71

After payment your links will be activated automatically after 1 confirmations.

waiting for your payment

Powered by COINGATE

Figure 15.2: CSAM scam payment page

From the off-chain data, it seemed apparent that these sites were connected. This assumption was challenged and then confirmed when comparing the uncovered off-chain data with the on-chain information for all these addresses. The original address, along with some of the newly discovered addresses, were all part of the same Bitcoin co-spending cluster, and all the addresses had similar sending exposure, confirming a strong connection between them all. This case is a prime example of how off-chain intelligence sheds light on the on-chain data, revealing a much clearer picture of our suspect's activity, much like the *Dirty White Trash* exhibit.

Search engines can help you to find quick wins when it comes to attributing addresses. Sometimes when searching on an address, you will find online chatter discussing your address of interest. This chatter can help you to attribute your address to a particular entity. Of course, with our ABCs of investigative mindset in mind, just because someone says it online doesn't make it true, so you will almost always have to spend time verifying any attribution you come across.

If you have read Nick's first book, or taken any of our crypto training courses, you may be familiar with Bitcoin address 3EGy678G659Rnev CA1pmfzVrrC5DEaiqAt. When searched, this address suggests a connection to the Turing Trust, a UK-based charity that provides refurbished IT equipment and educational software to students in Africa, Asia, and the UK (see Figure 15.3).

(The search phrase here uses the modifier **-block**. The dash can be understood as "not." So it is searching for the Bitcoin address but will ignore any site using the word *block*. This will remove many of the blockchain explorers from the results and hopefully help with finding the information we are looking for.) This attribution is indeed correct; however, when encountering any attribution via OSINT we should endeavor to confirm it. An early hit from Google directs us to a WordPress site from 2018 claiming that 3EGy is connected to the Turing Trust (see Figure 15.4).

Verifying this should be as simple as visiting TuringTrust.co.uk and browsing their website looking for references to donation addresses. However, if you visit their site, select How To Help and then Donate, then scroll down to Donate Crypto Currencies, you will find two crypto addresses:

```
Bitcoin: 3Eb1Gnp7ye8mu6d2KcrRr3MZfLP1mM7Hqk
ETH: 0xc4683D91a38Ac07AD15a6085B07813a15821C35f
```

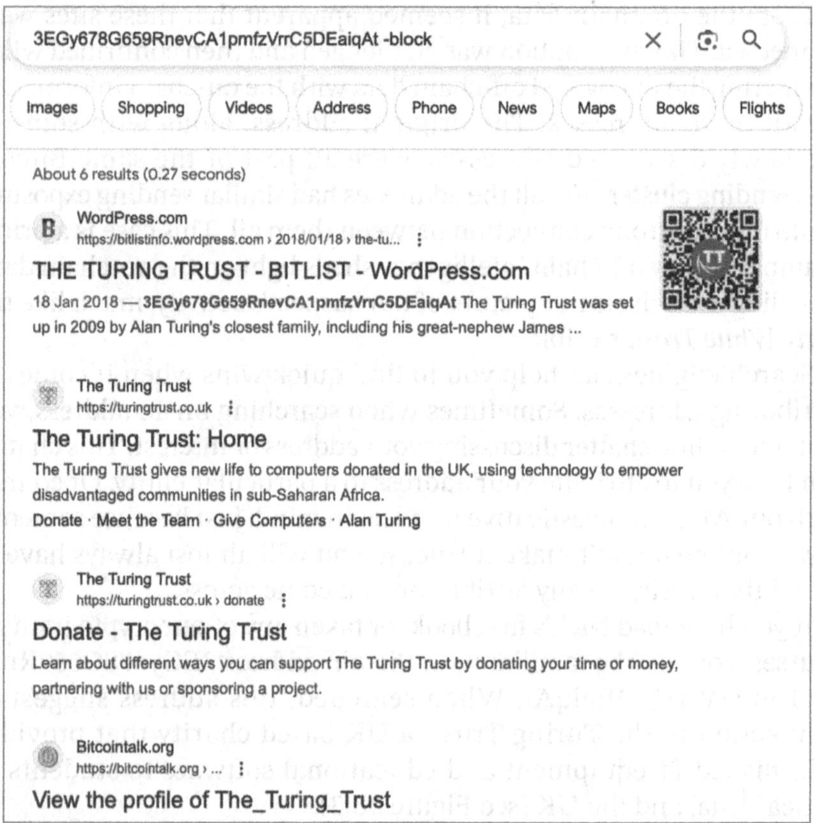

Figure 15.3: Google results for "3EGy678G659RnevCA1pmfzVrrC5DEaiqAt -block"

Neither of these addresses matches the expected 3EGy address. Why? Well, in this case it would seem apparent that the Turing Trust had previously used 3EGy6 as their donation address but now use 3Eb1G and 0xc4683. How can we combine off-chain intelligence and on-chain data to confirm this assumption while building the picture of activity?

Let's start by confirming that 3EGy was indeed used by the Turing Trust. As with all things OSINT, data regularly changes. If you do not capture or record the data that you have uncovered as you go, there is every possibility that the data will be gone the next time you look for it. Thankfully there are several online resources that you can use to find and record historical website data. The most common is the Internet Archive at `https://archive.org`. This is a site that attempts to create an archive of the Internet, backing up web pages and data for the last 26 years.

THE TURING TRUST
3EGy678G659RnevCA1pmfzVrrC5DEaiqAt
The Turing Trust was set up in 2009 by Alan Turing's closest family, including his great-nephew James Turing, in honour of his remarkable legacy. Today they are keeping Alan's legacy alive by providing quality technology and IT training to schools in sub-Saharan Africa.
turingtrust.co.uk

Figure 15.4: An older website related to the Turing Trust, which displays a Bitcoin address, `https://bitlistinfo.wordpress.com/2018/01/18/the-turing-trust`

Source: `wordpress.org` / `https://bitlistinfo.wordpress.com/2018/01/18/the-turing-trust/` / last accessed February 22, 2024.

If we use the Internet Archive's "Wayback Machine," we can look up a historical version of the Turing Trust's web page and find evidence that 3EGy was indeed used by them. To do this, consider when 3EGy was in use. Looking up this address in a blockchain explorer reveals that this address was first seen on the blockchain on April 2016 and last seen on May 2018. If this address was indeed used by the Turing Trust, you would expect it to appear on their website during this time.

Returning to the Wayback Machine, there are several saved versions of the Turing Trust's website in the archive. I have selected the snapshot from March 21, 2017. Browsing the web page from this snapshot, you can uncover the donation addresses for both Bitcoin and Litecoin used in 2017. In Figure 15.5 you can see that the Turing Trust did indeed claim that 3EGy was their donation address.

So, from digging into our initial Google search, we now know that the Turing Trust uses cryptocurrency on multiple blockchains, accepting donations from Bitcoin, Litecoin, and Ethereum. It used 3EGy for its Bitcoin donations between 2016 and 2018 and is now using 3Eb1. . .7Hqk and 0xc468. . .C35f for its donations. Can we use OSINT to further expand this understanding?

Figure 15.5: 3EGy appearing on an archived version of `turingtrust.co.uk`

Thinking back to *Dirty White Trash*, the more information we gather, the clearer the digital shadow becomes of our suspect, in this case the Turing Trust. So when did the Turing Trust begin using 3Eb1? Well, we could scour the Internet Archive to see if we can find the first time 3Eb1 appears on the site, but considering the nature of the Internet Archive, there is no guarantee we would find the day or even the month the address went live on the Turing Trust website. The best way to answer that question would be to consider the on-chain activity for 3Eb1G. . .M7Hqk.

Using a blockchain explorer, we learn that 3Eb1 was first seen on July 22, 2023, and, as of this writing, was last seen on October 23, 2023. So, what happened to the Turing Trust's crypto activity from March 2018 and July 2023?

By browsing snapshots from the Internet Archive between these dates, we can uncover two other addresses that were used for donations between March 2018 and July 2023. These addresses are 31y3Suzuew JAjxMvne1tARrtWQ46SiTypp (Bitcoin) and M8azmpVFHuQ6aTX sxk8YGkmLbxXuudCJ5t (LTC). If we were to continue examining both the on-chain and off-chain data for these addresses, we would continue to build a clearer picture of the charity's activities.

If you want a challenge, take a moment to dig into each of the Bitcoin addresses. Can you attribute them to an entity besides the Turing Trust? (Explorers like `WalletExplorer.com` can help with open source attribution.) Where did the initial address, 3EGy, send its final amounts of Bitcoin to? Can you attribute this cash-out point? What may this information indicate about the on-chain activity of the Turing Trust?

OSINT can provide you with some great attribution, especially when you dig deeper into the "trash," building that picture. It is also worth noting that when attributing addresses to entities, two things can be true at once. Take for instance, 31y3S, the address that appeared on the Turing Trust's website from 2018 to 2023. If asked who owns this address, what would you say? After working through the steps, many would confidently say the Turing Trust. This, however, is not the whole picture when it comes to attribution.

When the Turing Trust first accepted Bitcoin donations using 3EGy, this address was set up as a 2-of-3 multisignature address. Essentially this means that two out of three private keys were needed to unlock the received donations and to then send those funds on. Thus, funds were likely protected by anyone person having total control over the digital currency. Considering these funds belonged to a charity, it's understandable why they decided to do this. When funds were ultimately cashed out from the 3EGy address, the money was sent to 3JRNA2Q3Q9xsvQF FrfNPN1fh4uhqp3yD1g, an address controlled by Coinbase.

Following the cash-out of 3EGy, the Turing Trust's new address 31y3 appeared on their site. This address was not 2-of-3 multisig, which suggests a change in wallet infrastructure. When we search the new address on sites like `WalletExplorer.com`, or using commercial blockchain intelligence tools, they all have attributed 31y3 to Coinbase. Likewise, the charity's current address 3Eb1 is also controlled by Coinbase.

So, the question of attribution of 31y3 and 3Eb1 is that both the Turing Trust and Coinbase would be acceptable answers. By comparing the on-chain and off-chain information for these addresses, we are more accurately able to attribute these addresses. By posting the addresses as their donation addresses the Turing Trust has, in a sense, claimed responsibility for this address. However, the attribution of Coinbase tells us that the charity is not in control of the addresses' private keys, and hence is not responsible for any outgoing payments, relying on Coinbase to credit their account with the appropriate amounts of value.

In a criminal investigation, this dual attribution is incredibly helpful, since it allows us to accurately trace the funds of a suspect, with the accurate understanding that if we wanted to trace funds being paid from the address, we would need the support of the exchange. It also opens multiple lines of inquiry for us to investigate—the suspect itself—and of course we could request information from the exchange regarding our suspect.

In the previous examples, you have seen how OSINT can be leveraged to gather lots of individual chunks of "trash," slivers of information that, when combined, can build a clearer picture of our suspect. Most notably, OSINT can significantly impact our ability to attribute an address to an entity, illicit or otherwise. How, though, can we use off-chain information to attribute the on-chain activity of individuals rather than larger entities?

Attribution of Individuals

The whole idea behind cryptocurrencies is to give the user enhanced privacy and control over their financial activity. A person's financial activity on most blockchains, however, is only pseudonymous (pseudo-anonymous). We can trace crypto activity clearly and freely, but linking this activity back to a person is a real challenge. This pseudonymization is the reason we strive to find connections to compliant exchanges and other services that can deanonymize aspects of crypto activity linking it back to an individual or group of individuals.

Although there is no central database linking addresses to people across the cryptoverse, there are methods by which we can link an individual's on-chain activity to their off-chain online presence.

Let's start by considering ways in which we can leverage social media in this regard. First, you may be surprised by how many people post their address on social media, especially with the promise of a free NFT, a token airdrop, or even just a crypto giveaway. For example, if you search on X (Twitter), the social media formerly known as Twitter (X), for the phrase **my ETH address** you will be inundated with results where people are dropping their address in response to a chance to win an NFT or some sort of token. Simply change **ETH** for the currency of your choosing for addresses on different chains. Surprisingly, there are even a few people dropping their Monero address, seemingly working against the logic of the idea of a privacy coin. Being able to link someone's social media account to their on-chain activity is clearly a win when it comes to OSINT investigations.

Realistically, you will not begin an investigation by searching for random addresses on Twitter (X). What is likely, however, especially in an OSINT investigation, is that you come across a username or an online profile in your investigation. When conducting analysis on these accounts, what can you do if you encounter or suspect the use of crypto?

With the advent of NFTs, there are a few ways now to connect a social media profile with crypto activity. One way is via ENS names; another is to analyze the NFT in someone's profile picture. The former is by far the easiest way to uncover on-chain activity. An ENS (Ethereum Name Service) is the cryptocurrency version of a DNS. The ENS takes a human-readable string like `csitech.eth` and converts it into a machine-readable string, like a cryptocurrency address.

ENS names allow for the easy sharing of your crypto address, without having to type out the entire address or send cumbersome QR codes. You will often see ENS names that reflect someone's username or website. You can search for an ENS on Etherscan.io, where it will resolve to the relevant address. Or you can search for them directly on `app.ens.domains`. I prefer searching for them on the ENS site as it provides much more data, if available, than Etherscan does.

If you try searching for an ENS on Etherscan, you will be directed to the Domain Name Lookup page. If the ENS you have searched for is valid, you will be provided with the resolved and controller address for the ENS name. The controller is the one who controls the rights to edit the domain record, essentially the registrar. The resolved address is primary addresses resolved by the domain, essentially the address that would receive funds if you sent it to the ENS name. Try searching for **`taylor.wtf`** on Etherscan and examine the results (see Figure 15.6).

If you then click the Click To Show More button, you will be able to see the text records associated with `Taylor.wtf`. These records can be customized by the controller to store additional information if so desired. In the case of Taylor, it links us to his email, website, and Twitter (X) handle, and even a link to his Discord channel. This is an incredible amount of information as it provides us with multiple avenues of investigation for more traditional OSINT (see Figure 15.7).

Result for: taylor.wtf

Overview of ENS

Resolved Address:	0x550e970E31A45b06dF01a00b1C89A478D4d5e00A	
Controller:	0x550e970E31A45b06dF01a00b1C89A478D4d5e00A	Lookup names

+ Click to show more

Figure 15.6: `Taylor.wtf` on `Etherscan.io`

DNS Owner:	0x550e970E31A45b06dF01a00b1C89A478D4d5e00A Lookup names	
Token ID:	100684598744991014107387857008536826619213074580251939265848713875256460558892	
Text Records:	email	taylor@taylor.wtf
	url	www.taylor.wtf
	avatar	https://lh3.googleusercontent.com/grJOy9WSe3TdKfjY9azP96TqOK49E5lL4LLnqlWlkp_c7wVdJFpZ6WvoModQt9SQj1ncUc9raQlpXDHumivH6fM7HtEmaPhFOidJ=s0
	description	I create the future.
	keywords	nft, artist, nft artist, crypto art, punk, ape, deebie, cryptopunk
	com.twitter	TAYL0RWTF
	snapshot	ipns://storage.snapshot.page/registry/0x550e970E31A45b06dF01a00b1C89A478D4d5e00A/taylor.wtf
	com.discord	9EKFAQcVBb

Figure 15.7: Taylor.wtf details

In addition to this text data, `app.ens.domain` allows you to locate additional domains that resolve to a target address. By searching for Taylor's Ethereum (ETH) address on the ENS app, you will uncover additional ENS names that link to his address. These domains link Taylor to a variety of projects (my personal favorite is the JPEGLAND metaverse project.) Each of these domains potentially provides us with additional usernames and sites for us to carry out off-chain analysis upon (see Figure 15.8).

Figure 15.8: Taylor.wtf Twitter (X) page

On many occasions when digging through Discord chats, forums, Telegram, and other social media conversations, you will come across NFTs as profile pictures. Typically, this signifies ownership of the NFT, but realistically anyone can take a screenshot and use an NFT as their profile picture. If you assume that an NFT profile picture means ownership, you may be able to find additional information regarding the user, information that will hopefully allow you to challenge your assumption and verify it.

Most NFTs in a collection have specific attributes. Look at Taylor's profile on Twitter (X), `@TAYLØRWTF`. His profile picture is an NFT from the Bored Ape Yacht Club collection. It has distinct characteristics; a moustache, classic shades, and a mohawk. These attributes are not just descriptive of the image but are hard-coded into the collection, allowing you to use them to filter out and locate a specific NFT.

Consider the following NFT. This NFT is one of the most expensive NFTs ever purchased. It sold for 8,000 ETH, worth $23 million at the time of transaction. From the image alone, it is possible to locate the buyer of the NFT and the individual who currently controls it (see Figure 15.9).

Figure 15.9: CryptoPunks NFT

The first thing, and sometimes the hardest thing, you need to do is identify the collection to which the NFT belongs. Often a simple reverse image search will indicate the collection. Other times, you will need to do some digging where you encountered the NFT to identify the collection.

In this case, the NFT in question is part of the CryptoPunks collection. You can use an NFT marketplace to help locate the NFT. OpenSea.io is one of the largest NFT marketplaces available, if not the largest, and it's a good starting place to locate an NFT. If you search for the CryptoPunks collection on OpenSea, you will come across the collection page for CryptoPunks (see Figure 15.10).

From this page, you can filter on the various attributes of the NFT to locate the one of interest. This NFT has two noticeable attributes: a blue bandanna and blue skin. If you scroll through the Traits portion of the filter, you can choose from a variety of accessories. In this case, you are looking for the Bandana accessory. This narrows the collection down to 481 options. Next, if you select Type, the only one that has blue skin is the Alien option. This gives you two possible options and identifies your desired NFT as CryptoPunk #5822.

Once CryptoPunk #5822 has been selected, you can view significant on-chain information regarding this NFT's provenance. For instance, as of this writing the NFT was under the control of 0xA88F5de056eAcEf4812da3569F27C552f4B8Dc10. More significantly, you can trace its ownership back to the first sale of the NFT. Initially it was sold by "Straybits" to an unidentified address. From here it was transferred and then sold for 8000 ETH. Is it possible to use OSINT to enhance the on-chain data provided here to uncover the purchaser?

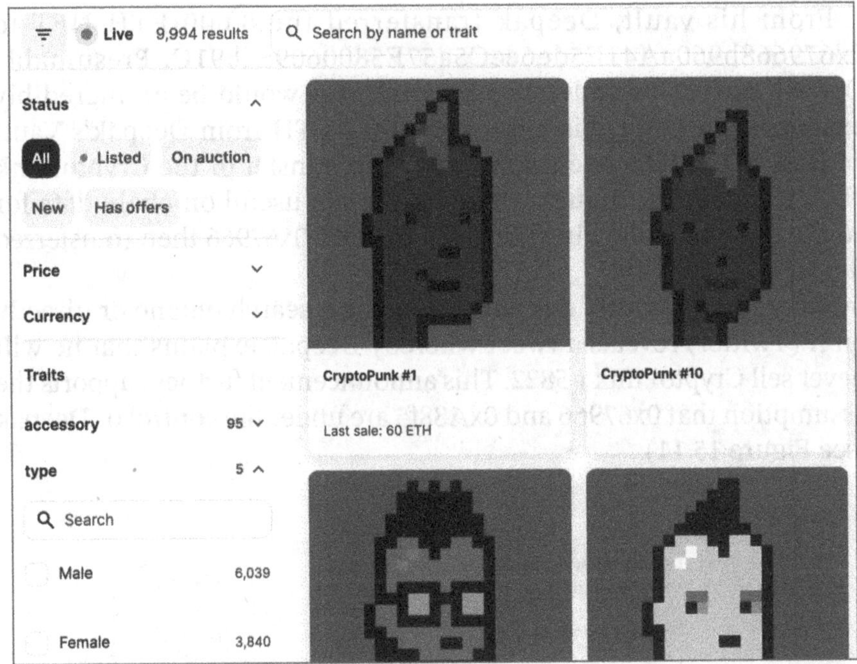

Figure 15.10: CryptoPunks OpenSea page

After the purchase of the NFT, it underwent a series of transfers until it arrived at its current destination, 0xA88F5. These were simple transfers between addresses, with no money changing hands. This pattern would tend to indicate a single owner of all these addresses. It's unlikely that someone would freely transfer such an expensive NFT to a wallet outside their control for free. What's more, you see the same addresses being reused to send and receive this NFT.

Your first clear indication of who owns this NFT comes from the ENS tagged as `vault.deepak.eth`. By comparing the on-chain activity of the NFT and its addresses with off-chain intelligence, you can establish a clearer picture of the NFT's provenance and hopefully confirm or deny your assumption.

You can start by confirming the identity of `vault.deepak.eth`. A search online indicates that this handle belongs to the former CEO of Chain, Deepak Thapliyal.

From his vault, Deepak transferred the 8,000 ETH NFT to 0x679668b960aA41E5de6eeC5a57E58006095db91C. Presumably Deepak owns this address; otherwise, this would be an incredibly expensive gift! There is a transfer of 0.3 ETH from Deepak's Vault address to 0x67966 one minute after the transfer of the CryptoPunk NFT. Besides this, though, there isn't much useful on-chain data for you to dig into. Following the same pattern, 0x67966 then transferred the NFT to 0xA88f5.

Searching for **vault.deepak.eth** using a search engine or directly on X (Twitter) reveals a tweet whereby Deepak explains that he will never sell CryptoPunk #5822. This announcement further supports the assumption that 0x67966 and 0xA88f5 are under the control of Deepak (see Figure 15.11).

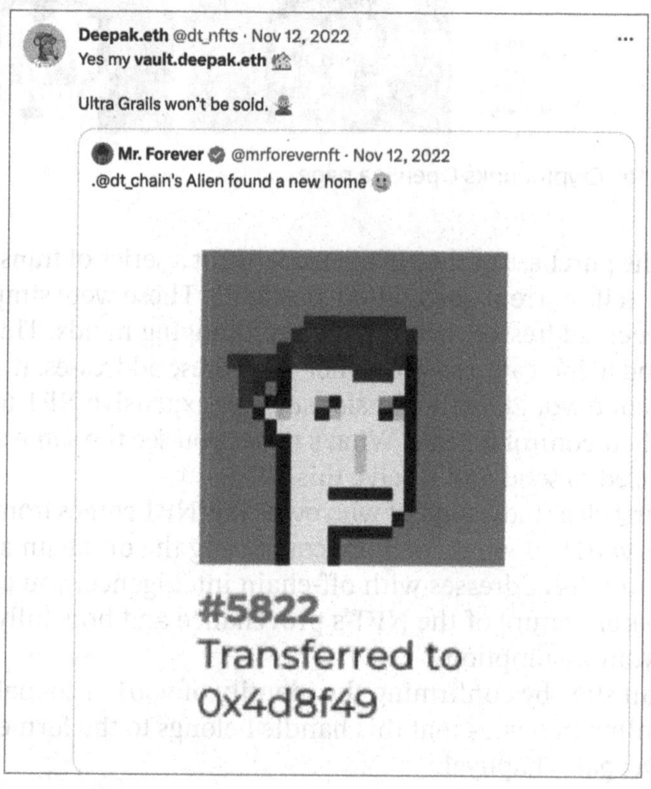

Figure 15.11: Deepak confirming ownership

This also provides you with a Twitter (X) handle for Deepak: `@dt_nfts` (previously `@dt_chain`) with the username `Deepak.eth`, which when resolved on `ens.domains` reveals further social media profiles you could analyze, including a link to his Telegram channel. Notice that under the "subnames" record for `Deepak.eth` you find an entry for the vault ENS, confirming the off-chain connection between these addressees.

From a single NFT, you now have three addresses that are under the control of Deepak. What about the addresses that also held the NFT after the record-breaking sale? Starting with the actual sale on OpenSea, you see that the NFT was sent to "8483383," which is the OpenSea username for the profile belonging to 0x69c488Bcda156379B 6661f08A35dB627E5D467Dd. This profile page has a link to the X (Twitter) user `@dt_chain`, which was Deepak's previous Twitter (X) handle. In addition to this, there are several references to Deepak and Chain in 0x69c4's NFT collection. What's more, 0x69c4 resolves to several ENS domains on `ens.domain`, further indicating the connection to Deepak, as well as some new lines of inquiry for additional OSINT (see Figure 15.12).

From here, the NFT was transferred to a new address, 0x7DDFFb c38121a7b21AA4B0bc96318E86EF2D0cb7. There is little to no off-chain information regarding this address, but there are some on-chain connections that indicate Deepak's ownership. For instance, the first payment into 0x7DDFF came from Deepak's 0x69c4 address for a meme value of 420.69 ETH. From here 0x7DDFF sent additional NFTs back to 0x69c4 as well as 419ETH and ultimately the original #5822 NFT.

There were then several transfers of the NFT back and forth between addresses. Little to no off-chain data exists for these addresses, but on-chain data reveals multiple payments of crypto between these addresses, in addition to the actual NFT transfers.

When you dig through these transfers and their subsequent address, an address of particular interest stands out: 0x685ACAC8CffCD 235255BFFb25982B96e066E2370, which received 40 million DAI (DAI is a stablecoin whose value is kept as close to one US dollar as possible) from an address tagged as "`tgl.eth`." It is unclear who this ENS belongs too, but it's interesting that `tgl.eth` also owns the ENS `tomgriffinlove.eth`. Both addresses, `tgl.eth` and 0x685A (possibly Deepak's), have on-chain connections to `FTX.com` and Alameda.

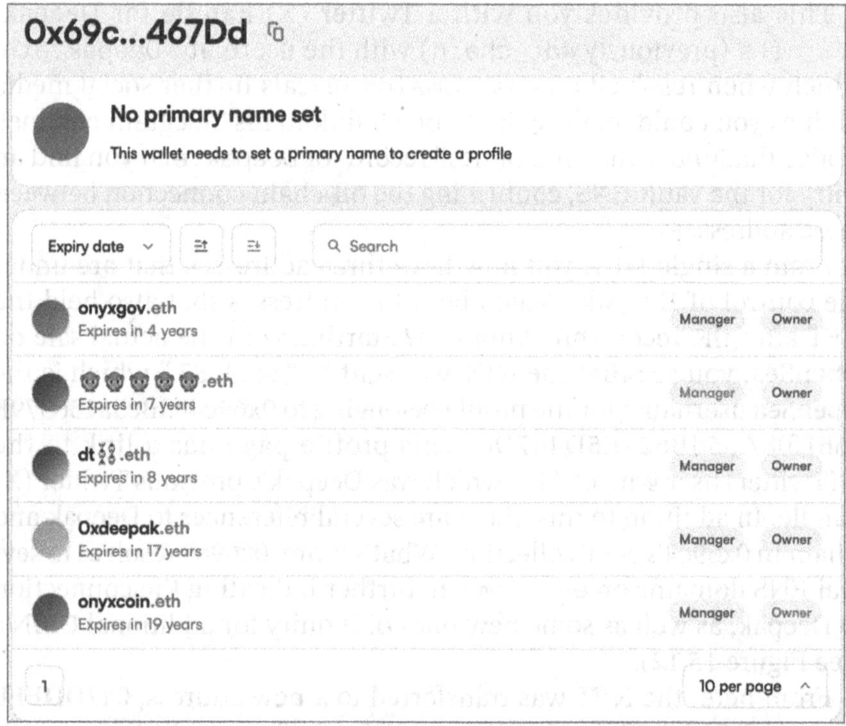

Figure 15.12: Connection between Deepak and 0x69c48

Researching this connection leads to several articles stating that "FTX contagion victim Deepak.eth puts NFT collection up for sale," linking to a series of now deleted tweets by Deepak during November 2022. Perhaps the transfer of such a large volume of funds is indicative of the on-chain connections to FTX and Alameda.

In any case, the multiple transfers of CryptoPunk #5822 allow you to interrogate several lines of both on-chain and off-chain information. These lines of inquiry help clarify the provenance of the NFT as well as establish multiple addresses owned by Deepak. It's these connections that can aid your investigations significantly; the more addresses you can uncover and connect to your suspect, the more likely it is that you will be able to find on-chain connections to virtual asset service providers (VASPs) that may be able to provide you with closed source but vital real-world information regarding your suspect.

NFT Metadata

NFT images are rarely if ever stored on the blockchain. Instead, a tokenization of the image is stored on the blockchain. The images and metadata of the NFTs are often stored off-chain. Depending on how the NFT collection is created, it may therefore be possible to locate the website, server, or service where the original NFT image is located. From an OSINT perspective, if you are dealing with fraudulent NFTs you may be able to uncover additional resources that can be tapped for OSINT.

When you're trying to identify the hosting location of NFTs in a collection, the best thing to do is view the NFT contract directly. As mentioned, different projects store NFTs differently. Some host each individual NFTs on the projects web page, others use the InterPlanetary File System (IPFS) or Arweave, and some host it on file sharing services like Google or Amazon.

Reading the contract of an NFT can reveal much about the collection and its creators and/or owners. When locating the hosting point for the NFT image and/or metadata the string "tokenURI" will be valuable in uncovering additional information. Consider the example of an NFT that immortalized some Islamic State news on the blockchain via a blockchain-enabled social media.

In this example, we will begin by interrogating an NFT contract via `PolygonScan.org`, which will lead us to where the NFT's metadata is hosted. The NFT contract address is 0x017A1653c0cB7B561c50717336c1F7fd912ed310 on the polygon blockchain.

Using `PolygonScan.org` we can look up the contract address for the "posts (POST)" token. Then, we can navigate to contract "tokenURI" on the Contract ➤ Read Contract tab. Next, enter the tokenID **149033** and notice that the URL that is returned points to Arweave, a decentralized, permanent network for data (see Figure 15.13 and Figure 15.14).

This is the location on the Arweave network where the metadata for the NFT is stored. This data then provides us with additional on- and off-chain intelligence, which we can then analyze (see Figure 15.15).

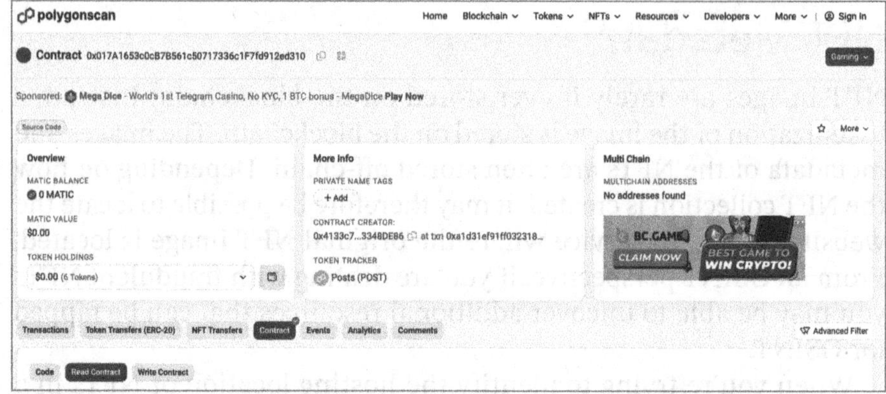

Figure 15.13: 0x017A1653c0cB7B561c50717336c1F7fd912ed310 contract page

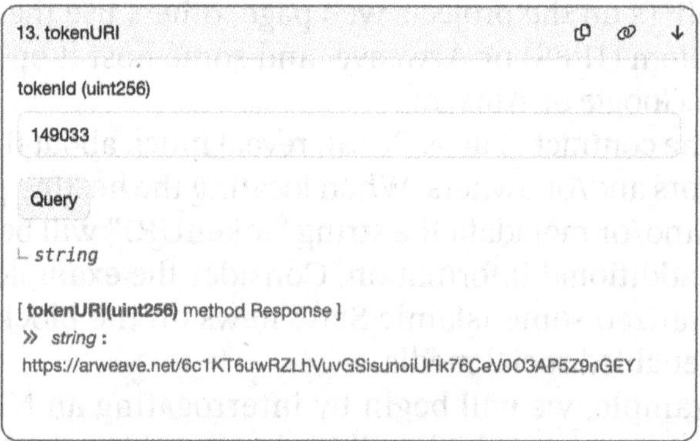

Figure 15.14: 0x017A1 tokenURI -`https://arweave.net/6c1KT6uwRZLhVuvGSisunoiUHk76CeV0O3AP5Z9nGEY`


```
{"name":"IS-NEWS #01","description":"![]
(https://ipfs.io/ipfs/QmbtNgoktsS3isjEcDnEepTRbzanssDZ4NBpDjewMp3f1V)\n\n\n
\nKhorasan Province\n\nBy the grace of Allah Almighty, the soldiers of the
Caliphate detonated an explosive device on a vehicle of the apostate
Taliban militia, in the (Khugyani) area in (Nanjarhar), which led to its
damage and the wounding of 4 members in it, and praise be to
Allah.","external_url":"https://beta.cent.co/+o50neb","image":"https://ipfs
.io/ipfs/QmcCuQoc3VpH1DMYDj4TQv6XbxbKcTJwCQAVsLP1kZx41P","metadata":
{"postTime":"2022-08-26
08:56:16","postID":149033,"userName":"YEC","userID":120122,"channelName":"I
slamicStateNews","channelID":4828,"message":"# IS-NEWS #01\n\n![]
(https://s3.amazonaws.com/cent-img-prod/29aa245d-f6f6-4e00-b863-
b4abefce754f.jpeg)\n\n\n\nKhorasan Province\n\nBy the grace of Allah
Almighty, the soldiers of the Caliphate detonated an explosive device on a
vehicle of the apostate Taliban militia, in the (Khugyani) area in
(Nanjarhar), which led to its damage and the wounding of 4 members in it,
and praise be to
Allah.","signer":"0x5d205a74094E7D979b73B065ca8DC33d5326f599","signature":"
0x08bd276870684d796dc67dcee335eef5ad0315493d4286cfc3b2dc70a753b660295208399
44654caf8f1021e59543a37a02770f4aa79c590e26a0919bd994ecb1c"}}
```


Figure 15.15: NFT metadata on Arweave

In this example, information pertaining to where the NFT was posted can be found. References are made to the IPFS, along with a social media called `beta.cent.co` and a more traditional reference to the Amazon Cloud. Each of these locations at one time hosted the image of the NFT. It has since been removed from the IPFS and `cent.co` but, as of this writing, is currently available to view using the Amazon AWS link (see Figure 15.16).

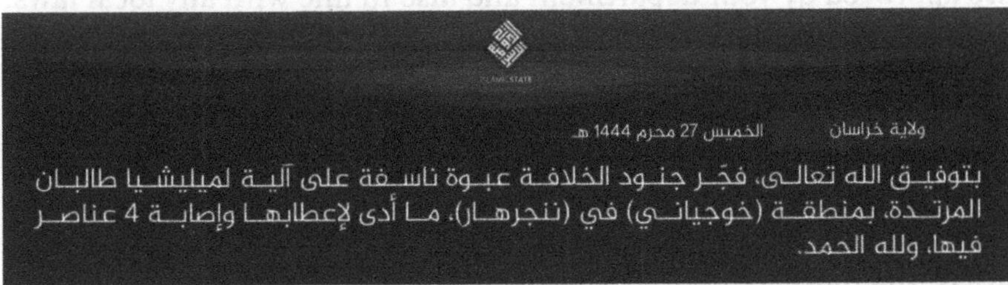

ولاية خراسان
الخميس 27 محرم 1444 هـ
بتوفيق الله تعالى، فجّر جنود الخلافة عبوة ناسفة على آلية لميليشيا طالبان المرتدة، بمنطقة (خوجياني) في (ننجرهار). ما أدى لإعطابها وإصابة 4 عناصر فيها، ولله الحمد.

Figure 15.16: ISIS NFT

Also, of note within the NFT data is the date that the image was posted on `cent.co`, along with the username and ID. Interestingly, the post time on `cent.co`, according to the NFT metadata, was August 26, a day after the timestamp found on the NFT, which corresponds to August 25 when converted from the Islamic calendar to Georgian. In addition to the off-chain data, there is the important on-chain intelligence of the "signer" address. This is the address of the individual who minted the NFT originally. When researching this address, you will find another two NFTs minted by this user with no other on-chain activity. (Although the OSINT trail goes somewhat cold in this example, you may wish to challenge yourself by attempting to identify the individual who created the POST token and identify how they connect to the founders of Cent.)

Each NFT you encounter in an investigation will, of course, be different from the ones mentioned here, using different methodologies to host and store the NFTs and their corresponding data. Regardless, looking into the contract and finding the hosting location, among other things, can lead to some significant off-chain data points.

OSINT and the Dark Web

No section on OSINT would be complete without commenting on how to access data from other sources besides the clear web. The regular

Internet, also known as the clear net or the surface web, will be where most OSINT investigators spend most of their time. But when working cryptocurrency cases, significant evidence can be found on networks other than the clear web. The most notable network is known as the dark web. Using the dark web in an investigation is fraught with complications and dangers, so we will not discuss it at length in this book. I recommend getting commercial training and defining processes that are approved by your department and also in line with any local laws.

Accessing the dark web isn't as hard as it sounds. It's only called the dark web due to the nature of much of the material contained on it, such as criminal services, child sexual abuse material, and extremist material. It's just a different network from the main Internet and needs a different type of connection software to access it. All you need is specialized software to access the specific network on which the dark web exists; the most common is Tor Browser. Tor Browser connects to The Onion Routing network, which allows for connection to sites with the .onion extension. Simply installing this software from the Tor Project will allow you to browse the dark web.

Before accessing and diving into the dark web, address any operational security concerns. Malware and cybersecurity risks abound, as does the possibility of leaking your own personal information or data about your investigation. A quick way of protecting yourself would be to access Tor using a VPN to protect your originating IP address (Tor is slow at the best of times, so don't expect fast browsing) and/or using a virtual machine to silo your data and protect it from any potential malware.

When searching for data on the dark web, do not expect to find results as easily as you might on the clear web using Bing or Google, as they do not index the dark web. Data on the dark web is much more volatile than data on the clear web. Sites regularly go down due to hosting issues, and so data that is indexed today may be gone tomorrow. Likewise, if a site is not up when a Tor-based search engine like Ahmia .fi or Torch indexes it, that data cannot be captured.

There are services that spider and index the dark web constantly, but often these tools charge a huge premium, which makes it unfeasible for individuals or even small teams of investigators to use. A particularly useful and free tool is a daily dark web report from `Hunch.ly`. This daily report provides a list of online, offline, and new hidden services.

This is an excellent way to keep track of target sites and identify potential investigative opportunities.

Even though searching functionality is limited on the dark web, it is still worth trying. In my experience, Ahmia.fi has a decent indexed database and works better than most. It also has an .onion mirror so it can be used from Tor. Neither of these sites contains NSFW or illegal advertisements, which makes it a more pleasant experience than most dark web search tools.

However, when searching on Ahmia or any dark web site, take extreme care. Typically you are only ever one click away from viewing illegal material. Try using a dark web search engine search on Ahmia for the phrase **Mixer**, and you will be inundated with cryptocurrency mixers, almost all of which are scams themselves. Or try searching for **1TorjL4GNKvGynZhvtJ1EXkaqVN26pc1B**—as of this writing, only one person has fallen victim to this mixer scam that this address relates to.

Summary

Rather than focusing on the plethora of tools and techniques that can be used to gather OSINT, this chapter has demonstrated examples of how you can apply an investigative mindset. Although knowledge of OSINT tools and techniques is important, of far more value is the ability to think critically on the data, challenge all assumptions or beliefs, and connect your off-chain data with any on-chain information you encounter. This way, you will not simply be building a pile of digital data or "trash"—you will be building a clear picture of your suspect's digital activity.

The primary benefit of connecting on-chain data with off-chain intelligence is enhanced attribution of individuals and their cryptocurrency holdings and activity. From a simple Google search to an analysis of an individual's NFT profile picture, off-chain information can help you better understand someone's on-chain activity. The example of CSAM scams demonstrated how on-chain and off-chain data can be used to confirm a relationship across multiple scam sites, all from the power of multiple search engines. In the case of the Turing Trust, we went from a single address to building an understanding of their entire cryptocurrency activity over the past several years. Applying this knowledge to a real-world investigation is invaluable. Using NFTs not only to identify social media accounts for crypto enthusiasts but also to connect their usernames to their financial assets is a great way of attributing individuals to crypto activity. And in the case of NFT collections, where scams and fraud are everywhere, locating and identifying the hosting points of NFTs can lead to significant real-world information.

16 Using Wallets for Investigations

In this chapter, we will consider an area of blockchain investigations that is often overlooked. In the past few chapters, you have learned how to track and trace funds on the blockchain. But that process can only begin once you have located crypto addresses during a premises or computer search, as you saw in Chapter 8, "The Importance of Discovery," or perhaps from a suspicious activity report (SAR). Once you have a target address, you can start looking at the inputs and outputs and begin to build a picture of the activity of that address over time. When looking at Bitcoin type blockchains, you may be able to use clustering techniques, as discussed in Chapter 10, "Bitcoin: Investigation Methodology," to locate other addresses as well as trace their activity.

However, there is a way by which you can circumvent all that hard work and be able to learn exactly what addresses a suspect used and see all the timed and dated transactions in and out of that address. How? Simply by re-creating the user's wallet in some appropriate wallet software. So often the reason for re-creating a user's wallet is purely to be able to seize any assets still held in a suspect address, as you will see in a lot more detail in the next chapter. However, if you can successfully re-create a wallet, you can learn much more, even if all the funds have already been spent.

Much of what we will cover in the next few pages relates directly to Chapter 17, "Crypto Seizure," so don't skip this chapter thinking that the next chapter will be more interesting!

Understanding Cryptocurrency Wallets

Before delving into the forensic process, it is important to understand what a cryptocurrency wallet is and how it functions. As you learned earlier in the book, a cryptocurrency wallet does not store any crypto coins. Instead, it securely holds cryptographic keys—public and private keys—that allow users to receive and spend the cryptocurrency associated with those keys. Wallets are often software-based, sometimes stand-alone programs or often an Internet browser extension. There are also hardware-based wallets, as we covered in Chapter 8, "The Importance of Discovery"; paper-based wallets with a series of seed words; or a hexadecimal string written on paper.

Seed Words and Wallet Recovery

One of the most critical components of a cryptocurrency hierarchical deterministic wallet is its recovery phrase, commonly known as *seed words*. This is usually a series of 12–24 words generated by the wallet software during the initial setup. The seed words (also known as a mnemonic phrase) are essentially a human-readable form of the wallet's private keys and are used to regenerate the keys if the wallet is lost or damaged. If you have the seed words, you may be able to re-create the wallet. When I teach this to a room of investigators, some find that it is a little counterintuitive that you are able to re-create a wallet that already exists elsewhere. To help with that concept, I often get all the students in the room to re-create a wallet from a series of seed words so that everyone ends up with the same wallet. I often drop a little crypto in the wallet and have a race to see who can "seize" it first. In some ways, it is no different from my wife and I both being able to access the same bank account simultaneously.

Step-by-Step Guide to HD Wallet Re-creation

Re-creating a wallet can range from extremely simple to highly complex. Let's start with a basic review of the process and then build from there.

1. Obtaining the Seed Phrase In an investigative context, the seed phrase may come from physical evidence (e.g., a written note), digital evidence (e.g., a text file stored on a computer), or through legal means such as court orders to surrender such information during an investigation.

2. Using a Standard Wallet Application Once the seed phrase is obtained, the next step is to input these words into a reputable and secure wallet application that supports the type of cryptocurrency involved in the investigation. It is crucial to use software that adheres to industry standards, such as those that comply with the Bitcoin or Ethereum protocols, for example, which outline how mnemonic phrases are converted into a binary seed. This involves something called a *derivation path*—more on that soon.

3. Re-creating the Wallet After we enter the seed phrase, the wallet software will regenerate the master private key, which in turn may generate every key ever created by the original wallet. This includes both current and past addresses, allowing investigators to track the flow of funds in and out of these addresses. The last two sentences are accurate in a simplistic sense, but you'll see that when we apply derivation paths things get a little more complicated.

What Can Be Seen?

Once access to a wallet is established, several types of data can be accessed that can be very useful during an investigation:

Transaction History Every transaction made with the wallet's addresses, including date, amount, and the corresponding transaction hash. It cannot be overstated how useful transaction history is, as we have all the users' transactions in one place from all the addresses they had generated in that wallet.

Balance The current balance of all cryptocurrencies contained in the wallet. Even though a wallet's balance may be zero, we are often able to see the wallet balance as it increased and decreased over time. This can be useful when associated with timestamps and when we're creating timelines of transactions.

Receiving and Sending Addresses Lists of incoming and outgoing addresses associated with transactions.

Timestamps Exact times when transactions were recorded on the blockchain, which can be crucial in establishing timelines for legal cases.

Let's look at a simple example. (Thanks to my good friend Matt "Billy" Humphries for the examples in this chapter.) I'm going to use the Electrum wallet, which you can download from `https://electrum.org`. It's available for most operating systems and is simple to install and use. I won't talk you through the installation process, as I would expect a reader of this book to be able to install a program on their operating system of choice.

Once Electrum is installed, select the Standard Wallet and the I Already Have A Seed options on the appropriate screens. (If you already have Electrum installed, then just choose File ➢ New/Restore from the menu.) When the Create/Restore Wallet screen appears, enter the following in the text box (see Figure 16.1):

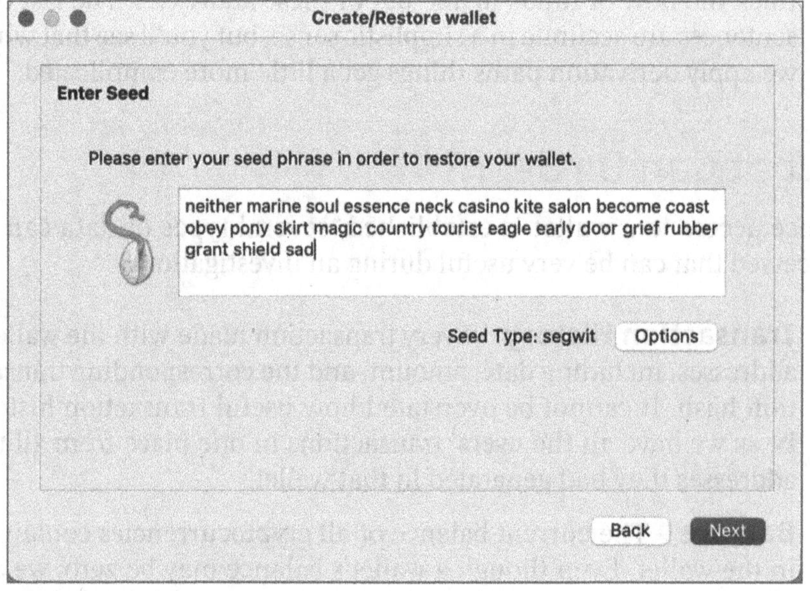

Figure 16.1: Entering seed words

> *neither marine soul essence neck casino kite salon become coast obey pony skirt magic country tourist eagle early door grief rubber grant shield sad*

Note that there is an options box that lets you specify the seed type. It defaults to *segwit* and uses the Electrum protocol. It's important for investigators to understand that at this point the Electrum protocol is being used because the software has recognized that the 24 words adhere to the Electrum format. This simply means that this seed phrase was generated to comply with the Electrum format. Although all these words appear in the BIP39 wordlist, this unique seed phrase would be deemed invalid by BIP39 standards because it does not meet the checksum requirements. To test this, change the last word, *Sad*, to *Saddle*, and you will notice that the Electrum format is no longer available. If you click the Options button, you will see that Electrum has the ability to create a wallet using Electrum or the BIP39 or SLIP39 seed types. If you are playing along with this, just leave it on Electrum. Then click Next (see Figure 16.2).

Figure 16.2: Seed Options

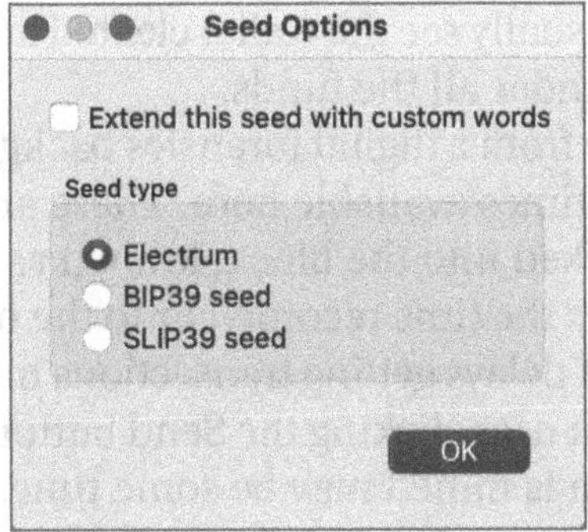

The seed words using the Electrum seed type generate a wallet with some historical transactions. You can see them in Figure 16.3.

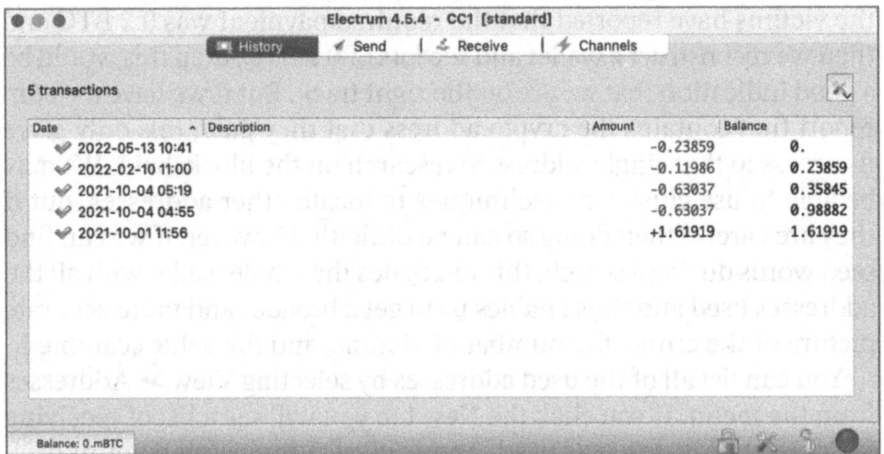

Figure 16.3: Transaction history

Once the wallet is generated, you can see in the wallet a history of five transactions from 2021 and 2022. There is just one inbound transaction, providing a balance of 1.6 Bitcoin and also four outbound transactions resulting in an empty wallet. Even though there are no funds to seize from this suspect, this is still useful information for an investigator as you can immediately see the "life" of this wallet from its first use to when it was emptied. I use the word *emptied* very specifically as a payment for a particular chosen amount from a wallet, with accompanying fees that are hard to precalculate and that will almost certainly result in some change returning to the wallet. However, when you see a zero balance, this will almost certainly be the result of a decision by the user to clear the wallet. When you are investigating scams and the like, you will usually see the wallet cleared at the end of the scam period in order to launder all the funds.

If you come from a digital forensics background, you will appreciate the dates and times available here. These are the times that the transaction was locked into the block, known as the *block time* for obvious reasons. This is the time recorded onto the blockchain. Just remember that because of delays getting transactions mined, especially on Bitcoin, the time from a user clicking the Send button in their wallet to the time the transaction is mined may be some time. In the past, when Bitcoin has been very busy it was not unusual to see many hours pass before a transaction was confirmed.

Obviously, the History tab also provides values that again can be useful to reveal patterns and explain the extent and likely value of a crime. As a simple example, if we are investigating a ransomware attack and the victims have reported that the required payment was 0.2 BTC and then we reconstruct a wallet and see lots of 0.2 BTC, then this would be a good indication that we are on the right track. But if we have a victim report that contains the crypto address that they paid, this only gives us access to that single address to research on the blockchain. We may be able to use clustering techniques to locate other addresses, but if they are careful then doing so can be difficult. However, if we can find seed words during a search, this re-creates the whole wallet with all the addresses used and thus enables us to get a broader and more accurate picture of the crime, the number of victims, and the value scammed.

You can list all of the used addresses by selecting View ➢ Addresses from the menu. If you click the New tab you will see a list of receiving addresses; only one was used, and it gives a transaction count of 4.

If you scroll down, you will see the change addresses; just one has been used a total of twice (see Figure 16.4 and Figure 16.5).

Type	Address	Label	Balance	Tx
receiving	bc1qknf7yeyw6ftnyt7rsy0wfajqre4svqnwe0ren0		0.	4
receiving	bc1qqjgfldcn32e38yrdtzzqs7yxnela358dh207p0		0.	0
receiving	bc1qd9vxn05mgqek0xjttdxxtfv7246g7jsjxezlft		0.	0

Figure 16.4: Receiving addresses

change	bc1q6x807n9sd9ysptglpduhpjj24gtdjka9s73nqu	0.	2
change	bc1qvyceypnxcst2clhed4a9t38yhjf0t4ptv4apag	0.	0
change	bc1qc59k7uvz2ss5f4z2mxr36fx7v8uygflnrxpczz	0.	0

Figure 16.5: Change addresses

If other addresses had been used by a suspect in this wallet, then you would see them listed here along with the amount of transactions that the address had been involved in. This would enable you to extend your investigation and give you more onward tracing paths.

Return to the History tab. If you double-click one of the transactions—for example, the second to last on February 10 at 11 a.m. UTC—you see movement of funds from their address bc1qknf7 to bc1qufz. This screen also identifies the change address bc1q6x80, which is in yellow if you are looking at a screen (see Figure 16.6).

Inputs (1)

703454x817x1	bc1qknf7yeyw6ftnyt7rsy0wfajqre4svqnwe0ren0	0.35845

Outputs (2) ■ = Wallet Address ■ = Change Address

722614x2564x0	bc1qufzeywdltd4fyevfkl2gnknkfx0uslx7nyz6l4	0.11326
722614x2564x1	bc1q6x807n9sd9ysptglpduhpjj24gtdjka9s73nqu	0.23859

Figure 16.6: Transaction screen

Again, this is very useful as we do not have to guess, even intelligently guess, at the change address and so we can trace the funds onward with confidence.

The Benefits of Wallet Re-creation in Investigations

When we find seed words that we can directly attribute to a suspect and then re-create a wallet, we know that we are tracing funds that are definitely owned by the suspect rather than looking for other evidence of ownership. Sometimes we may find an address that would appear to be owned by a person of interest, but it's only when we trace funds to an exchange and are able to request and receive KYC information that we get a definitive identification of ownership. However, when we find seed words that are being hidden in the suspect's personal safe, or in encrypted files, or related to a hardware device only they have access to, we then have a definite identification before we begin. I've seen this investigative step missed on a number of occasions when investigators assume that the only reason to re-create a wallet is for asset seizure. On an investigation two years ago, the officer I was assisting with seizure of crypto was disappointed that the wallet we re-created was empty and there was "nothing we could learn." In reality, we now knew all the suspect's addresses from this wallet and there was a huge amount to be learned, even though there were no funds to seize.

Let's take a brief look at some of the benefits of wallet investigations:

- **Financial Tracking and Asset Recovery:** By re-creating the wallet, investigators can trace the origins of funds and follow their movement across the blockchain, potentially leading to the identification of criminal activities such as money laundering or fraud. This can also play a critical role in asset recovery, enabling law enforcement to locate and seize illicit or stolen funds.
- **Evidence Gathering:** Re-created wallets provide concrete evidence that can be used in court to prove ownership of the wallet and establish connections between individuals and criminal activities. This evidence is immutable and highly reliable due to the nature of blockchain technology.
- **Timeline Reconstruction:** Investigators can reconstruct the timeline of a suspect's crypto transactions to create a detailed profile of their financial behavior over time. This can be instrumental in identifying co-conspirators, proving or disproving alibis, and understanding the financial motives behind criminal activities.

- **Enhancing Investigative Techniques:** The ability to access and analyze detailed transactional data in cryptocurrency wallets equips investigators with deeper insights into the digital financial dealings of suspects, improving overall investigative strategies and outcomes.

Understanding Derivation Paths in Cryptocurrency Wallets

Almost all modern crypto-wallets are hierarchical deterministic (HD) in nature. These wallets play a crucial role due to their ability to generate a structured tree of keys from a single seed. If you can imagine a tree with many branches carrying their own fruit but all stemming from the same trunk, you can go some way to picturing the concept of derivation paths, which all come from one seed but have their own addresses and crypto assets. If you set up a wallet with the wrong derivation path, you may find yourself on the wrong branch where there are no assets, and conclude that there is nothing to find. However, other derivation paths may have assets. This section explores the concept of derivation paths, contrasts the typical paths used for Bitcoin and Ethereum, and provides detailed guidance on how to adjust derivation paths in software wallets.

The Importance of Understanding Derivation Paths for Investigators

For investigators dealing with crypto investigations or seizure, understanding derivation paths is crucial. This knowledge plays a vital role in successfully re-creating suspect wallets, which is a key step in locating, tracing, and seizing all associated cryptocurrency assets.

Each derivation path can lead to numerous addresses under which assets or historical transactions might be available. If an investigator understands the structure and significance of these paths, they can ensure that no illicit funds are missed. For instance, a suspect might use multiple accounts (denoted by different account numbers in the derivation path) to segregate funds from different sources or activities. Recognizing and following these paths allows investigators to access and evaluate all associated accounts, not just the primary one.

To reiterate, each path potentially represents unique transactions and balances. By inputting the seed phrase and using the same derivation path that the suspect used, investigators can restore the wallet in its entirety, exactly as the suspect maintained it.

Avoiding Oversight and Ensuring Legal Admissibility

Overlooking funds stored under different derivation paths could not only lead to incomplete asset recovery but might also affect the outcome of any criminal case due to incomplete evidence. It is also vital that an investigator demonstrate a thorough understanding of these technical aspects in court, which can then help establish the credibility of the evidence and potentially of the investigator as well.

Given the technical complexity associated with derivation paths and HD wallets, ongoing training for investigators is vital. Such education ensures that law enforcement is kept up to date with the latest in cryptocurrency technologies and wallet structures. If you do not consider yourself to be particularly technical, then collaboration with digital forensic experts who specialize in cryptocurrency recovery will be vital.

The Concept of a Derivation Path

Derivation paths are a fundamental component of HD wallets, which adhere to the BIP32/BIP44 Bitcoin Improvement Proposals. As described, these paths allow for the deterministic generation of cryptocurrency addresses from a single seed phrase. A derivation path defines a direct route to a particular address within the hierarchical tree of keys, ensuring that each address can be regenerated if the wallet is recovered from the seed.

Derivation paths follow a structured notation that outlines the journey from the master seed to the specific child key:

m / purpose / coin_type / account / change / address_index

- **m:** Refers to the master seed from which all keys are derived.
- **purpose**: Often set to 44 in accordance with BIP44, which dictates the structure of the derivation path.

- **coin_type:** A constant that specifies the cryptocurrency type, ensuring that each coin has a unique derivation path to prevent cross-coin key usage.
- **account:** Allows for multiple account derivations under the same seed, enabling users to have separate accounts for the same cryptocurrency.
- **change:** Differentiates between external addresses (0) used for receiving funds and internal change addresses (1) used for transaction change.
- **address_index:** Specifies the index number of the key within the category of external or change addresses.

This technically is BIP44 notation, not purely BIP32. However, it builds upon the BIP32 standard by adding specific levels of hierarchy for multi-account and multi-coin support. The basic BIP32 path notation is:

m: The master node (root key)

m/0: The first child of the master node

m/0/0: The first grandchild of the master node, and so on.

BIP32 provides the fundamental structure for HD wallets, whereas BIP44 defines a specific path format for different types of cryptocurrencies and accounts.

For example, the BIP39 seed *aerobic chef vault finish lonely champion child victory umbrella fish amazing jelly* will produce different addresses based on the two different protocols:

m/44/0/0/0/0 1H2es9g7eJopS9CBMcJFyctReQTq7JyxTW

m/0/0 1J9MN6iXnP1TKt71T5WQzCwrGa67zgZTwq

Bitcoin vs. Ethereum Derivation Paths

The standard derivation path for Bitcoin wallets is m/44/0/0/0/0. This path is based on the BIP44 proposal and breaks down as follows:

- **44:** Adheres to the BIP44 purpose.
- **0:** Coin type for Bitcoin.
- **0:** The first account.

- **0:** External chain for receiving Bitcoin.
- **0:** The first address in this external chain.

For Ethereum, wallets typically use the path m/44/60/0/0/0, which also follows the BIP44 standard but with adjustments appropriate for Ethereum:

- **44:** BIP44 purpose.
- **60:** Coin type for Ethereum, differentiating it from other cryptocurrencies.
- The remaining structure mirrors that of Bitcoin, accommodating Ethereum's unique requirements within the same framework.

The critical difference between Bitcoin and Ethereum derivation paths lies in the coin_type segment, which ensures that addresses for each cryptocurrency are uniquely derived without overlap, enhancing security and organizational clarity.

Investigators often ask why the Ethereum structure includes the change placeholder when Ethereum does not use a change address. The reason Ethereum adopts BIP44 is to ensure compatibility across various wallet implementations, making it easier to switch between wallets and recover addresses using the same seed phrase. In addition, this allows for flexibility in the case of any future use cases where that placeholder position might be beneficial.

Changing Derivation Paths in Software Wallets

Adjusting the derivation path when setting up a recovered wallet from seed words can be vital for an investigator to find assets, or the history of assets, they may not have been aware of. You can often do the following:

1. **Access Wallet Settings.** When setting up a new wallet or when adjusting an existing wallet, most advanced software wallets have an option in their Settings menu to configure derivation paths. This option is typically found under Advanced Settings, Options, or similar.

2. **Input the Custom Derivation Path.** Once in the settings, you can input a new derivation path. It's crucial to use the correct

notation to avoid errors in address generation. Some tools such as Electrum have a tool for scanning paths to try and find assets.

3. Save and Implement Changes. After configuring the new path, save the changes. The wallet will use this new path, accessing any assets or history of assets on that path.

If you return to the wallet you re-created earlier, you are able to see the derivation paths of any of the addresses. If you double-click one of the receiving addresses, perhaps the one that has been used four times, you will see a list of transactions that this address was involved with but also the derivation path of the address. Here it is set to the standard derivation path of m/0/0. Try double-clicking the change address that was used; what is its derivation path? It's m/1/0, with the 1 indicating that it is reserved for change.

Figure 16.7 shows setting a custom derivation path using wallet software. Recovering assets from this wallet would be highly unlikely unless you were aware of this custom derivation path.

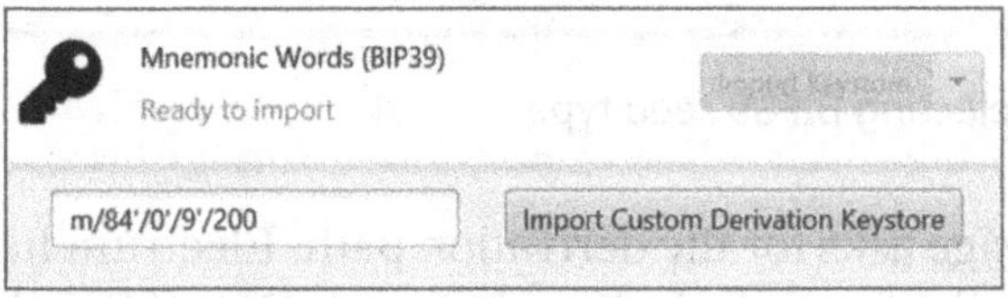

Figure 16.7: Adding a custom mnemonic

Let's take a look at another example. Using Electrum, set up a wallet almost as you did before, choosing Standard Wallet and I Already Have A Seed. Use the following seed words:

subway total push please correct page mesh top human brother bitter float

Feel free to play with this and see if you can find any assets. Once you are done, continue reading.

When you enter the seed words, if you click Next using the standard Electrum settings and derivation path, the Next button will not even be available. However, on the seed word page, if you click the Options button you can select BIP39 and the Next button will appear.

This is because this is not recognized as an Electrum string, but it is a BIP39 string (see Figure 16.8).

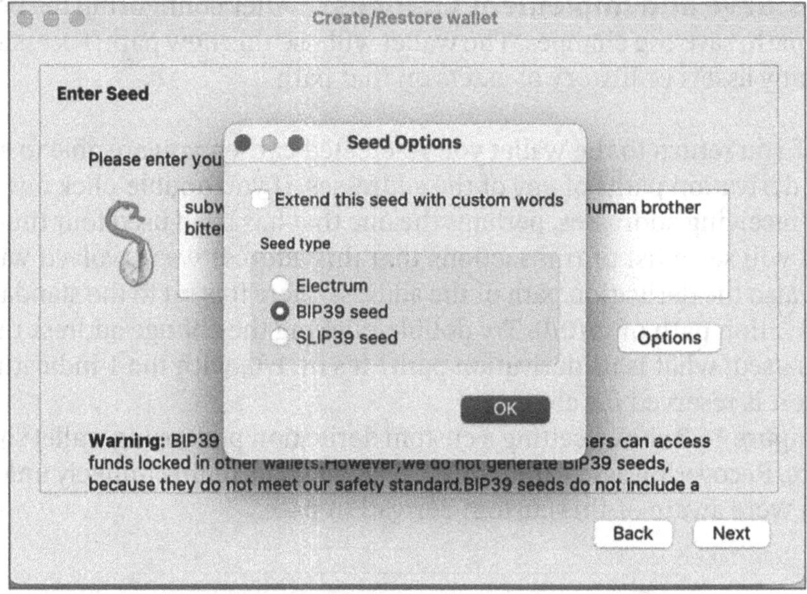

Figure 16.8: Selecting BIP39 seed type

The next page asks for the derivation path. Electrum has a great tool to help you in the form of a button that reads Detect Existing Accounts. If you click it, it will scan for paths that have transactions on the blockchain (see Figure 16.9 and Figure 16.10).

If you select Account0, the wallet will create addresses based on the account 0 path and you will find a transaction (see Figure 16.11).

But what about the Account1 that was found by the scanner? Set up a new wallet, same settings and seed words, but this time select Account1. Are there any transactions there? Indeed there are, as Figure 16.12 shows.

This brief example illustrates how important it is that you understand and actively look for different derivation paths because assets can so easily be missed. This, of course, is also vital when you consider seizure of criminal assets, which we will focus on in the next chapter.

Electrum is a Bitcoin-only wallet, and we have managed to find Bitcoin on two different paths, but you might want to try a wallet that supports more assets. I recommend trying the Exodus (`http://exodus.com`) wallet. Is there more to find using the same seed words? Try directly importing the same key into Exodus and you will find another asset from a different blockchain. I'll leave that with you to experiment.

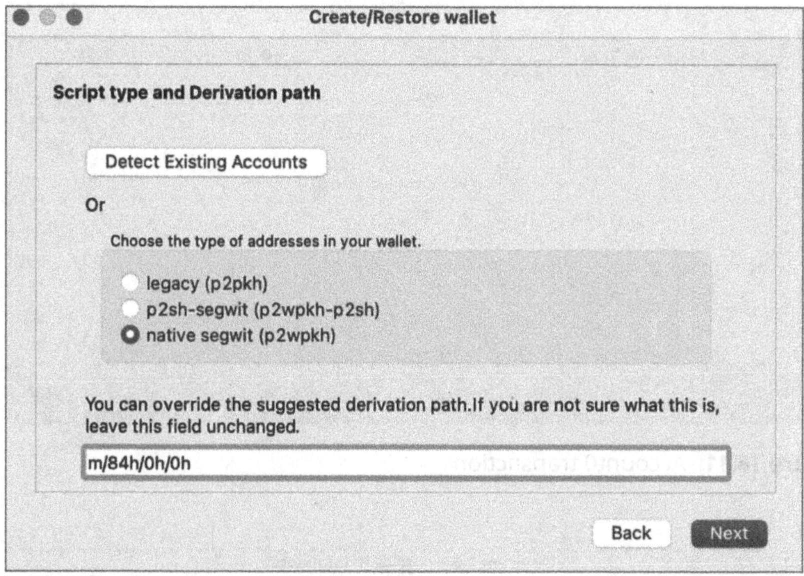

Figure 16.9: Screen to scan for existing accounts

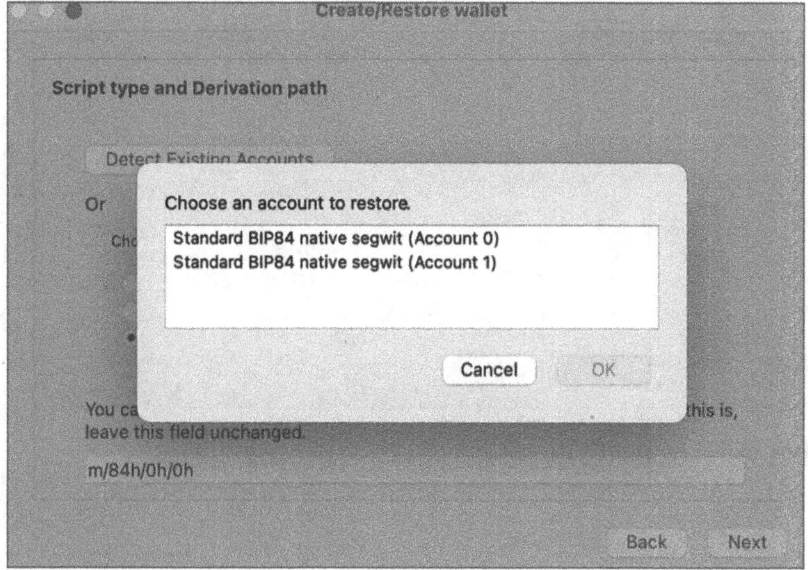

Figure 16.10: Detected accounts

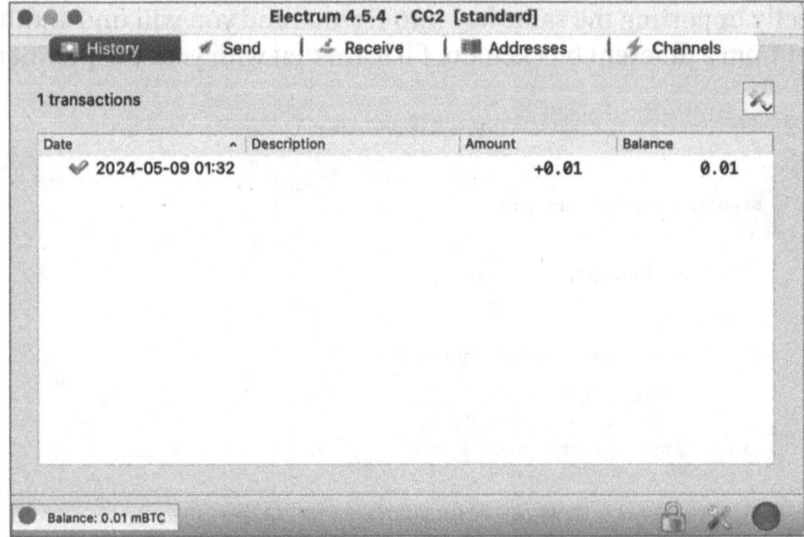

Figure 16.11: Account0 transaction

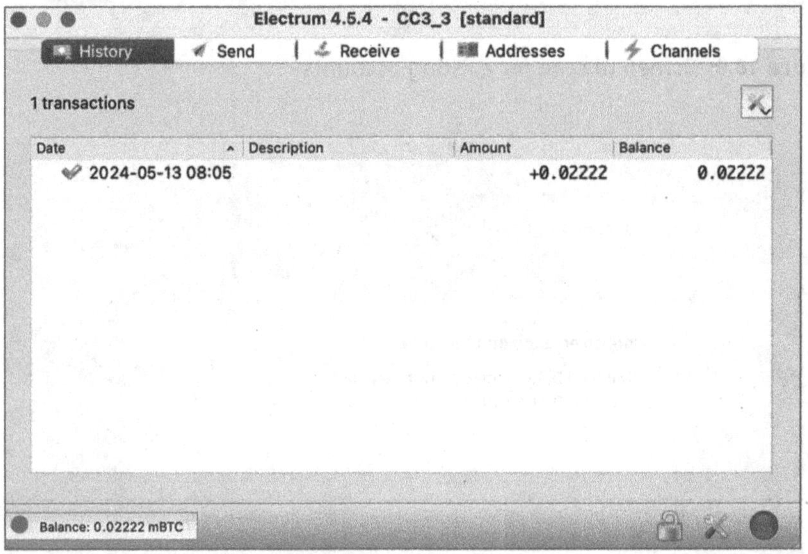

Figure 16.12: Account1 transaction

UNDERSTANDING GAP LIMITS

When working with wallets, you may come across something called *gap limits*. Gap limits are an important concept in the context of cryptocurrency wallets, particularly those that generate multiple addresses from a single seed phrase using hierarchical deterministic (HD) wallets. The gap limit is the maximum number of consecutive unused addresses in a hierarchical deterministic wallet. HD wallets generate addresses in a sequence, and the gap limit helps the wallet determine how far ahead it should look for used addresses when scanning the blockchain for transactions. The gap limit is important for two reasons:

Efficiency in Scanning When a wallet scans the blockchain to find transactions involving its addresses, it starts with the known addresses and continues generating new ones until it encounters a series of unused addresses greater than the gap limit. This mechanism prevents the wallet from scanning an infinite number of addresses, thus saving time and computational resources.

Recovery of Funds If a user loses access to their wallet and later attempts to recover it using their seed phrase, the gap limit ensures that the wallet can correctly identify and restore all addresses that have been used, provided they fall within the gap limit.

Different wallets may set different default gap limits. However, a common standard is to have a gap limit of 20. This means that if there are 20 consecutive unused addresses, the wallet will assume there are no further used addresses and stop scanning.

Imagine you have an HD wallet with a gap limit of 20. If you use the first address, skip the next 21 addresses, and then use the 22nd address, the wallet will not automatically find the 22nd address when recovering because it encountered 21 consecutive unused addresses, exceeding the gap limit of 20.

The implications for an investigator should be obvious. An advanced user could exploit the standard gap limit by putting funds in the 30th address, for example, meaning that wallets with a gap size of 20 will miss the funds. Some advanced wallets allow users to adjust the gap limit manually.

When recovering a wallet, you should be mindful of the gap limit if you are dealing with an technically advanced suspect. It may be worth using a wallet that enables the gap limit to be changed and perhaps set a much higher limit.

For more detailed technical information, you can refer to the Bitcoin Improvement Proposal (BIP) 44, which outlines the gap limit concept in hierarchical deterministic wallets: Adapted from `https://github.com/bitcoin/bips/blob/master/bip-0044.mediawiki`.

To Sum Up

Although this is a short chapter, it is an important part of understanding and conducting a crypto investigation. With discovered seed words, an investigator can re-create a wallet and locate all used addresses, which can then be traced backward and forward on the blockchain using a standard blockchain viewer such as blockchain.info or Etherscan.io. This is even a vital aspect of an investigation if you are fortunate to have a shiny blockchain intelligence tool available to you. To make use of a commercial tool, you still need to have a starting address, and the tool may not have sufficient transaction information to be able to cluster addresses to give you a broader picture. The re-creation of a wallet gives you all of those addresses and hence you will get the best use from your tracing tool.

Of course, being able to re-create a wallet may expose assets that are still held on those addresses, and once you have access to the wallet, you are able to move those assets. The next chapter will discuss seizure of crypto assets and the issues involved.

17 Crypto Seizure

This chapter will discuss some of the processes and issues that surround the legal seizure of crypto assets. I use the term *legal seizure* because the same processes could be used to acquire crypto that doesn't belong to you, and without the correct approvals and legislation it would be called theft. This is another one of those chapters that could easily be fleshed out into an entire book, but I will cover the fundamentals and then hopefully you can work to build a seizure process and policy from that point.

Everything we discuss in this chapter should be taken under advisement, and any seizure of crypto assets should be in line with your local laws, applicable legislation, agreed processes, and the security of assets at the forefront of the procedures you define. Any processes you decide to use should be tested, and all investigators who will be involved in your seizure operations should be trained on those processes.

In this chapter, we will hear from two contributors: Chris Recker, a U.K.-based lawyer who has worked with me on a number of crypto investigations, and Aidan Larkin, an ex–HM Revenue & Customs (HMRC, in the U.K.) investigator and close friend who probably knows more about international asset seizures than anyone else I know.

We will also discuss what equipment you need to carry out seizures and the tricky decision as to where seized assets should be stored and secured.

Let's start by enjoying a contribution from Chris, who along with his colleagues Brian Pandya, Charlyn Cruz, and Taylor Hertzler, looks at the legal challenges that exist when carrying out seizures in both the U.K. and U.S. jurisdictions.

THE LEGAL CHALLENGES AND OPPORTUNITIES SURROUNDING CRYPTO SEIZURE

About the Contributors

Chris Recker is a senior associate at Kingsley Napley LLP. He is an international fraud and investigations lawyer with an emphasis on matters relating to digital assets and/or cybersecurity. He regularly advises on complex multijurisdictional asset recovery strategies (particularly where digital assets are involved) and also on a range of cybersecurity issues (including incident response following ransomware).

Brian Pandya is a partner at the Washington, D.C., office of Duane Morris LLP. He represents technology companies and executives in high-stakes litigation, arbitrations, investigations, and appeals. Brian has served as lead trial counsel in a range of intellectual property, antitrust, complex commercial, and white-collar matters. He is also an experienced strategic counselor, regularly advising clients on data privacy, cybersecurity, artificial intelligence, and national security issues, and providing advice on corporate compliance programs. Brian previously served at the U.S. Department of Justice as Deputy Associate Attorney General.

Charlyn Cruz is an associate in the London office of Duane Morris LLP. Her practice focuses on complex commercial litigation in a number of different sectors, such banking and finance, technology, and transportation. Recently, she has increased her focus on litigation, investigations, and asset recovery in the digital asset space. Her work is often cross-border in nature, and her experience spans multiple jurisdictions in Europe, the United States, and Asia.

Taylor Hertzler is an associate at the Philadelphia office of Duane Morris LLP. He practices primarily in the area of health law, working on matters of digital-asset recovery on the side. He advises providers, hospitals, and other healthcare entities on regulatory concerns, including state licensure, federal kickback issues, Medicare and Medicaid rules, and FDA matters. Taylor also has experience working in insurance litigation.

Litigation to recover stolen digital assets is a constantly evolving arena, one that spans international borders. The courts are sympathetic to victims of fraud and are grappling with the challenges that arise from this specific asset class. This chapter aims to provide quick insights into some of these challenges and how the issues are practically managed in both England and the U.S.—two of the most active jurisdictions for these types of cases.

Getting Away With It: One Step behind the Wrongdoer

The first and million-dollar (sometimes literally) question that has to be answered is this: Where is the asset? And once that is known, we face the important question *How do I get it back?*

It sounds simple; blockchain technology provides an immutable and verifiable record of the transactions undertaken on it. This is one of the very benefits of this technology. Many victims, therefore, assume that the blockchain can just be followed (with the help of a specialist investigator and software) and their cryptocurrency located. This is partly true. The challenge is that the wrongdoers who cause these types of problems also understand the technology and know how to obfuscate transactions or slow down the tracing process.

The first action for a legal team working to recover stolen assets is to instruct a specialist blockchain tracer to interrogate the relevant transaction IDs and map out what has happened.[1] In theory, transactions between private addresses can be easily identified, and that could lead you straight to the wrongdoer. But in practice, rarely is the situation ever so simple. A wrongdoer may use a mixing service to combine unlawful transfers with other (often lawful) transactions, making the money trail hard to follow. The bad actor may transfer wallets within clusters of other wallets, again increasing the number of transaction "hops" and work required to draw the line between the asset leaving the victim's wallet and reaching its last known location.

While the initial instruction to blockchain tracers is a crucial first step, it is also important that the tracers continue to monitor

[1]It is important that the instructions come from the legal team, to ensure that the investigation is privileged. To further enhance work product protections, the instructions should be made once the legal team has concluded that litigation is reasonably likely.

and report on any subsequent movement of assets. Although this continued monitoring will likely involve an extra cost, it is just as critical as the initial report. Funds can be moved at the click of a mouse, so it is best to have an eye on the live movements of the assets so that when it comes time to litigate, you are not chasing outdated asset locations.

Another key question to consider is how the wrongdoer plans to cash out your misappropriated cryptocurrency. The answer is that unless the wrongdoer happens to have an "off-chain" transaction lined up (e.g., where someone is prepared to pay you a sum of money in exchange for you handing over a private key, thus giving them control of the address without recording the transaction on the blockchain), they will have to find an "off-ramp." Those off-ramps will likely be in the form of an exchange, a peer-to-peer trading platform, or an over-the-counter broker. Each of these off-ramps leaves a "hook" for where to direct the line of inquiries for potential recovery.

Using the Discovery (U.S.)/Disclosure (U.K.) Process

The disclosure process in the U.K., or the more expansive discovery process in the United States, is a key tool for asset recovery once the initial tracing report has been prepared. Although wrongdoers are usually not amenable to the disclosure/discovery process, most transactions traverse reputable exchanges that will respond to properly issued discovery. Disclosure (discovery) requests focus on getting onward-transaction information (if dealing with a centralized exchange) and/or information on the individual(s) who opened the account that received the victim's crypto assets (by way of know-your-client [KYC] information). This detail is vital, as it allows you to continue the tracing process and can potentially identify defendants or sources of further information (e.g., sources that may need to be interrogated using open source intelligence techniques).

In England, the legal process for getting disclosure has evolved over the last few years. The process generally requires obtaining a court order, which ultimately compels the third party to provide the information sought. To obtain a court order, you must provide the court with a sufficient basis for pursuing the information in question. Examples of bases that courts have found sufficient include identifying the wrongdoer who misappropriated the assets or obtaining enough information from an exchange for a victim to progress their claim. An application for a court order will need to be supported by evidence, usually in the form of a witness statement. Once granted, the court order then allows exchanges (and other third parties) who are usually resistant to providing such information in isolation, because they would likely need to disclose confidential and/or personal data, to legally disclose such information. A common challenge, however, is that entities that hold the information are based in other jurisdictions, or their contact information is difficult to find. Many exchanges will voluntarily comply with court orders, but others will require those orders to be domesticated or reciprocated in their jurisdiction before they comply. Thus, having a strong network of local counsel across foreign jurisdictions is beneficial to any asset recoveries.

In the United States, the Federal Rules of Civil Procedure presume comparatively expansive discovery, including for domestic litigants seeking discovery against entities domiciled abroad and to foreign litigants seeking discovery against entities domiciled in the U.S. For domestic litigants, 28 U.S. Code Section 1783 provides that a federal court can issue a subpoena against a U.S. national located in a foreign jurisdiction.

(It is worth interjecting here a comment from John Valkovci, who was an assistant U.S. attorney for 28 years. He states that Section 1783 provides that the subpoena can be issued "if the court finds that particular testimony or the production of the document or other thing. . .is necessary in the interest of justice. . .and that it is not possible to obtain his testimony in admissible form without his personal appearance or to obtain the production of the document or other thing in any manner." What this means is that the party seeking such a subpoena (court order) must demonstrate certain facts before the court will authorize the issuance of the subpoena. The decision to issue the subpoena is within the sound discretion of the court.

In addition, the issuance of such subpoenas—or most discovery devices in the United States—is contingent on the existence of a civil case being filed in federal court. In other words, the discovery process is tethered to an existing case—it does not exist in a vacuum. A federal court can also issue a letter rogatory through the U.S. Department of State asking a foreign court for assistance in performing a judicial act.

For foreign litigants, 28 U.S. Code Section 1782 provides that a federal court may compel a citizen within its jurisdiction to comply with a foreign discovery request. Seeking discovery against foreign citizens through letters rogatory can be unpredictable and slow, since it relies on foreign courts to effect civil action against their own citizens. However, U.S. subpoenas issued under such methods can be fast and effective (and potentially quicker than the process in England), as failure to produce discovery within the subpoena's deadline may result in court-imposed penalties.

Although these disclosure/discovery measures are useful to have in your arsenal, cryptocurrency exchanges may not always be in a position to provide the requested information, even if an order is granted. Whereas some of the well-known exchanges take onboarding information from custodians of their crypto asset wallets, wrongdoers will inevitably be drawn to platforms that take little to no KYC information. That said, in complex cases it is often worth rolling the dice with this route due to the possibility that a disclosure order may uncover more information about transactions or links than would have otherwise been uncovered.

Seizing Control: To Freeze or Not to Freeze

Courts all over the globe are grappling with issues surrounding crypto assets. In traditional fraud cases, if an asset is misappropriated, then the usual course is to move swiftly and obtain an injunction to restrain the asset's onward transmission. The same strategy often applies in crypto asset cases. However, there are nuances depending on the jurisdictions involved (which limit, for instance, whether a claim or injunction could be advanced against categories of unknown parties—aka *persons unknown*—or whether a defendant must first be identified).

Assuming an order can be obtained, the questions that follow are: (1) how that order can be enforced against exchanges/defendants/respondents (including in other jurisdictions), and (2) how that order can be policed (i.e., how can we make sure that an asset is actually frozen?).

Centralized exchanges are often prime targets for injunctions. This is because, generally speaking, they have the ability to freeze/restrict accounts that are within their control.

But what if the funds are parked in private addresses? One of the unique aspects of cryptocurrency is the fact that a private key or seed phrase is the mechanism by which someone controls a wallet/address. With a private address, it may mean that the wrongdoer (or controller of that wallet/address) is the only party who can restrict an onward transaction, as there is no third party that the injunction can simply be served on in the same way that a centralized exchange or a bank can be served with an injunction.

These cases have advantages—for example, if the tokens are being moved between private addresses, then a victim will know where their assets are. The disadvantage, however, is the difficulty you face when trying to freeze and recover those assets once their location is identified. Knowledge of where an asset sits on the blockchain does not give you the ability to move that asset. Nor does it reveal who possesses that asset. So unlike addresses that are held by centralized exchanges, addresses held only by private individuals may be less-than-prime targets for injunctions.

As with disclosure orders, the extent to which any injunctions apply overseas (and entities voluntarily comply with them) will vary. Therefore, local lawyers are often needed in the jurisdiction where the injunction is to be policed to ensure that the injunction can be enforced. This process often involves working with an international law firm that can operate in the relevant jurisdictions.

The real power of injunctions of this nature is that they are usually coupled with a penal notice, which makes a contravention of the injunction's terms punishable by contempt of court (or an equivalent penalty), which can lead to criminal or civil liability. The gravity of the punishment would depend on, among other things, how blatant any disregard of the injunction was and if an offender was deliberately trying to mislead the court. The enforceability of any contempt order, however, will depend on whether the bad actor is located within the court's jurisdiction. If not, freezing the actor's assets may be the only punishment with any teeth.

The game changers here (particularly when dealing with private addresses) are intelligence and innovation. Open source intelligence investigations often play an important part in these kinds of cases. There is a huge amount of publicly available information that can be identified and interrogated to help to identify someone or provide hooks for further inquiries. Doing so could include identifying social media channels from usernames on NFT platforms, or identifying other victims of the same scam. With the intelligence piece in hand, the question is how you get the injunction in front of the wrongdoer so that (1) they have been served with it, and (2) they are on notice of it.

This difficulty has led to a number of court-approved innovations. If your cryptocurrency or NFT sits in a private address and you do not know who controls that address and, by extension, have no means of controlling the crypto assets within it, the latest trend is to serve the injunction and other court documents by way of an NFT that contains a hyperlink to a repository of documents, which can then be accessed by the wrongdoer. That NFT (which is often just an image of a covering letter) is then airdropped to the wallet(s) of interest. This method of service has been accepted by courts in both the United States (the New York Supreme Court recognized it in June 2022) and the U.K. (the High Court of England and Wales recognized it in July 2022). This innovation is a very welcome development, and we expect it will continue to be used in cases of these natures (particularly to ensure that a wrongdoer is put on notice and/or validly served with an injunction, which is a requirement in both the U.S. and the U.K.).

However, without the ability to obtain a private key or (with the assistance of a specialist receiver) to transfer any frozen cryptocurrency to a wallet that is "safe" (even once a defendant knows about a service order), a victim is still reliant on an unknown party (potentially the wrongdoer, or someone associated with the wrongdoer) to comply with the order. In an age where technology allows someone to mask who they are and where they are, it is perhaps expected that a wrongdoer may feel that they will never be identified (and so would see less risk in not engaging with or simply ignoring an order). The penalty of contempt of court becomes a rather empty threat in these situations.

Funding: Why Is There Uncertainty in These Cases?

Potential claimants in these cases are often startled at the potential cost of taking action to recover their misappropriated assets. Claimants are often required to look at alternatives. As cryptocurrencies are a new asset class, traditional insurance products (which apply to cover legal costs) may not be available to fund efforts to recover them.

Litigation funding (i.e., the process by which a third party pays for some or all of the costs of advancing a claim) has developed as a separate service line on potential matters. So have insurance solutions, which cover a portion of legal costs in the event that a successful recovery is not made. These developments may allow claimants who cannot otherwise afford sophisticated counsel to pursue asset-recovery claims. However, the trade-off is that the victim must give away a slice (sometimes a large slice) of the funds that are recovered. Given these competing concerns, a best practice may be to work with a broker that assesses all options for financing a claim.

From a funding (or insurance) perspective, the real difficulty is determining the confidence with which a victim can say that their funds will be recovered. Victims must also show that the losses are at such a level for funding to be worth the time and expense of the prospective funder. Often the tracing piece will go only so far, as there is a significant element of the unknown—for example, where did the funds go after they left the exchange (if anywhere) and what needs to be done to continue tracing the funds or to recover what can be found? These issues will be carefully explored by a funder or insurer. However, for cases that warrant funding or insurance, there is ample money available and ample interest in using it; litigation funding has become a multibillion-dollar, international business in both the U.K. and the U.S.

Legal teams who pursue litigation funding in the U.S. or the U.K. must understand the evolving regulatory landscape that governs this tool. A few courts in the U.S. currently require legal teams or their clients to disclose litigation-funding agreements. While the industry remains largely unregulated, several states have proposed (and a few have passed) laws that require disclosure of litigation-funding agreements, require registration or licensure for litigation funders, regulate interest rates or fees for litigation funding, or regulate such funding the same way they regulate normal loans. For example, Wisconsin enacted Wisconsin Act 235 in 2018, which requires automatic disclosure of all funding agreements in civil litigation. And in 2020, Utah enacted the Maintenance Funding Practice Act, which requires entities to register before acting as a "maintenance funding provider."

The position in the European Union (EU) is also developing in similar vein (and it is possible that the U.K. will follow). On top of these concerns, procuring a litigation funder requires providing key information to the funder, some of which information may be covered under attorney-client privilege. While litigation funders should know the laws that regulate them, it is the lawyer's responsibility to know the laws of their jurisdiction when procuring funding and to ensure that they do not violate either those laws or attorney-client privilege.

Law Enforcement: Cost vs. Control

In any fraud case, one of the first conversations that often happens (when options are set out) is discussing the "cost vs. control" challenge. Civil litigation comes at a cost, but it allows a party to speed up, slow down, apply pressure on, and take complete control of a matter. Referrals to criminal authorities cannot necessarily be sped up or slowed down. However, criminal authorities generally have faster and more powerful mechanisms for requesting information from third parties (including exchanges). And where a criminal referral is made, the main costs will be incurred by the authorities. The overarching strategy you take with these options will depend on the jurisdictions involved. Assessing this challenge is a conversation that almost always happens in U.K. cases, but it is not always followed through.

U.S. litigants in particular have ample opportunity to partner with federal law enforcement. The Federal Bureau of Investigation (FBI) and its parent agency, the Department of Justice (DoJ), regularly work with private actors to investigate cryptocurrency fraud (and both agencies have reported significant successes in recent years). And these partnership opportunities are poised to grow: Pursuant to a March 2022 executive order, numerous federal agencies have begun developing interagency task forces to address cryptocurrency crimes, and in September 2022, the DoJ announced several new initiatives to increase expertise and enforcement efforts in this area and increase collaboration with international prosecutors. Note, however, that federal law enforcement efforts can take years before any recovery occurs, and agencies are likely to take or prioritize only those cases that involve large-scale scams with lots of money involved.

Conclusions

Despite the increasingly mainstream nature of crypto assets and the corresponding advancements in law and technology, victims of crypto-related fraud may find recovery to be a hard road ahead. However, there is a growing cadre of tracers, lawyers, funders, and other specialists who can assist with this sort of work. It is therefore vital for victims of crypto asset fraud to engage with these experts as soon as possible to keep pace with fast-acting wrongdoers and, in turn, increase their chances of recovery.

We hope that this contribution has been informative and provided food for thought on some of the issues that practically need to be considered in these types of cases (and how the legal systems deal with these challenges).

Disclaimers

None of these materials is offered, and the materials should not be construed, as legal advice. Your receipt or use of such information is not intended to create, and does not create, an attorney-client relationship with Duane Morris or any of the firm's attorneys. You should not act or rely upon information contained in these materials without specifically seeking professional legal advice. Any opinions expressed in this publication do not necessarily reflect the views of the firm or its clients. Any examples are solely intended to be illustrative. Any opinions expressed should not be assumed to be the individual opinion of any one contributor.

Any sections contributed to by Kingsley Napley LLP are based on English law, are provided for information only, and are not advice. Those sections are expressions of opinion; they do not deal with all possible options or strategies and cannot and should not be relied on by any person or entity. Independent advice should always be taken.

Thanks very much to Chris and his colleagues for those interesting insights.

Before we get into the specifics of how we technically carry out crypto seizes, let's hear from Aidan Larkin. Aidan is one of the world's foremost experts in seizure and management of criminal assets and ran the first ever auction of cryptocurrency. He now runs Asset Reality.

SEIZING CRYPTO ASSETS

Aidan Larkin, Contributor

I recall my first asset seizure involving crypto vividly. A digital investigator rang me from his police department in England, and the call went something like this—we'll call him Steve for the purposes of this story.

"Hi, Aidan, just looking at our seized-asset contract with your company. It says you guys recover, manage, and realize any asset?"

"Well, within reason, Steve," I nervously joked.

"We've got some Bitcoin."

"Ah, yes. . .Bitcoin," I said, trying to sound reassuring despite having little knowledge of this cryptocurrency that I'd only heard about a few times by that point in 2017.

"We've managed to seize it but need a home for it until the case is concluded. It might need to be sold or returned to the suspect if he's acquitted. Is this something you can look after for us?"

I had more questions than answers, and we hadn't even delved into the technical details yet.

"We'll come up with a plan and get back to you in the morning. Just need to check with the insurers. Is that okay?"

"Absolutely," he agreed. I could detect a bit of relief in his voice, mixed with surprise that we could assist and potentially get this off his plate. "I'll also connect you with a guy named Nick Furneaux who's assisting us with the investigation. He literally wrote the book on the topic and has a training course on this subject if you're interested."

"Nick Furneaux? Never heard of him. Yes, please, I'd be happy to meet him."

As someone tasked with managing government-seized assets, we had understandably high standards for processes, auditing, insurance, and procedural considerations regarding the chain of custody. My mind was racing with multiple threads: How do you transfer it? How do you set up a wallet that would satisfy our insurance providers? Could you even insure it, and if so, had one of these policies ever successfully paid out? Were they worth the paper they were printed on? We still hadn't touched on the KYC/AML and other regulatory issues around this asset class.

We couldn't just throw it onto a hardware wallet and hope for the best, could we? Could we get away with using a spreadsheet to track multiple blockchain addresses? How robust would that be? No other inventory tools existed at that point—what other options did we actually have? What had other agencies done?

We were a private sector company registered with the Financial Conduct Authority in the U.K. Surely there'd be rules governing these sorts of activities, or were there? How would we safely return it to an acquitted defendant or cash out in a compliant way? Then the "scale" issue came up in conversations with my colleagues. The general consensus was that we could figure this out for this particular seizure, but how do we scale a solution that will allow dozens, hundreds, and eventually thousands of officers to safely and simply seize digital assets in the future as demand for these services inevitably grew?

And so my journey into seizing cryptocurrency began. I met Nick, and the seed for creating a company to specifically tackle the challenges faced by agencies seizing and managing assets was planted—we just didn't know it yet.

Fast-forward to 2024, and we've collectively investigated, recovered, managed, and realized billions of dollars' worth of seized crypto—from the infamous Silk Road Bitcoin seizures, the world's earliest crypto-freezing orders, to the first seized crypto auctions. We've had the opportunity to work with some of the greatest minds in the space and build asset forfeiture programs in multiple countries, problem-solving in this fascinating and ever-changing sector. All this is to say that we're practitioners first and foremost. We've made the mistakes, got the scars, and regularly share cautionary tales on the subject. We've seen everything from the brilliant and innovative to the downright crazy, dangerous, and illegal practices (like officers stealing the seized crypto). So, how should we approach it today, and what issues do we need to be aware of?

"If You Can Seize Cars, You Can Seize Crypto"

In Nick's first book, the challenges highlighted regarding crypto asset seizure are reassuringly evergreen and haven't changed much. How do I actually seize it? Where and how do I store it? When do I sell it? The mechanics of asset seizure don't vary just because it's crypto rather than, say, a car. As Nick summed up, "The differences are only technical." Just as you wouldn't use a tow truck to seize a Rolex, there is no one-size-fits-all approach. The main challenges now lie in having the right toolkit, knowledge, and experience to successfully (and safely) seize crypto from wherever it's located in an auditable, effective, and robust way.

In this look at crypto asset seizure, we also have the benefit of hindsight and experience to review and dissect a diverse range of previous cases. We no longer have to theorize what the processes might look like, as we're currently living through a seized crypto boom with all the best practices and what-not-to-do readily available.

You might be wondering why assets are seized in the first place. Asset seizure is an incredibly powerful tool commonly categorized into achieving four key outcomes: deter, deny, deprive, and disrupt criminals. Primarily, though, effective asset recovery is usually the act of returning what was taken from a victim, which could be a person or an entire country. Additionally, it's important for society, as the proceeds from seized assets fund law enforcement, repay victims, and support wider societal causes like education campaigns targeting crime prevention strategies.

Asset seizure has been around for a long time. Assets have been getting seized for centuries, from as early as ancient Rome, where the state confiscated property from individuals deemed enemies or traitors. This practice, known as *proscription*, was both a punitive measure and a means to enrich the state. During the Middle Ages in Europe, asset forfeiture became more structured, serving as both punishment and deterrent. The modern concept of asset forfeiture, particularly in the United States, began to take shape during the Prohibition era of the 1920s, when the government targeted the assets of bootleggers and organized crime syndicates to disrupt their operations. This period highlighted the effectiveness of using financial tactics in combating crime.

In the late 20th century, the focus shifted toward the much-publicized war on drugs. Governments worldwide enacted laws allowing for the seizure of assets linked to drug trafficking. The United States, through the Comprehensive Crime Control Act of 1984, expanded its asset forfeiture laws, enabling the confiscation of assets connected to a broader range of criminal activities. Today, asset forfeiture is a crucial tool in the fight against various forms of organized crime globally, including terrorism, fraud, human trafficking, and money laundering. However, it remains controversial, with ongoing debates about its implementation, potential for abuse, and impact on civil liberties.

How Do I Actually Seize Crypto?

Sticking with the car analogy, if governments wanted to cover all the bases for every type of potential vehicle seizure, they would need to maintain a costly fleet of every type of tow truck for every potential type of car they might end up seizing. That simply wouldn't happen for a multitude of reasons, primarily cost. Instead, we've seen years of collaboration with private sector contractors to procure recovery services from a managing agent that can be called upon when needed. This level of public and private sector collaboration isn't new to asset seizure. From hardware and software solutions, including digital forensic tools, scientific, medical, and ballistic analysis, it's utilized daily around the world to support law enforcement agencies and has been for decades.

The same logic applies to crypto to be effective. Gone are the days of having a solution for Bitcoin only. With over 2 million cryptocurrencies in existence and almost 10,000 actively used, agencies need to consider whether they have an infrastructure that allows them to deal with the unexpected. Even those agencies with the luxury of deep sectoral experience and are more than qualified to go it alone still draft in the support of private sector partners as and when needed.

As of 2024, many of the largest agencies in the world have launched and implemented contracts with companies to assist with seizing, managing, and liquidating digital assets. The sector has matured to the extent that there are now companies and software solutions for every stage of the crypto asset recovery process. We've witnessed the creation of software to scour digital devices for artifacts of crypto asset ownership, like addresses and seed phrases that can control and, most importantly, move the asset from the suspect to a government-controlled wallet.

There are a range of seized-asset software solutions that allow agencies to generate a QR code on an app (or secure platform) to access a government-controlled wallet. Some enterprise-grade solutions have more advanced blockchain-based inventory functions to live-track seized crypto and actively monitor addresses controlling seized assets. Advances in building governance structures to allow for multiple signatories who can authorize transactions via an easy-to-use platform have removed the need to rely on basic multisig on a hardware wallet. No more managing dozens of individual wallets with single points of failure.

Government audits of existing public infrastructure and how seized crypto is being managed are being published online, and opportunities for improvements are being implemented around the world. Embarrassing headlines regarding losses of seized assets, thefts by serving members of law enforcement, and an overall lack of transparency have triggered an overhaul of how seized crypto is dealt with.

Just like the maturity in many of the large crypto exchanges that now have law enforcement liaison teams, staffed with former police investigators, many companies are in the market offering dedicated asset-recovery tools to make it easier to seize, manage, and liquidate crypto assets. As witnessed with some of the high-profile collapses or criminal charges and fines against some of the biggest exchanges in the industry, a new risk for agencies involved in seizing assets is choosing the right partner. It's essential that agencies ensure they run robust procurement processes to identify suitable solutions.

Putting the Recovery Back in Asset Recovery: The Wider Impact

> *Police pounds and storage facilities are usually not geared to managing the volume and types of assets typically made subject to seizure orders.*
>
> *Opportunities to increase the revenue derived from confiscated property are often not exploited due to a lack of focus, specialist skill, and resources.*
>
> `https://www.unodc.org/documents/corruption/Publications/2017/17-07000_ebook_sr.pdf`

For decades, with the exception of a few standout agencies, asset seizure has been an afterthought in many criminal and civil investigations, and the sector has a well-documented and damning track record. Most of the largest intergovernmental agencies in the world agree that only 1 percent of illicit assets are recovered from criminals. Even more bleak is the fact that those statistics primarily relate to illicit financial flows pre-2015 and before the explosion of crypto usage. You'd be forgiven for being pessimistic and perhaps a bit cynical, thinking that if we have a broken asset-recovery system and we often struggle with managing everyday assets like cars, then things are only going to get worse with the arrival of this new and complicated asset class. Right?

Not so. On the contrary, asset seizures involving crypto have become the white knight on the horizon, combatting that shocking 1 percent statistic, and we're seeing jaw-dropping seizures all around the world that eclipse the biggest non-crypto seizures.

"...Government Seized $3.6 Billion in Stolen Cryptocurrency..."

You've probably seen the news headlines about these enormous billion-dollar crypto seizures and might be wondering what is fueling them. It would be remiss of me not to explore this. A combination of the stratospheric rise in the value of the sector overall and maturity in blockchain investigation skills appears to be paying off. It's the equivalent of miners discovering a new location abundant with rare valuable gemstones and having precisely the right tools and resources to recover and reap the rewards.

As Nick summed up beautifully in his last book, what's the point if all your hard work at the investigatory stage doesn't result in taking assets off the bad guys and/or returning them to the rightful owners? For us to build effective programs to seize assets, we first need to appreciate that the existing infrastructure faces a number of challenges that have existed for almost two decades. Positively, crypto asset recovery contains the blueprint to improve asset recovery overall.

The seized-asset life cycle is the same (in principle) for all assets:

1. Pre-seizure
2. Seizure (aka Recovery)
3. Management
4. Liquidation (Realization) or Return/Reinvestment, even auctions!

It can be argued that agencies need less capital to run an effective asset forfeiture program. You don't need a warehouse or expensive tow truck to recover and manage billions of dollars' worth of crypto assets.

Global Outlook

One other major factor that will drive improved standards and a probable increase in crypto seizures is a renewed focus on asset recovery improvement from the Financial Action Task Force (FATF; `www.fatf-gafi.org`). Crypto asset recovery is a key part of that new strategy. Everything from handling crypto-related intel (the lifeblood of future seizures), to how quickly agencies respond to requests to freeze fast-moving illicit assets, to how many cases have resulted in asset confiscation/forfeiture will be measured in future country evaluations.

Interesting technology developments are also being witnessed, such as reusing seized crypto in undercover operations to snare criminals, which in itself creates new challenges in terms of asset management and auditing. This will potentially lead to more seizures. Everything from targeting individual scammers to fighting with nation-state actors who use crypto thefts to fund nuclear proliferation will be played out in the crypto asset recovery arena.

"You Don't Need to Train to Be a Mechanic to Seize a Car. . ."

Despite the many billion-dollar seizures, there are still many agencies not taking the plunge into crypto asset recovery and doing the basics. This leads to a tragic cycle of victims of scams involving crypto assets not being offered support as the force "doesn't do crypto cases."

I've lost track of how many times I've heard "Once we amend our legislation. . ." or "Once we finalize our standard operating procedures . . ." explaining why an agency hasn't dealt with seizing any sort of crypto. Additionally, there is often the argument of the knowledge barrier or high cost of entry to purchasing many of the blockchain analytic and visualization tools, but the reality is they assist and enhance crypto asset seizure but are not necessary.

A lot of the groundwork has been laid by those early pioneers, and rather than go to court and explain to a judge what a Bitcoin is, you have the advantage of referring to case after case where crypto has been successfully frozen and forfeited. If you encounter a suspect with crypto in a well-known exchange, seizing, recovering, managing, and liquidating those assets is now as common as dealing with a bank account or a car.

If you seize a car, you don't need to understand the intricacies of the internal combustion engine. It has value, and you can link it to illicit activity of some sort—that's what matters. The same applies to crypto. Happy seizing!

Thank you, Aidan, that was very interesting indeed. Let's now take a look at the kit and processes needed to carry out a seizure.

What Do You Need to Carry Out a Crypto Seizure?

If you think back to what you learned in the previous chapter regarding recovering wallets from seed words, all the same knowledge applies but with the additional step of moving the assets from a recovered wallet into secure storage. The word *secure* was the key word in that sentence. As we have mentioned many times in this book, if you have the seed words you have access to the assets and so security of the crypto both pre- and post-seizure is critical. If you feel you need to, head back to Chapter 8, "The Importance of Discovery," to review how discovered seed words belonging to a suspect need to be carefully managed. We need to take steps to avoid a co-conspirator moving the funds before we are able to, or for seeds to fall into the wrong hands through use of body-worn camera footage or see-through evidence bags and subsequently stolen. Once the funds are moved to a wallet controlled by us, we face the prospect of having to secure those seed words for perhaps an extended period of time.

A crypto seizure may be proactive or reactive. We may have intelligence that a suspect has illicit crypto funds in their possession and so when we carry out a premises or device search we will obviously be prepared to move any funds that are found. However, seizure may be reactive as we may stumble across crypto-wallets when searching paper files, computers, or phones and may have to reactively seize funds if we have reasonable suspicion that they are proceeds of crime (depending on your legislation). My colleague Ari Redbord said on the "Seize and Desist" podcast (Episode 7) that crypto is becoming the new digital evidence. Going back 25 years we might have found a cell phone or computer being used by a suspect that had useful evidence; today *every* case has some type of digital evidence associated with it. Going back 5 years or so you might find crypto involved in a case; today we see some crypto being used by suspects in almost every case with a financial element that we look at. Reactive seizure is becoming more regular.

It is a bit pointless for me to outline the kit bag and software tools that you will need—if you are reading this in 5 or 6 years' time, then there will undoubtedly be shiny new software and hardware tools that will help you, aside from the many new crypto-wallets that will be in use. However, if you stop and think about the likely scenarios, then it's quite straightforward to build a kit list. Remember that no matter what equipment and software you have available to you, no seizure should be carried out without training, practice, and planning. Let's look at two scenarios:

Seizure Directly from a Suspect's Device. If you have access to a suspect's device and have the legal right to examine it, you may be able to move crypto directly from the phone or computer to your prepared addresses. There are significant challenges to being able to work on a live running device, and training should be completed before any "live" device investigation is undertaken. Using a digital device changes it in real time, and so it is impossible for a defense investigator to be able to re-create the data or steps that the officer took in exactly the same way. This is why digital forensics always works primarily on the "do no harm, make no changes" principle and powers down digital devices before making a bit-for-bit copy using a write blocking device. However, if your legal powers enable you to, a device is on and running, and you have access to the suspect's wallet, although there are risks I would advise, on balance, to go ahead and seize the funds. Just be aware that phones can be remotely wiped if they are switched on, cloud storage backups continue to be made, and remote access to the device by a third party is possible. In the past we would disconnect the device from the Internet, but if you do that, you can't seize the crypto!

It is worth bearing in mind that with most crypto-wallets a password, dual-factor authentication, or biometric login is required to access them; in this case, the cooperation of the suspect is likely vital. Don't expect too much from your decryption department, reasoning that you will power off the phone and get them to crack any passwords, they do their best but usually the mathematics is against them.

I'm discussing this topic with a friend who just suggested that you could always disconnect the device from the Internet, access the wallet if you are able, and then just find and record the seed words. Pretty good idea actually, but again some wallets require an extra word that is not recorded and that is remembered by the user, so that may get in the way. If you have access to the wallet, think about seizing immediately.

In the case of seizing from a suspect's device, you don't need any kit or software at all—just the prepared addresses that you are seizing to.

Seizing from a Recovered Wallet or Seed Words. If you locate seed words or a wallet file from a software wallet, then you will need some equipment to be able to recover the wallet and move the funds. This would include:

Laptop. As of this writing, I suggest using a Windows laptop since almost every wallet is available for that operating system. Consider the security of the laptop; make it dedicated to the task of seizure and don't use it for anything else. Perhaps turning off cloud backups would be a good idea and ensuring that the OS, firewalls, and so on are kept up to date. Antivirus (AV) is generally a good idea, of course, but *not* if the laptop is going to be used for any forensic recovery as you may recover a file only for AV to immediately delete it. That has happened to me many times! Preinstall a series of software wallets and the software needed to configure a hardware wallet and learn how to use them. You may want to consider making a copy/image of the newly set-up laptop and wiping it and restoring the clean copy after each case.

Cell Phone. I prefer an iPhone because the Apple App Store is more secure with fewer apps that are suspect than other app stores, in my personal opinion. Install software wallets that enable the importing of seed words and learn to use them so that you are not fumbling around trying to find the right function when on scene. Again, you might choose to wipe and reinstall apps after each seizure.

Hardware Wallets. Assuming you are going to seize to your own wallet, the decision of which we will discuss later in this chapter, you will absolutely need to implement a key storage system based around hardware wallets. As of this writing, there are many available, including Trezor, Ledger, and SafePal. Please ensure that you purchase from the manufacturers or another approved website, as there are counterfeit versions of many of the best-selling wallets available online. If you are planning to set up a hardware wallet to seize illicit funds, give considerable thought to the securing of the seed words, the access PIN, and any software passwords.

Recording Seed Words

As you have learned, the seed words for a wallet enable the re-creation of the wallet and access to the funds controlled by the resulting private key. This means that the seed words need to be treated, arguably, even more securely than cash. Although stealing cash from a crime scene is easy, seed words can be stolen after they are seized if they have been captured by body-worn cameras or on-scene photography, or even if they have been put in a see-through evidence bag.

You may want to consider using an obfuscation method for securing seed words such as the Shamir backup method. This method spreads the seed words over three lists with words missing in each list; however, only two lists are needed to re-create the entire list.

You can find an implementation of this at `https://iancoleman.io/bip39`. (As of this writing, this site was not working when using the Safari browser. Chrome and Firefox seem to work fine.)

If you enter the seed words you want to split (remember to do this in a offline version of the page), then select the option Show Split Mnemonic Cards. This splits these seed words

small excess prize push aerobic nerve economy slogan hood session cannon alert caught caught please federal asthma stone cram diagram vendor job climb dust

into the following three lists, which can be put on individual cards and separated:

```
Card 1: small XXXX prize XXXX aerobic nerve economy slogan hood
XXXX cannon XXXX caught XXXX please federal asthma XXXX cram
diagram XXXX job climb XXXX
Card 2: small excess XXXX push aerobic XXXX XXXX slogan hood
session XXXX alert caught caught XXXX federal XXXX stone XXXX
diagram vendor XXXX climb dust
Card 3: XXXX excess prize push XXXX nerve economy XXXX XXXX
session cannon alert XXXX caught please XXXX asthma stone cram
XXXX vendor job XXXX dust
```

Simply give a card to three trusted individuals or put them into safes. The wallet can only be re-created if two of the three cards are combined. Simple and clever.

Although it is possible to brute-force the missing words if you only have one card, doing so is difficult and time consuming.

Seizing to Your Own Wallet

Later in this chapter we will discuss the pros and cons of seizing to your own wallet or seizing to a wallet owned and managed by a custodian. However, if you decide to set up your own wallets, then give considerable thought to the process, especially the process of securing the seed words. I'm not a great fan of long bullet-pointed or numbered lists, but I'm going to make an exception in this section. It is so important that a strong and secure process is defined that I've listed the key aspects of a good process so that it can be used as a checklist if you are tasked with setting up a process for your organization.

Considerations for a Software Wallet

When managing a software wallet, several factors must be considered and solutions recorded to ensure the security of the seized assets. A software wallet will often have its own password or other types of authentication, so the management of the wallet can be about multiple elements of security.

Managing the Access Password. Securely manage the password to the computer or phone where the wallet is installed. Unauthorized access to this device can potentially compromise the entire wallet.

Managing Backup Seed Words. Sorry to reiterate yet again, but the seed words are crucial for recovering the wallet if the device is lost or compromised but also give anyone with access to the seed words the ability to transfer the funds. Store these words securely and separately from the device, preferably split using a method similar to the Shamir backup method covered in the previous section.

Managing Wallet Access Password or PIN. The password or PIN to open the wallet should be strong and stored securely. This adds an extra layer of security to the wallet.

Managing Wallet Names. If multiple wallets are used, clearly manage and document the names to avoid confusion and the potential of assets being assigned to the wrong case.

Securing the Hardware Post-Seizure. Ensure the device on which the wallet is installed is securely stored to prevent unauthorized access.

Wiping and Reinstalling Device between Seizures. To maintain security and prevent contamination, wipe and reinstall the device's operating system between different seizures.

Considerations for a Hardware Wallet

Hardware wallets provide an additional layer of security as they store the private keys on a physical device that is usually not connected to the Internet. Key considerations for managing a hardware wallet include:

Managing Device Security. The physical security of the hardware wallet is paramount. Ensure that it is stored in a secure location to prevent theft or loss.

Managing the Access PIN. The PIN for accessing the hardware wallet must be securely managed and should not be stored with the device.

Managing Backup Seed Words. Just like with software wallets, the security of the backup seed words is critical. Store these securely and separately from the hardware wallet, preferably split using a method similar to the Shamir backup.

Managing Security for Computer-Based Access Software. If the hardware wallet requires connecting to a computer, ensure that the computer is secure and free from malware. You may wish to consider using the computer only for seizure tasks.

Some hardware wallets are entirely stand-alone, whereas others require connection to a computer. Understand the specific requirements of the hardware wallet being used and ensure that all security protocols are followed.

Establishing an Organizational Process

Defining a clear process within your organization is vital for the secure management of any seized cryptocurrency. An example process might include the following steps:

1. **Top-Level Management.** Ensure that top-level management is aware of the processes and storage locations for seed words. This oversight is crucial for accountability and security.

2. **Supervisors.** Designate supervisors to oversee the creation of wallets. Supervisors ensure that procedures are followed correctly and securely.

3. **Staff Members.** Involve three staff members in splitting and recording the seed words onto three separate cards. This division adds an additional layer of security.

4. **Verification.** Ensure that any two of the three cards can be used to re-create the wallet. This redundancy ensures that the wallet can be recovered if one card is lost or compromised.

5. **Storage.** Place the cards in envelopes, seal them in evidence bags, and store them in three different secure locations. This dispersal minimizes the risk of all seed words being compromised simultaneously.

6. **Hardware Devices.** Store any hardware devices in sealed evidence bags and secure them appropriately.

Document Your Processes

Documentation plays a crucial role in the process of seizing cryptocurrency by law enforcement. It ensures adherence to approved methodologies, provides necessary evidential support, prevents mistakes, aids in learning from any mistakes that do occur, and prepares for all eventualities, including corruption and false accusations. As the saying goes (well, a saying from my friend Billy), "If it wasn't recorded, it didn't happen."

Proper documentation ensures that law enforcement officers follow approved methodologies during the seizure of cryptocurrency. This adherence not only maintains procedural integrity but also strengthens the credibility of the evidence collected. Documentation may also be required evidentially in court to support the legality and correctness of the seizure process.

Production of thorough documentation helps prevent mistakes by providing clear instructions and records of all the actions you have taken. In cases where mistakes do occur, detailed records can aid in understanding what went wrong and how to avoid similar issues in the future. This is particularly important in law enforcement, where personnel turnover is a reality, and new officers must quickly learn established procedures.

Documentation also serves as a safeguard against corruption and false accusations. By meticulously recording each step of the process, it becomes significantly harder for a corrupt staff member or officer to tamper with the procedure or for false accusations to gain traction.

Methods of Recording

When documenting the seizure process, consider various recording methods while maintaining the security of sensitive information like seed phrases or PIN codes. Common methods include video recordings and paperwork, each with its own set of advantages and risks.

Paperwork

Utilize checklists and task allocation processes to ensure that every step is completed and documented.

Document who performed each task, when it was done, and how it was executed. This includes noting evidence bag numbers and maintaining the continuity and chain of custody.

Video

Record video evidence of key steps in the seizure process to provide visual proof of actions taken.

When using any recording method, be aware of the risks of disclosing sensitive information. Ensure that seed phrases or PIN codes are not recorded in a manner that makes them accessible to unauthorized individuals.

Preparation and Administration

Effective preparation and administration are important for a smooth and secure seizure process. The head of the unit should be briefed, and storage locations for seized assets should be chosen carefully. Designate an officer in charge of the overall process and specific officers responsible for each Shamir card if this method is used for splitting seed phrases.

Documentation in Law Enforcement Systems

To maintain a comprehensive record within law enforcement systems, the following information should be documented:

- Wallet description
- Whether the wallet is secured by a password or a PIN code
- Evidence bag numbers
- A circle of knowledge indicating who is aware of the seed phrases and wallet details

By following these procedures, law enforcement can effectively and securely manage their seizures. Proper setup, adherence to local laws, secure management of wallets, and well-defined organizational processes are crucial for maintaining the integrity and security of your seized assets.

Questions to Ask before Carrying Out a Crypto Seizure

The seizure of cryptocurrency is often a time-sensitive operation and, as we have discussed, necessitates well-defined processes and toolkits, clearly established roles, and a meticulous chain of custody. But there are other questions to ask before heading to a search scene where we may be asked to seize crypto assets.

Preparing for a Time-Sensitive Seizure

Cryptocurrency seizures require swift and precise actions. To ensure readiness, law enforcement agencies must define processes and toolkits ahead of time. Roles need to be clearly considered and defined, determining whether a cyber investigator can handle the seizure or if a financial investigator's involvement is necessary as is required in some countries. Establishing a defined chain of custody is critical to maintain the integrity of the seized assets. Working in a buddy system, where one officer checks the work of the other, is also advisable to minimize errors and ensure accuracy.

On-Site Seizure Considerations

As we discussed earlier in the chapter, seizing assets on-site or as quickly as possible should be a priority. Immediate seizure prevents potential loss of assets due to unauthorized transfers by a third party. There are a couple of key questions to address before heading to a scene:

- Who else has the private keys or seed words? Understanding who has access to the assets is crucial. This includes co-conspirators or other individuals who might have the ability to move the assets.
- Are the assets linked to, or suspected of being linked to, criminality? If the assets are tied to criminal activity, immediate seizure is necessary to prevent further illicit use.

Before arriving on-site, law enforcement should ask:

- Do we have the right skills and toolkit available? Ensuring that the team has the necessary expertise and equipment is essential.
- Do we have destination addresses? Prepared destination addresses on a number of key blockchains are needed ahead of time. Trying to set up wallets and addresses while on scene is time-consuming and can result in errors.
- Do we have the legal right to seize the assets? Confirming legal authority is crucial to avoid legal complications post-seizure.

Managing Access and Potential Threats

I'm going to say it again! Anyone with seed words or private keys can move the assets. If possible, we may be able, through intelligence methods, to become aware of potential co-conspirators, who might be trusted family members or friends with access to the assets. Law enforcement must either gain control of these individuals simultaneously or seize the assets as quickly as possible, ensuring that the operation is conducted safely and securely.

On-Site Toolkit and Practice

I cannot overemphasize how important it is to have a prepared toolkit on-site. If no prepared option is available, an officer might use a personal device to seize the assets, but this should be avoided due to potential security risks. Officers should also ensure that they have recently practiced the techniques and procedures for seizing cryptocurrency to maintain proficiency and confidence in their actions.

Where to Store Seized Assets?

I should declare at the start of this section that in addition to my work with blockchain intelligence company TRM Labs, I'm a founder and minor shareholder of a company called Asset Reality, which assists with the management of seized assets, including crypto assets for governments and law enforcement globally. I will, however, attempt to be neutral.

Determining the best destination for seized cryptocurrency assets is a critical decision that requires the careful consideration of various options, each with its own advantages and disadvantages. This section explores three primary options: seizing assets to an exchange, to a specialist custodian, or to a law enforcement–controlled wallet. Each option presents unique challenges and benefits.

Seizing to an Exchange

Seizing cryptocurrency assets to an exchange may initially seem like an obvious and straightforward choice due to the robust infrastructure exchanges typically offer. Many exchanges provide several specific custodian services designed to handle a wide range of currencies and tokens, making them a convenient option. The advantages of using an exchange include having a contract in place, easy account management, and the ability to generate addresses on request.

However, there are significant drawbacks to consider. Fees associated with using exchanges can be high, depending on the contract terms, of course, but many agencies have found that the costs of storage and eventual conversion to fiat currency can be very high. Also, not all exchanges comply with local law enforcement legislation and can even be resistant to working with government agencies, which can be difficult. You would not want to sign up your department to an exchange only for them to be indicted in some money-laundering scheme or other criminal activity.

Converting seized assets to cash may not yield the best price, which is often a requirement in legislation related to proceeds of crime, and funds stored on exchanges are not always insured—assets are often "self-insured" by the exchange.

Although any company or agency can be a target for criminals, exchanges are frequent targets for hackers, raising concerns about the security of the seized assets. The commingling of funds on exchanges can also lead to visibility issues, where other parties, including criminals, might see where their funds were transferred. Finally, time delays in accessing assets can pose significant challenges during critical moments.

Given these issues, it must be said that there are some legally compliant and trustworthy exchanges operating in most jurisdictions around the world. Just be very careful who you choose.

Specialist Custodians

Specialist custodians represent another option for managing seized cryptocurrency assets. These organizations are specifically designed to support law enforcement with the management and storage of crypto seizure. It is essential to conduct thorough research to find the most suitable custodian for your needs.

The advantages of using some specialist custodians include segregated accounts, contracts that clearly define the relationship and responsibilities, and the ability to generate addresses on request. Some custodians offer management software, which enables a department to see all seized assets, no matter where they are stored on a "dashboard," and to be able to see current fiat values and even carry out conversion to other currencies such as stable coins or fiat currency. These custodians offer comprehensive asset management features, support for most or all currencies, and defined costs, which can provide a department with financial predictability.

However, the costs associated with using specialist custodians can be high, both for management and for converting assets to fiat currency. These costs are typically dependent on the contract terms. Another potential drawback is that some custodians may not comply with local law enforcement legislation, which could complicate the seizure and management process.

Seizing to a Law Enforcement–Controlled Wallet

Some law enforcement agencies opt to manage their own wallets, allowing for full control over the seized assets. This option enables agencies to set up wallets quickly and for any currency, providing instant access to the funds. Having full control means law enforcement can respond promptly to any developments related to the seized assets.

However, the control that comes with managing your own wallets also brings significant responsibilities and risks. The complexity of key management across multiple seizures can be daunting, and securing the keys is a critical challenge. Other considerations include ensuring proper insurance for the assets and dealing with staff issues such as turnover and redeployment, and maintaining sufficient training and trust within the organization can be a significant task. Additionally, the software and hardware used for managing these assets may not have been fully tested and risk-assessed, leading to potential vulnerabilities. Human factors, such as the risk of staff being socially engineered, corrupted, or otherwise coerced, must also be considered.

Given these factors, it is essential to carefully evaluate whether your department has the capacity and knowledge required to effectively manage seized crypto assets. Without this capacity, self-storage and self-management might introduce considerable risks.

Deciding where to send seized cryptocurrency assets is not a straightforward decision and requires careful consideration. Each option, whether using an exchange or a specialist custodian, or managing assets in-house, presents unique benefits and challenges. Unless your department has substantial expertise and resources, managing seized assets independently might not be advisable due to the complexities and risks involved. Ultimately, the chosen method should align with your agency's capabilities, legal requirements, and strategic objectives to ensure the secure and effective management of any seized cryptocurrency assets.

We have to be honest that seizing crypto is quite a daunting task. My good friend Phil Ariss, who contributed a piece to Chapter 4 of this book, recently wrote,

> *. . .one of the most nerve wracking parts of my police career was signing a [seizure] transaction for nearly $400k. It took me several minutes to pluck up the courage to click "send."*
>
> *Why? There is something really unnerving signing off an irreversible transaction for assets that didn't belong to me. What if I had made a mistake, what if I lose all the assets. . . lots of what ifs.*

This is very true. Another colleague at a U.K. agency had to click Send to seize hundreds of millions in sterling, and he described the fear of the situation in similar terms. The reality is that whether transferring $10 of crypto or $100 million of crypto, the process is exactly the same, but the pressure of the transaction increases with the value. This fear can only be reduced through preparation and practice. Knowing your tools, having carried out many test transactions and knowing that they work, trusting the wallets that will receive the crypto, knowing that the processes and documentation protect you—all these things help the officer to have confidence.

Several companies in the blockchain intelligence space have excellent training programs that will help you define your processes and become more confident with the steps involved, and if you are likely to carry out seizures in the future it may be worth investing in one of them. Having a certificate under your proverbial belt can also help when proving your competency in court.

Seizure of crypto assets will only become more frequent as crypto gains a more substantial foothold in the broader criminal space. This chapter has given you the right questions to ask if you and your department want to set up a sound and verifiable process.

Final Thoughts

I sincerely hope that you have enjoyed this book. I understand that for some of you the more technical chapters may have been tricky to wrap your head around. For those of you who are more experienced, much of the content would likely have been just good reminders. Whatever your skill level when you started Chapter 1, I hope that you have benefited in some way from the content. Maybe one or two of you have read this book and think you can do better, or feel that more time should have been spent on subjects such as contracts or DeFi. If you feel that way, I urge you to pull out your laptop and start writing; our community desperately needs dissemination of knowledge to be able to stop criminals in their tracks. I always enjoy the books written about certain frauds or successful hunts for cyber criminals, but we need more books to teach us how to investigate these crimes. If you are able, write one!

I'm proud of this book. I've done my best—especially writing through difficult times such as the loss of my father—but I am not so deluded as to think that someone out there couldn't do a better job of it.

I'm going to repeat exactly what I said in the introduction to the book as it is very important for all investigators to consider:

> *If you are working in the crypto investigations space, I urge you to focus on the victims. Investigation of areas such as fraud, pig-butchering, and other such scams ruins people's lives. I've had people in tears on the phone and even reports of those who take their own lives as a result of losing all they had. Being an investigator is not all about the "tech," the prosecution targets set by our bosses, or even "getting the bad guys." First and foremost, you should focus on the victim, bringing them justice and hopefully the return of lost funds. Having a victim focus also helps to stop you from becoming jaded when wading through bureaucracy or intransigent criminal systems. Investigate for the* person, *rather than just the* crime, *and you will feel better about your life and the good you can do for others.*

Some readers of this book may be the perpetrators of the crimes we have been discussing, hoping to learn how to evade detection and capture. Because of this I have not included techniques for tracing through mixers or capabilities related to privacy coins and other techniques. I know that for some of you, a life of crime is about putting food on the table for your family, for others just sheer greed. As I mentioned earlier in this book, I am often amazed at the creativity and utter brilliance of some criminal schemes, but surely you can use the same abilities for good. Your choices hurt real people, people raising kids like yours, people caring for elderly parents, normal people who you would probably like if you met them in the real world. One day, you will be facing the last moments of your short life, when your memories "flash past your eyes"—who do you want to see? A person who helped others, who will be remembered for being a force for good and decency in the world, or a person who was no more than a parasite, a person despised by others in life and in death? I truly respect your skills and your abilities, but consider turning your life around and use your talents to make money doing good. You will never regret it.

I hope that you have enjoyed the contributions from some of the world's most extraordinary crypto investigators. I thank them for their wisdom and all that I continue to learn from them. I will leave the final words to our last contributor, the extraordinary Carole House. I first met Carole when I was teaching crypto investigation techniques to FINCEN (Financial Crimes Enforcement Network) in the United States. Her work within both the military and government, including at the White House National Security Council (NSC) as the Director for Cybersecurity and Secure Digital Innovation, has given her a unique perspective as to the role of crypto in the international criminal space.

Over to you Carole! Thank you all for reading.

By the time I was 12 years old, my father had taught me to don my chemical protective mask within 9 seconds—the Army standard. My family lived an hour south of the most heavily defended border in the world between North and South Korea. Dependent families of U.S. servicemembers like my father, a U.S. Army colonel, were issued gas masks upon arrival in country to be able to protect ourselves in the case of a chemical weapons attack by North Korea. That was and remains an unfortunate reality for those living under the shadow and potential threat from rogue nations—my status as a noncombatant child, nor that of my friends and family, did not change the devastating consequences we could face if the situation escalated.

The driving forces affecting national, economic, and technological security have defined significant elements of my life, as I am confident is the case for many of those reading this book. Over a decade after learning to don my gas mask, I returned to South Korea, this time in uniform serving on a monthlong training exercise. Both in and out of uniform, I committed my life to serving the American people across different fields of national security. As a civilian, I worked across executive and legislative branches of government on cybersecurity and critical infrastructure protection. Next I stepped into the realm of countering illicit finance, which brought me to my first real introduction to cryptocurrency *and Nick's first book* on crypto investigations—as we know, cryptocurrency sits right at the nexus of cybercrime and financial crime.

It was an incredibly impactful moment of realization for me when, another decade after my Army service, sitting on stage on a panel at a cryptocurrency conference, I was asked if it was *really* important and the cryptocurrency sector's responsibility to stop North Korea from funding half of its proliferation activities with cryptocurrency heists and cybercrime. Interactions like this helped me understand where so many differences existed between what I saw and how some strong voices in the cryptocurrency sector feel about what responsibility and accountability in finance and technology can and should look like.

As with any technology or financial system, cryptocurrency can be leveraged for the good of or to exploit societies, consumers, and markets. Cryptocurrency and blockchain technology have been used to facilitate humanitarian aid delivery and disbursement, to lower costs of cross-border remittances, and to enhance auditability and transparency for finance and supply chains. However, they have also been used to promote a wide spectrum of illicit activities and national security threats, ranging from cybercrime and ransomware, proliferation and terrorism financing, to human and drug trafficking. Features attractive to licit users, like instant cross-border reach of payments from one person to another, are also attractive to illicit users seeking tools to enhance their money-laundering capabilities.

Cryptocurrency's ability to be exploited, and to *prevent* abuse, depends on the design and implementation of a complex ecosystem of technology, policy, operations, and the people and businesses affecting them. Never before have we had a technology that could permit such public visibility and auditability of financial flows.

However, we also have not before had a financial instrument that holds simultaneously in one asset many of the risky features of wire transfers—like speedy cross-border reach of electronic funds transfers—with the risky features of cash—like disintermediated, peer-to-peer value transfers. Even the potential lowering of risk we have with public traceable ledgers and analytics is not enough on its own in a world of off-chain transactions, obfuscating methods like mixers and anonymity-enhanced cryptocurrencies, and a growing interest to implement privacy-enhancing technologies to address the concerning consumer risks from publishing financial transactions publicly.

It is not an accident that criminals are using cryptocurrency as a preferred means of payment on darknet marketplaces, for child sexual abuse materials, and in cybercrime economies. But this is also not an inevitability. We must, *and absolutely can,* shape this system and our own capabilities to keep pace with the risks.

Key elements mitigating risks across this ecosystem are the investigators, analysts, supervisors, and regulatory technology that can leverage the public and transparent nature of blockchains to help identify and combat illicit activity. As cryptocurrency continues to grow in adoption and as technology continues to evolve, so too must the scale and sophistication of these risk mitigants.

Nick, this book, and its readers are some of those risk mitigants. Both analytic platforms and our workforce are critical tools in that national security toolbox. This update from Nick and those who pick up this text in order to sharpen and hone investigative skills demonstrates a recognition of the very real reality of the threat and our capabilities to do something about it, to hold accountable the bad actors exploiting this technology and defend the vulnerable being targeted by despicable heists, scams, and ransomware extortion. As criminals update their tactics and typologies, and as markets and implementations of cryptocurrency and blockchain technology grow and evolve, so must our national security tools.

This feels especially poignant to write as the rise of democratized access to another cutting-edge technology capability, artificial intelligence (AI), is taking the world by storm, both in presenting incredible promise for higher-order economic developments and efficiencies and in foreboding significant challenges for trusting content, ensuring privacy of data, and combating cybercrime. These technologies together can help address each other's gaps but also can reinforce each other's worst traits if left unmitigated. As criminals increasingly leverage AI and cryptocurrencies to scale and automate already script-enabled money laundering to more deeply obfuscate financial trails, the speed, complexity, and explainability of tech-enhanced analysis must grow alongside the ability of investigators and legal systems to use it.

Against this backdrop, Nick Furneaux's book provides a critical, timely tool in the hands of investigators seeking a way to refine and sharpen skills to keep pace with emerging technology and the criminals of today and tomorrow. Understanding how to apply critical methodologies for forensic investigations involving cryptocurrency will aid those readers helping to recover assets for victims defrauded and stolen from, and to hold accountable the perpetrators behind these despicable crimes. These are very real victims being harmed by very real criminals and rogue regimes. My gratitude goes out to those readers and to Nick for his efforts with this book to be a force multiplier to the wider ecosystem of people safeguarding our financial system from abuse.

—Carole House, Senior Fellow, Atlantic Council, Former White House and Treasury Official

Acknowledgments

First, thank you to my wife Claire—you have my eternal love.

My son Tobias, I wish you happiness and peace on your chosen path, all my love.

My daughter Loulé, you are the best of us all; I hope that I can be like you when I grow up! (Loulé has Kleefstra Syndrome, a very rare genetic condition that affects every part of her brain and body. If you ever are looking to make a contribution to a small charity, please consider `www.kleefstrasyndrome.org`.)

Thank you to Jim and Danielle at Wiley for their extraordinary patience, as the challenges of life so often got in the way of me writing.

Many thanks to Luke Russell. From mathematician to world-class investigator, what a journey! Thank you for all your help at CSITech and then TRM. The student can truly become the teacher!

While on the journey of crypto-oriented investigations, I have been privileged to work with and be mentored by some extraordinary investigators and I'm incredibly proud that some have been able to provide contributions to this book. Their insights, expertise, and experiences bring the book alive. I thank you all and wish you health and happiness.

About the Author

Nick Furneaux has been working with and programming computers since his parents procured his first computer, a Sinclair ZX81, when he was 12. (At the age of 14 he designed a computer program to convince his teacher that he had gained access to his bank account.)

In the past 20 years, he has provided cybersecurity and forensics consultancy for companies and law enforcement institutions in the United Kingdom, Europe, the United States, Canada, Australasia, and Asia and has lectured on the subject to numerous organizations. Nick also has considerable knowledge of covert evidence extraction and covert data systems.

Previously through his company CSITech Ltd. (purchased by TRM Labs in 2022), he has been specifically involved in the prevention and investigation of cyber crime, including a specialization in forensic computer memory analysis and investigation of crimes involving cryptocurrencies. He has been privileged to be able to work with some of the top security researchers and investigators in the world.

In 2018 he published *Investigating Cryptocurrencies* (Wiley, 2018), which, until this book, was the only book in the world on the subject aimed at investigators. Since 2018, Nick has trained thousands of digital detectives on cryptocurrency investigative techniques, built software tools to assist with investigations, and worked on investigating over $27 billion in cryptocurrency assets.

Nick now works as a blockchain intelligence expert with TRM Labs and is an adviser to the board for Asset Reality in the U.K.

Offline, Nick can be found running on the clifftops of south Devon, paddleboarding, and attempting to play the piano.

About the Contributors

Erin West, Foreword

Erin West is an internationally recognized speaker and educator in transnational organized crime as well as the criminal investigation and prosecution of cases involving cryptocurrency. She has served as a deputy district attorney in Santa Clara County, California for 26 years and for the past 8 years has been assigned to the Regional Enforcement Allied Computer Team (REACT) high-technology task force, known for its arrests and prosecutions of "SIM-swappers" and for the recovery of cryptocurrency. Erin founded and leads the Crypto Coalition, a group of more than 1,700 local, state, federal and international law enforcement agents who specialize in cryptocurrency investigation. In response to the worldwide scam crisis, Erin founded Operation Shamrock, the first global cross-industry information-sharing organization focused on uniting the world against transnational organized crime originating in Southeast Asia.

Carole House, Final Thoughts

Carole House is a nonresident senior fellow at the Atlantic Council. She has previously served as an executive in residence at Terranet Ventures, as the chair of the Technology Advisory Committee (TAC) to the Commodity Futures Trading Commission (CFTC), and at the White House National Security Council (NSC) as the Director for Cybersecurity and Secure Digital Innovation. Carole first joined the NSC from the U.S. Treasury's Financial Crimes Enforcement Network (FinCEN), where she led cybersecurity, virtual currency, and emerging technology policy efforts as a Senior Cyber and Emerging Technology Policy Officer. Prior to FinCEN, she worked as a Presidential Management Fellow supporting the White House Office of Management and Budget's Cyber and National Security Unit and the U.S. Senate Committee on Homeland Security and Governmental Affairs on cybersecurity, supply chain risk management, and critical infrastructure protection policy issues. Carole is a former Army captain who served in chemical defense and military intelligence until November 2014, including a deployment to Kandahar Province, Afghanistan, from 2012 to 2013 in support of Operation Enduring Freedom. She holds a BA in international affairs from the University of Georgia and an MA in security studies from Georgetown University.

Erica Stanford, Author, Chapter 2 Contributor

Erica Stanford is the author of the award-winning *Crypto Wars: Faked Deaths, Missing Billions and Industry Disruption* (Kogan Page, 2021), which was awarded Highly Commended in the Business Book Awards. She is also author of the chapters "Risks Relating to Crypto and Digital Assets" in *Crypto and Digital Assets Law and Regulation*, edited by Charles Kerrigan, and "Ethical AI" and "United Kingdom" in *AI, Machine Learning & Big Data* by Global Legal Insights.

At international law firm CMS in London, Erica advises in a nonlegal capacity on crypto, AI, and strategy.

Erica is an industry expert on fraud and fraud prevention. She is associate guest lecturer on digital assets at Warwick Business School. She writes the weekly industry newsletter the *Crypto Currier*, which has a combined subscriber base of 14,000 across Substack and LinkedIn.

Erica has a master's degree from the University of Edinburgh in European Union Studies (Economics), with modules in French and Spanish; has studied AI at Oxford Saïd Business School; and is a Master of Science candidate in data and AI ethics at the University of Edinburgh.

She speaks and writes globally about crypto and digital assets, specifically about misinformation, risk and scams, and the integration of AI.

Ari Redbord, Interview in Chapter 3

Ari Redbord is the Global Head of Policy at TRM Labs, the blockchain intelligence company. Prior to joining TRM, Ari was the senior adviser to the Deputy Secretary and the Undersecretary for Terrorism and Financial Intelligence at the U.S. Treasury. In that position, Ari worked with teams from the Office of Foreign Assets Control (OFAC), the Financial Crimes Enforcement Network (FinCEN), and other Treasury components to use sanctions and other regulatory tools effectively to safeguard the financial system from illicit use by terrorist financiers, weapons of mass destruction proliferators, drug kingpins, and other rogue actors, including Iran, Syria, North Korea, and Venezuela. In addition, Ari worked closely with regulators, the Hill, and the interagency on issues related to the Bank Secrecy Act, cryptocurrency, and anti–money laundering strategies. Prior to Treasury, Ari was an assistant United States attorney for the District of Columbia for 11 years, where he investigated and prosecuted terrorism, espionage, threat finance, cryptocurrency, export control, child exploitation, and human trafficking cases.

Phil Ariss, Chapter 4 Contributor

Phil Ariss is a serving police inspector with 15 years policing experience, specializing in research and development, cyber crime, and cryptocurrencies and virtual assets. Phil was the first national coordinator for policing for cryptocurrencies while seconded to the UK's National Police Chiefs' Council (NPCC) cybercrime program. It was here that Phil built the United Kingdom's policing response, building a network of trained staff, writing national operational guidance documents, obtaining dedicated funding, and building the capability and capacity that is the foundation for the current model that is still in use today. Operationally, Phil was involved in some of the very first cryptocurrency investigations in the U.K., helping secure convictions and asset confiscations and seizing assets on multiple occasions. Phil is currently on a career break from the police service, working for TRM Labs as the Director of Public Sector Relations in the U.K.

Iggy Azad, Chapter 10 Contributor

Iggy Azad is a senior director at Coinbase, where he oversees the domains of investigations, intelligence, and law enforcement relations. With a keen focus on combating illicit activities within the cryptocurrency space, Iggy leads a dedicated team of investigators tackling issues ranging from fraud to terrorist financing.

Before joining Coinbase, Iggy had a decorated 20-year career with the Metropolitan Police Service in London. He began his career walking the beat before moving to the Criminal Investigation Department, where he honed his investigative skills tackling gang crime in South London.

In 2011, Iggy moved to the UK's National Cyber Crime Unit, where he served until 2019. During this period, he became an experienced financial investigator. He first began investigating illicit use of cryptocurrency in 2014. He lives in London and enjoys "doom-scrolling" crypto Twitter (X).

Helen Short, Chapter 10 Contributor

Helen Short is currently a global senior security lead at Accenture, where her role involves developing custom cyber solutions tailored to the evolving landscape of cybersecurity. Her ability to pinpoint vulnerabilities and offer strategic solutions has made her a trusted adviser in the field.

Helen's journey in cyber intelligence began with a distinguished 15-year tenure as a detective within the London Metropolitan Police Service. Her last 10 years were focused on intelligence, cyber crime, and financial investigations.

Luke Russell, Chapter 15 Author

Luke Russell is a dedicated senior blockchain intelligence expert and master instructor at TRM Labs, where he combines his extensive experience in crypto-related investigations, OSINT, and digital forensics. Before joining TRM Labs, Luke served as the lead investigator at CSI-Tech, overseeing investigations of over $6 billion in illicit crypto activity related to child sexual abuse material, fraud, and narcotics-linked funds. Having trained thousands of investigators worldwide, he has developed several courses on integrating digital forensics with cryptocurrencies, advanced OSINT investigations, and both intermediate and advanced cryptocurrency investigation techniques, including RAM analysis. Luke has contributed to various investigations for U.K. and international law enforcement, as well as private sector clients.

Aidan Larkin, Chapter 17 Contributor

Aidan Larkin is the co-founder and CEO of Asset Reality, a seized asset company. Asset Reality is the world's first end-to-end platform to seize, manage, and realize physical and digital assets securely. Utilized by public and private sector organizations worldwide, the company's expertise extends to investigating, recovering, and managing billions of dollars' worth of seized assets in some of the world's most high-profile asset recovery cases.

An Associate Fellow at RUSI (Asset Recovery & Crypto), he is a lecturer, consultant, and subject matter expert on seized assets for the United Nations and multiple international organizations.

Aidan's asset-recovery career began as a criminal tax inspector and then as an experienced seized asset manager, where he oversaw one of the world's first sales of seized crypto.

Chris Recker, Chapter 17 Contributor

Chris Recker is a senior associate at Kingsley Napley LLP in the UK. He is an international fraud and investigations lawyer with an emphasis on matters relating to digital assets and/or cybersecurity. He regularly advises on complex multijurisdictional asset recovery strategies (particularly where digital assets are involved) and also on a range of cybersecurity issues (including incident response following ransomware).

Brian Pandya, Chapter 17 Contributor

Brian Pandya is a partner at the Washington, D.C. office of Duane Morris LLP. He represents technology companies and executives in high-stakes litigation, arbitrations, investigations, and appeals. Brian has served as lead trial counsel in a range of intellectual property, antitrust, and complex commercial and white-collar matters. He is also an experienced strategic counselor, regularly advising clients on data privacy, cybersecurity, artificial intelligence, and national security issues. He provides advice on corporate compliance programs. Brian previously served at the U.S. Department of Justice as Deputy Associate Attorney General.

Charlyn Cruz, Chapter 17 Contributor

Charlyn Cruz is an associate in the London office of Duane Morris LLP. Her practice focuses on complex commercial litigation in a number of different sectors, such banking and finance, technology, and transportation. Recently, she has increased her focus on litigation, investigations, and asset recovery in the digital asset space. Her work is often cross-border in nature, and her experience spans multiple jurisdictions in Europe, the United States, and Asia.

Taylor Hertzler, Chapter 17 Contributor

Taylor Hertzler is an associate at the Philadelphia office of Duane Morris LLP. He practices primarily in the area of health law, working on matters of digital asset recovery on the side. He advises providers, hospitals, and other healthcare entities on regulatory concerns, including state licensure, federal kickback issues, Medicare and Medicaid rules, and FDA matters. Taylor also has experience working in insurance litigation.

About the Technical Editor

John Valcovci is the Senior Vice President of Learning and Development at Asset Reality, LLC, where he uses his extensive experience in cybersecurity, law enforcement, and education to develop and coordinate seized asset management and cryptocurrency education for law enforcement and industry professionals internationally. He has been recognized by the Council of Europe as an expert in digital assets and has delivered digital asset consultation and instruction to the governments of the British Virgin Islands, Ukraine, Kosovo, and Turkey, as well as multiday training programs in cryptocurrency analysis for agents and analysts of the U.S. Drug Enforcement Administration (DEA). Before joining Asset Reality, John was an assistant U.S. attorney with the U.S. Department of Justice, where he devoted 28 years prosecuting various cyber-related crimes, including fraud, narcotics, and online child exploitation. John is happiest spending time with Kathy, his wife of 41 years (and counting). After raising four wonderful children, John and Kathy look forward to planning their next adventure, traveling, cooking, and restoring classic automobiles.

Index

C

D

F

J

K

L

M

Q

R

U

V

W

X

Y

Z